PRINCE PHILIP'S CENTURY 1921–2021

THE EXTRAORDINARY LIFE OF THE DUKE OF EDINBURGH

ROBERT JOBSON

AD LIB

For Karen, for all her steadfast support and hard work
in helping this book become a reality.
For my late aunt, Maureen, I miss our funny conversations.

First published in 2021 by Ad Lib Publishers Ltd
15 Church Road
London, SW13 9HE
www.adlibpublishers.com

Text © 2021 Robert Jobson

Paperback ISBN 978-1-913543-09-9

A CIP catalogue record for this book is available
from the British Library.
Every reasonable effort has been made to trace
copyright-holders of material reproduced in this book,
but if any have been inadvertently overlooked the publishers
would be glad to hear from them.

Printed in the UK

10 9 8 7 6 5 4 3 2 1

'I, Philip, Duke of Edinburgh, do become your liege man* of life and limb, and of earthly worship; and faith and truth I will bear unto you, to live and die, against all manner of folks. So help me God.'

The Duke of Edinburgh's pledge of allegiance to his wife and sovereign Queen Elizabeth II at her Coronation, Westminster Abbey, 2 June 1953

---

* A 'liege man' is a devoted follower who owes allegiance and service to a feudal lord.

'Life is going to go on after me, if I can make life marginally and more tolerable for people who come afterwards or even at the time I'd be delighted.'

HRH Prince Philip,
Duke of Edinburgh

ACKNOWLEDGEMENTS

I would like to thank my publishers, John and Jon, at Ad Lib for investing in me and caring about this book, my fabulous editors, particularly Karen, for improving my work, my sources, for informing me and, of course, my friends and family for putting up with me during the writing of this book. I would also like to thank my old friend and colleague, Arthur Edwards MBE, for allowing me to showcase some of his brilliant photographs of the Duke of Edinburgh, the Queen and other members of the Royal Family that are used in this book. I hope you enjoy the book.

Robert D. Jobson
@theroyaleditor

1: STRENGTH AND STAY

'There is nothing like it for morale to be reminded that the years are passing —
ever more quickly — and that bits are beginning to drop off the ancient frame.
But it is nice to be remembered at all.'

Philip's response to being awarded an
'Oldie of the Year Award' in 2011.

Throughout his long and eventful life, Prince Philip had been a stickler for precision and military detail. The arrangements for his death and funeral, he vowed, would be no different. He could not abide commotion and confusion. He loathed it as much as he did in receiving personal praise. His mantra in life had, after all, always been, 'Just get on with it'.

Philip was as pragmatic about death as he was practical in life. His first instruction was that he would not die in hospital, but at Windsor Castle, his home. Further detailed instructions for his own funeral, known by the codename 'Operation Forth Bridge', were to be carried out to the letter and were incontestable. He ruled that there would be no state service at Westminster Abbey, even though as the Queen's husband he was entitled to one, nor would his body lie in state. Instead, Prince Philip settled on having a ceremonial military funeral at St George's Chapel, Windsor, the high-medieval Gothic style Royal Peculiar and the Chapel of the Order of the Garter, located in the Lower Ward of the castle built in 1475. In addition, the duke instructed that a palace official should not confirm or deny anything about his death until the designated footman, dressed in full livery, had attached the framed notice to the gates of Buckingham Palace. Then and only then could the Royal Family's team of communications officers at the palace press office be allowed to break the silence. Everyone with a role in this final piece of solemn theatre knew exactly what to do and when, so that it could be carried out, as Philip planned, with the minimum of fuss. When the COVID-19 pandemic first struck in March 2020 and both he and the Queen were forced to relocate and self-isolate at Windsor he agreed to simplify the funeral arrangements still further should anything happen to him. He never liked loose ends.

Robust and controversial, Prince Philip inevitably had detractors. They preferred to focus on his so-called 'gaffes', perceived blunders and crotchety remarks, rather than his huge achievements. He deserves his place in history on merit. Reducing Philip to a caricature of himself is a gross misrepresentation of one of life's great characters, leaders and innovators and does him a disservice. He often uttered his risqué comments simply to liven up dull proceedings, and at boring official events he often drew a laugh by saying: 'You're going to see the world's most experienced plaque unveiler at work.' He once got a roar of laughter from the crowd on a visit to Canada in 1969, 'I declare this thing open, whatever it is.' He would tell advisers that when he entered a room, he would look along a line and select one person he would try to make laugh.

I was fortunate to have met the Duke of Edinburgh many times in my capacity as a royal correspondent and author, both in public and private. He was president of my London club, the Naval and Military Club (known as the In & Out club) at 4, St James Square. Indeed, Naval history remained a keen interest throughout his life. He was appointed a Trustee of the National Maritime Museum in 1948. He was instrumental in saving the tea clipper Cutty Sark – now a museum ship stationed in Greenwich – and in establishing the Maritime Trust.

He was funny, sometimes audacious, and sharp-witted on each occasion. He didn't care about offending the politically correct brigade and spent even less time on any criticism they may have thrown his way. As for the ladies and gentlemen of the press, he had even less time and, despite having a number of friends who were journalists in his earlier years, took to referring to them as 'The Reptiles'. In 1983 in Bangladesh, the Queen and the duke were standing in the garden of a government building to meet guests waiting in line for a cocktail party. Ashley Walton, the then royal correspondent of the *Daily Express*, was with other members of the travelling 'Royal Rat Pack' of reporters at the end of the line. Philip, not realising he could be overheard, turned to the Queen and grimaced: 'Here come the bloody reptiles!'

When asked if he felt the press has been unfair to him or misrepresented him, he said, 'I suppose, yes, occasionally but I think it has its own agenda and, and that's it, you just have to live with it.' He saw journalists as fair game, as they saw the royals in a similar light. Whenever he came into direct contact with one, he would toy with his prey, but just like a cat with a mouse he was not actually playing.

When he was guest of honour at the 60th birthday dinner of the Foreign Press Association in London in 1948, he described journalists as 'the people's ambassadors' but then added caustically: 'I often wish the people didn't want to know quite so much.' The Parliamentary Press Gallery invited him as its guest of honour in 1956 and asked for his views on journalists in general. 'It is very tempting,' said the duke, 'but I think I had better wait until I get a bit older.'

Indeed, he had been making jokes at the expense of the press for years. Looking at the Barbary apes on a visit to the Rock of Gibraltar in 1950, accompanied by a posse of press, he joked, 'Which are the apes, and which are the reporters?' Even senior journalists who had been invited to his home were not safe. I remember at a media reception held at Windsor Castle in 2002 to mark the Queen's Golden Jubilee, which I attended, he was on top form.

'Who are you?' he demanded of Simon Kelner.

'I'm the editor-in-chief of *The Independent,* sir.'

'What are you doing here?' asked the duke?

'You invited me.'

'Well, you didn't have to come!'

His next victim was Martin Townsend, the bespectacled and affable then editor of the *Sunday Express.*

'Ah the *Sunday Express*,' said Philip. 'I was very fond of Arthur Christiansen.'

'Yes, there's been a long line of distinguished editors,' replied Townsend.

'I didn't say that!' Philip replied bluntly before walking away.

At the same reception I was chatting to two distinguished Irish journalists as the royals worked the room. Out of nowhere the duke appeared. He peered at the labels on our lapels and as soon as he had worked out that they were Irishmen he then proceeded to tell a completely inappropriate Irish joke. 'Did you hear the one about the Irish pilot who radioed the Air Traffic Control Tower saying he had a problem?' They clearly had heard it, but played along politely. 'Tower control then cleared him to land,' Philip said, 'but also asked for his height and position.'

'Well, I'm five foot eight and I am sitting in the cockpit at the front of the plane,' said the duke and delighted at being the first to laugh at the punchline of his own joke. We all dutifully joined in. Then he read my name badge which said, Robert Jobson, Royal Correspondent, *The Sun*. He also recognised my Naval and Military Club tie and just tutted, said, 'They'll let anyone in these days' and walked off to find his next victim with the enthusiasm of a naughty schoolboy.

But there was another side to the duke rarely seen, even when it came to interacting with media. His staff loved him too. Whenever he hosted a party for his team, he made sure everyone who had supported him and his work was invited from the cleaners to his private secretary. He always commanded fierce loyalty.

He was often unpleasant and impatient when dealing with photographers. He let fly with the f-word at an unfortunate photographer during a photo call that he deemed to be taking too long at an event to mark the 75th anniversary of the Battle of Britain on 19 July 2015. His temper exploded as the official photographer dithered. 'Just take the fucking picture!' At the Windsor Horse Trials he agreed to allow a woman member of the public to take a picture of her daughter and him together as he was about to leave. However, when the camera failed for the third time, he let out his familiar expletive and drove off, much to the little girl's surprise.

Despite his reputation, he wasn't always so rude to photographers and reporters and on rare occasions he could be generous and accommodating. Once *Sun* photographer Mark Sweeney, later the newspaper's Scottish picture editor, was sent to scout Balmoral with a colleague and they were getting nowhere. His friend had just taken delivery of a gleaming new BMW and they decided to abandon the royal watch and drive five miles south of Braemar to Loch Muick to take some shots of the car with a classic Scottish background. After a few minutes, a Range Rover Vogue SE pulled up towing a fishing boat, with Philip at the wheel. He was alone.

'Are you guys off duty?' Philip asked, mistaking the two photographers for policemen, 'Could you help me launch the boat into the loch?' Mark agreed and made sure the duke was aware that they were *Sun* photographers, which didn't faze him. They proceeded to help him get the small fishing boat into the water. Without the photographers asking, Philip said, 'I should get some fish in a while, do you want to get some shots of my pulling them out of the water?'. The pair, both unassuming in their approach, were delighted and sent the excellent and exclusive shots to the picture desks in Glasgow and London who were thrilled.

Most importantly, he was the Queen's most loyal and trusted supporter, somebody she could rely on completely to help her through the longest reign in British history. At this time of mourning and reflection, it is right to remember and respect his dedicated service to his wife Queen Elizabeth, his country, and the institution of monarchy. A tireless supporter of charity, industry, the arts, and education, he was founder, fellow, patron, president, chairman and member of more than 800 organisations. He was also the head of his family: by the time of his death, he was a father of four, grandfather of eight and great-grandfather of another ten.

For decades, Philip shared the Queen's burden of office without upstaging her, always privately providing reassurance and advice but never overstepping the boundaries of his supporting role. It was an unforgiving position – a challenge for anyone – but one that he met head on. He remained the Queen's adviser all her adult life and into his retirement and was instantly recognised the world over. That said, he was wise enough to acknowledge his limitations and the constraints that came with his public role. He always seemed to instinctively know when it was time to step back and let his wife take the lead. His job after all was always to allow her star to shine.

In his 90th birthday interview he told the BBC that he had to work out what his role would be for himself by trial and error. 'There was no precedent. If I asked somebody, "What do you expect me to do?" they all looked blank. They had no idea, nobody had much idea,' he said in a typically forthright manner.

Philip was very reluctant to talk about himself and his achievements too to BBC broadcaster Fiona Bruce, refusing to say what he was most proud of. 'I couldn't care less,' he said gruffly when asked if he thought he had been successful in his role. 'Who cares what I think about it, I mean it's ridiculous.'*

I am sure Philip did consider his legacy; he did 'after all' achieve a great deal in his life both as a role model and leader. He inspired young people to be the best they could be, to develop strength of character through action and experience and gave them a platform to help them achieve it. Perhaps his most far-reaching initiative was his eponymous The Duke of Edinburgh's Award, which has stretched the capabilities of millions of young people globally. Drawing on his experiences at Gordonstoun, and at the suggestion of his old headmaster, Kurt Hahn, he established the Award in 1956. He appointed Brigadier Sir John Hunt, leader of the British expedition that had scaled Everest three years earlier, as the scheme's first director. The activity programme was borne out of Philip's belief that the young should be given opportunities to learn and wanted to introduce young people to new experiences,

---

* He was particularly awkward with Fiona Bruce because he understood his friend the broadcaster Selina Scott was due to conduct the interview, but the BBC hierarchy had replaced her.

including physical, skills-based and community challenges*. 'I don't run it – I've said it's all fairly second-hand, the whole business. I mean, I eventually got landed with the responsibility or the credit for it,' he said when pressed about it. 'I've got no reason to be proud of it. It's satisfying that we've set up a formula that works – that's it,' he finally said grudgingly to Fiona Bruce. She seemed a little taken aback by the irascible duke, but she soon recovered her composure. Philip, never one for saying sorry, loved putting interviewers on the back foot and testing resolve.

When the at first bullish interviewer Alan Titchmarsh interviewed Philip for ITV's *Philip at 90*, the unfortunate television personality didn't fare much better.

'You were thrust into combat at a very early age,' he remarked, before the duke barked back, 'So was (sic) lots of other people.'

'Was fatherhood a role you were conscious of fulfilling?'

'"No, I was just a father,' came Philip's blunt response.

'It** has been a unique position,' Titchmarsh offered up limply, which Philip batted back, 'There have been several others, Prince Albert, Prince George.'

'Were you*** trying to make a difference?'

'I was asked to do it,' Philip replied with a deep sigh.

'You've been voted Oldie of the Year.' Titchmarsh added, his optimism draining from his voice, but this time hopeful of a lighter response.

'So what?' Philip responded irritably, 'You just get old.'

Philip had actually been touched at getting that title from *The Oldie* publication. In a self-effacing letter to the organisers of an awards ceremony to celebrate the achievements of the elderly, the duke

---

* Since it was founded more than four million young people from over 90 countries have taken part. When the scheme marked its 60th anniversary, more than 2.5 million awards had been earned. It was typical of the hands-on involvement that helped give many organisations a push and in some cases, in Philip's inimitable style, a good shove. At the 50th anniversary of the Duke of Edinburgh's Awards scheme he got a laugh when he joked, 'Young people are the same as they always were. They are just as ignorant.'

** The role of Queen's consort

***When appointed president of one of the 847 organisations he has headed

admitted that time was passing 'ever more quickly' as he prepared to enter his tenth decade, with the inevitable effect on his 'morale'. In accepting the award Philip showed he hadn't allowed physical frailty to affect his sense of humour. He apologised for not being able to appear in person at Simpsons in the Strand to collect it and added, 'I much appreciate your invitation to receive an 'Oldie of the Year Award'. There is nothing like it for morale to be reminded that the years are passing — ever more quickly — and that bits are beginning to drop off the ancient frame. But it is nice to be remembered at all.'

Prince Philip was much more, however, than a sharp-witted raconteur, who would walk two-steps behind his wife when carrying out public engagements. He was his wife's 'liege man', dedicated to the Crown and a resolute public servant. He was the Queen's rock throughout her long reign, and his death will be devastating to her.

For someone who has always kept her feelings a closely guarded secret, it is impossible it know the true depth of impact the loss of her husband will have upon the Queen. She will of course be comforted by her faith. But there is no doubt that she truly loved Philip. On 20 November 1997, after 50 years of marriage, her love and devotion were incontrovertible as she marked their golden wedding anniversary at Banqueting House, Whitehall. She let her guard down for a moment and gave a remarkably personal and heartfelt tribute to her husband. 'All too often, I fear, Prince Philip has had to listen to me speaking. Frequently we have discussed my intended speech beforehand and, as you will imagine, his views have been expressed in a forthright manner,' Queen Elizabeth told the audience that included the then British Prime Minister The Rt Hon Tony Blair. 'He is someone who doesn't take easily to compliments but he has, quite simply, been my strength and stay all these years, and I, and his whole family, and this and many other countries, owe him a debt greater than he would ever claim, or we shall ever know.'

Elizabeth and Philip's marriage was not a dynastic arrangement to cement a treaty or an alliance with a foreign power as in days gone by. It was a true love match, built on foundations of romance and loyalty. Philip, who presented the Queen with an engraved 'E and P' diamond and ruby bracelet to mark their fifth anniversary, romanced his wife throughout their long lives with love tokens and personal trinkets. At times, like any husband, he infuriated her, but they shared a similar sense of humour and those close to the couple said he always managed to make her laugh. Her Majesty's life with Philip was never dull. As their beloved daughter-in-law Sophie, Countess of Wessex, wife of their fourth child, Prince Edward, and a close confidante of the Queen, said when she gave a rare glimpse into the dynamic of the relationship, 'For her to have found somebody like him, I don't think she could have chosen better. And they make each other laugh – which is half the battle, isn't it?'

Whenever possible Elizabeth and Philip made time to take afternoon tea together when they were in residence at the same time and would talk over their experiences of the day. Philip lived almost full-time at Wood Farm on the Sandringham Estate in Norfolk after he retired, and while Her Majesty continued with her official duties, such intimacy was less frequent. But when Philip informed his wife, five years Philip's junior, that he wanted to effectively step down from royal duties, she rightly felt he had earned his rest after nearly 70 years of public service as a working member of the Royal Family.

The COVID-19 lockdowns in 2020 changed this. Forced to shield together in Windsor Castle in isolation from the rest of the Royal Family, Philip and the Queen spent more time together than ever and it brought the couple as close as any time in their 72-year marriage. Having Philip at her side again, and being able to spend quality time with her husband, appeared to give her a new lease of life, those close to her said. They were cared for by a small team of loyal staff, who were dubbed 'HMS Bubble'. They were able to relax and finally live relatively normal lives, as people in their 90s perhaps should be able to. They de-camped to Balmoral, Aberdeenshire, the Queen's privately owned Scottish estate, for their summer break, but cut short their trip after six weeks as they found it a little tedious, with all the social distancing rules and restrictions due to coronavirus. They spent a further two weeks on her Norfolk estate, Sandringham before she returned to Windsor, with Philip remaining on Wood Farm, his usual residence after retiring. In early November 2020, the Queen and the Duke of Edinburgh reunited at Windsor Castle for the second national lockdown, where they spent a quiet Christmas without their family, again due to the coronavirus. It was the first time in 32 years that the couple had not been at Sandringham, normally marked by a procession of royals walking from the big house to nearby St Mary Magdalene church to attend the morning service, watched by members of the public, for the festive period. The Queen also announced that she would not attend a Christmas Day Service at St. George's Chapel, Windsor Castle to avoid attracting crowds. The Palace said the couple hoped 'things would get back to normal' in 2021. Sadly, that was not to be the case. Without Philip at the head of the table, how could it be?

Philip was admitted to the King Edward VII Hospital in London on 17 February 2021 as a 'precautionary measure' on the advice of a palace doctor. After being taken to the private hospital by car he walked in unaided. It was not an emergency admission or COVID-related, but it was a warning. Sadly, it came on the day that his retired page Christopher Harry Marlow, who had been honoured with a bar to his Royal Victorian Medal (Silver) by the Queen upon his retirement in 2003, had died. The duke had been 'feeling unwell for a short period and the doctor was called' and the phrase that was used by his doctors was 'an abundance of caution'. Boris Johnson led the nation in sending his best wishes to the duke for a speedy recovery and wished him well while he rested in hospital. The Prince of Wales made a 100-mile trip to visit the Duke of Edinburgh in hospital three days later and spent half an hour at his bedside, leaving shortly before 4pm. Observers described him as looking sombre as he climbed into his car.

During the time they spent together at the castle in lockdown, Elizabeth and Philip were able to rediscover some of the happiness of their earlier years and this will surely give Her Majesty memories to cherish and strength in her time of need and mourning.

2: NOMADIC PRINCE

'I didn't know any different, you just get on with it.'

Prince Philip when asked about his upbringing

The Queen and Prince Philip's marriage is seen as the bedrock of our modern monarchy. For 75 years he was her rock, somebody she could rely on without question. So it seems hard to imagine now that there were many leading figures, including her father, the king, who were against the union. It meant their journey to the altar of Westminster Abbey to pronounce the marital vows was far from smooth. Elizabeth, headstrong and determined despite her comparative youth, had to fight for what she wanted, and what she wanted without question was Philip.

Philip, as a young man, was seen by some in the British establishment as an outsider and a threat. Born Prince Philippos of Greece and Denmark, the man destined to wed the most eligible woman in the world and be elevated to HRH Prince Philip, Duke of Edinburgh, was born on a kitchen table at his family's villa Mon Repos, south of Corfu City on the Greek isle of Corfu on 10 June 1921*.

Philip may have had the bloodline, connections and good looks to marry well, but events meant he didn't have the fortune to match. His mother, a great-granddaughter of the last monarch

---

* He was actually born on 28 May 1921 – adjusted to 10 June only when his birthplace Greece adopted the Gregorian calendar.

of the Hanoverian dynasty Queen Empress Victoria, was Princess Alice of Battenberg. Born congenitally deaf, she was a Hessian princess by birth as the Battenberg family was a morganatic branch of the House of Hesse-Darmstadt.

The first member of the House of Battenberg was Julia Hauke, whose brother-in-law Grand Duke Louis III of Hesse created her Countess of Battenberg with the style Illustrious Highness in 1851 on her morganatic marriage to Grand Duke Louis' brother Prince Alexander of Hesse and by Rhine. Julia was elevated in her title to Princess of Battenberg with the style Serene Highness (HSH) in 1858.

Two of the sons of Alexander and Julia, Prince Henry of Battenberg and Prince Louis of Battenberg, became associated with the British Royal Family. Prince Henry married Princess Beatrice, the youngest daughter of Queen Victoria. Prince Louis married Victoria's granddaughter, Princess Victoria of Hesse and by Rhine, and became the First Sea Lord of the British Royal Navy.

Due to understandable anti-German feelings in Britain during the great 1914–1918 war, not even the King, George V, and the Royal Family and their close relations were safe from criticism. Author H. G. Wells confirmed King George's worst fears in his *Times* newspaper column, in which he referred to Britain's 'Alien and uninspiring court'. George V, who thought Wells to be 'impertinent', famously responded, 'I may be uninspiring but I'll be damned if I'm an alien.'

Lord Stamfordham, George V's private secretary, in cahoots with Prime Minster David Lloyd George, felt the King needed to distance himself from his blatant German ancestry given the wave of anti-German feeling sweeping the country at the time. On 17 July 1917 the Privy Council proclaimed, 'Henceforth the royal family would be called the House of Windsor, having divested itself of its previous surname, as well as all other German degrees, styles, titles, dignitaries, honours and appellations'. After a number of alternatives were considered, including Plantagenet, York, England, Lancaster, d'Este and Fitzroy, Lord Stamfordham's suggestion of Windsor was adopted, after a minor title once held by Edward III.

His cousin the Kaiser, himself a grandson of Queen Victoria, saw the funny side and remarked he looked forward to attending a performance of *The Merry Wives of Saxe-Coburg-Gotha*. A more serious and altogether grander disapproval came from the Bavarian Count Albrecht von Montgelas, who commented that, 'The true royal tradition died on that day in 1917 when, for a mere war, King George V changed his name.'

It was not just the immediate family, but all branches of the family that were impacted. The Teck family became the Cambridges and took the Earldom of Athlone, the Battenbergs, Philip's mother's family, overnight were transformed into the Mountbattens with the Marquisate of Milford Haven. Prince Louis, his children and his nephews (the living sons of Prince Henry) were effectively forced to renounce their German titles and changed their name to the more English-sounding Mountbatten. (They rejected an alternative translation, Battenhill.) Their cousin, George V, compensated the princes with British peerages. Louis became the 1st Marquess of Milford Haven, while Prince Alexander, Prince Henry's eldest son, became the 1st Marquess of Carisbrooke. He was offered a dukedom by the King but declined as he could not afford the lavish lifestyle expected of a duke.

As for George, who had always been quintessentially British and found German 'a rotten language', he felt the move was timely and necessary, given the hostility to royal houses across Europe which had led to their collapse, and it received a positive reaction in the press. It proved a wise move as one of the most important roles of the Windsor monarchs was to act as national figureheads during the two devastating wars of 1914–1918 and 1939–1945 ostensibly against Germany.

Although Prince Philip's uncle on his father's side was King Constantine I of Greece, he did not have a drop of Greek blood as he was descended from both Danish, German and British royalty. Philip's father was the son of King George I of Greece, a former Danish prince installed as the Greek monarch in 1863 and later assassinated in 1913. Andrea was a major-general in the Greek army and had already left to take up his command the day before his son's birth and did not see him for months.

Philip's mother wrote to inform her husband of the 'splendid, healthy child' who at birth was sixth in line to the Greek throne. But this was an insecure royal house, one that could be toppled by its volatile people at any given moment. Philip was born into dangerous times. Greece was again involved in a bloody war with old enemy and neighbour Turkey (Asia Minor at the time) and when the military campaign, led by the Greek king, proved an unmitigated disaster, the people and politicians looked to their royal family as scapegoats. After the humiliating defeat was confirmed, discontent spread among the middle-ranking officers and men and it boiled over into a full-scale armed revolt led by anti-royalist senior officers. The destruction of the Greek forces in Anatolia led to calls for those responsible for the shambles to be punished. The government of Petros Protopapadakis resigned on 28 August and the new government headed by Nikolaos Triantafyllakos replaced it. Within days, on 11 September, the revolution was declared, with the formation of a Revolutionary Committee headed by Colonels Nikolaos Plastiras as representative of the army in Chios and Stylianos Gonatas as representative of the army in Lesvos and Commander Dimitrios Fokas as representative of the navy.

The next day, the troops boarded their ships and headed to Athens. Before they arrived there, a military aeroplane delivered a manifesto demanding the resignation of King Constantine I, the dissolution of the parliament and the formation of a new politically independent government. On 13 September, King Constantine resigned and went into exile, in Italy. His son, George II, was declared king. On 15 September, the troops of revolution entered the city of Athens and blocked the efforts Theodoros Pangalos was making to take advantage of the situation and take control of the government. Soon a new government was formed with Sotirios Krokidas as chairman.

With the king forced to leave his country, angry mobs demanded a scapegoat and Philip's unfortunate father, Andrea, fitted the bill.

He was arrested and charged with poor leadership and disobeying a direct order. He was warned by a member of the newly installed government that his son and four daughters would soon be orphans. A date was set for his court-martial in Athens. Philip's older sister, Princess Sophie of Greece and Denmark, noted the family's trauma in her private memoir. 'My father's trial ended with him being sentenced to death. Many governments tried to save his life including King Alfonso XIII of Spain and the Pope. But finally my father's first cousin Britain's George V succeeded in having the death sentence remitted.'

He may have been spared his life by the intervention of his powerful extended family but Andrea felt he had been stripped of his honour. What followed was difficult for the proud prince to live with, the humiliating prospect of a perpetual exile from his country. Indeed thanks to George V* the family was spirited to safety in the battleship cruiser HMS *Calypso*. Unsurprisingly, it was a chaotic and dangerous time for the whole family, and they didn't have enough time to make sure Philip had a proper cot or carriage to carry him in. They had to think quickly to work out a way to transport the infant Philip, so the family got creative and carried him aboard in an orange crate. It might not have been the most comfortable means of travel for Philip, but it managed to help him and his family successfully flee to safety.

With little money and no papers, the royal refugees sailed to Britain dreaming of a calmer existence. But if they thought they would be welcome there due to George's intervention, they were soon to be disappointed. It was only five years after the Russian Revolution when another of George V's cousins, Russian Emperor Tsar Nicholas II, his wife Empress Alexandra and their five children, Olga, Tatiana, Maria, Anastasia and Alexei, had been shot and bayoneted to death by Communist revolutionaries in Yekaterinburg. European royalty was on the run with the rise of socialism and the King did not welcome the idea of having exiled

---

* Philip's future wife's grandfather

royals on display in England reminding his subjects that royalty and monarchy was not permanent and could be overthrown. The prospect of living in London among a rather hostile people didn't appeal to Andrea and his family either so instead he decided to take his family to Paris where he was lent a suite of rooms in a palais on the edge of the Bois de Boulogne.

There was always a sense of impermanence for Andrea and his family. The exiled prince soon realised he didn't have the capital to pay for the household that came with the accommodation so they moved across the Seine to a lodge in the garden of the impressive mansion 5 Rue du Mont-Valérian, situated in the hill-top suburb of St Cloud, a few miles west from the centre of Paris. The property surrounded by apple trees, belonged to the heiress wife of Andrea's elder brother Prince George of Greece and Denmark, known to the family as 'Big George'. Princess Marie Bonaparte, who was a great-grandniece of Emperor Napoleon I of France, had inherited her huge wealth from her maternal grandfather François Blanc, the principal real-estate developer of Monte Carlo. She was destined to be a disciple and benefactor of Sigmund Freud and thus central to the establishment of psychoanalysis and sexology in France.

The dramatic escape and fall from power took its toll on Philip's parents leaving them scarred mentally. They were broke too. Although Marie was a gracious and generous hostess who did her best to support her husband's brother and his family and small staff, Andrea's finances were a mess. He had managed to bring some money with him during the hurried exit from Greece and had a bequest from Constantine, his brother, as well as an annuity from his late father but it was not enough to sustain him and his family. He had inherited villa Mon Repos but feared his property in Greece would be confiscated by the revolutionary government. To his surprise it was not and in 1926 he secured a deal to lease it to his wife's wealthy brother, Lord Louis 'Dickie' Mountbatten; that provided another modest source of much-needed cash. He eventually sold Mon Repos to his nephew King George II of Greece in 1937 having won a legal case legitimising his ownership.

Philip's mother, who had inherited a tenth of the estate of her father Prince Louis of Battenberg, suffered terribly from the family's enforced refugee status. Her inheritance had been radically reduced due to the war and the Russian Revolution. Philip, sensitive to his surroundings and his family's plight, appreciated that there was a need to economise and to value what he had, so much so that he acquired a reputation of being mean.

Philip, however, recalled his childhood as a happy time. His resilient family had learned to always make the best of their situation. Supported by his uncle Christopher, in 1927 Philip, aged six, was enrolled at an American school known as the Elms. He settled in quickly insisting on being called 'just Philip' (dumping the princely title) when he was asked to introduce himself, as he wisely was reluctant to stand out by letting the other boys know of his high birth.

Princess Alice encouraged the headmaster, Donald MacJannet, known to the boys as 'Mr Mac', to establish a Cub Scout group so that her son's 'great vitality' was put to good use. Another key figure of constancy in the young Philip's life was the family nanny, Emily Roose, a down-to-earth English woman, who instilled a sense of the importance of the English language and values in him.

Philip enjoyed his first school and the challenges it threw up. 'I had four sisters and we were living in quite a small house just outside Paris and I went to an American children's school. I was French and English speaking because I had an English nanny and the family spoke about four languages so one got a bit confused,' he recalled. 'Often a conversation would start in English then somebody couldn't remember the word so it went on in French then it went into Greek and then into German and this would happen all the time,' he added. Another time he recalled, 'If anything, I've thought of myself as Scandinavian, particularly, Danish. We spoke English at home.*"

---

* In 2008, France's First Lady Carla Bruni-Sarkozy was surprised and impressed by Philip's 'impeccable French'.

His cousin, the late Countess Mountbatten of Burma, said she couldn't recall the first time she met her cousin Philip. 'He was boisterous and full of fun and got up to all sorts of things you hadn't dare get up to yourself.' Constantine II of Greece said Philip had a unique ability to make the person he was talking to feel the most important person in the room. Lady Myra Butter, another cousin, described him as, 'Very boyish but great fun and very kind. He hasn't really changed as a person at all.'

Exile took its toll on Philip's mother who began to suffer a rapid deterioration of her mental state. Her marriage to Andrea was in crisis too. His mother's ill health would always be something Philip played down throughout his life, but it undoubtably had a huge impact on him. Dismissed as a religious crisis, her family tried to cover up her mental frailty. For Andrea, his wife's heightened state of mania and her religious fervour became impossible to cope with. She became obsessed with spiritualism and the supernatural too, repeatedly dealing her cards to predict her future path and obtain messages. Alice also became obsessed with a mystery Englishman in 1925 with whom she fell hopelessly in love but she repressed her feelings for him.

Another suggestion is that Alice was suffering from manic depression, or bipolar disorder as it would later be known, a mental condition that can lead to dramatic mood swings and periods of prolonged manic energy. In October 1928, just two weeks after she and her husband marked their 25th wedding anniversary at St Cloud, Alice converted to the Greek Orthodox faith. But the following year her mental state deteriorated and her behaviour became even more odd. She took to lying on the floor in a bid to converse with God and became convinced she had been given a divine power to heal. By November the situation had reached crisis point.

When her mother Princess Victoria went to Paris for a visit in January 1929, there was serious concern for Alice. The family turned to Marie Bonaparte for advice, as she had recently undergone psychoanalysis with Sigmund Freud. Marie recommended that her sister-in-law go to a clinic run by Freudian Dr Ernst Simmel outside Berlin in Tegel, the first to use psychoanalysis to treat patients. Alice was diagnosed by Simmel as a ' paranoid schizophrenic' and he also claimed she was suffering from a 'neurotic-pre-psychotic libidinous condition'.

On 2 May 1930, Victoria contacted Professor Wilmanns and agreed to section Alice at his psychiatric clinic Bellevue Sanatorium at Kreuzlingen on Lake Constance. When he arrived at 5 Rue du Mont-Valérian Alice was alone as it had been arranged for her children to be out. She needed to be sedated before being bundled into a car and driven away without the opportunity to say goodbye to her son and daughters. Philip had been taken for a walk, and when he came back his mother had gone. Believing that her reported visions were the results of sexual frustration, it was recommended she receive therapy involving electro-shock treatment. Alice pleaded her sanity, but was kept in the sanatorium for over two years.

Philip had to learn to take whatever life threw at him. He would not see his mother for the rest of his childhood. His father Andrea moved in with his mistress and effectively abandoned his young son now his daughters were married. He headed south to Monte Carlo for pastures new. It was the beginning of Philip's nomadic existence. At just nine years old with his mother in a psychiatric clinic and his father mostly absent, Philip had to learn to face the world alone. 'I just had to get on with it. You do. One does,' Philip said when reflecting on his childhood. 'I didn't notice it at the time, no. It seemed to be perfectly normal as far as I was concerned. How could I compare it to anything else?' It was a fair point, but it could have left many boys of his own age emotionally damaged.

Alice's brother George Mountbatten, 2nd Marquess of Milford Haven, effectively became Philip's guardian. George and his wife, Nada, the flamboyant and sexually fluid great-granddaughter of the Russian poet Alexander Pushkin and the daughter of Grand Duke Michael Mikhailovich, sent for him to join them at their home Lynden Manor, England for the next stage of the young Philip's life's journey. Within weeks he joined Cheam School, Surrey – then Britain's oldest preparatory school – as a boarder. The athletic Philip delighted his uncle by excelling on the sports field, winning a clutch of trophies and being selected to join the cricket first XI. The school afforded him stability as his family network practically disappeared. By the end of 1931, his four older sisters had all married members of the German nobility and, from the summer of 1932 to 1937, Philip did not hear from his mother. Meanwhile his father Andrea, who by now had closed down the family home at St Cloud, moved to Monte Carlo full-time with his mistress French film actress and wealthy widow Andrée Lafayette (also known as Andrée de la Bigne) aboard a yacht, *David*.

Philip attended all his sisters' weddings in Germany. He briefly joined his brother-in-law's school at Salem, despite the fact that it was being taken over with Nazi doctrine as Hitler's power and influence rose in Germany. The school's co-founder, Dr Kurt Hahn, had already fled the country amid the rise of the Nazi Party and sustained persecution of the Jewish population by the brown-shirt SA or Sturmtruppen led by Hitler's brutal henchman, Ernst Röhm. In enforced exile the Jewish intellectual went on to found an outward-bound boarding school in Duffus to the north-west of Elgin, Scotland.

'I went to Salem; it seemed to be the sensible thing to go because it was owned by my brother-in-law so it was the cheapest way of educating me,' Philip recalled. 'After I'd been at Salem for about a year the Nazis had more or less taken over and life was getting a bit tricky, because my brother-in-law and sister were not really enthusiastic about the Nazis and didn't think it was very good for me to be there.' Dr Hahn later recalled Philip's irreverence to the Nazis: 'Whenever the Nazi salute was given he roared with laughter.' This was apparently because his pals at Cheam used to make a similar gesture when they wanted to go to the lavatory.

The year 1934 saw Hitler's infamous 'Night of the Long Knives' on 30 June when the Nazi leader, fearing that the paramilitary SA had become too powerful, ordered a purge and sent his elite

SS guards to murder Röhm. With political turmoil in Germany increasing, Philip returned to Britain. 'We thought it better for him,' explained his sister Theodora.

Eventually, after consulting his father, it was decided that Philip would be sent to Kurt Hahn's new school, Gordonstoun, on the Morayshire coast close to Elgin and Lossiemouth in Scotland where he had developed a testing, Spartan regime for his pupils. A visionary educationalist, Dr Hahn believed that young people flourish when their horizons are broadened beyond just their academic potential. Despite his rank Philip never asked for any privilege on account of his birth. Years later in 1961 Dr Hahn gave an interview and said, 'One thing you can definitely say is that early on he was one of those boys who very early on rendered disinterested service and who never asked for any privilege on account of his birth.'

On his return to Britain Philip flourished, excelling academically demonstrating what his masters described as a 'lively intelligence' and a determination to 'exert himself more than was necessary.' His chief faults were his 'intolerance and impatience' they said, but although often 'naughty' he was never 'nasty'. His sporting prowess reached new heights too when he became both captain of the hockey and cricket teams, culminating in him later acting as head boy.

The robust system at Gordonstoun suited Philip. The boys were up at 6.30 a.m. for a cold shower and a run. From 10.30 a.m. they had a break from lessons for sporting activities. After lunch adult boys would read to the younger ones. At this time the most stable influence on Philip was his grandmother Princess Victoria, Marchioness of Milford Haven, an amazingly strong and intelligent woman. She could be a little overbearing but she kept a watchful eye on him, ensuring he had his school uniform and making timely visits to Scotland so he didn't feel isolated and alone. 'I admired her enormously. She was hugely intelligent and well read and had fascinating conversation. She knew about everything as far as I was concerned,' he said of her. The school and Philip were a perfect fit. His time there taught him self-reliance with a motto, 'Plus est en vousin' ('There is more in you').

Competing at your best level to achieve something for yourself was its ethos. It was to stay with Philip all his life.

At 16, Philip was hit by tragedy. That November his pregnant and beloved eldest sister Cecilie died in a plane crash after setting off from Frankfurt aerodrome in a three-engine Junkers monoplane (operated by the Belgian airline Sabina) to London airport for a family wedding. Cecilie was travelling with her husband, George Donatus, known as ' Don' who had just succeeded his father as the Grand Duke of Hesse and by Rhine, his widowed mother the Dowager Grand Duchess and the couple's two young sons, Prince Ludwig, six, and Prince Alexander, four. Their baby sister Princess Johanna* was deemed too young to attend the wedding and didn't travel.

The plane, flown by experienced captain Tony Lambotte, a personal friend and pilot of Belgian King Leopold III, was due to touch down on route near Brussels, but thick fog forced the pilot to fly to Steene Aerodrome near Ostend. Fog had swept in there too and it meant the pilot was 'flying blind'. Three rockets were fired to help him find his way but only the first one worked. During the descent tragedy struck as the plane hit the top of a brickworks chimney at around 100 mph and then crashed into the roof killing all on board. When firemen sifted through the burnt wreckage they found the remains of a baby lying next to the body of Cecilie, which gave rise to the theory that the pilot had tried to land as the Grand Duchess was giving birth.

It was left to his headmaster Dr Hahn to break the devastating news to Philip. He recalled that Philip's sorrow 'was that of a man'. He kept a piece of wood recovered from the wreckage for the rest

---

* After the tragedy her paternal uncle Ludwig still married his bride Margaret Geddes. The couple adopted Johanna, their orphaned niece, and planned to raise her as their own daughter, but she developed meningitis and died 20 months later at the age of two and a half. Her maternal grandmother, Princess Alice of Battenberg, said later that the unconscious Johanna so closely resembled her mother at the same age that it felt like losing her daughter Cecilie all over again. Following Johanna's death, she was buried with her parents and brothers at the Rosenhöhe.

of his life. Philip's cousin, Lady Myra Butter, recalled, 'That was totally horrendous. Somehow he has had to bear with that one. He just gets on with it, that's his motto, "just get on with it." Sometimes what are the alternatives?'

Alice reunited with her family at the funeral in Germany. It was the first time the teenager had seen his mother in almost five years. But she did not stay long in his life and went on to found a nunnery in Greece, funded with her own jewels, and was never seen in civilian clothes after 1949. Philip suffered another blow the next April when George Mountbatten, his mentor and benefactor, died from cancer at just 45. His care now fell to his other maternal uncle Louis 'Dickie' Mountbatten. Mountbatten's daughter, the late Patricia, Countess Mountbatten, recalled Philip as a vibrant youngster who was a regular guest at their home. 'He was three years older than me. He was very boyish, full of fun. Loved to play pranks, quite nice pranks, and just somebody that one welcomed rather than think oh it's a bit of a bore so and so is coming,' the Countess said. 'It was "how nice he's going to come and enliven life."'

In 1935 for a brief moment Philip was torn between his influential English relatives and his role as a prince of Greece. That year Georgios Kondylis, a former military officer, became the most powerful political figure in Greece. On 10 October, he compelled Panagis Tsaldaris to resign as Greek prime minister and took over the government himself, suspending many constitutional provisions in the process. Kondylis, who had joined the Conservatives, decided to hold a referendum in order to restore the monarchy in Greece. It took place on 3 November 1935 and, incredibly, the proposal was approved by 97.9 per cent of voters. Philip's first cousin (a maternal nephew of Wilhelm II the last German Emperor), George II of Greece, who had reigned as King of Greece from 1922 to 1924, returned to Athens after 12 years of exile, the latter part of which had been spent living at Brown's Hotel in London. The crown was formally restored on 30 November 1935.

The move meant that Philip was now sixth in line to the Greek throne and it gave his father, Andrea, who was living in Monte

Carlo, a renewed purpose. He said in one newspaper interview, 'We shall not return as avengers but as symbols of the love of the people on whose will alone the restoration will be founded.' The body of Philip's uncle, Constantine I, was duly returned to Athens for burial and Philip, in morning coat, attended the ceremony. His future journey was at a crossroads.

The new King of Greece wanted his cousin, Philip, to join the Greek navy, but Dickie Mountbatten persuaded him otherwise. He had come to see Greece as an undeveloped, backward Balkan country inhabited by a romantic but volatile and feral people. Dickie advised Philip that Greece was not a stable enough country to nail his colours to, and was determined to steer his nephew and protégé towards a career in the British Royal Navy.

Britain's George V was equally unconvinced by the stability of the newly restored Greek monarchy and felt it would not last long either. He was advised, confidentially, by the British Ambassador, Sir Sydney Waterlow, that the experiment of restoring the monarchy in Greece was almost certainly 'doomed to fail' and that the new king was ill-advised to insist on restoring his uncle, Andrea, and his brother, Nicholas, to their elevated positions back in Greece and out of exile. But the decree that banished Andrea was lifted in 1936 and by the autumn he was once again living in Athens, serving as the main aide-de-camp to his nephew, the new monarch.

If Philip's head was turned by the pomp and perceived importance of being a prominent member of the Greek royal family, he didn't show it. His headmaster, Dr Hahn, later recalled that when Philip returned to school he seemed more determined than ever to sit the Special Entry Examination for the Royal Navy. He made it clear, Hahn said later, that England was his home. It was, in terms of his life's journey, the most consequential decision he would ever make.

Once a close confidante of King Edward VIII, Dickie Mountbatten had deftly switched his allegiance to the new king, George VI, after the shock of the 1936 abdication crisis. He had big plans for his nephew and saw Philip as the perfect consort to the Princess Elizabeth, heir presumptive. His striking good looks, strength of character and his regal-blooded ancestry more than qualified him for that role in Mountbatten's view. 'I toyed with the idea of going to the Royal Air Force but my uncle persuaded me to try the navy and I had to sit the civil service exam to become a special entry cadet in Dartmouth in 1939,' Philip later recalled.

His father, Andrea, remained involved in Philip's education but from a distance. He soon tired of life in Athens and, with World War II approaching, returned to living his playboy existence and only saw his son fleetingly in the years that followed. In 1944 Philip lost his father, who remained in Vichy France from the beginning of the war, whilst his son fought on the side of the British. They were unable to see or even correspond with one another. Andrea died in the Metropole Hotel, Monte Carlo, of heart failure and arterial sclerosis as the war was ending and substantially in debt owing £17,500 (around £782,000 today). The playboy prince left his only son some trunks containing clothing, an ivory shaving brush, a solitary pair of cufflinks and a signet ring that Philip would wear for the rest of his life.

Philip's mother, Princess Alice, had made a satisfactory recovery by this time and had returned to Greece where, during the Nazi occupation of Athens in the war, she hid a Jewish family and saved them from certain death at the hands of the SS and Nazis. Evy Cohen, later spoke about how her father Alfred Haimaki Cohen, head of a prominent family with ties to Greek royalty, sought out Princess Alice as their only hope of refuge from the Nazis. 'At the beginning of [19]43, it became obvious that the decisions against Jews, to take them to concentration camps, was starting to be obvious, my family had to go into hiding. If it hadn't been for her, I wouldn't be alive today to say all this. My parents would not have met, and so many other things,' Evy revealed in the documentary *Princess Alice: The Royals' Greatest Secret*. 'She didn't even think for a minute, she just heard that there were people in danger, and she thought she could do something for them. The story of Princess Alice and my family is a beautiful one, and I hope it can be an example for young people today to continue to do good things in life, and to be human.'

Many years later Princess Alice was honoured for her courage. She was to spend the last two years of her life at Buckingham Palace with her son and his young family.

As Nazi Germany's tanks rolled across Europe, beginning with the German annexation of Sudetenland in 1938 and continuing in March 1939 with the invasion of the Czech lands and the creation of the Protectorate of Bohemia and Moravia, Philip left school and enrolled as a cadet at Dartmouth Naval College. Hitler's annexation of Czechoslovakia breached the written guarantee he had issued to British prime minister Neville Chamberlain in Munich in 1938, stating that he had no further territorial demands to make in Europe. Therefore, on 31 March 1939, Chamberlain issued a formal guarantee of Poland's borders and said that he expected Hitler to moderate his demands. Hitler was not deterred and on 3 April 1939 he ordered the Wehrmacht to prepare for the invasion of Poland on 1 September. Hitler was convinced that Chamberlain would not go to war to defend Poland and that France would lack the will to act alone.

Prince Philip, meanwhile, was ready to serve his adopted country. As soon as he graduated he was determined to be assigned to a warship, do his duty and fight against the Nazi tyranny. He didn't have to wait long to get his chance.

3: BRIEF ENCOUNTERS

'The first time I remember meeting Philip was at the Royal Naval College, Dartmouth, in July 1939, just before the war. (We may have met before at the coronation or the Duchess of Kent's wedding, but I don't remember.) I was 13 years of age and he was 18 and a cadet just due to leave.'

Princess Elizabeth's recollections about her romance with Philip

Prince Philip and Princess Elizabeth's paths first crossed at the wedding of his first cousin, Princess Marina of Greece and Denmark, to Prince George, later the Duke of Kent. Elizabeth, the groom's niece, was an eight-year-old bridesmaid and was included in all the main photographs. Thirteen-year-old Prince Philip of Greece and Denmark was really a bit part player and did not feature. The wedding on 29 November 1934 at Westminster Abbey was a grand affair on a rather dull day. Coming a decade after the last royal wedding, that of his brother, the Duke of York and Lady Elizabeth Bowes-Lyon, Princess Elizabeth's parents, it was the first royal nuptials to be broadcast on the radio too.

Tens of thousands of people lined the route and gave the bride and groom 'a warm hearted crescendo of cheers', the commentator said on the *Movietone* news special, as they rode in the Glass Carriage. Westminster Abbey accommodated 1,500 guests including members of the extended British Royal Family as well as the royal families of Denmark, Greece, and Yugoslavia. There were also members of the former reigning royal families of Russia, Prussia and Austria, and other lesser royals who had also lost their thrones after World War I. Among the guests was the American-born British shipbroker Ernest Simpson and his American wife, Wallis, who would soon become a household name.

The bride's gown was in white and silver silk brocade, designed by couturier Edward Molyneux, and worked on by a team of seamstresses including, at Marina's request, a number of Russian émigrés. The dress featured a sheath silhouette, a draped cowl neckline, trumpet sleeves and a wide train. A tiara, given to her as a wedding gift, secured her tulle veil which Princess Elizabeth and ten-year-old Lady Mary Cambridge carried. After the bride reached the altar, the hymn 'Gracious Spirit, Holy Ghost' was sung.

Upon return to Buckingham Palace, a Greek Orthodox wedding ceremony was held in the private chapel officiated by the Metropolitan Dr Strinopoulos Germanos, Head of the Greek Orthodox Church in England. The Prince of Wales caused a stir when he decided to smoke and lit his cigarette using one of the many candles alight inside.

Until then, Princess Elizabeth of York's life's story had been far more stable than her exotic foreign male cousin Philip. Protected and secure, she had been raised embraced by love and affection. She may not have been born to be monarch but, as third in line to the throne, Elizabeth was a star attraction as far as the press was concerned.

★★★

Hot coffee and sandwiches were sent out to reporters waiting in a huddle in the dark outside the house. The weather had been foul for a week, and the pervading mood in London was one of gloom. Britain was in serious crisis, with the threat of a general strike uppermost in people's minds. Inside 17 Bruton Street, Mayfair, the scene was one of undiluted joy. For at 2.40 a.m. on 21 April 1926, Elizabeth, the first child of the Duke and Duchess of York, came into the world.

The duchess had been in labour for several hours, and the surgeon, Sir Henry Stratton, took the decision to perform a caesarean section. Thankfully, everything went well. The baby girl stood third in line of succession to the throne, after her uncle, the Prince of Wales, and her father, the Duke of York. At the time it was not expected that her father would become king or that she would ever become queen.

News of the birth was kept private for an hour or two, to allow the King and Queen to be told first. At 4 a.m., George V and Queen Mary were woken at Windsor Castle and given the happy news. That afternoon they drove to London to see the baby girl. 'A little darling with a lovely complexion and pretty fair hair,' the Queen later wrote in her diary. The following day the Duke of York wrote to his mother: 'You don't know what a tremendous joy it is to Elizabeth & me to have our little girl. We always wanted a child to make our happiness complete, & now that it has at last happened, it seems so wonderful & strange.'

Despite their royal rank, they were attentive parents. On 28 October 1926, Elizabeth wrote to her mother, Lady Strathmore, from Sandringham, Norfolk, 'My Darling Mother... The baby is very well, and now spends the whole day taking her shoes off & sucking her toes! She is going to be very wicked, and she is very quick I think.'

The little princess was christened in the private chapel of Buckingham Palace eight months later by the Archbishop of Canterbury, Dr Cosmo Gordon Lang, a complex character said to have 'a jangle of warring personalities.' The gold, lily-shaped font was brought from St George's Chapel, Windsor, and the water for the baptism came from the River Jordan in Palestine. The royal child was named Elizabeth Alexandra Mary: Elizabeth after her mother, while her two middle names were those of her paternal great-grandmother, Queen Alexandra, and paternal grandmother, Queen Mary. The King and Queen were among her godparents. Also present were Lady Elphinstone (the baby's aunt and godmother); Arthur, Duke of Connaught (great-great-uncle and godfather); the Countess and Earl of Strathmore (maternal grandparents; the earl was also a godparent); and Princess Mary, Viscountess Lascelles (aunt and godmother). They appeared together in a group photograph by Herbert Vandyk, a second-generation court photographer with a studio in close proximity to the palace, taken at the palace on 29 May 1926.

In January, on the King's orders, the Yorks embarked on a six-month tour of several colonies and dominions, including New Zealand and Australia, leaving their tiny baby in the care of the unflappable, no-nonsense nanny, Mrs Clara Knight, affectionately known as 'Allah'. The duchess particularly dreaded the trip as it meant being parted from her baby daughter for so long. Her diary recorded her misery. 'Thursday 6 January 1927. Up by 8.30. Feel very miserable at leaving the baby. I drank some champagne & tried not to weep…'

With her parents away, the little princess often brightened the afternoons of her grandparents, George and Mary. George V, a stern father by all accounts to his own five children, was transformed into a soft and besotted grandfather for his little 'Lilibet', the nickname she later gave herself as she could not pronounce Elizabeth properly.

Elizabeth's early life was blissfully happy, spent in the top-floor nursery at 145 Piccadilly, the London house taken by her parents on their return from their overseas visit. The InterContinental Hotel, London, Park Lane, now stands proudly on the very site. Back then Elizabeth would play ensconced with Allah and her assistant Margaret 'Bobo' MacDonald. The King adored Elizabeth and often asked for her to be brought to the palace so that they could play. When they were not together he would telephone the nursery and then focus on the window with a pair of binoculars to see his beloved granddaughter waving back at him. When the King became seriously ill, requiring lung surgery to be carried out on 12 December 1928, Elizabeth was taken to stay with him in Bognor, the seaside resort in West Sussex, to help make his convalescence bearable. He would later bestow the suffix 'Regis' which means, 'Of the king', on the town as he had spent so much time there.

At that time Princess Elizabeth was not expected to become the monarch given that her uncle, David, was still expected to marry a suitable bride and produce a legitimate heir. Winston Churchill, then Chancellor of the Exchequer in Stanley Baldwin's government, observed something special about the child on their first encounter. Within the Churchill papers is his earliest recorded reference to Elizabeth in a letter to his wife, Clementine. Churchill, then 53, imagines the destiny of the future sovereign during a stay at Balmoral Castle on 25 September 1928. 'There is no one here at all except the family, the Household & Queen & Elizabeth — aged two. The last is a character. She has an air of authority & reflectiveness astonishing in an infant,' he recalled.

When Princess Elizabeth was four years old, the Duke and Duchess of York were offered a new house, Royal Lodge, situated within Windsor Great Park, as a retreat. Elizabeth's beloved 'Grandpa England', as she called the King, presented her with a Shetland pony that ignited Elizabeth's lifelong love for horses. The following year when most of her contemporaries were attending school she remained at home and was taught to read by her mother.

The Yorks' second daughter, Margaret Rose, was born on 21 August 1930 at Glamis Castle, the Scottish estate of her mother's parents, the Earl and Countess of Strathmore and Kinghorne. Her parents felt so sure the child would be a boy that they had no girls' names ready. Elizabeth announced she would call her sister 'Bud'. When asked why, Elizabeth responded, 'Well, she's not a rose yet, is she? She's only a bud.' If Margaret had been a boy, Elizabeth's importance would have waned as the law of primogeniture, still in place then, meant the younger male child would have taken precedence in the line of succession. In fact, Margaret's birth brought the York family, that her father dubbed 'we four', into sharper focus.

George V's illness had taken a great toll on him, but his obdurate heir, the popular 36-year-old Prince of Wales, showed no sign of settling down with a suitable bride and starting a family of his own. His offspring would have taken precedence in the line of succession to the throne. George V had little time for his other sons. The love the Prince of Wales felt towards twice-divorced American, Wallis Simpson, not only caused a rift between the King and his direct heir, but growing concern among government ministers and leading establishment figures.

By now, George V had come to the conclusion that the Yorks were a safe pair of hands and that in Bertie*, despite his speech impediment, there was a man of inner strength who had the courage to be a leader. Princesses Elizabeth and Margaret, despite their tender ages, could not be shielded from the growing tensions within the family. But they were, perhaps, too young to fully understand how the unfolding abdication would one day impact on their young lives. To them, the Prince of Wales was their golden-haired, favourite uncle, David, a charming, mischievous, joyful man who around them was above all always fun to be with. They would spend hours with him miming the characters in A. A. Milne's bestselling *Winnie the Pooh* and they simply adored him.

For the Duke of York the situation had become intolerable. The prospect of him becoming king in place of his older brother, should David abdicate his responsibilities, filled him with dread. In 1936, which was to become known as 'The Year of the Three Kings', his worst nightmare would come true and his blissful private world, and that of his young family, would change forever.

Over Christmas 1935, George V's health deteriorated rapidly and he developed a debilitating viral respiratory infection. Eight years earlier, on 9 December 1928, the King, who suffered from bronchitis and numerous lung problems throughout his later life, had only been spared death by the skilled intervention of his physician, Sir Bertrand Dawson, who located and drained the abscess that had gravely complicated an attack of pleurisy. That crisis, and the long months of recovery, inspired a surge of popular feeling towards him and the crown he served. Now ennobled, Lord Dawson of Penn could do very little to help the King, apart from making him comfortable in his final hours of life. Years later it emerged that, as the King lay comatose on his deathbed in 1936, his personal physician injected the monarch with fatal doses of morphine and

---

* The Queen's father

38

cocaine to ensure a painless and timely death, according to his own notes, for the announcement to be carried 'in the morning papers rather than the less appropriate evening journals.'

This remarkable act of royal euthanasia remained a secret for half a century until in 1986 it was revealed that he administered the two lethal injections at about 11 p.m. on 20 January 1936. An hour and a half earlier, Dawson had written a classically brief and now famous medical bulletin that declared, 'The king's life is moving peacefully toward its close.' The physician had already taken the precaution of phoning his wife, Minnie Ethel, in London to ask that she, 'Advise *The Times* to hold back publication.' The next morning, 21 January, under the headline, 'A Peaceful Ending at Midnight,' *The Times* led the tributes to the monarch. Lord Dawson was satisfied too, that he had played his part in ensuring such important news was published in the newspaper of record and the other morning newspapers, rather than the 'less appropriate evening journals'.

George V's death at 70 was not unexpected. He had been a very heavy smoker all his life and by 1925 he was diagnosed with chronic obstructive pulmonary disease. A few years later, he fell seriously ill with an inflammatory disease and never fully recovered. It meant in his final year he was often administered oxygen. It was noted officially that his death was due to bronchial problems and a weak heart, not an act of euthanasia.

George V was succeeded by his direct heir, his eldest son, who took the name King Edward VIII. Prophetically, before his death, George had confided in Prime Minister Stanley Baldwin, who would later become a key player in the abdication crisis that soon unfolded, 'After I am dead, the boy will ruin himself in twelve months.' His last words were reportedly, 'How is the Empire?' Within weeks of his statement the father's concerns appeared to have become reality, as Edward's reign, that began with such promise, started to unravel.

Hampered by a pronounced stammer, the Duke of York loyally carried on with his royal duties but soon tensions developed between the two royal brothers and their respective partners. The

King's mistress, Wallis Simpson, was cruelly dismissive of his sister-in-law, the Duchess of York, referring to her as the 'Fat Scottish cook'.

Princess Elizabeth was astute enough to know a family and public drama was unfolding but she wasn't sure exactly what. In answer to one of her sister Margaret's incessant questions the princess, herself just ten years old, answered, 'I think Uncle David wants to marry Mrs Baldwin, and Mr Baldwin doesn't like it.'

Elizabeth's father had a sense of foreboding as preparations were going ahead for the new king's coronation. Up to this point the detail of Edward's love affair with twice-married Wallis Simpson was largely kept out of the British newspapers. But within the Royal Family the possibility of the monarch abdicating had been discussed at the highest levels and was now a very real possibility. The King said later he had only ever wanted to be an up-to-date king and hadn't wanted to bring the institution to its knees. Far from it, he wanted to modernise what he saw as an outdated and increasingly irrelevant institution. 'I had lots of political conceptions,' he said, 'I kept them to myself.' In an interview with Kenneth Harris in October 1969 he revealed he had a secret plan to change things, especially to do with the court, but time had not been on his side. Indeed some historians believe it was his interpretation of kingship and not only his relationship with divorcee Mrs Simpson that brought him into direct conflict with Baldwin's government and led to the constitutional crisis that unfolded.

Whatever the truth the Simpson affair gave a hostile Baldwin the perfect excuse to topple him and replace the monarch with his more amenable younger brother. His earlier visits as Prince of Wales to depressed areas in Wales and different parts of Britain, such as Northumberland, had deeply troubled Baldwin. So much so that the Prime Minister had called him to the House of Commons and asked him why he was making such visits. The future king insisted it was very important that he showed his face to give the men hope as there were some who had been out of work for a decade.

'Mr Baldwin suddenly became conscious of the fact that he and his Government has actually done very little to alleviate the plight of the unemployed of which there were thousands at that time.'*

The crisis gathered pace in October when the American press published that a marriage between the King and Mrs Simpson was imminent. Alec Hardinge, private secretary to the King, wrote to him on 13 November, with a blunt warning. 'The silence in the British Press on the subject of Your Majesty's friendship with Mrs Simpson is not going to be maintained ... judging by the letters from British subjects living in foreign countries where the press has been outspoken, the effect will be calamitous.'

On 16 November the King invited Baldwin to the palace where he informed the hostile Prime Minister that he intended to marry Mrs Simpson. Baldwin's response was that such a union would not be acceptable to the people. 'The Queen becomes the Queen of the country. Therefore in the choice of a queen the voice of the people must be heard.' The Prime Minister's position was shared by Stanley Bruce, former Australian prime minister and the then incumbent High Commissioner to Britain, who was horrified at the prospect of such a marriage.

There could be no going back now, either for the King or his government. It was a full-blown constitutional crisis and something had to give. Within weeks it did. On 10 December 1936, just 326 days after ascending the throne, Edward's turbulent reign was at an end. It has been one of the shortest reigns in history**.

---

* In the same interview in 1969, the Duke of Windsor revealed how he was rebuked by his father, George V, for including a joke in a speech. Asked what his father would have made of Prince Philip, who loved to include jokes in his addresses, he replied, 'I think that any audience that Philip talks to would be very disappointed if he didn't have some jokes and maybe some pretty forceful criticisms as well.

** Although her reign was disputed, Lady Jane Grey ruled for nine days from 6 July until 15 July 1553, although she was only proclaimed queen by the Lords of the Council on 10 July. The king with the shortest definitively known reign was Edgar the Ætheling who ruled for two months, 12 days in 1066 before submitting to William the Conqueror. Some records indicate that Sweyn Forkbeard reigned for only 40 days in 1013–1014.

Edward's decision to abdicate inflicted a wound in the Royal Family that never healed. Bertie, 18 months the King's junior, was devastated by his brother's decision. He wrote in his diary, 'I went to see Queen Mary and when I told her what had happened I broke down and I sobbed like a child.' As children and young men, they had been very close although David, a charismatic winner who oozed self-confidence, did occasionally mock his knock-kneed younger brother over his stammer, as some siblings are of a mind to do.

The historic decision shattered their relationship and their brotherly love was further destroyed forever in the vicious feud between their wives, Wallis and Elizabeth, that followed. The loyal Bertie had continued to doggedly support his older brother until he lied to him about his finances when negotiating the abdication pay-off.

There was more to the feud. Elizabeth knew that a secret report had been drawn up on Bertie's psychological fitness to rule. And she was all too aware that, because of the doubts over his capability, a holding operation had been constructed, involving his mother, Queen Mary, becoming Queen Regent, followed by the enthronement of his youngest brother, Prince George, Duke of Kent. Bertie knew it was by no means certain he would inherit the throne because of all this, which was humiliating in itself. The fact that he would now have to speak – and often – to the public and expose himself to their scrutiny lowered his self-esteem still further. The feud was to last until Edward's death. The new king hated the fact that his elder brother had plunged him into what he described as 'this ghastly void'. Following her sudden elevation to Queen Consort the new Queen Elizabeth wrote to her brother-in-law that she and her husband were 'overcome with misery' at being unexpectedly thrust on to the throne.

When the Duke of York arrived from seeing the King, he told his wife who, in turn, went to the nursery and broke the news to their eldest daughter. The Princess Elizabeth was now the Heiress Presumptive, and unless her parents were to have another child and that child was a boy, she would be Queen after her father's death. Her sister Margaret, despite her age, seemed to appreciate the significance. She asked her sister, 'Does that mean that you will have to be the next queen?' Elizabeth paused for a moment and replied, 'Yes, someday.' Margaret replied, 'Poor you.'

***

Princess Elizabeth and Prince Philip of Greece's first meaningful face to face encounter came on 22 July 1939 when she joined her parents and sister on an official visit to Dartmouth Naval College. Philip's wily uncle, Louis Mountbatten, was present and Philip, now a dashing 18-year-old naval cadet, was charged with looking after Princess Elizabeth and her younger sister Princess Margaret. Mountbatten, as a consequence of the death of his older brother George, had now assumed the position of Philip's mentor-in-chief at the behest of his sister, Alice and Philip's father, Andrea.

Unlike the affable previous father figure George, 'Dickie', as Mountbatten was known among the close family, was a man of ferocious ambition, and at the heart of his ambitions was his handsome nephew, Philip, now his charge. Married to the hugely wealthy but unfaithful heiress, Lady Edwina Mountbatten (née Ashley) he had the financial means and high society connections at his fingertips that enabled him to groom Philip into the perfect suitor for the young Princess Elizabeth.

Lord Mountbatten's wife's maternal grandfather, the international magnate Sir Ernest Joseph Cassel, a friend and private financier to the future King Edward VII, became one of the wealthiest and most powerful men in Europe. The merchant banker died at his Park Lane residence in 1921 and his estate was probated at £6,000,000, the equivalent of around £268 million today. He bequeathed the bulk of his vast fortune to Edwina, his elder granddaughter, and Mary, on whom he doted. Edwina inherited around £2 million, which equates to around £89 million today, as well as his palatial

43

London townhouse, Brook House, at a time when Louis' naval salary was £610 per annum (just £30,000 today).

Edwina would go on to inherit the country seat of Broadlands in Hampshire – with its Grade 1 listed Palladian-style mansion designed by Capability Brown and finished by architect Henry Holland – from her father, Wilfred William Ashley, 1st Baron Mount Temple, and the former home of nineteenth-century UK prime minister Henry John Temple, 3rd Viscount Palmerston.

Lord Mountbatten was very impressed by his nephew, loved his forthright manner and would later treat him like a surrogate son. In 1938, whilst Dickie's brother, George, was close to death fighting bone marrow cancer, Philip stayed at Broadlands. Louis wrote to George's wife, Nadejda Mountbatten, who was the daughter of Russian Grand Duke Michael Mikhailovich Romanov. 'He really is killingly funny, I like him very much.' The two men, Louis and Philip, were destined to become much closer and – with Philip's father, Andrea, consciously playing such a minor role in his life – their relationship was almost like that of father and son.

At Dartmouth, after a few hours in Philip's company, the young Elizabeth, then just 13, was quite taken with the young officer. As Philip's cousin, the late Countess Mountbatten said, 'I think quite early on she was quite smitten. His background was not very different at all to that of the Queen so he wasn't overawed or worried by it.'

The charming cadet Philip took her and sister Margaret off to play croquet and to the tennis courts to have 'some real fun' jumping over the nets. 'How good he is, Crawfie. How high he can jump,' she told her nanny Marion Crawford. In truth, George VI had hardly noticed Philip until it was time to leave.

As the royal yacht sailed away, Philip and a few cadets took charge of several small craft and set off in pursuit. A gale set in and his fellow cadets turned back, but Philip kept on rowing while Elizabeth watched him through her binoculars, captivated. The King eventually spotted him and remarked: 'The young fool. He must go back!' Philip's boldness, however, had made a lasting impression on the young princess. He was no fool in her mind.

44

Lord Mountbatten wanted to strike a spark of love between the two young royals that day and it worked. There is no doubt that the teenage Elizabeth fell for the dashing 18-year-old adonis Philip. As far as she was concerned, from then on he was the one for her. Privately, Lord Mountbatten was overjoyed but he and Philip would soon realise there were many in royal circles who were less keen on seeing this romance flourish.

***

After the uncertainty of the abdication crisis of 1936, his leadership throughout World War II had cemented George VI's place in the affections of the nation. During the Blitz, he visited bombed areas in London to see the devastation caused by enemy air raids. On these regular visits, with his queen at his side, they both took a keen interest in what was being done to help people who had lost their homes. After Buckingham Palace was bombed on 13 September 1940, Queen Elizabeth famously said she felt she could now 'look the East End in the face'.

In 1939 the security services were not as convinced by the new king as members of the public. Like his brother, Edward VIII, who has repeatedly been accused of having Nazi sympathies, George VI sided with Neville Chamberlain and Foreign Secretary, Lord Halifax, and favoured the policy of appeasement. The secret services in the UK had long monitored George's elder brother and his wife. The pair, by now styled the Duke and Duchess of Windsor, later enjoyed decades-long semi-exile living in continental Europe. Years later, secret documents, including some papers that have only recently been declassified, bolstered speculation that the couple harboured pro-Nazi sympathies and were even involved in a failed plot to overthrow the British crown during World War II.

While Edward's strong apparent pro-German sentiments were shared by others, his outspokenness even as heir to the throne made his words potentially dangerous. His support for Oswald Mosley and other fascist organisers (many of whom would be imprisoned after Britain went to war with Germany) increased doubts about his political beliefs. The intelligence services kept a close watch on Wallis Simpson too. Rumours of her veracious sexual appetite and taste in men abounded. Some claimed she had begun a long-term affair with Nazi official Joachim von Ribbentrop while he served as Germany's ambassador to Britain in the mid-1930s. Even more salacious were allegations that Simpson had passed along confidential British government secrets gleaned from private despatches.

In January 1936, fearful that the new king (and his relationship) might be a danger to national security, Prime Minister Stanley Baldwin stepped in, ordering MI5, Britain's domestic intelligence agency, to start state-sponsored surveillance of the couple. Both their phones were bugged and members of their Scotland Yard security team were asked to provide detailed information about the King whom they were also charged with protecting.

In October 1937, four months after their marriage and despite the strenuous objections of the British government, the duke and duchess travelled to Germany. While the duke claimed he was making the trip to inspect housing and working conditions (a long-time passion of his), he likely hoped the trip would burnish his reputation both at home and abroad and possibly improve Anglo-German relations.

His private secretary later wrote that the duke also planned to use the trip to showcase his new wife, who had not been granted the title of 'Her Royal Highness' upon the couple's wedding, and who had been shunned in royal circles. And the couple were indeed treated like stars during the two-week trip, which took on the trappings of a mock-state visit. They were met by massive, cheering crowds, many of whom greeted the former king with a Nazi salute, which Edward frequently returned. The duchess, meanwhile, was met with the royal curtsies and bows she had been denied elsewhere.

The couple were feted at lavish receptions packed with VIP guests and dined privately with several high-ranking Nazi officials, including Hermann Goering and Joseph Goebbels. The pair even visited a training school for future members of the Schutzstaffel, his feared SS guard. On 22 October, the couple were invited to Hitler's country home in the Bavarian Alps, known as the Berghof. Hitler and the duke spoke privately for over an hour, while the duchess met with Deputy Führer, Rudolf Hess. Some accounts of the duke's conversation claim that he openly criticised some of Hitler's policies, while others maintain he happily gave Hitler his tacit support. A typed transcript of their meeting, that was subsequently lost, was possibly destroyed by the Nazis before the end of the war. Edward and Wallis were all smiles as they departed following taking afternoon tea with Hitler. It was clear to most observers that they were awestruck by their host and succumbed to the flattery and lavish treatment doled out by the Nazis. The reaction back in Britain, however, was quite different. As feared, the trip heightened concerns about Edward and Wallis's loyalties, with many horrified by the Duke of Windsor's complete lack of judgement and loss of common sense.

A planned trip to the United States was soon scuttled when prominent members of American Jewish organisations protested the couple's seeming willingness to ignore Germany's persecution of Jews. In the waning days of the war a large cache of files from the German Foreign Ministry were discovered at Marburg Castle near the Harz Mountains. Among the 400 tons of paperwork were a smaller collection of some 60 or so documents and telegrams, which became known as the 'Windsor File', detailing German communication with the Duke and Duchess of Windsor before and during World War II. The file included details of a secret plan, codenamed Operation Willi. In the summer of 1940, the duke and duchess fled Nazi-occupied Paris and travelled to neutral Spain and Portugal. German Foreign Minister Joachim von Ribbentrop ordered local Nazi officials to meet with the couple, who, the Windsor File documents claimed, voiced their displeasure with both the British royals and Churchill and his government.

That July, in an effort to get him out of Europe and away from German influence, Churchill ordered the duke to take up a new position as the Governor of the Bahamas. Edward was reluctant to go, and von Ribbentrop played on those fears, allegedly feeding false information to the couple that they were in danger of attack or even assassination by British secret operatives. Nazi officials also tried to get the couple to return to Spain, by force if necessary, and lend their support to the German war effort, which, if victorious would see the overthrow of George VI with Edward in his place as a puppet king and Simpson as his queen.

According to the Windsor File, the duke and duchess did not dismiss the plan, nor did they inform British authorities of these conversations. They delayed their departure by nearly a month, but despite last-minute efforts by the Nazis, including calling in a false bomb threat on the ship the couple were booked on, the duke and duchess finally left Portugal in August, and spent the rest of World War II in relative obscurity in the Bahamas, from where Edward continued to publicly cast doubt on Britain's ability to win the war.

Initially, British, French and American officials agreed to declassify and release the Marburg papers, as the top-secret archives discovered in May 1945 became known. A team of eminent historians were tasked with sorting through the massive trove, which took more than a year. As government files released in 2017 show, Winston Churchill moved quickly to block the Windsor File, including details of Operation Willi, from being published. He claimed the documents were biased and unreliable, and likely to cast the former king in the worst possible light. He asked US General Eisenhower, the Supreme Commander of the Allied Expeditionary Force in Europe, to prevent the public from seeing them for 'at least 10 or 20 years'.

Many in the US intelligence community agreed with Churchill's assessment, and Eisenhower wrote to Churchill in July 1953 that the documents were 'obviously concocted with some idea of promoting German propaganda and weakening western resistance.' Eisenhower restricted any of the documents from being released in the initial publication, but they were finally leaked in 1957. The Duke of Windsor later strenuously denied any involvement in anti-

British plots and called the Marburg Files a 'complete fabrication', and the British Foreign Office stated on the record that the duke, 'never wavered in his loyalty to the British cause'.

In his memoirs, the Duke of Windsor would dismiss Hitler as a 'somewhat ridiculous figure, with his theatrical posturing and his bombastic pretensions.' But, in private, he claimed that Hitler was 'not such a bad chap' and frequently blamed any number of groups, including the British government, America and even Jews themselves for causing World War II. While most modern historians are in agreement about the duke's pro-German beliefs, there is continued debate over whether those sympathies crossed the line into treason, or if the famously weak-willed and easily swayed former king played right into the Nazi's hands, making him the most high profile of propaganda tools.

As Hitler pushed the world to the brink of war Britain's then prime minister Neville Chamberlain returned from Germany on 30 September 1938 and declared 'Peace for our time' concerning the Munich Agreement and subsequent Anglo-German Declaration. The phrase echoed Benjamin Disraeli, who, upon returning from the Congress of Berlin in 1878, stated, 'I have returned from Germany with peace for our time'.

At Heston Aerodrome, as he disembarked the aircraft, Chamberlain spoke to the crowd waiting for him, and said, 'The settlement of the Czechoslovakian problem, which has now been achieved, is, in my view, only the prelude to a larger settlement in which all Europe may find peace. This morning I had another talk with the German Chancellor, Herr Hitler, and here is the paper which bears his name upon it as well as mine. Some of you, perhaps, have already heard what it contains but I would just like to read it to you: "…We regard the agreement signed last night and the Anglo-German Naval Agreement as symbolic of the desire of our two peoples never to go to war with one another again".' Later that day Chamberlain stood outside 10 Downing Street and again read from the document, claiming to bring peace with honour. 'I believe it is peace for our time. We thank you from the bottom of our hearts. Go home and get a nice quiet sleep,' he said. He would soon have to eat his words. Churchill was having none of it. 'An appeaser,' he said with gusto, 'is one who feeds a crocodile – hoping it will eat him last.'

It was a victory of deception. Hitler had no intention of halting his Nazi expansion leaving Neville Chamberlain's failed policy to be exposed within weeks. Many saw it as a PR stunt. A large crowd of 15,000 people protested in Trafalgar Square against the Munich Agreement on the same day, three times more than welcomed the exhausted Prime Minister at Downing Street, a fact that never made the BBC broadcasts.

At the same time Chamberlain was proclaiming peace the British secret services were preparing for what they saw as an inevitable European war that would escalate to world war. They even had doubts about the new king, George VI, and viewed him sceptically, believing him to be an appeaser after the monarch granted Chamberlain a Buckingham Palace balcony appearance following his 'Peace for our time' declaration, thus publicly aligning himself to the supporters of appeasement.

Remarkably, according to documents released later, the King was actually vying with Chamberlain to establish a personal rapport with Hitler. The monarch even drafted a letter to Hitler in which he says this is not a letter from one statesman to another but from one ex-serviceman to another. The security agencies were troubled by this. Eventually, the Foreign Office blocked the King's letter and Hitler's invasions of Czechoslovakia and Poland ended any serious talk of appeasement. The King's pro appeasement stance meant some senior figures in the security services never fully trusted him with state secrets. He had to find a way to earn their confidence.

Chamberlain had failed to fully estimate the intentions of Hitler's Nazi regime and, following a series of events which led to the crisis in Norway in April 1940, he faced heavy criticism in the Houses of Parliament. On 9 May 1940 he resigned and requested a meeting with Conservative MP Lord Halifax and with Winston Churchill, certain that one or the other was his successor. When Halifax flatly refused, Churchill jumped at the chance.

With Chamberlain out of the picture, Churchill set about reforming the government and creating a coalition of national unity to tackle the crisis head on. Churchill also appointed himself Minister for Defence and head of a Defence Committee. He surrounded himself by complementary military staff, among them Air Chief Marshal Hugh Dowding, General Hastings Ismay, Admiral Dudley Pound and Field Marshal John Dill. Later service heads included Field Marshal Alan Brooke and Sir Charles Portal. These men were essential to Churchill's vision of a war machine, unflinching in its belief in ultimate victory over Hitler's tyranny.

Churchill, after all, was experienced in warfare, from both the civilian's and the soldier's point of view. He had seen active service in the Anglo-Sudan war, and British India, where he famously engaged in hand-to-hand combat. Before he secured a narrow victory in Oldham to become a Member of Parliament at the age of 25, Churchill also used his position as a journalist for the *Morning Post* to fight for peace in the Boer War. He also saw action on the Western Front from 1915–1916, during World War I.*

***

A few weeks after the infamous meeting between Princess Elizabeth and Prince Philip came the outbreak of World War II on 3 September 1939. Hitler's invasion of Poland from the west, two days earlier, gave France and Britain no choice but to declare war on Germany. On 17 September, Soviet troops invaded Poland from the east. Philip was desperate to prove himself and do his duty.

---

*   At the outbreak of war in 1914, Churchill was serving as First Lord of the Admiralty. In 1915 his involvement in the planning of the disastrous Dardanelles naval campaign and the military landings on Gallipoli, both which saw huge casualties, led to him being demoted and his resignation from government. He joined the Army as an officer and became a Lieutenant Colonel of the 6th Scots Fusiliers and served in France on the Western Front until early 1916.

As he was still technically a Greek citizen, however, he was at first deployed as a 'neutral foreigner' serving on escort and convoy missions. When he went to sea as a midshipman aboard HMS *Ramillies* he surprised his captain, Vice-Admiral Harold Tom Baillie-Grohman, by indiscreetly letting slip his uncle Dickie's masterplan for him to become Princess Elizabeth (the future monarch)'s husband. His captain noted the conversation in a typewritten unpublished memoir, *Flashbacks on the past, Vol 2*. The account – alongside a photograph of a youthful looking Prince Philip – makes it clear that, despite Elizabeth's tender age, Philip clearly believed he was a potential suitor.

Baillie-Grohman noted he told Philip that being born in Greece to a German–Danish father of the House of Schleswig-Holstein-Sonderburg-Glücksburg and a German mother of the House of Battenberg might be a hindrance to him serving in the British Royal Navy. Philip then told Baillie-Grohman that he was focused on becoming a naturalised British subject because he planned to pursue a naval career. What he revealed next 'surprised' his senior officer. 'He went on to say, "My uncle Dickie (Mountbatten) has ideas for me; he thinks I could marry Princess Elizabeth."' When the taken aback Baillie-Grohman asked if he was really fond of her, Philip told him, 'Oh, yes, very. I write to her every week.'

His captain was so taken aback by Philip's claim that he wrote a note of the conversation directly afterwards so he knew it was pretty correct. The entry clearly shows that Philip was already well aware of his uncle's plans for him, especially when you consider Elizabeth was then just 13 years old. It suggests too that Philip was a willing participant in Lord Mountbatten's ambitious scheme to install him as a lead player in a new royal dynasty which, he believed, would be the House of Mountbatten.

4: THE FOG OF WAR

*'To have been spared in the war and seen victory, to have been given the chance
to rest and to re-adjust myself, to have fallen in love completely and unreservedly,
makes all one's personal and even the world's troubles seem small and petty.'*

Extract from a letter written by Prince Philip to
Princess Elizabeth, 1946

Relations between Winston Churchill, resolute and confident to
the core, and his new king, George VI, got off to a tricky start.
Like MI5 the Prime Minister believed the monarch's leanings
towards Chamberlain's belief in appeasement with Nazi Germany
to be both fatal for British democracy and naive, as Hitler was not
somebody who could ever be trusted.

For years, when others tried to placate Nazi Germany, Churchill
saw the dangers. In his foreign affairs article in the *Evening Standard*,
17 September 1937, he wrote under the headline, 'Friendship with
Germany' 'I find myself pilloried by Dr Goebbels' Press as an enemy
of Germany. That description is quite untrue.' He had made many
efforts on Germany's behalf in recent years, Churchill continued, but
it was his duty to warn against German rearmament: 'I can quite
understand that this action of mine would not be popular in Germany.
Indeed, it was not popular anywhere. I was told I was making ill-will
between the two countries.' Thankfully, by 1939, many people in the
UK had begun to listen to Churchill and had woken up to the threat.

George VI and Churchill had very different temperaments too.
Perhaps in awe of the bullish, great orator Churchill, the King's
stammering affliction made communication difficult. Caroline

Erskine, the daughter of the indomitable courtier Sir Alan 'Tommy' Lascelles, private secretary to George VI, remarked about their weekly audiences, 'Word got around that it wasn't very easy for either of them. They were very different people and Winston to begin with didn't know how to cope with the King as a person. The King was rather frightened by Winston, over-awed by him.'

In the autumn of 1940, the British secret services informed the Prime Minister that they had reliable intelligence that a Nazi invasion of the country by elite German paratroopers, the Fallschirmjäger, led by Luftwaffe General Kurt Student, was imminent. Churchill had no reason to doubt it. The general, who would later serve five years for war crimes, had led the first major airborne attack in history, the successful Battle of the Hague on 10 May the same year, enabling the German troops to secure a bridgehead. Despite brave resistance by the Dutch people, Nazis troops eventually swept into and occupied Holland. Britain's intelligence agencies expected General Student to do the same in Britain, leading his crack airborne troops into the Home Counties ahead of a full-scale invasion.

Fearing the worst, Winston Churchill immediately instructed the intelligence services to prepare a top-secret plan to evacuate the King and the Royal Family to Canada by ship via the port of Liverpool. But when the Prime Minister put the elaborate plan to the monarch the King rejected it outright. The King, who was after all Commander-in-Chief of the British Armed Forces and a war veteran having manned a gun turret aboard HMS *Collingwood* during the Battle of Jutland as a midshipman during WWI, made it clear he was not going anywhere and neither were his wife, the Queen, and children, the direct heirs to the throne. The Queen backed her husband completely. 'The children will not leave unless I do. I shall not leave unless their father does, and the King will not leave the country in any circumstances whatever,' was her response to the plan*. As a former serviceman

---

* Prince Albert was promoted to sub-lieutenant in May 1916 and made an acting lieutenant aboard HMS *Collingwood* by the end of the WWI in 1918.

who had seen combat, he was not going to shirk his duties if the Nazis invaded. As the only British sovereign to have seen action in war since King George II, who led his troops at the Battle of Dettingen on 27 June 1743 against the French, he made it abundantly clear he would fight to the bitter end to defend his family and the palace.

This presented Churchill with a problem that he dealt with in his own indomitable way, as Richard Aldrich, Professor of International Security at Warwick University, revealed. 'He [the King] says everybody is going to stay and going to fight. He says, "I want to get my German. I want to at least kill one of the invaders and we will all fight to the last,"' Professor Aldrich said. When Churchill learned of the King's defiant stance, he sent him a Thompson M1928 submachine gun, known colloquially as a 'Tommy Gun', with an effective firing range of 164 yards. Upon receipt, the King was thrilled with his new weapon.

From that moment George VI insisted that his family and the staff at Buckingham Palace become a fully functional fighting unit. His immediate family as well as the members of the Household, such as equerries, and servants, were all drilled with handguns and rifles and took turns to unleash a round or two from Churchill's 'Tommy Gun' gift. Queen Elizabeth, his consort, particularly enjoyed taking potshots at rats in the palace's gardens.

Throughout World War II, the King never went anywhere in his car without his trusty Lee Enfield No. 4 Mk.1 rifle and a British Army standard issue Enfield No. 2 Mk. I.38/200 calibre revolver strapped to his side. It was his way of demonstrating leadership as well as showing defiance to those in the war cabinet who felt he should leave the country for his own safety and the preservation of the monarchy and Empire. On a wartime visit to RAF Tempsford near Bedford on 9 November 1943 the King and Queen were shown a variety of weapons used by agents in the field. While there the Queen called her husband over to show him an innovative new weapon being used against Hitler, exploding horse manure, which both intrigued and amused her.

With remarkable maturity, on 13 October 1940, Princess Elizabeth made her first public speech with an address on the radio to the children of the Commonwealth, many of whom had been evacuated from Britain to America and Canada. It was first broadcast on the BBC's *Children's Hour*, urging them to have courage. She delivered her broadcast without a hint of nerves. She said, famously, 'Thousands of you in this country have had to leave your homes and be separated from your fathers and mothers. My sister, Margaret Rose, and I feel so much for you as we know from experience what it means to be away from those we love most of all. To you, living in new surroundings, we send a message of true sympathy and at the same time we would like to thank the kind people who have welcomed you to their homes in the country. All of us children who are still at home think continually of our friends and relations who have gone overseas, who have travelled thousands of miles to find a wartime home and a kindly welcome in Canada, Australia, New Zealand, South Africa and the United States of America.'

Princess Elizabeth then went on to thank 'our gallant sailors, soldiers and airmen' and said the children back home were trying, too 'to bear our own share of the danger and sadness of war.' She signed off with a flurry of optimism saying, 'When peace comes, remember it will be for us, the children of today, to make the world of tomorrow a better and happier place.'

Philip couldn't wait to report for duty and do his bit. He would go on to serve with distinction during World War II, proving his mettle and leadership skills on the dangerous high seas. After Italy invaded Greece in 1940, he was assigned to HMS *Valiant*, a battleship that was deployed in the Mediterranean. As a midshipman, an officer of the lowest rank, above naval cadet and below sub-lieutenant, Philip was 'Mentioned in Despatches' for his operation of searchlights during the night Battle of Cape Matapan in 1941, when the British destroyed several Italian warships. On page 554 of the *London Gazette*, 3 February 1942, it read, 'Midshipman His Royal Highness Prince Philip of Greece and Denmark, Royal Navy HMS *Valiant*.' He was also awarded Greece's War Cross of Valour, at the time (and until 1974) the highest military decoration the Greek State awarded for acts of bravery or distinguished leadership on the field of battle.*

Philip recalled: 'I seem to remember that I reported that I had a target in sight and was ordered to "open shutter". The beam lit up a stationary cruiser, but we were so close by then that the beam only lit up half the ship. At this point all hell broke loose, as all our eight 15-inch guns, plus those of the flagship and Barham's started firing at the stationary cruiser, which disappeared in an explosion and a cloud of smoke. I was then ordered to "train left" and lit up another Italian cruiser, which was given the same treatment. As well as the two cruisers identified by the Duke, a third Italian cruiser and two destroyers were sunk by the British fleet, with the loss of 2,300 sailors. It was Italy's worst defeat at sea. The next morning the battle fleet returned to the scene of the battle, while attempts were made to pick up survivors. This was rudely interrupted by an attack by German bombers. The return to Alexandria was uneventful, and the peace and quiet was much appreciated.' Allied losses during the battle amounted to a single torpedo bomber which was shot down with the loss of its three-man crew. Allied ships picked up 1,015 Italian survivors, with another 160 saved by the Italians.

Even at such an early age Philip knew he had a tendency, due to his bluntness, to 'rub people up the wrong way'. He acknowledged this character flaw in a letter of condolence to a relative who had lost a son during the war at the age of 21, saying: 'I know you will never think much of me. I am rude and unmannerly and I say many things out of turn which I realise afterwards must have hurt someone. Then I am filled with remorse and I try to put matters right.'

---

* The Duke opened up about his courage during the battle which resulted in him being Mentioned in Despatches by the fleet's Commander-in-Chief, Admiral Sir Andrew Cunningham in *Dark Seas: The Battle of Cape Matapan*, the first in a series of books about some of the great naval actions and campaigns of the war.

When asked, Philip was always modest about his brave war service at a young age. He said, 'So were lots of other people of my generation. The most active part was when I was on the east coast escorting convoys from the Firth of Forth down to Sheerness and that was through E-boat alley and that was quite active. Yes, there was a bit of activity before that in the Mediterranean.' He had little time, it seemed, for the serious mental health problems service personnel could suffer as a result of fighting on the front line, a cause his grandson Prince Harry champions. For Philip, a man of his time, it was a case, as the wartime slogan went, of 'keep calm, and carry on.' When asked about counselling for servicemen in 1995 Philip replied in a matter of fact manner, 'We didn't have counsellors every time somebody let off a gun. You just got on with it.'

The full extent of his heroics, however, only came to light in 2008, when fellow veteran Harry Hargreaves, then 85, spoke to the BBC. He recalled that Philip had been assigned as first lieutenant to the destroyer HMS *Wallace* by the time of the Allied invasion of Sicily in June 1943. Mr Hargreaves, recalled how Philip saved the entire crew after a German bomber attacked the warship at night. During a lull in the bombardment, Philip came up with a plan to dump a wooden raft overboard with smoke floats that would give the appearance of blazing debris. The pilot was duped and the *Wallace* sailed away under cover of darkness. 'Prince Philip saved our lives that night,' Mr Hargreaves later recalled. 'He was always very courageous and resourceful and thought very quickly. You would say to yourself, "What the hell are we going to do now?" and Philip would come up with something.' In 1944 Philip transferred to HMS *Whelp*, a destroyer that saw action in the Pacific as part of a British fleet involved with joint operations with the US navy, including the landings at Iwo Jima.

While Philip was away at sea, Princess Elizabeth was blossoming from a susceptible teenager to an accomplished and beautiful young woman. She spent the war years at Windsor where her cousin Philip was a regular visitor when home on leave. At Christmas

1943 he was among the audience who watched her play Aladdin in a pantomime with her sister Margaret. Her governess Marion Crawford noted the event, 'I have never known Lilibet so animated. There was a sparkle about her none of us had ever seen before.' But the princess's parents, the King and Queen, were not quite as keen and certainly did not encourage the match. One courtier noted that the family was 'horrified' when they saw Philip was making up to Elizabeth.

During the Blitz, the German bombing campaign against Britain from 1940 to 1941, George VI visited many bombed areas to see first-hand the devastation caused by enemy air raids. On regular visits, with his queen at his side, they both took a keen interest in what was being done to help people who had lost their homes.

Apart from a short stint in Scotland, the princess remained at Windsor Castle with her sister Margaret and, like many other British children, they were often apart from their parents, although they were regularly drafted in to be photographed with the King and Queen in order to project an image of stability and fortitude on the Home Front.

At this time, Princess Elizabeth and Alathea Fitzalan Howard had become best friends, while the aristocrat lived on the Windsor Castle estate. The pair shared dancing and drawing lessons together and confidences too. Had she been born a male, Alathea would have eventually assumed the title, the Duke of Norfolk, as well as become Earl Marshal, and the leader of England's leading Catholic aristocratic family. She would also have inherited the magnificent Arundel Castle. Alathea's parents had separated and when she was 15 years old, she was sent to live at Cumberland Lodge in Windsor Great Park with her grandfather, Viscount Fitzalan of Derwent, for the duration the war.

While she was living in Windsor, Princess Elizabeth, 13, and Margaret, 9, who were also being educated by governesses at home, became her constant companions. In her diaries, written in October 1941, she reveals how she and Elizabeth had a crush on the same Guards officer, Hugh, Earl of Euston, a descendant of

Charles II. Elizabeth had admitted that she 'adored' the 22-year-old Cape Town born aristocratic officer, while Alathea herself had a tremendous crush on him. In an entry on 23 October Alathea gave some insight into the princesses' lives at Windsor when she wrote, 'I biked to the Castle for drawing; we painted designs on our clay horses. They [Princess Elizabeth and Princess Margaret] wore their old brown check skirts and red Aertex shirts, which they ought not to do — their clothes have gone down a lot since the war. They talked about their new lot of officers [guarding the castle] and are v. sorry Hugh [Hugh Euston was the officer both Princess Elizabeth and Alathea were keen on] has gone. Lilibet said she'd had her hair permed — it looked v. nice in front but too stiff behind.'

In another entry in her diary, dated 'Saturday, 7 February, 1942', Alathea wrote, 'Lilibet looked v. pretty. She showed me a letter from Hugh E. thanking her for her Christmas card — "it's miserable him going abroad, I shall never see him again now".' Hugh Euston became a recurring theme in the teenager's diary and there was more than a hint of jealousy over Elizabeth's fondness for him, which shows, although Philip was her 'beau', he was far from being the only candidate for the future queen's affections.

Alathea penned on Friday, 29 May, 'Everyone congregated in the Green Drawing Room [for a dance at the Castle] and then we all filed past the Royal Family, shaking hands and curtsying. The Q wore white lace embroidered with pale blue and silver, and the princesses pink taffeta picture frocks, embroidered with seed pearl bows — they ought not to have been alike. P.E. [Princess Elizabeth] didn't look pretty tonight somehow — she's v. Hanoverian and has reached the age now when she needs make-up. Hugh was there. He sought me out to dance with him and we sat in the White Drawing Room after and talked easily and happily. But everyone's talking of the way in which the Royal Family single him out — he's staying the night there and he sat by the princess at supper and [P.E.] began liking him at the same time as I did, though unbeknown to each other! She was so sweet tonight and told me that it was she who pointed me out to him when he was vaguely

60

looking for me to make sure he danced with me! If it is [the King and Queen's] intention that P.E. should marry an English commoner, then I think this match quite probable — he is not in love with her, but I believe fondness of them all would greatly tempt him. If this be the case, I would make a willing sacrifice of him to my future sovereign! And meanwhile it gives a zest to life to combat my charms with hers!'*

An entry on 7 June 1942 shows that Elizabeth, still an impressionable teenager, was confused about her future and romance. 'We began about her family, which she's never breathed about before, and I said things to her I would never have thought I would say! She said she wondered if she'd ever marry, and I assured her she would, and she said if she really wanted to marry someone she'd run away, but I know she wouldn't really — her sense of duty is too strong, though she's suited to a simpler life. But tonight I learned to know a new Lilibet: I saw behind the outward calm and matter-of-factness into something lovable and sincere.'**

But Alathea also referred to Philip as Elizabeth's 'beau' so even then she clearly had a place in her heart for her handsome cousin. In another entry she wrote, 'She told me Philip, her beau, had been for the weekend and that I must come and see him if he came again! She said he's very funny, which doesn't sound my type actually — the only thing that does bore me about the Royal Family is that they all will tell one jokes they've heard on the wireless, etc. No one else I know is in the least interested in those sort of silly jokes, but then the K and Q and the princesses are v. simple people.'

The Queen would write regularly to her eldest daughter and even raised the issue of being killed. On 27 June 1944, Queen

---

* Eton and Oxford educated Hugh became the 11th Duke of Grafton KG DL in 1970 when he succeeded his father. He was known from 1936 to 1970 as the Earl of Euston. On 12 October 1946, he married Ann Fortune Smith (the current Mistress of the Robes to Queen Elizabeth II) and they had five children. He was made a Knight of the Garter in 1976. He died in 2011 at Euston Hall, Suffolk.

** Alathea wed in 1953. She married the Hon. Edward Ward whom she outlived. They settled in Lausanne. She died in 2001.

Elizabeth wrote to Princess Elizabeth from Buckingham Palace, alongside the King. Her letter read,

'My Darling Lilibet …
This is just a note about one or two things in case I get "done in" by the Germans! I think that I have left all my own things to be divided by you & Margaret, but I am sure you will give her anything suitable later on … Let's hope this won't be needed, but I know that you will always do the right thing, & remember to keep your temper & your word & be loving – sweet –

Mummy'

Elizabeth made it clear to her father that despite her role as heir to the throne, she didn't want to be wrapped in cotton wool and wanted to do more to contribute towards the war effort. As Allied troops advanced across Europe towards Nazi Germany, Elizabeth told her father that she felt she must enlist; she wanted to do her bit for the war effort like millions of his subjects. He finally agreed and she joined the Auxiliary Territorial Service in 1945 on her 18th birthday. The King felt he had no choice but to bow to Elizabeth's request. Headstrong, young and determined she set out to do her bit.

She proudly became known as No 230873 Second Subaltern Elizabeth Windsor, the first female royal to join the Armed Services as a full-time member. By the end of World War II the princess had attained the rank of junior commander, having successfully completed her course at No.1 Mechanical Training Centre of the ATS and she also passed out as a fully qualified driver.

At 6 p.m. on Victory in Europe (VE) Day, 8 May 1945, the King made an historic broadcast to the nation. 'Let us salute in proud gratitude the great host of the living who have brought us to victory,' His Majesty said. 'I cannot praise them to the measure of each one's service, for in a total war, the efforts of all rise to the same noble height, and all are devoted to the common purpose. Armed or unarmed, men and women, you have fought and striven and endured to your utmost. No one knows that better than I do, and as your king, I thank with a full heart those who bore arms so valiantly on land and sea, or in the air, and all civilians who, shouldering their many burdens, have carried them unflinchingly without complaint.'

Throughout the afternoon and evening, the monarch, in his splendid blue Royal Navy uniform, and his immediate family made eight appearances on the balcony of Buckingham Palace to acknowledge the crowds gathered below. Nineteen-year-old Elizabeth, who had appeared on the balcony wearing her ATS uniform, and Margaret, 14, after asking for their father's permission, were allowed to leave the palace and secretly take part in the celebrations. No one recognised the teenage princesses as they walked through the crowds incognito.

The princesses were escorted by 16 members of the Royal Household, including the Queen's cousin Lady Margaret Rhodes, lady-in-waiting Jean Woodroffe, members of the Grenadier Guards and the King's newly appointed Equerry Group Captain Peter Townsend, a dashing decorated wartime flying ace and recipient of the Distinguished Flying Cross and Bar and Distinguished Service Order, who had caught the eye of the impressionable Margaret.

The Queen recalled in an interview with the BBC war correspondent Godfrey Talbot. 'I remember the thrill and relief. I remember we were terrified of being recognised.' She went on to describe how she pulled her ATS uniform cap down low over her eyes in a bid to cover her face, but a Grenadier Guard officer amongst the group accompanying her informed the princess, who was now a junior commander in the ATS, that he would not be seen in the company of another officer improperly dressed, so the princess had to wear her hat according to regulation.

'My parents went out on the balcony in response to the huge crowds outside. I think we went on the balcony every hour, six times. And then, when the excitement of the floodlights being switched on got through to us, my sister and I realised we couldn't see what the crowds were enjoying ... so we asked my parents if we could go out and see for ourselves,' she said. 'We cheered the king and queen on the balcony, then walked miles through the streets.

I remember miles of unknown people linking arms and walking down Whitehall, all of us just swept along on a tide of happiness and relief,' she said.

The King recorded in his diary that evening, 'The Prime Minister came to lunch. We congratulated each other on the end of the European war. The day we have been longing for has arrived at last, & we can look back with thankfulness to God that our tribulation is over. No more fear of being bombed at home & no more living in air raid shelters. But there is still Japan to be defeated & the restoration of our country to be dealt with, which will give us many headaches & hard work in the coming years... The Prime Minister broadcast his statement that the European War had ceased at 3.00 pm. The Germans had signed the Capitulation in Berlin itself. The rest of the day was a General Holiday. Great crowds had collected outside Buckingham Palace & we went on to the Balcony to see them. We were given a great reception. We went out several times during the afternoon... I made a broadcast at 9pm to the British Empire. Several buildings in Whitehall besides Buck. Pal. were floodlit & we were called for to go out on to the balcony repeatedly. We went out eight times altogether during that afternoon and evening. Lilibet & Margaret with a party of friends walked in the crowd after dark to see London in festive mood. Poor darlings they have never had any fun yet.'

Now the war was over, Elizabeth was overjoyed at the prospect of being reunited with the man who had occupied her thoughts, her secret love, Lt. Philip Mountbatten R.N. There was of course a number of suitable aristocratic, spirited young gentlemen around the princess at that time, recalled Lady Anne Glenconner, whose family were friends and neighbours of the King and Queen at Sandringham. 'Elizabeth realised her destiny and luckily set her heart on Philip at an early age. He was ideal – good-looking and a foreign prince,' she said. The King, overprotective and reluctant to let her go, still had reservations about Philip's suitability as a marriage match, her mother's concern was more to do with his German roots and Nazi-supporting relations. She dubbed Philip 'The Hun'.

5: A SECRET ENGAGEMENT

'People will say we're in love.'

From Rodgers and Hammerstein's
1943 musical *Oklahoma*

It seemed nothing, not even the heat of war, could distract the ever-resourceful Dickie Mountbatten from matchmaking. Amid his heroics in battle, he still had his sights set on securing a marriage between his nephew, Philip, and the world's most eligible heiress. Lord Mountbatten, who knew first-hand the advantages of marrying well, having wed an English heiress himself, never missed an opportunity to press Philip's bloodline and credentials as a suitable husband for his second cousin, the King's eldest daughter. He believed the match would suit everyone, not least of course the Mountbatten name. In the early days of Philip and Elizabeth's courtship, there were occasions when Philip toyed more than once with throwing in the towel and returning to Greece, worried that the restrictions that would be placed on him in the future would be suffocating. But he was persuaded by Mountbatten to stick with it.

Mountbatten's daughter, Patricia, explained, 'The characters of Prince Philip and Princess Elizabeth matched extremely well. And I thought he genuinely thought that this was something that should be seriously considered and would be a very good idea.' On a trip to London in 1944, Dickie suggested to George VI that they should open talks with the Greek king, George II, about a possible marriage between Philip and Elizabeth. Exasperated by Dickie's persistence he firmly knocked him back. 'I know you like to get things settled at once, once you have an idea in mind but I've come to the conclusion that we are going too fast,' George VI wrote to the over-enthusiastic Mountbatten.

At the time, Philip, by now promoted to the rank of first lieutenant – having become one of the youngest officers in the Royal Navy to hold the rank at just 21, when he was promoted in 1942 – was serving aboard HMS *Whelp* in Tokyo Bay when the Japanese surrendered in 1945. Philip had served his adopted country with distinction having seen service with the British Pacific Fleet in the 27th Destroyer Flotilla as the war in the East came to an explosive end with US President Harry S. Truman's decision to drop the world's first 5-ton 'Little Boy' atom bomb, made of highly enriched uranium-235, over Hiroshima.

Three days later President Truman, who had only become president a few weeks before upon the sudden death of Franklin D. Roosevelt, ordered a second more complex atom bomb, 'Fat Man', made of plutonium, to be dropped at Nagasaki. These nuclear attacks – the first immediately killing 80,000 people, the second 40,000, with tens of thousands dying later of radiation exposure – played a decisive role in Japan's unconditional surrender. After 1,364 days, 5 hours and 14 minutes, the bloody war in the Pacific officially ended at 0904 on 2 September 1945 with the signing of the Instrument of Surrender on the battleship USS *Missouri*, anchored in Tokyo Bay.

On board were representatives of the Allied Nations. Japanese Foreign Minister Mamoru Shigemitsu signed on behalf of the Emperor of Japan and General Yoshijiro Umezo signed on behalf of Imperial General Headquarters. The ceremony was conducted by General of the Army Douglas MacArthur, Supreme Commander, with Fleet Admiral Chester W. Nimitz, signing for the US and Admiral Sir Bruce Fraser for the UK. Admiral Nimitz, remembering those who gave their lives in the Pacific War, said, 'They fought together as brothers in arms; they died together and now lie side by side. To them we have a solid obligation – the obligation to ensure that their sacrifice will help make this a better and safer world in which to live.'

Philip recalled, 'Being in Tokyo Bay with the surrender ceremony taking place in the battleship which was, what, 200 yards away and you could see what was going on with a pair of binoculars, it was a great relief.' After Japan's surrender, HMS *Whelp* took former prisoners of war on board. 'These people were naval people. They were emaciated… tears pouring down their cheeks, they just drank their tea, they really couldn't speak. It was a most extraordinary sensation,' he recalled.

Throughout the war Elizabeth kept a photograph of her cousin Philip in her room and the couple wrote letters to each other. He occasionally visited Windsor Castle on shore leave, but the blossoming relationship was never made public. In January 1946, Philip returned from the war for good aboard HMS *Whelp* and he was posted to the Royal Navy Petty Officers' School in Corsham, Wiltshire. In a letter, Elizabeth, who had turned 20 that April, wrote that this was the turning point in their relationship and afterwards she and Philip 'started seeing more of each other'.

After the adrenalin buzz of real front-line action, Philip found this home posting dull, which left him restless and disillusioned. In a letter to Elizabeth, he admitted he was 'still not accustomed to the idea of peace, rather fed up with everything and feeling that there was not much to look forward to and rather grudgingly accepting the idea of going on in the peacetime Navy.' It did at least allow for more frequent trips to London, and Marion Crawford, Princess Elizabeth's former governess, described seeing Philip's black, green-upholstered MG sports car roaring into the forecourt of Buckingham Palace and the prince getting out 'hatless' and 'always in a hurry to see Lilibet'.

For her part, the princess remembered having 'great fun' being driven around in the car – of which Philip, she wrote, 'was very proud'. Ms Crawford noted, 'He came into the palace like a refreshing sea breeze. A forthright and completely natural young man given to say what he thought.' According to 'Crawfie', Elizabeth began to take more trouble with her appearance, and to play the tune 'People will say we're in love' from the musical *Oklahoma*.

Elizabeth recalled how the pair were pursued in his sports car by paparazzi through the streets of post-war London during their courtship. In a handwritten note with a Balmoral letterhead, the then 21-year-old princess details their shared love of dancing and Philip's love of fast driving in his MG sports car. The letter was written to Betty Shew, an author, just months before the Queen and Prince Philip were due to marry in 1947. Mrs Shew was writing a book called *Royal Wedding* as a souvenir of the marriage, and the then Princess Elizabeth agreed to share details of her relationship.

Elizabeth, who also detailed his love of riding and how the couple danced at nightclubs Ciro's and Quaglino's, wrote, 'Philip enjoys driving and does it fast! He had his own tiny M.G. which he is very proud of – he has taken me about in it, once up to London, which was great fun, only it was like sitting on the road, and the wheels are almost as high as one's head. On that one and only occasion we were chased by a photographer which was disappointing.'

When in London, Philip would stay either with his grandmother, Princess Victoria, Marchioness of Milford Haven, at Kensington Palace or on a camp bed at the home of his uncle Dickie. In visitors' books at the time, he declared himself 'of no fixed abode'. Mountbatten's butler, John Dean*, was struck by the fact that the prince's civilian wardrobe was 'scantier than that of many a bank clerk.' Often, Dean recalled, all Philip brought with him was a razor for his morning shave. When he had gone to bed, Dean would wash and iron his shirt and darn his socks. 'He was very easy to look after and never asked for things like that to be done for him, but I liked him so much that I did it anyway.'

While Philip's romance with Elizabeth progressed apace, the royal establishment did not welcome him with open arms. The Queen, Elizabeth's mother, who had lost a beloved brother, Captain The Hon. Fergus Bowes-Lyon in World War I on 27 September

---

* Dean later became Philip's personal valet, married palace servant Betty Burns and eventually wrote a memoir, *H.R.H. Prince Philip, Duke of Edinburgh: A Portrait by his Valet*, published by Hale, 1954.

1915 at the Battle of The Hohenzollern Redoubt, in particular was against it. Although he had been born in Greece, Philip was descended from German and Danish princely stock and, given that World War II had only just finished, she feared the British people would not warm to such a union. Given the Royal Family's own Germanic ancestry, it hardly seemed fair even though in post-war Britain anti-German feeling was still running high.

The more difficult issue was Philip's three surviving older sisters, all of whom had married German aristocrats. Worse still was that their husbands had been fully signed up members the Nazi party – two of them from the aristocratic Von Hessen family, whose ancestral home Schloss Wolfsgarten, established 1722, was a former hunting seat of the ruling family of Hesse-Darmstadt, located in Hessen, approximately 10 miles south of Frankfurt am Main. Philip had been a regular visitor before the war enjoying many family holidays there.

Philip's nephew, Prince Rainer Christoph Friedrich of Hesse, was the son of Philip's youngest sister, Sophie of Greece and Denmark, and Christoph of Hesse, himself a nephew of the Kaiser, Wilhelm II. Prince Rainer's father was a Nazi and German SS officer who was killed on active duty in a plane crash during World War II. His mother Sophie's memoirs describe Hermann Goering, one of the most powerful figures in the Nazi regime, in glowing terms. She noted that Goering talked a lot about the new political party which he had joined and especially about the charismatic party leader, Adolf Hitler. She wrote, 'As Goering was insistent that we should meet Hitler personally we decided to invite him to lunch at our flat. I have to say here that although Chri [Christoph her husband] and I changed our political view fundamentally some years later, we were impressed by this charming and seemingly modest man [Hitler].'

Philip's sister and her husband Christoph, who became a Nazi member in 1933, also attended Goering's wedding to actress Emma Sonnemann at Berlin Cathedral on 10 April 1935. At the reception in the Hotel 'Kaiserhof' in Berlin, Philip's sister Sophie was photographed at the top table sitting opposite Adolf Hitler, who was Goering's best man. Sophie's husband by this time had become an SS colonel and was head of an espionage network that gathered intelligence for the Nazis.

It is understood that the network helped Hitler prepare for the 1939 invasion of Czechoslovakia and to deceive British prime minister Neville Chamberlain, who thought he had gained a lasting peace in negotiations with Hitler at Munich the previous year. Christoph's son, Prince Rainer, admitted that he had wrestled for years about his family's close relationship with Hitler and his Nazi henchmen and said it 'haunts him'. It was a problem too for his cousin Philip who, as part of Dickie Mountbatten's grand plan, needed to be, or at least appear to be, an English Royal Navy sailor rather than a prince of German blood. Another concern of the King and Queen was Philip's reputation as a playboy. Long before the official engagement in 1947, 'Blondes, brunettes and redhead charmers, Philip gallantly and I think quite impartially squired them all,' said Philip's cousin and exact contemporary, Alexandra of Yugoslavia. But was Philip really doing anything wrong?

Philip is adamant that he did not think seriously about marrying Elizabeth until more than a year after the war had ended when he went to stay at Balmoral in 1946. By then, as Lieutenant HRH Prince Philip of Greece, he had applied to become a naturalised British subject. If he had thoughts of marriage much then, he kept them private.

In 1943 Philip was 24, barely recognisable sporting a full beard and still on active duty in the Pacific. Along with his friend Commander Mike Parker, an Australian and fellow naval officer, he enjoyed his Antipodean shore leave to the full. Parker was an affable and independently spirited Australian whose personality clicked with Philip. In 1944 Parker and Prince Philip came together again in the Far East, where they served in sister ships of the 27th Destroyer Flotilla, and their friendship grew.

According to Philip's cousin, Alexandra, who incidentally was not there, 'Philip, with a golden beard, hit feminine hearts, first in

Melbourne and then in Sydney, with terrific impact.' Mike Parker, who was there, tells a different story. 'Philip was actually quite reserved. He didn't give away a lot. There have been books and articles galore saying he played the field. I don't believe it. People say we were screwing around like nobody's business. Well, we weren't.'

It was a different story to what Parker, who died in 2001 aged 81, told author Tim Heald, during the research for his 1991 biography *The Duke: Portrait of Prince Philip.* 'Yeah, there were always armfuls of girls,' he said. When pressed on it, Parker said, 'Jesus, I wish I'd never used that phrase. What I meant was this: we were young, we had fun, we had a few drinks, we might have gone dancing, but that was it. In Australia, Philip came to meet my family, my sisters and their friends. There were girls galore, but there was no one special. Believe me. I guarantee it.'

Philip, a healthy and handsome young man, inevitably did go out on dates before a marriage to Elizabeth became a serious prospect. Elegant Australian, Robin Dalton, born 1920 and who enjoyed a colourful career as a literary agent and film producer was 23 years old in 1945. The Australian was working as secretary to the commanding officer of the ordnance department of the Southwest Pacific Area and remembers it a little differently.

'I met Philip through David [Milford Haven, Philip's cousin and, later, best man]. They were like brothers, you know.' She recalled Philip had two 'special' girlfriends in Australia at the end of the war: 'A society girl called Sue Other-Gee, and then Sandra Jacques – that was a terrific love affair … a very full love affair,' Robin claimed. When another alleged old flame of Philip's was asked if she had been Philip's girlfriend, Georgina Kennard (mother of Sacha Hamilton, Duchess of Abercorn with whom Philip also enjoyed an intimate friendship later) replied, 'Everybody said he was in love with me. My mother used to say that his mother – who was a saintly person, deaf but lovely – would have been very happy for Philip to marry me, but it never came up.

'I said to him, "Are you still in love with me?" and he said, "Yes, of course, I am." The truth is, he was wonderfully attractive – he still is – and we were friends, best friends, and we went out together and had just the best time, but nothing really serious happened. It wasn't like that. He was young and handsome and, of course, I loved him. At that age, you fall in love all the time, don't you? Philip knew lots of girls. There was Osla Benning, wasn't there? We were just young people having fun.' In 1944, however, both Georgina and Osla, an attractive Canadian debutante, became engaged to other men.

Getting an insight into Princess Elizabeth's feelings about Philip at this time is much more straightforward than pinning down his. The Queen is happy for you to know that, in her heart and in her way, she has been committed to Prince Philip from the age of 13. As it was with her horses – and her dogs, and her faith, and her duty – so it was with Philip. Her first cousin, near-contemporary and friend, Margaret Rhodes, and from 1991 to 2002 Woman of the Bedchamber to Queen Elizabeth The Queen Mother admitted, 'Princess Elizabeth was enamoured [by Philip] from an early age. She never looked at anyone else. She was smitten from the start.' However smitten Elizabeth was, and no matter how interested Philip declared himself to be, establishment figures were far from happy with the prospect of this handsome 'German' marrying the heir to the throne. Sir Alan Lascelles, who Philip dubbed one of the 'moustached men at the palace' felt he was 'rough, uneducated and would probably not be faithful.'

Philip still had an ace in his pack – Uncle Dickie. The war had launched Mountbatten on a meteoric rise. He had been promoted to the Supreme Commander of Allied Forces, South East Asia Command (SEAC), a position he held until 1946. Working with General William Slim, he helped halt the Japanese offensive towards India, pushing them back, and masterminded the reconquest of Burma. In September 1945, he received the Japanese surrender at Singapore. Many saw this charismatic figure as a national hero.

Despite his immaculate war record, among the aristocracy Lord Mountbatten was mistrusted and still seen as a pushy newcomer. 'The older members of the establishment were very frightened of the very fresh air coming along and he certainly produced a gale of fresh air with him,' his daughter Countess Patricia explained. 'They thought that change was not for good, my father thought change was nearly always excellent,' Lady Pamela Hicks, her younger sister, confirmed this.

Just as Philip was warming to the idea of a future with Elizabeth, strong rumours of a romance began to appear in the British Press about the intimacy between the couple. On 27 October 1946, in the splendour of Romsey's Norman abbey before 1,300 guests, the wedding of Patricia Mountbatten to Coldstream Guards Captain Lord Brabourne marked a turning point, as far as the media were concerned. As guests, ranging from farm and domestic employees of the two families to generals who had served under Viscount Mountbatten in Asia, toasted the couple, newspaper reporters were focused on Elizabeth and Philip, who was an usher at the ceremony conducted by the Archbishop of Canterbury, the Bishop of Winchester and two other clergymen.

Elizabeth and Margaret attended to the 22-year-old bride, a Wren officer during the war, and when they arrived Philip was immediately on hand to escort them from their car. As she removed her fur coat, Elizabeth turned and the newspaper photographers captured an image of them gazing at each other lovingly. Nothing short of a media frenzy followed that alarmed the King and Queen. Indeed, off camera, Lady Pamela Hicks was more forthcoming about the Royal Family's reaction. She told *Vanity Fair* journalist James Reginato in 2013 that the King and Queen were 'appalled' by the prospect of a serious romance. He wrote, 'When Philip casually took the coat of Princess Elizabeth as they arrived, the press assembled outside caught this first hint of a royal romance, and a media frenzy ensued.'

Lady Patricia and Lady Pamela had long known about Elizabeth's crush on Philip. Lady Pamela recalled how Elizabeth had to convince her parents to let her marry Philip when she came of age. Lady Pamela continued: 'The King and Queen were appalled. The thought that he might become a son-in-law was most unwelcome. Why wasn't she marrying some respectable English duke? Yes, he was a Prince of Greece and Denmark. But very suspect, Greece – they get rid of their royal families regularly. And he had no money.' She went on to say that Philip's infamous bluntness was also an obstacle to endearing himself to the Royals too. 'He's never been one to flatter. He was not the courtier they were used to,' Lady Pamela added.

No official confirmation followed and the couple kept up an active social life. Elizabeth's guardsmen friends served as her innocent escorts to restaurants and fashionable clubs, while Philip would take Elizabeth and Margaret out to a party or to the theatre. It was Elizabeth's first experience of this new kind of public interest. Her personal life had become public property and she did not like it. When she arrived at engagements, people in the crowd would shout, 'Where's Philip?'

Different witnesses give different assessments of the temperature of Philip's ardour. His loyal friend, Mike Parker, insisted Philip 'was completely in love with her [Elizabeth], absolutely.' Lord Brabourne agreed saying it was a 'love-match'. Gina Kennard too said Philip was 'extremely fond' of her before they were engaged. Crucially, at 24, he had sensed his Uncle Dickie's well-meaning meddling was not actually helping the romance develop naturally. 'Please, I beg of you, not too much advice in an affair of the heart, or I shall be forced to do the wooing by proxy,' Philip wrote to his uncle.

The King was still not convinced Philip was the right man for his beloved Elizabeth. He was certainly not happy with the speed of the developments, but by now it was beyond his control. Unexpectedly, Philip proposed to the princess at Balmoral in 1946. Her father believed his eldest daughter and heir was still far too young to marry. He stalled the couple's plans only giving his blessing providing any formal engagement was delayed until Elizabeth's 21st birthday, the following April. Their engagement was officially announced on 9 July 1947 and Philip presented Elizabeth with a 3-carat round diamond ring consisting of a centre stone flanked by ten smaller pave diamonds, the diamonds taken from a tiara that belonged to Philip's mother.

The delay and secrecy was to ensure the princess would have time to reconsider her acceptance should she have a change of heart. All concerned agreed. The King, perhaps hoping absence and distance would cool his daughter's ardour, took the young princess with him on a tour of South Africa meaning she would be away from her secret fiancé for months.

It was on this overseas visit on her 21st birthday in 1947 during a radio broadcast – it was also filmed – from Cape Town that Princess Elizabeth made the historic public declaration that she would dedicate her life to the service of the Commonwealth. She said, 'I declare before you all that my whole life, whether it be long or short shall be devoted to your service and the service of our great imperial family to which we all belong.' If her parents thought this might weaken her resolve to marry Philip, they would be disappointed. She had made a promise to serve for life, but she had also made a promise to the man she loved and she would keep it.

6: FANFARE OF TRUMPETS

*'When I handed your hand to the Archbishop,
I felt I had lost something very precious.'*

Letter from George VI to Princess
Elizabeth after her wedding

Earl Mountbatten of Burma was a brilliant networker throughout his life. By 1947, as a rear admiral and the last Viceroy of India, his multitude of contacts included powerful players in the new Labour government and on Fleet Street. A decorated war hero, Mountbatten's political contacts may not have been the 'firm friends' he described them to be, but they were often in his debt and many owed him favours.

Indeed, it was one of those so-called 'firm friends', the sitting prime minister Clement Attlee, who persuaded Mountbatten to accept the poisoned chalice of overseeing the British withdrawal from India. His instructions were, effectively, 'Keep India united if you can, but whatever happens, get Britain out.' On 18 March 1947 Clement Attlee wrote to Mountbatten effectively ordering him to negotiate an exit deal for Britain by no later than October that year. 'It is, of course, important that the Indian States should adjust their relations with the authorities to whom it is intended to hand over power in British India; but as was explicitly stated by the Cabinet Mission His Majesty's Government do not intend to hand over their powers and obligations under paramountcy to any successor government. It is not intended to bring paramountcy as a system to a conclusion earlier than the date of the final transfer of power, but you are authorised, at such time as you think appropriate, to enter into negotiations with individual States for adjusting their relations with the Crown. The princely states would be free from orders and treaties of British Rule in India. They can either join the two dominions or stay separate,' he wrote.

Among others Mountbatten's wartime mentor, Churchill, by now in failing health and Leader of the Opposition, was furious with the Labour government's India strategy and would later fall out with his old friend over the way he handled Britain's exit from the subcontinent. Suspecting underhand political movements were afoot, Churchill wrote to Attlee on 1 July 1947:

'My dear Prime Minister,
I'm worried to hear that you'll call the India Bill, "The Indian Independence Bill". This is completely against what we'd been told before. The only reason why I gave support to plans agreed with Mountbatten is because they'd establish Dominion status. Dominion status is not the same as Independence, although it may lead to independence. It's not true that a community is independent when its Ministers have in fact taken the Oath of Allegiance to the King. This is a very serious issue and the correct process and naming should be used. The correct title would be, it seems to me, "The Indian Dominions Bill". I'll also support it if it were called "The India Bill, 1947" or "The India Self-Government Bill". I'm glad to hear you're thinking about these changes. Believe me,

Yours sincerely, WSC'

The India question polarised many leading figures across Britain. The Left wanted to ditch the old Raj and instead focus on rebuilding post-war Britain, by now a bankrupt country. Others like Winston Churchill, who famously said that he had not been made the King's first minister to preside over the liquidation of the empire, still saw Britain as a major player on the world stage. He was appalled by what he saw as Mountbatten's betrayal by his handling of the withdrawal from India. For Mountbatten, India presented a snake-pit of challenges. He knew it was a position that would need all his guile; not everyone would get what they wanted and he soon realised the timetable he had been set was unattainable. His role would mean he would gather enemies, but it also meant he would be owed favours too.

Eventually, Attlee's government decided that Britain would leave India with no deal by June 1948. Mountbatten's hopes of overseeing a peaceful transition to an independent, united India were dashed as communal violence intensified between Muslim and Hindu communities. Hoping to force a compromise and to end the violence, Mountbatten decided to accelerate independence, a move that was much criticised and that many believed worsened the violence and he eventually agreed, with much reluctance, to India's partition and the creation of Pakistan.

The decision to speed this up and leave on 15 August 1947 was Mountbatten's. The decision to grant such power to the 'master of disaster', as his detractors at the Admiralty dubbed him for his propensity to damage warships by precipitate action, was Mr Attlee's. On 3 June 1947, Dickie finalised the 'Mountbatten Plan' after giving up hope of a united country. On 14 and 15 August 1947, British India was partitioned into the new states of India and Pakistan.

The result was a catastrophe, not only for many individuals, but also for the system that was failing around them: an unpopular and chaotic British Empire. Riven by political violence for its entire existence, the British Empire had long resisted democratisation and had institutionalised differences based on identity between its subjects as a matter of policy. What followed was widespread inter-communal violence, particularly in the Punjab region, now divided between East India and West Pakistan. There were huge population movements as three and a half million Hindus and Sikhs fled from the areas that had become Pakistan and around five million Muslims migrated to the new country of Pakistan, created by Muhammad Ali Jinnah. Entire communities that had coexisted for a thousand years turned on each other in a terrifying outbreak of bloody sectarian violence, with Hindus and Sikhs on one side and Muslims on the other, a terrible and unprecedented genocide. In Punjab and Bengal, provinces adjoining India's borders with West and East Pakistan respectively, the slaughter was appalling. Massacres, arsons, savage sexual violence ensued with 75,000 women raped, and many then disfigured or dismembered. By the end of it in 1948 more than 15 million people had been uprooted, and between one and two million were dead.

In his radio broadcast on partition Mountbatten concluded hopefully, 'I have faith in the future of India and am proud to be with you all at this momentous time. May your decisions be wisely guided and may they be carried out in the peaceful and friendly spirit of the Gandhi-Jinnah appeal.' It was, at best, wishful thinking. Many placed the blame for the catastrophe of partition squarely, but unfairly, on Mountbatten. He was considered for other status positions, having served as the first governor general of independent India between 1947 and 1948, but he elected to continue his naval career and became commander-in-chief of the Mediterranean Fleet based in Malta, where he would soon be reunited with his nephew, Philip.

Lord Mountbatten had good contacts among leading figures in the British press too. So while the King and Queen and Princess Elizabeth and Princess Margaret were on the South African tour, Dickie busied himself trying to secure his dynastic ambitions. His opportunism is demonstrated in a letter written at the time to influential journalist and Labour MP Tom Driberg, a homosexual, whose associates later included East End gangsters Ronnie and Reggie Kray, which led to MI5 keeping a file on him amid allegations that they provided 'rent boys' for him. Mountbatten's new mission was to convince those that mattered of Philip's Britishness and eradicate chatter of him being a 'Johnny foreigner' at a time when there was still so much anti-German feeling. 'He left Greece at the age of one, and has only spent three months of his entire life since in Greece and cannot even speak the language,' he wrote.

According to Philip Eade's 2011 biography, *Young Prince Philip: His Turbulent Early Life*, Lord Mountbatten divulged his nephew's political leanings to Driberg just after it was announced that Philip and Elizabeth were engaged in July 1947. Mountbatten told Driberg he was 'agreeably surprised' to see only the left-wing American newspaper the *Daily Worker* 'condemned my nephew's engagement on political grounds'. He went on, 'As you know, I am an ardent believer in constitutional monarchy as a means of producing rapid evolution without actual revolution, but only if monarchy is wisely handled. I am sure Philip will not let the side down in this respect.' Influenced by Mountbatten Philip had become relatively progressive politically and, in 1945, he had told his uncle that he was not in the least 'antagonistic to principles of socialism'. Philip even wrote to Elizabeth in December 1946 apologising for starting a 'rather heated discussion' on politics, in which he said he hoped she would forgive him 'if I did say anything I ought not to have said'. Philip added that he hoped she did not consider him 'violently argumentative and an exponent of socialism' – showing he was more left-leaning politically than the royals.

No matter how exemplary his record in World War II, Philip's surname, Schleswig-Holstein-Sonderburg-Glücksburg was clearly a stumbling block for him being accepted as Princess Elizabeth's suitor. Mountbatten's solution was simple; for his nephew to adopt the Mountbatten name.

Ahead of the royal wedding, George VI decreed that his future son-in-law, the new Duke of Edinburgh, should be addressed as 'His Royal Highness'. His official livery colour was dark green, known as Edinburgh Green, which was used for his cars and his staff's uniforms. His coat of arms represented his lineage as a Prince of Greece and Denmark on his paternal side and his descent from the Mountbatten family on his maternal side. His motto read simply, 'God Is My Help'.

His exact rank and level of importance was debated at the highest levels of government – with Churchill suggesting Prince Consort – but he rejected any additions and only received his British princehood from the Queen in 1957, despite the fact he had been born a prince. Although he was a privy counsellor, the duke had no other constitutional role and, unlike Queen Victoria's husband,

Albert, he was not given access to state papers. Until 1999, he was a member of the House of Lords but his position as a member of the Royal Family meant he never spoke in the chamber owing to his close proximity to the Queen, who had to remain politically neutral.

As he had discovered after the wedding, whether he was a royal duke or not, he was not considered by senior courtiers to have any real role. When one member of the Royal Household remarked to him disdainfully that he would get used to Windsor Castle in time, he retorted: 'Thank you very much – my mother was born here.' Philip knew these new circumstances would be challenging and decided to turn them to his advantage. He recalled: 'There were plenty of people telling me what not to do. "You mustn't interfere with this." I had to try to support the Queen as best I could without getting in the way. The difficulty was to find things that might be useful.'

With two days to go, on November 18, the King hosted a celebratory ball. Dramatist Noël Coward, one of the guests, said the happy couple looked radiant. 'The whole thing was pictorially, dramatically and spiritually enchanting.' The King led a conga line through the staterooms of the palace with the party ending after midnight. Philip handed out gifts to his fiancée's attendants: silver compacts in the Art Deco style with a gold crown above the bride and groom's entwined initials and a row of five small cabochon sapphires, dealing them out 'like playing cards', recalled Lady Elizabeth Longman, one of Elizabeth's bridesmaids.

Philip was finally naturalised as a British citizen on 28 February 1947. In the *London Gazette*, 19 March 1947, page 1,271, the now very English-sounding 'Mountbatten, Philip; Greece; Serving Officer in His Majesty's Forces, 16 Chester Street, SW1' (a property owned by Dickie) was now an English subject. A few months later on 9 July 1947 the engagement was announced, the newspapers and newsreels portraying Philip as a thoroughly British Royal Navy officer. 'The King has gladly given his consent,' read the statement. The next day they made their first public appearance as a royal couple, at a garden party. Newspaper baron Lord Beaverbrook's

Daily Express trumpeted: 'Today the British people, turning aside from the anxieties of a time of troubles, find hope as well as joy in the royal romance.'

Philip had wooed and won his princess and presented her with the 3-carat round diamond and platinum engagement ring. The King had his own method of dealing with Philip's Nazi relatives but it was tactless. Philip was effectively ordered not to invite his beloved sisters by the King and Queen. George decided their connection to Nazi Germany was still too shaming.

It wasn't until 2006 that Philip broke a 60-year public silence about his family's Nazi ties. Like many Germans, he explained, his family had found much to admire in Hitler's early attempts to restore Germany's power and prestige. 'There was a great improvement in things like trains running on time and building,' Philip said. 'There was a sense of hope after the depressing chaos of the Weimar Republic. I can understand people latching onto something or somebody who appeared to be appealing to their patriotism and trying to get things going. You can understand how attractive it was.' He stressed, however, that he was never 'conscious' of anyone in the family expressing anti-Semitic views.

Philip and his close friends were determined to keep details of his stag night on the eve of his wedding secret. Their secret held for nearly 70 years which is no mean feat, given among the throng were major Fleet Street figures from the newspaper industry. There was an official stag party at the Dorchester Hotel, Central London, where the press photographers were invited to take official pictures. That was a relatively tame affair. But a few days earlier there was a private dinner which Philip hosted with some of his closest friends held at the Belfry Club on 14 November 1947 located in the heart of Belgravia. Built in 1830, the building served as a Presbyterian church, a spiritualists' meeting place and, finally, is now one of London's most famous luncheon and dining clubs, Mosimanns, run by Swiss chef and restaurateur Anton Mosimann OBE.

Philip celebrated giving up his single status with some of his closest friends in style. A bespoke menu and seating plan, created by artist Feliks Topolski, read, 'Dinner to Distant Country Member Lt. Philip Mountbatten, Royal Navy, who is to be married on the 20 November 1947'. There was no mention of the bride. Attached was a 25-person seating plan and menu which shows guests dined on foie gras, turtle soup, mixed grill and crêpes suzette. There also still exist black-and-white photographs of the black-tie event, with the now 26-year-old Philip sitting down at the luxurious table while other friends gather round in a group pose.

His bachelor party guests were a raffish collection of friends, mostly pals from the infamous 'Thursday Club' that met for lunch at Wheeler's restaurant, in Old Compton Street, Soho, every week. It's colourful bon vivant members, who Elizabeth labelled Philip's 'funny friends', included actors such as David Niven, James Robertson Justice, and Peter Ustinov as well as the yet to be exposed Soviet spy and traitor Kim Philby.

Philip's cousin and best man, David Milford Haven, was the only aristocrat, which showed how classless and what a man of his time Philip was. Most had risen from humble beginnings but were high achievers. Surprisingly for a man who was later so critical of the media, many present were newspapermen, editors and writers. Arthur Christiansen, editor of the *Daily Express* from 1933 to 1957, under his stewardship the world's biggest-selling newspaper, was close to Philip. The son of a shipbuilder, he became a reporter at 16 at the *Wallasey and Wirral Chronicle* before being hired by Press baron Lord Beaverbrook. His mantra was 'always, always tell the news through people.' Journalists Sean Fielding, a former wartime colonel and Anglo-Irish reporter who established *Soldier* magazine, Canadian war correspondent Matt Halton, and Jack Broome DCS, a Royal Navy veteran who became editor of *Sketch* magazine, as well as an author and film director, were present. Others at the table included artist and writer Bobby St John Cooper, a war correspondent who created the 'Young Bert' cartoons from France inspiring the song 'We're Going To Hang Out The Washing On The Siegfried Line'.

Also among the invitees was Michael Eddowes a lawyer, author and restaurateur, who later became embroiled in the Profumo scandal, which dragged on from 9 July 1961 to 4 June 1963 culminating in the Secretary of State for War, John Profumo, resigning after it emerged that a girl he had been seeing, Christine Keeler, had also been sleeping with a Soviet naval attaché. The man at the heart of the scandal, society osteopath and alleged pimp, Stephen Ward, had also introduced Eddowes to Keeler in 1962, and he fell for her and wanted to set her up in a flat in Regent's Park.

Bernard Walsh, proprietor of Wheeler's restaurant, was also in Philip's inner circle of friends, along with actor Guy Middleton, who specialised in playing cads, and Vivian Brodzky, Fleet Street's first industrial correspondent, who penned the 1966 book, *Fleet Street – The Inside Story of Journalism* for which Philip wrote the foreword.

The stag night photo was taken by photographer Baron Nahum, a descendant of Italian Jews from Libya. He founded the Thursday Club and often hosted parties in his Mayfair flat where aristocrats met showgirls. He introduced Philip to this bohemian circle, including stage star Pat Kirkwood. Later she and the (by now) married Philip dined together alone at a Mayfair restaurant before dancing at a club and ending up eating scrambled eggs at dawn in Nahum's flat. Nahum was another friend of the subsequently disgraced Stephen Ward, who was convicted of living off the immoral earnings of Christine Keeler and Mandy Rice-Davies. He died suddenly aged 50 and Philip sent a wreath to his funeral.

Others with a seat at Philip's table were Sam Boal, American-born London bureau chief for the *New York Daily Post* and Warsaw-born artist Feliks Topolski, who encouraged Philip to paint. The Prince commissioned many of his works, including a 200-foot mural of the Queen's coronation, still hanging in Buckingham Palace. Philip 'Pip' Youngman Carter, an illustrator and writer, who created dust jackets for novels by Graham Greene and John Steinbeck; W. T. 'Skipper' Coulton, London office boss of *The Times of India* and co-founder of the Thursday Club; Tony Wysard, a cartoonist and illustrator; writer Paul Holt, solicitor Roger Slade, Dan Sangster and John Myers completed the group seated around the horseshoe-shaped table.

Included in the personalised Belfry menu is a verse about marriage by Dr Samuel Johnson which reads: 'Marriage is the best state for a man in general; and every man is a worse man in proportion as he is unfit for the married state…'

The humour and sense of fun is clearly evident among Philip's circle, from the menu art by Feliks Topolski to the selection of each course. It was one of the last times Philip could be truly free. The wedding was just six days away.

On the way to the wedding rehearsal, Philip was stopped by police for driving too fast. 'I'm sorry, officer,' he said, 'but I've got an appointment with the Archbishop of Canterbury.' The wedding would certainly raise his standing in society, but also help with his bank balance. At the time of his wedding, he had 12 pennies in the bank.

His wedding present from George VI was a pair of Purdey shotguns*. But he never forgot what it was like to have little money and was always frugal. In 2008, he gave his Savile Row tailor, John Kent of Kent, Haste and Lachter, a 52-year-old pair of trousers to be altered.

★★★

On his marriage to Elizabeth, he removed himself from the line of succession. As a descendant of Queen Victoria, Philip had a distant claim to the top job, but that was the least of his concerns. On the morning of their wedding, however, some nervousness crept in. He had just given up smoking and at breakfast he and his best man drank a gin and tonic. 'I saw him just after breakfast that morning,' said Countess Mountbatten – Lord Mountbatten's elder daughter, heiress and one of Elizabeth's eight bridesmaids. 'We were alone together – we were cousins and we knew each other very well – and I said something about what an exciting day it was and, suddenly, he said to me, "Am I being very brave or very foolish?"'

---

* Following the death of the King in 1952, Philip reorganised the shoot at Sandringham and for many years achieved his target bag of 10,000 pheasants during the annual seven-week stay. He gave up shooting in 2011. It was feared the gun's recoil could dislodge a stent he had to remedy a heart problem.

although not because he doubted his love for Lilibet, rather, he worried that he would be relinquishing other aspects of his life that were meaningful. 'Nothing was going to change for her,' his cousin recalled. 'Everything was going to change for him.'

'He was apprehensive, he was uncertain, not about marrying Princess Elizabeth, but about what the marriage would mean for him. He was giving up a great deal. They have, indeed, done a lot together, and everything did change for him.'

Elizabeth saved her rationing coupons to buy the essential materials for her wedding dress, helped along by a gift of 200 coupons from the government. At the time rationing was still imposed. She even had to return the many hundreds of coupons sent in by the public as it would have been illegal to accept them. Despite the unconventional funding, couturier Sir Norman Hartnell's design included ivory silk, duchesse satin, silver threads, crystals and 10,000 seed pearls, and the dress featured full-length sleeves, a fitted bodice, a heart-shaped neckline, a floor-length panelled skirt and a dramatic 14.8 foot-long train.

On the big day Philip's best man, David Mountbatten, the Marquess of Milford Haven, was at his side as they left Kensington Palace by car. Among those waiting to cheer them was a chimney sweep, complete with his brush, who waved his cap in the air with delight, and was seen by commentators as a lucky omen. Philip was cheered all the way along the route via Hyde Park Corner to the Abbey, where crowds were ten deep. A Captain's Escort of Household Cavalry in full-dress uniform was in attendance on the Queen and Princess Margaret who were driven to the Abbey in the Glass Coach from the palace. After the Queen and Margaret had passed by, the crowds waited with tense excitement for the appearance of the King and the bride Princess Elizabeth in the Irish State Coach.

The weather smiled on the couple too. It may have been a grey day but it remains the mildest 20 November on record in the UK which encouraged an immense crowd to gather outside Westminster Abbey. Almost as one, the loyal royalists applauded and cheered as the King and the beaming princess arrived at the Great West Door. His Majesty paused briefly to help his daughter alight.

Two thousand VIP guests waited eagerly inside for the 11.30 a.m. ceremony which started right on cue. Her smiles belied the fact that the princess had to cope with her own fair share of wedding hitches that some brides might have interpreted as a wedding-day disaster. Her 'something borrowed' – her grandmother's diamond-spiked tiara – snapped hours before she walked down the aisle. Elizabeth's mother suggested she simply swap out tiaras, the princess wouldn't. With just two hours until the wedding was to begin, a court jeweller – on standby – rushed it to his workshop so that it could be speedily welded. Although the emergency repair was mostly successful, it was noticeable in wedding-day photos, which show a larger gap between the centrepiece and diamond spike to its right.

With her tiara in place, all was not yet smooth sailing for the bride: she also recalled that she had left an antique two-strand pearl necklace – given to her by her parents as a wedding gift – at St James Place, where over 2,500 wedding gifts sent to her and her groom from around the world were displayed. Elizabeth's private secretary was despatched to retrieve the necklace – commandeering the King of Norway's car in the process. As traffic on the day was gridlocked due to the crowds, the secretary was forced to leap out of the car and make a dash for it on foot. The hour-long wedding ceremony – described as 'solemn and reverent' – itself went smoothly.

Officiated by the Archbishop of Canterbury, Geoffrey Fisher, and the Archbishop of York, Cyril Garbett, it was recorded and broadcast by BBC Radio with 200 million people around the world tuning in. The almost 15-foot wedding gown train was held by the two five-year-old pages, Prince William of Gloucester and Prince Michael of Kent, who wore Royal Stewart tartan kilts and silk shirts. Her tulle veil was embroidered with lace and secured by Queen Mary's diamond tiara, and Philip's naval uniform glinted with his new Order of the Garter insignia pinned to his jacket. The Archbishop of York, Cyril Garbett, presided, telling the young couple that they should have 'patience, a ready sympathy, and forbearance'.

The organist and Master of the Choristers at the Abbey, Australian William Neil McKie, was the director of music for the wedding. He had composed a motet (a vocal musical composition) for the occasion: 'We wait for thy loving kindness, O God.' The hymns were 'Praise, my soul, the King of Heaven' and 'The Lord's my Shepherd' to the Scottish tune 'Crimond' attributed to Jessie Seymour Irvine, which was largely unknown in the Church of England at the time. The service would start with a specially composed fanfare by Arnold Bax and finish with Felix Mendelssohn's 'Wedding March'. The bride signed the certificate 'Elizabeth' and listed her profession as 'Princess of the United Kingdom of Great Britain and Ireland.' Philip simply signed his Christian name and listed his profession, 'HRH The Duke of Edinburgh KG', the title the King had conferred on him shortly before his marriage*.

After the service, the bride and groom led a procession down the nave. Behind them were the King and Queen, followed by five kings, five queens and eight princes and princesses that included the crowned heads of Norway, Denmark, Romania, Greece, Iraq and from the Netherlands, Princess Juliana and Prince Bernhard. The Mountbattens, given their family rank, followed behind. The Duke of Windsor and his wife Wallis, like Philip's sisters, didn't make the guest list. The national anthem was played as the newly-weds were driven to the palace in the Glass Coach, flanked and preceded by the Household Cavalry on horseback. It was the most elaborate public display since the coronation of Elizabeth's father before war, and the crowds responded with ecstatic cheers.

Winston Churchill called it 'a flash of colour on the hard road we have to travel.' Lady Pamela Hicks, Mountbatten's younger daughter, said of the wedding 'It was unforgettable, the first bit of colour anyone had seen since the war. It was like a fairy story.' But this was a fairy tale with a twist. Many who had witnessed

---

* He was also made Earl of Merioneth and Baron Greenwich at the same time.

the couple making their vows inside the Abbey would prefer the wedding was not happening at all. They thought that Philip was not a gentleman, that he was bluff, rude, arrogant. He was not one of them. Some were ferociously hostile to the match.

Only 150 guests attended the wedding breakfast which was, in reality, a lunch in the Palace Ball Supper Room, a nod to the post-war austerity and the royals not wanting to appear profligate. The menu featured filet de sole Mountbatten, perdreau en casserole, and bombe glacée Princesse Elizabeth. The tables were decorated with pink and white carnations, as well as small keepsake bouquets of myrtle and white Balmoral heather at each place setting. The bride and groom cut the wedding cake – four tiers standing 9-foot high – with Philip's Mountbatten sword. The King, who had a stutter that made it difficult for him to make speeches, simply lifted his glass of champagne and toasted 'the bride'.

Philip's mother, Princess Alice, wrote to him afterwards: 'I was so comforted to see the truly happy expression on your face and to feel your decision was right from every point of view.' Countess Patricia Mountbatten noted it was a 'fantastic occasion' but said it was 'A little sad for him as it was too soon after the war for his sisters who were married in Germany as it would feel perhaps rather tactless to invite them.' Her sister Lady Pamela Hicks added, 'So soon after the war, you couldn't have "the Hun" … I think Philip understood, but the sisters certainly didn't. For years afterwards, they would say: "Why weren't we allowed to come to your wedding?" They weren't exactly Stormtroopers.'

The King was more reticent in a deeply personal letter he wrote to his daughter: 'I was so proud of you and thrilled at having you so close to me on our long walk in Westminster Abbey, but when I handed your hand to the Archbishop I felt that I had lost something very precious.'

7: ROSES AND CARNATIONS

'I think the main lesson that we have learnt is that tolerance is the one essential ingredient of any happy marriage. You can take it from me that the Queen has the quality of tolerance in abundance.'

Philip speaking on his golden wedding anniversary in 1997

Once the brouhaha of the royal wedding was over, Philip was anxious about what was next for him personally. He found life at court was very frustrating at first. Lord Brabourne, whose wife was Philip's cousin, Patricia, recalled, 'It was very stuffy. Sir Alan Lascelles, the private secretary to the King, was impossible. They were bloody awful to him. They patronised him. They treated him as an outsider. It wasn't much fun. He laughed it off, of course, but it must have hurt. I'm not sure Elizabeth noticed it. She probably didn't see it. In a way, marriage hardly changed her life... She was able to carry on much as before. In getting married, she didn't sacrifice anything. His life changed completely. He gave up everything.'

There was no doubt the young couple were very much in love and could not have been happier. After being showered with rose petals on the forecourt of Buckingham Palace, the newly-weds were transported in an open carriage drawn by four horses, the bride kept snug by hot-water bottles, to Waterloo Station. The train took the newly-weds to Romsey, Hampshire where they honeymooned at Broadlands, Lord Mountbatten's Grade 1 listed Palladian-style mansion in Hampshire. When they left for Birkhall on the Balmoral estate in Scotland for the second part of their romantic break, Philip wrote to his mother-in-law, the Queen. In his letter he revealed that he wanted 'to weld the two of us [himself and Elizabeth] into a new combined existence that will not only be able to withstand the shocks directed at us but will also have a positive existence for the good'. Philip, however, could not understand why Elizabeth's long-serving maid Bobo MacDonald had to join them on honeymoon, along with the Queen's beloved corgi, Susan. He had not expected Bobo to be constantly at his bride's side, even when the princess used the bathroom. It irritated him and he resented not being able to be alone with his wife whenever he wanted. Elizabeth genuinely could not understand why Philip was making a fuss about it. She was so used to being constantly surrounded by palace servants and members of the Royal Household that she had learned to zone out and just ignore their presence.

The battle over Bobo was something that was never satisfactorily resolved between Elizabeth and Philip. Like many female retainers who had devoted their lives to royal service, Bobo too faintly resented the presence of her mistress's husband. Philip, instead of trying to befriend her, did his best to make the servant feel uncomfortable, believed Bobo's role was to open the curtains each morning and let the dogs in – nothing more.

Eventually, Philip and Bobo came to an understanding to keep out of each other's way. As for Elizabeth, she viewed Bobo, who went on to serve Elizabeth for a total of 67 years, as a friend and a vital link with her childhood, as the servant had been her nanny. Not only was Philip unable to escape the maid on his honeymoon, but he was forced to live with his in-laws at Buckingham Palace for the first year of his marriage, while Clarence House was being refurbished at a cost of £50,000. The costs escalated and, due to a public outcry, her father the King stepped in to settle the outstanding amount.

Princess Elizabeth was conscious that it would be difficult for a man, so used to doing what he wanted, to be tied to a suite of rooms in a huge, old-fashioned palace, where everything seemed subject to protocol and tradition. It seemed George VI had spoken prophetically, but also with foresight, when he told a guest at the royal wedding, 'I wonder if Philip knows what he is taking on. One day Lilibet will be Queen and he will be consort. That's much harder than being a king, but I think he's the man for the job.'

Philip, after all, was his own man: complex, bristling with ideas and fiercely independent. She found his irreverence funny and would often burst out laughing at his risqué asides. Thankfully, like his wife, he was a man of duty, a loyal servant to the crown and someone who knew the value of service too. Describing what made him tick, he said, 'Everyone has to have a sense of duty; a duty to society, to their family.' According to their mutual cousin, the late Countess Patricia Mountbatten, 'Philip had a capacity for love which was waiting to be unlocked, and Elizabeth unlocked it. She was beautiful, amusing and gay. She was fun to take dancing or to the theatre'.

Buckingham Palace courtiers and some members of Elizabeth's extended family viewed Philip with suspicion. Influential politicians did not warm to him either. Harold Macmillan, later Conservative prime minister, summed up the attitude when he wrote in his diary: 'I fear this young man is going to be as big a bore as Prince Albert… it was really much better when royalty was just pleasant and polite.' Irked by his lack of deference and his foreign roots, it didn't seem to matter to them that he had been educated in England and Scotland and had served with distinction in the Royal Navy. He knew that a number of influential courtiers regarded him as a foreign interloper with no constitutional importance. His role was simple: provide the heiress presumptive with an heir and secure the line of succession.

Within weeks of exchanging their marriage vows, Princess Elizabeth was pregnant, but Buckingham Palace took the decision to keep the joyous news from the public. The princess effectively hid her baby bump under loose-fitting blouses, boxy coats, and eventually retreated from public life when it became so pronounced she could no longer hide it. The practice reflected the time and the general attitude toward pregnancy. There was no official confirmation that the royal couple was expecting their first child. Buckingham Palace simply released a statement announcing that the princess would not be seen in public. 'Her Royal Highness the Princess Elizabeth will undertake no public engagements after the end of June,' the statement read. It, of course, created more questions than it gave answers. In effect it was as close to official confirmation as the press, that had been busy speculating about a baby, was going to get.

Elizabeth, at just 22, gave birth to a baby boy weighing a healthy 7 pounds, 6 ounces, at 9.14 p.m. on 14 November 1948 via caesarean section in the Buhl Room at Buckingham Palace. Ordinarily it was used as a guest room, but it had been especially converted into what was described as a 'miniature hospital' for the royal birth.

Prince Philip was not at his wife's bedside at the birth. It was not common practice in the 1940s for fathers to be present during the delivery of a baby. Instead, he got so restless pacing up and down an equerry's room waiting for news that his private secretary, Mike Parker, took him off for a game of squash on the palace court. Sir Alan Lascelles gave Philip the good news. He was ecstatic and ran to the Buhl Room, and held his firstborn son in his arms, still wearing the sporting flannels and open-neck shirt he had been wearing on the squash court.

Philip declared to his wife and those in the room that his newborn son looked just like a 'plum pudding'. Hazy and feeling nauseous, Princess Elizabeth's doctors decided to administer her extra oxygen when the anaesthetic wore off. It was then that her overjoyed husband presented her with a beautiful bouquet of flowers, red roses and carnations, that Parker has sent out for and popped open a bottle of champagne. At Philip's insistence, for which he got the King's backing, the new parents were not joined by any senior government officials, such as the Home Secretary, as had been the custom for royal births over the centuries.

A proclamation was posted on the palace railings just before midnight announcing: 'Her Royal Highness Princess Elizabeth had been safely delivered of a son who had been named Charles Philip Arthur George.' Outside loyal fans had gathered and started chanting, 'We want Philip', such was the popularity among the general public for this handsome Royal Naval officer.

A 41-gun salute was fired to mark the new arrival by the King's Troop, Royal Artillery, and in Trafalgar Square the fountains were floodlit blue; outside Buckingham Palace almost four thousand gathered to watch the comings and goings of the medical team.

According to Philip's cousin, Marina, the Duchess of Kent, he was similarly entranced by the new arrival. 'I am so happy for Philip, for he adores children and also small babies,' she wrote in a letter to her mother. 'He carries it [the baby] about himself quite professionally, to the nurse's amusement.' Nevertheless, Philip showed no inclination for being a nappy-changing, hands-on kind of father. At the time, he not only had his career in the Royal Navy to consider, but he was also scheduled to carry out royal duties as well as trying to maintain a remnant of his former bachelor lifestyle with late night outings with Mike Parker.

Philip certainly saw nothing wrong in handing his baby son over to the care of nursery staff. He had, effectively, been raised by a nanny himself. So, each morning at 9 a.m., baby Charles would be taken to see his mother. In the evening, if her engagement schedule allowed it, Princess Elizabeth would join her baby in the nursery. Essentially, the infant and his parents lived separate lives. 'To my knowledge, she never bathed the children,' recalled Mrs Parker, Mike Parker's wife. 'Nanny did all that.' It was therefore to his nanny, Helen Lightbody, that Charles, a shy and sensitive child, naturally turned for the affection he craved. Helen, whom he affectionately called 'Nana', was the one who got him up in the morning, dressed him, slept in the same room as he did and comforted him if he awoke frightened during the night.

Of course, he adored his mother, but it was from afar. She was, Charles's biographer Jonathan Dimbleby revealed in his book, a 'remote and glamorous figure who came to kiss you goodnight, smelling of lavender and dressed for dinner'. Aside from this nightly ritual, Elizabeth always found it difficult to hug or kiss her son, preferring to leave such tactile displays of emotion to the nannies. She was physically undemonstrative by nature.

This was probably one of the happiest periods of Philip and Elizabeth's married life. There is no doubt this was a love match and there was a mutually strong physical attraction between the couple. They had time for each other too and he made sure he romanced his young wife, buying her flowers and love tokens as well as taking her dancing. In October 1949, Philip was posted to Malta as the second-in-command of the destroyer HMS *Chequers* and Elizabeth first flew to him there on 20 November, their second wedding anniversary. Elizabeth then divided her time between Malta, where Lord Mountbatten and his wife, Edwina, played host to the couple, and Britain, where she carried out her public duties as heiress presumptive. Baby Charles did not join his parents when they were in Malta and instead he was cared for at their London residence, Clarence House.

Philip's Royal Navy career was proceeding forcefully. He was promoted to lieutenant-commander and then appointed to his first and as it transpired, only, command, the frigate HMS *Magpie*, a modified Black Swan-class sloop, on 2 September 1950. At last, he felt he was fulfilling his potential and was clearly destined for a highly successful career in the Royal Navy. For Elizabeth, the time she spent in Malta with her husband was filled with fun. It was a carefree existence when she could forget about her royal destiny and becoming Queen, and try to lead as normal a life as possible.

Between 1949 and 1951, the couple lived in the townhouse, Villa Guardamangia, formerly known as Casa Medina, built around 1900 in Pietà. It was leased by the owners, the Schembri family, to Philip's uncle, Mountbatten.

Lady Pamela Hicks, Philip's cousin, said, 'It was a period that he [Philip] described as among the happiest days of his sailor life, as well as being the closest he and his young bride came to living an ordinary married life. It was the only place where she felt she could live without the pressure of being next in line to the throne. The princess really loved Malta because she was able to wander through the town and do some shopping. She was able to live the life of a naval officer's wife, just like all the other wives. It was wonderful for her and it's why they have such a nostalgia for Malta.'

It was an idyllic, carefree existence, a life of swimming, coastal picnics and the princess was able to drive around the quaint, cobbled streets on the outskirts of Valetta in her Morris Minor, unrecognised and not pestered by locals or photographers. But the princess rapidly came to realise something she has had to deal with throughout her marriage – that it could never be quite so carefree for Philip. One day in Malta, when they had been out, they got back late to the Villa Guardamangia, where they were living with the Mountbattens, and missed dinner.

In polite society, particularly when one was a guest in someone else's home, this simply was not done. Philip was summoned by Lord Mountbatten. Elizabeth Pule, now a retired nurse who was there with her mother, Jessie Grech, the housekeeper, still remembers it clearly, recalling Mountbatten shouting: 'Philip, Philip, I want to talk to you, come to my office NOW.' She recalled: 'We could hear him – everyone could hear him. He was saying: "Don't you dare do it again. Remember, she is the queen of tomorrow and please never forget that."' For Mountbatten this was just an old-fashioned bawling out for his naval officer nephew, but it was a chastening which hit Philip, and hit him hard. Was this how his life was going to be?

When she was six months pregnant with her second child, Elizabeth returned home for good. Princess Anne was born in August 1950. Philip was well on the way to an accomplished career as commander of the frigate HMS *Magpie*. An ambitious officer he always had his eye on the main chance and hoped, even then, to go right to the top of the Admiralty. It is no overstatement to say that he felt that it was his destiny. Malta clearly had a special place in both their hearts, for it was where they chose to celebrate their diamond wedding anniversary 60 years later. As in *The Aeneid*, Philip and Elizabeth discovered that fate is stronger even than divine intervention and the duke soon learned that his lot was to be one of endurance. Their Maltese idyll would come to an abrupt end.

In the summer of 1949, George VI had his first brush with death. His condition was so worrying, the idea of a regency whilst he recovered was flirted with as he lay in bed in Buckingham Palace following an operation to block a nerve at the base of his spine. Word had it that he was dying, or at best, would not recover sufficiently to again take up the reins of state. Prime Minister Winston Churchill observed that 'Bertie now walked with death'. The lumbar sympathectomy was designed to counteract the arteriosclerosis – a stiffening of arteries – that the King suffered from as a result of too much stress and smoking far too many cigarettes every day. Miraculously, the King made an excellent recovery, although it took its toll on him. The traumatic times through which he led Britain left him physically and mentally exhausted and those close to him, including his wife the Queen, believed it contributed to his faltering health.

On Sunday 23 September 1951 sombre crowds gathered outside the palace awaiting news of their king following an operation to remove part of his lung. A bulletin on his health posted on the palace gates in the afternoon read: 'Anxiety must remain for some days … but his immediate post-operative condition is satisfactory'. It was signed by the five doctors who attended the monarch and who spent the night at the palace prior to the operation.

The decision to operate had been taken after doctors noticed 'structural changes' in the monarch's lung. Nurses moved into the palace and oxygen cylinders and other medical equipment arrived during the day. The operation began at around 10 a.m. and took most of the morning. The Queen was at Buckingham Palace and was the first to hear from the doctors of the King's condition after the surgery.

News of the monarch's condition was then telephoned to Princess Elizabeth and the Duke of Edinburgh at Clarence House and to his mother, Queen Mary, at Marlborough House. The King was moved to his own bedroom immediately after the operation and was attended by nursing staff around the clock. Elizabeth and Philip went to Buckingham Palace that evening to see him after his mother, Queen Mary, had left. Princess Margaret flew in from Scotland to join her parents and drove directly to the palace from London Airport.

The situation was so worrying that Prime Minister Clement Attlee also flew back to London from Scotland, and was kept informed of the King's progress at Number 10 Downing Street. Special prayers were being said in churches throughout the country for the King's recovery. Recover he did. But by February 1952 his doctors confirmed what they had feared; he was suffering from lung cancer. As preparations were made for Princess Elizabeth to take on more of his royal duties, Prince Philip had no choice but to support her and to leave the Royal Navy on 'indefinite leave'. flying home from Malta in July. A successful tour to Canada and America followed and, at the end of January the next year, Philip and Elizabeth prepared to travel to Kenya on a stopover on route to Australia and New Zealand.

Frail and wan, and ironically with his pack of strong Chesterfield cigarettes in his pocket, the King went to London Airport to see off his beloved daughter and son-in-law. He was greeted with a cheer from his loyal supporters and responded with a customary wave of acknowledgement. It was bitterly cold evening and he waved them goodbye. As she climbed aboard a royal flight bound for Africa, he looked heartbroken. He then turned and told Margaret 'Bobo' MacDonald, Elizabeth's loyal assistant, 'Look after the princess for me.' Miss MacDonald later admitted that she had never seen him so upset.

8: BECOMING QUEEN

'For fifteen years George VI was King. Never at any moment in all the perplexities at home and abroad, in public or in private, did he fail in his duties. Well does he deserve the farewell salute of all his governments and peoples.'

Sir Winston Churchill

The King had appeared in good spirits the previous evening after returning from a shooting party with his friend, Maurice Roche, the 4th Baron Fermoy. He had spent the early evening playing with his young grandchildren, Charles and Anne, and then had dinner with his daughter, Princess Margaret, before retiring to bed. A short time after drifting off to sleep he suffered a fatal blood clot in his heart and died. His post-mortem later revealed that the 56-year-old monarch had severe vascular disease in his legs, 99 per cent due to smoking; a carcinoma of the lung, 99 per cent due to smoking; and recorded the cause of death as coronary thrombosis, 90 per cent due to smoking.

His valet, James McDonald, prepared his bath the following morning at 7.30 a.m., knowing the running water was usually enough to wake him. But the King did not stir and McDonald and His Majesty's page, Maurice Watts, sensed something was seriously wrong and called for the doctor. Shortly afterwards, Dr James Ansell, Surgeon Apothecary to the Royal Household at Sandringham, examined the body and confirmed that the King had died in his sleep.

At 8.45 a.m., Sir Alan Lascelles, the late king's principal private secretary, telephoned his assistant, Lieutenant-Colonel Sir Edward

Ford, in London and gave him the codeword that validated the death of the monarch. 'Hyde Park Corner,' he said. 'Now go and tell Mr Churchill and Queen Mary,' Lascelles told him. At just after 9 a.m. Sir Edward arrived at 10 Downing Street the bearer of 'bad news' for the Prime Minister. 'Bad news? The worst,' Winston Churchill responded before calling a cabinet meeting to discuss the constitutional issues arising from the monarch's death.

The news of his death was conveyed to Queen Mary at Marlborough House. The King's younger brother, The Duke of Gloucester, immediately travelled to Sandringham from his Northampton home and the Princess Royal cancelled her projected journey to Switzerland. Finally, at 10.45 a.m. Greenwich Mean Time, news agencies were given the green light to release the official confirmation of George VI's passing. The BBC's John Snagge – a British newsreader who infamously during the 1949 University Boat Race amusingly reported, 'I can't see who's in the lead but it's either Oxford or Cambridge' – broadcast the sombre news at 11.15 a.m. to radio listeners around the world. 'This is London. It is with the greatest sorrow that we make the following announcement. "It was announced from Sandringham at 10.45 a.m. today, 6 February 1952, that the King, who retired to rest last night in his usual health, passed peacefully away in his sleep earlier this morning."'

Widowed Queen Elizabeth was devastated. In a letter to her mother-in-law, Queen Mary, dated 6 February 1952 from Sandringham, she wrote,

'My Darling Mama,
What can I say to you? I know that you loved Bertie dearly, and he was my whole life, and one can be deeply thankful for the utterly happy years we had together. He was so wonderfully thoughtful and loving, & I don't believe he ever thought of himself at all...'

She would spend the next three months dressed in black in official mourning. After the Prime Minister in the House of Commons and Lord Salisbury in the House of Lords had expressed their grief at the news both Houses adjourned, as did also the courts of justice.

Still Elizabeth, who was now the new queen, was unaware of her father's passing because the urgent telegram that had been sent had not reached her. It transpired later that it had been sent to Government House in Nairobi and had not been decoded because the keys to the safe holding the codebook had gone missing. Conscious that the Queen had not been told Buckingham Palace officials decided to delay the announcement of the monarch's death for three hours while desperate attempts to contact her continued. Oblivious, Philip and Elizabeth had just returned from Treetops hotel and observation tower to Sagana Lodge in Kenya.

In London Churchill, who was back as prime minister after defeating Attlee's Labour Party in a snap election in October 1951, was inconsolable. His private secretary, Jock Colville, found Churchill sitting at his desk with tears in his eyes: 'I had not realised how much the King meant to him,' the official noted later. When he tried to console the 78-year-old statesman, by assuring the Prime Minister that he and the new queen would work well together, Churchill replied that he barely knew Elizabeth and that she was 'only a child'. Colville, who had served as private secretary to the princess from 1947 to 1949 in between his periods of service as a principal private secretary, was confident the two would develop a good rapport.

At around lunchtime in Kenya the editor of the *East African Standard* managed to contact Princess Elizabeth's private secretary, Martin Charteris, by telephone to ask if reports of the King's death were true. As soon as he had confirmed the sad news, Charteris contacted Sagana Lodge, where he asked to speak to Commander Mike Parker, Prince Philip's closest friend and confidante, who was accompanying the royal couple on the visit. Once Charteris had imparted the news, it fell to Parker to tell Philip of the King's death. Parker later admitted when he told the duke the news it was 'as if you'd dropped half the world on him.'

At that moment, Philip's first duty was to his wife and his new sovereign. He steeled himself as he prepared to tell her and invited her for a walk in the garden. At 2.45 p.m., local time, Princess Elizabeth finally learned that she was now the queen. Her stoicism and deep sense of duty to the crown, her late father and the people of her country somehow gave her strength in her hour of need. She discussed practicalities, such as how they were to get back home, and organised letters of apology for cancelling the royal tour. Throughout, she demonstrated great poise and appeared composed. Outside the residence press photographers, including John Jockinson who had been covering the royal tour, assembled after being sent by their picture editors.

The Queen formally requested that no photographs be taken at this point. It was a more deferential age and the gentlemen of the press obliged, every one of them lowering their cameras out of respect. With her permission, she was photographed later walking through the Sagana Lodge alongside Sir Philip Mitchell, Governor of Kenya, a few hours after learning of the King's death.

Arrangements were hurriedly made for the new queen and the royal party to return to London. Under considerable strain, the royal couple quietly boarded the plane with none of the usual pomp and ceremony that usually accompanies a royal departure. With Imperial Airways pilot Captain Ronald Ballantine at the controls of the BOAC Canadair Argonaut airliner, Atalanta G-ALHK, on which she had flown to Kenya a week earlier, the plane took off and flew first from Nanyuki, a nearby town, and then onto Entebbe airport in Uganda. The Queen was delayed for several hours when a storm hit Entebbe. Finally, they left Uganda just before 9 p.m. on 6 February and climbed to 16,500 feet. It then flew across the Sahara on the 2,260-mile flight to RAF El Adem in Libya. After the aircraft was refuelled, Captain R. C. Parker and his crew took over and Her Majesty eventually arrived at London Airport the following afternoon, 20 hours after taking off from Entebbe.

During the flight, the Queen realised that her mourning outfit had already gone ahead and she only had a totally inappropriate floral dress to wear when she exited the aircraft; during the refuelling in Libya a message was despatched so that a second black outfit could be taken to London airport. It was only then, inside the cabin, that her mask slipped and she left her seat for a while to cry alone. Elizabeth knew she had to compose herself for her first public appearance as the new monarch as the eyes of the world would be upon her. Once the plane had touched down and taxied, her mourning outfit was taken aboard so that the Queen could change. When the aircraft door finally opened her uncle, the Duke of Gloucester, walked up the steps, followed by the late king's private secretary, Sir Alan Lascelles, and went inside to offer his condolences to his new queen. Knowing the world's cameras were waiting, Elizabeth took a few extra moments to compose herself. She then descended the steps alone, her husband, in what would become a familiar routine, was told by the forthright Lascelles to wait at the top of the steps for a second or two. She was then officially greeted by her uncle, the Duke of Gloucester, who had left the plane to join the welcoming party, Prime Minister Winston Churchill, Leader of the Opposition Clement Attlee and Anthony Eden, the Foreign Secretary.

The new queen did not go straight to Sandringham to comfort her grieving mother, Queen Elizabeth, and sister, Princess Margaret, as she had to carry out a number of formal functions connected with the Accession in London. On the morning of 8 February, Elizabeth presided over her first Privy Council meeting. It was there, with her assembled ministers standing as they always do, that she read out her Declaration of Sovereignty. She said, 'I pray that God will help me to discharge worthily this heavy task that has been laid upon me so early in my life.' Tired and emotional she managed to get through it without faltering, despite having to mention her father several times.

Like so many of her generation, Elizabeth was in awe of Churchill due to his imperturbable personality and resolute leadership during World War II. Churchill's daughter, Mary, revealed to her own daughter, Emma Soames, that that respect was mutual, 'The Queen very quickly captivated him, he fell under her spell. I think he felt early on her immense sense of duty, and he looked forward to his Tuesday afternoon meetings with the young monarch.'

It was to Churchill that the British people turned again in this hour of need and grief at the loss of the King. Acknowledging the importance of the institution of monarchy, the inspirational statesman excelled in his broadcast to mark the death of the King and the ascension of the new Queen Elizabeth. He was effusive about the reigns of earlier queens too. 'Now that we have the Second Queen Elizabeth, we understand why her gifts, and those of her husband, the Duke of Edinburgh, have stirred the only part of our Commonwealth she has yet been able to visit. She has already been acclaimed as Queen of Canada and tomorrow the proclamation of her sovereignty will command the loyalty of her native land and of all other parts of the British Commonwealth and Empire. I, whose youth was passed in the august, unchallenged and tranquil glories of the Victorian Era, may well feel a thrill in invoking, once more, the prayer and the Anthem, God Save The Queen!'

On 18 February 1952, Queen Elizabeth, now the Queen Mother, wrote to Churchill from Buckingham Palace.

'My dear Mr Churchill ...
It is very difficult to believe that the King has left us ... He was so well, the day before he died, so gay, & full of plans & ideas for the future ... One thing I am very thankful for, and that is that you returned as his Prime Minister before he died...'

George VI had been totally unprepared for the burden of kingship. Leading his country and Empire through the horrors of World War II had taken an immeasurable toll on his mental and physical health. His profound sense of duty had pushed him to find the strength to lead and his people loved him for his courage and tenacity. He had tried to prepare his direct heir, Princess Elizabeth, for her future role but his life had been cut short at the age of 56 and he had just run out of time. Elizabeth would now have to learn the complexities of the role of monarch whilst on the job. Her lifetime of duty, sacrifice and public service had just begun in earnest*.

From the outset of her reign, Philip sat on the sidelines as his wife fulfilled her duty. He knew his was to be a supporting role and nothing more. He knew his life, however, would never be the same either. His wife's ascension meant his ambitions in the Royal Navy were dashed, along with many of his hopes and dreams. He was just 30 years old, when many men in leadership roles are beginning to find their feet.

Many years later, in 1992, the then Admiral of the Fleet, Terence Lewin, who would later become Baron Lewin, a contemporary of the duke's (b.1920, d.1999) said that had Philip's naval career not been cut short he would have risen to the very top. 'Prince Philip was a highly talented seaman,' Lewin said. 'There was no doubt about it. If he hadn't become what he did, he would have been First

---

* When Queen Elizabeth II came to the throne in February 1952, she became Queen of Great Britain and Northern Ireland; the Channel Islands and the Isle of Man; Queen of Canada; Australia; New Zealand; the Union of South Africa; Pakistan and Ceylon. India had become a republic during her father's reign, but acknowledged her as Head of the Commonwealth. Southern Rhodesia, a self-governing colony, and many dependent territories – some colonies, some protectorates, some protected states, some in United Kingdom trusteeship – all looked to the Queen as their Head. The principal among them were Aden; the Bahama Islands; Barbados; Bermuda; British Guiana; British Honduras; Brunei; Cyprus; the Falkland Islands and its dependencies South Georgia, South Orkney, South Sandwich, South Shetland and Graham Land; Fiji; Gambia; Gibraltar; the Gold Coast, including the Trust territory of Togoland; Hong Kong; Jamaica, with its dependencies the Cayman Islands and the Turks and Caicos Islands; Kenya; the Leeward Islands, including Antigua, Montserrat, St Christopher and Nevis and Anguilla, and the Virgin Islands with their dependencies; the Federation of Malaya, consisting of the nine Malay states of Johore, Pahang, Negri Sembilan, Selangor, Perak, Kedah, Perlis, Kelantin, Trengganu and the two British settlements of Penang and Malacca; Malta; Mauritius; Nigeria, including the Cameroons, under UK trusteeship; North Borneo; Northern Rhodesia; Nyasaland; St Helena and its dependencies, including Ascension Island and Tristan da Cunha; Sarawak; the Seychelles Islands; Sierra Leone; Singapore and its dependencies of Christmas Island and the Cocos Keeling Islands; Somaliland protectorate; Tanganyika; Trinidad and Tobago; Uganda; the Western Pacific islands, consisting of the Gilbert and Ellis Islands colony, the British Solomons protectorate, the protected state of Tonga, the New Hebrides condominium and Pitcaim Island; the Windward Islands, comprising the colonies of Granada, Dominica, St Lucia and St Vincent, with their dependencies; and the protectorate of Zanzibar.

Sea Lord and not me.' George VI's death and Elizabeth's destiny put paid to any chances of that. Perhaps conscious of his sacrifice the Queen presented Philip with the title and office of Lord High Admiral of the Royal Navy, a post that dates back to the fourteenth century, to mark his 90th birthday*. Throughout his life Philip, who was appointed a Trustee of the National Maritime Museum in 1948, enjoyed a keen interest in naval history. In that role he was instrumental in saving the famous tea clipper *Cutty Sark*, now a museum ship stationed in Greenwich – and in establishing the Maritime Trust.

---

* His other British service appointments were Field Marshal of the Army and Marshal of the Royal Air Force.

9: FIRST DUTY

'Where did you get that hat?'

What Prince Philip said to the Queen during the
rehearsal of her Coronation, 1953

At just age 26, the new queen was not minded to start making
wholesale changes to the institution when she ascended the
throne. Indeed, Elizabeth, who was cautious by nature, made a
conscious decision to follow the template for kingship established
by her father, George VI, and grandfather, George V, before her.
It had, after all, served the institution well in the aftermath of the
1936 abdication crisis and it enabled George VI to lead his people
through World War II too. 'So often she would say "my father did
it this way, my father told me that"', said long-serving courtier,
Lieutenant-Colonel Sir Malcolm Ross, former Comptroller of
the Lord Chamberlain's Office, who served the Queen from 1987
when he joined the Royal Household (d. 27 October 2019).

Queen Elizabeth always valued order and structure too and
generally favoured the status quo. Her husband, Philip, was the
complete opposite. He often bemoaned the rigidity of his wife's
routine and convention. 'If it was customary to have porridge at
every meal,' Philip once remarked, 'Lilibet would have it.' A born
innovator, Philip believed that when methods change, mankind must
change too with them to achieve success. He was a man of action
and never one for standing still. His restlessness was undoubtedly
caused by his transition from being a respected commanding officer
in the Royal Navy, where he was a leader, to playing a supporting

role to his wife in a hierarchy where it was her orders that counted, not his. The King's death had sadly come far earlier than many, including Philip and Elizabeth, had anticipated. Worse still, it came just at the moment when Philip had achieved a rank where he could command his own ship. Philip had hoped he might have at least another decade, or maybe even longer, of active service before his duty as monarch's consort would take precedent over his Royal Navy career. Instead, his call-up to work as a full-time royal came just four years into their marriage.

When asked years later, in an ITV interview with broadcaster Alan Titchmarsh, what was the impact on him of relinquishing his Royal Navy career, Philip was reticent at first, but honest. He replied, 'I was naturally disappointed because I'd just been promoted to Commander and in fact the most interesting part of the naval career was just starting.' He went on, 'Being married to the Queen and it seems to me that my first duty was to serve her in the best way I could.' In another interview Philip went even further when he said, 'I thought I was going to have a career in the navy, but it became obvious there was no hope. There was no choice. It just happened. You have to make compromises. That's life. I accepted it. I tried to make the best of it.'

Philip was not someone prone to brooding about an issue. Once a decision was made, it was done, he saw no point in looking back. He was, after all, one of life's doers. Just weeks after the Queen's ascension, however, Philip again clashed with the old guard of the Royal Household, knowing that in doing so he consciously risked turning up the pressure on his marriage. The moment the Queen became the monarch, the whole apparatus of the institution embraced her. The veritable army of courtiers who had served the King now served her. As far as senior courtiers in her private office were concerned, the duke had no formal constitutional standing and his only duty, like theirs, was to serve the Queen as a supporter. He felt, as he put it, like the 'refugee husband' of the Queen.

His foreign antecedents also meant many at court and among the aristocracy and British establishment regarded him and his intentions with suspicion. Some of them, including the Queen Mother, would have preferred Elizabeth to have married a British duke or other aristocrat. Some, whose families had served the monarchy for many generations, were actively hostile towards Philip, who they regarded as a brash interloper. Philip's cousin, Lady Pamela Hicks, summed up the antagonism the duke faced. She said 'He had been a very active head of the family; he would now be cast in the supporting role which for a very active, a real action man, that was very hard to begin with because he had to find out the kind of career he could make for himself.' Philip knew he had to shape up and make the best of his lot. There was no point, he believed, in wallowing in self-pity, it was just not his style anyway.

The duke's private secretary between 1993 and 2010, Brigadier Sir Miles Hunt-Davis (d. 23 May 2018), explained, 'He has made a very, very busy extremely influential life for himself. And that perhaps more than anything else is a lesson in duty. Just getting on, head down, getting on with your job. Sometimes very much in the public eye, sometimes just working away quietly. He had to make a role of his own. There was nobody to follow. He made what he made of himself by force of circumstance. He has been able to play a part in all sorts of areas that the Queen couldn't have got involved in and [which] wouldn't have got where they are as organisations without a push and sometimes a jolly hard shove.'

It was difficult to see how an alpha male like Philip could fit into the rigid palace system. There was no template for the role and certainly no established infrastructure to support him, unlike in the US where the 'First Lady', the President's wife, has her own office and staff already in place when her husband is sworn in. There was no doubt that this confusion and perceived lack of respect led to growing resentment.

There was one part of the marriage, however, of which he was determined to maintain control. For any man at that time it was important to have certain emblems in your life that represented who you were. One of them, according to the tradition and practice at the time, was that one's wife on marriage always adopted the surname of the husband and the resulting children of the legal union would also use it as their last name. His determination for this to happen, however, set him on a collision course with the establishment and the palace old guard, not least with his mother-in-law, Queen Elizabeth the Queen Mother.

The Queen Mother had long been the quiet power behind the throne during her husband, George VI's, reign. Now she was a widow, Queen Elizabeth appeared reluctant to relinquish that role and wanted to maintain her influence at court. She dug her heels in and on her daughter Elizabeth's ascension, she made it clear she was in no hurry to leave her home, Buckingham Palace, the seat of royal power. A letter she wrote in late February 1952, to the Queen, which is now in the royal archives, revealed how she felt at the time. She wrote, 'I could be quite self-contained upstairs, meals etc... You'd hardly know I was there.' Behind this request was her desire to be on the spot and therefore able to walk into her daughter's room and give her opinion. It would put the new queen in an invidious position, especially as her husband, Philip, was not shy in sharing his own views with her on how the institution of monarchy could be changed and should be run. It would put the two people closest to her on a collision course. The Queen agreed to let her mother live at the palace as she wanted, which was a blow for Philip and his desire to modernise the institution.

The Queen Mother, after all, was not only sceptical about Prince Philip but also of the ambitions of his uncle, Lord Mountbatten. Philip's rough manners and overbearing demeanour and direct way of addressing the Queen irritated her. It would be her, more than anyone, who would dig her heels in when it came to protecting the Windsor dynastic name in the fight that was about to ensue. After all, following the abdication crisis of 1936, her husband had been forced to take his brother's discarded crown and saved the Windsor dynasty, established by his father, George V, in the process. A widow at just 51, Elizabeth firmly believed the heavy responsibility of kingship had driven her husband to an early grave. Now, no matter how hard Philip and Mountbatten pushed, she was determined that his sacrifice would not be marked by the end of the Windsor name and dynasty. The royal matriarch, her mother-in-law, Queen Mary, George V's widow, backed her daughter-in-law. She remarked, 'What does that damn fool Edinburgh think the family name has got to do with him?'

Together the two dowager queens wielded considerable influence over the impressionable Queen Elizabeth. They both expected her to side with them on such an important issue. To ensure their success, the pair enlisted support from the most powerful man in the land, Winston Churchill, who had privately admitted that he neither 'liked nor trusted' Philip. On 18 February 1952, the Prime Minister and his ministers discussed the issue in the cabinet room at Downing Street. The minutes of the meeting stated, 'The Cabinet was strongly of the opinion that the Family name of Windsor should be retained and they invited the Prime Minister to take a suitable opportunity of making their views known to Her Majesty.'

Winston Churchill, who was determined to head Philip and Lord Mountbatten off at the pass, said his government believed monarchy was an institution that had relied on the past and tradition and they would not support such a name change. Philip, blunt and forthright, made it clear to his wife that he felt strongly that his surname should be acknowledged. By denying him what every other man in her kingdom took as his right, Philip believed, would be effectively to emasculate him. Elizabeth, not for the first time, was torn, caught between the devil and the deep blue sea. She knew unless she found in favour of her husband she heaped huge pressure on the marriage, but if she defied her mother, grandmother and the advice of her government she faced a far greater crisis.

On 9 April 1952, Elizabeth's decision over the dynastic name was made public. A statement issued from Clarence House read: 'The Queen today declared in council Her Will and Pleasure that She and Her children shall be styled and known as the House of and Family of Windsor, and Her descendants who marry, and their descendants, shall bear the name Windsor.'

Philip had lost and it undoubtedly hurt him. 'I am just a bloody amoeba … the only man in the country not allowed to give his name to his children,' he is said to have shouted before storming out on learning of the news; he had already given up everything else for Elizabeth, his freedom and his career, now to put it candidly he was simply the producer of the Queen's children. For a time relations between him and Elizabeth cooled.

Ever the adventurer, Philip needed something to take his mind off the disappointment over the failure over the dynastic name change. Out of the blue, he told his wife that he wanted to learn to fly. Despite concerns from the government, and Churchill in particular, the Queen gave his plan her blessing. His flying training began on 12 November 1952 at White Waltham under the instruction of Flight Lieutenant Caryl Ramsay Gordon (later RAF Group Captain, d. May 2018), the son of a former Indian Army cavalry officer. Gordon, who had been instructing at the Central Flying School, was moved to White Waltham to join the Queen's Flight, which had been allocated two Chipmunk and two Harvard training aircraft for the duke's training. After a few hours, Philip flew solo in the Chipmunk on 20 December 1952.

Gordon remained the duke's personal instructor for the next two years, which included flying twin-engined training aircraft before he took delivery of a de Havilland Heron as his personal aircraft. At the end of 1955, when Gordon's royal appointment had run its course, he was appointed MVO, which was later upgraded to LVO, a personal honour from the monarch. The Chief of the Air Staff, Marshal of the RAF, Sir William Dickson, presented Philip with his wings on 8 May 1953. Philip went on to gain his helicopter wings in 1956 and pilot's licence in 1959, achieving 5,986 hours in 59 types of aircraft, that included becoming the first member of the Royal Family to fly himself out of Buckingham Palace in a helicopter. His final flight was on 11 August 1997 from Carlisle to Islay after which he stopped flying aged 76.

Within a month of the royal surname announcement, Elizabeth and Philip moved into Buckingham Palace. Philip was shocked by the way the place was run, that had hardly changed since the days of Queen Victoria. In his opinion it was over-elaborate and loaded down by tradition that greatly irritated him. At the time palace footman still powdered their hair, as they had done during the days of Queen Victoria's uncles in Hanoverian times, with flour and water. Defeated over the use of his name, Philip was determined to put an end to what he regarded as these archaic practices and ring in the operational changes in their new 775-room home. He took the lead of the much-needed modernisation of Buckingham Palace and its systems, visiting every room in the palace and questioning staff to discover precisely what their role was. He listed, what he regarded as, unnecessary and time-wasting procedures. When electric frying pans came on the market he purchased one and proceeded to fry his own breakfast every morning. Eventually, the Queen put a stop to it as she couldn't stand the smell in their private apartments lingering until lunch. Philip forged ahead regardless, determined to carve out a useful and challenging role for himself. The Queen's courtiers were equally determined to push back and fought a rear guard action to keep Philip and his new ideas at arm's length. Surrounded by the 'blockers' as he called them, the duke became increasingly frustrated by the situation. He confided to those closest to him that he would have to curb his ill humour for the sake of his own sanity.

The Queen, ever the pragmatist, wanted to avoid any unnecessary confrontation between her husband and her senior courtiers. She found what she hoped would be a solution, albeit a short-term one, by appointing Philip to the role of Chairman of the Coronation Committee, which she hoped would focus his attention on a specific project with a specific remit and time frame. Elizabeth's coronation was, after all, a global event. In early 1953, the influential *Time* magazine, anticipated the excitement by naming Queen Elizabeth as 'The personality who best expressed the world's new sense of hope for the future.' The editorial went further, claiming the fascination with the coronation ceremony as proof of a general resurgence of public belief in the ancient power of monarchs 'to represent, express and effect the aspirations of the collective sub-conscious'. The *New York Times* wrote an editorial claiming the act of crowning was a symbol of the civilisation that would protect the world from the barbarians of 'another dark age'. This is one of the most explicit statements on the meaning of the coronation in the post-war period, but it was widely echoed in newspapers around the world.

Philip embraced his new challenge with typical enthusiasm. He immediately introduced a radical idea that ruffled the feathers of the establishment when he suggested the coronation should be televised. At first, Elizabeth, the Queen Mother, and the British government were vehemently against Philip's idea. Not only had it never been done before (in a country still dominated by the class system, only the upper classes and establishment were deemed fit to witness the ancient and sacred event), but many felt that bringing television cameras into Westminster Abbey was 'not right and proper'. One of the staunchest defenders for banning television coverage was Winston Churchill. The BBC reported that the Prime Minister was 'horrified' at the thought of using cameras inside the Abbey.

'It would be unfitting that the whole ceremony, not only in its secular but also in its religious and spiritual aspects, should be presented as if it were a theatrical performance,' Churchill told the House of Commons. When it was announced that television coverage would just be an edited film of the ceremony shown after the event had finished, there was a public backlash. Philip, not for the first time, had his finger on the nation's pulse, while Churchill and the palace old guard did not. BBC viewers protested in their hundreds of thousands and MPs questioned the wisdom of the decision, forcing Churchill to reopen discussions and eventually back down.

Philip and his new-found friends and allies at the BBC were set against overturning the decision. The final ruling lay with the Queen who had the prescience to change her mind and side with Philip. Emboldened by Philip, the Queen told Churchill, 'All my

114

subjects should have an opportunity of seeing it.' Realising that televising the coronation would be a way to break down class barriers too, Elizabeth officially sanctioned Philip's project and on 8 December 1952 it was announced that most of the coronation would be televised live. Philip knew it was a huge undertaking but was determined to keep control of it. It was agreed that there would be four cameras in the Abbey, one above the high altar, one by the south transept, one in the organ loft and one at the west end. In all there were 26 microphone points, most of them near the Queen's throne.

John Snagge, who wasn't a clergyman as was first suggested, was chosen to commentate on proceedings for the BBC Home Service. He was housed in a tiny, unventilated box in the gallery above the nave. Above him, in slightly more comfort, sat Richard Dimbleby, who had been the BBC's first war correspondent. Below Dimbleby and Snagge, the television cameramen was positioned, again in very cramped surroundings. In addition, there were overseas commentators who needed to be accommodated too. In all, on the day, there were more than 2,000 journalists and 500 photographers from 92 nations who had been assigned to cover the coronation, including reporting on the route too. Among the many foreign journalists assigned to cover the story, was Jacqueline Bouvier (who would later marry future US President John Fitzgerald Kennedy), who was working for the *Washington Times-Herald* at the time.

On 2 June 1953, London was once again the media centre of the world. The news that New Zealander, Edmund Hillary and Nepalese Sherpa, Tenzing Norgay, of the British expedition, led by Colonel John Hunt, had become the first to conquer Mount Everest, was released on the morning of the coronation. Many interpreted it as a portent for a reinvigorated British Commonwealth after the painful and slow death of the British Empire. Hotels and boarding houses were full and it was said that wealthy Americans were in exclusive occupation of the rooms overlooking the coronation parade.

Seats in the newly erected stands were expensive at £20 (£562 today) more than double the average weekly wage of around £9

(£253 today). Black market tickets went on sale for up to £50 (£1,405 today) while the huge sum of £3,500 (£98,350 today) bought a balcony position. Others tried to get a vantage point wherever they could to watch the parade go by. The Diggers (Australian soldiers) included four recipients of the Victoria Cross and another VC holder from New Zealand: Private F. J. Partridge VC, Private E. Kenna VC, Sergeant J. D. Hinton VC (New Zealand), Private R. Kelliher VC and Sergeant R. R. Rattey VC. They were given the right to wear their khaki uniforms and the slouch hat in the procession after they were repeatedly mistaken for Royal Marines in their blue dress uniform.

The Canadians sent members of their famous Royal Canadian Mounted Police and the Nepalese members of the Gurkha Regiment, while the South Rhodesians caused a minor sensation by including a woman in their armed contingent. When the royal carriages rolled down The Mall, people cheered wonderful characters such Queen Salote of Tonga who captured the hearts of the people. The royal families rode last in golden coaches. Elsewhere, street parties took place all over the nation. Churchill's government spent more than £1 million on the coronation. It also recompensed local councils for some of the expense of decorations, souvenir publications, public carnivals and parties. It should have come as no surprise. Winston Churchill's wife, Clementine, would remind him: 'You are Monarchical No. 1 and value tradition, form and ceremony.'

Just days before the coronation, Churchill had addressed the Commonwealth Parliamentary Association in the presence of the Queen. He told them, 'Here today we salute fifty or sixty Parliaments and one Crown. It is natural for parliaments to talk and for the Crown to shine,' he said. He then continued: 'Well do we realise the burdens imposed by sacred duty upon the Sovereign and her family. All round we see the proofs of the unifying sentiment which makes the Crown the central link in all our modern changing life, and the one which above all others claims our allegiance to the death.'

The Queen – carrying her coronation bouquet made up of orchids and lilies of the valley from England, stephanotis from Scotland, orchids from Wales and carnations from Northern Ireland and the Isle of Man – and the Duke of Edinburgh, in full-dress naval uniform, were driven from the palace to Westminster Abbey in the 24-foot-long, 4-ton Gold State Coach. It had been commissioned in 1760 and used at the coronation of every British monarch since George IV. It was pulled by eight grey gelding horses: Cunningham, Tovey, Noah, Tedder, Eisenhower, Snow White, Tipperary and McCreery. Elizabeth looked radiant in her coronation dress designed by British Fashion designer Sir Norman Hartnell, made of white satin and embroidered with the emblems of the United Kingdom and the Commonwealth in gold and silver thread, as she acknowledged the crowds. She would wear it a further six times including the Opening of Parliament in New Zealand and Australia in 1954.

The elaborate ceremony fell into six parts: the recognition, the oath, the anointing, the investiture, which included the crowning, the enthronement and the homage. The ancient coronation service used for Queen Elizabeth II evolved from that of King Edgar at Bath in 973; the original fourteenth-century order of service was written in Latin and was used until the coronation of Elizabeth I of England.

Shortly after 12.30 p.m., Elizabeth walked slowly towards her throne, dressed in a robe that was as unique as the coronation ceremony itself. It had been hand-crafted by Ede & Ravenscroft of Savile Row, London following the strict design guidelines of previous coronations. The robe featured a 6-yard train in best quality handmade purple silk velvet, trimmed with best quality Canadian ermine and fully lined with pure silk English satin, complete with ermine cape in the traditional manner including embroidery by the Royal School of Needlework.

Once Elizabeth was seated in King Edward's Chair, the ancient abbey fell silent. The Archbishop, Geoffrey Fisher, held the solid gold St Edward's Crown, made in 1661 and weighing 4 pounds and 12 ounces, aloft for a moment and then lowered it on to the

Queen's head, placing it first on her forehead and then pressing it down at the back. He then raised his arms high with a little flourish. A great cry went up: 'God Save the Queen!' Then in a cacophony of noise, the gothic abbey resounded with fanfares and loud shouts of acclamation.

Prince Philip's role as best supporting actor, Elizabeth's 'liege man' in this elaborate real life stage play was officially confirmed when he knelt before her and swore an ancient oath of fealty. Wearing a coronet, which he was entitled to as a peer of the realm, he looked immaculate in robes made especially for the coronation ceremony by Ede & Ravenscroft. Their ledger entry for '21 August, 1952' reads: 'A Royal Duke's Coronation Robe in the best handmade silk velvet trimmed with finest Canadian ermine. Coronet in metal gilt with airtight case with name inscribed. A page's uniform complete.' He was pin sharp.

As husband of the sovereign, he may not have been crowned or anointed at the ceremony but millions watched on television as he was the first to pay homage to the new queen of the second Elizabethan age. He was faultless as he said, 'I, Philip, Duke of Edinburgh, do become your liege man of life and limb and of earthly worship.' He then stood and kissed her cheek before backing away.

At the rehearsal, perhaps wanting to relieve his wife's tension, he mumbled the words quickly, missed the Queen's cheek when planting the kiss and then moved backwards far too fast, for which the Queen admonished him. 'Don't be silly, Philip. Come back here and do it properly.' But he did make her smile when the crown was placed on her head, by whispering, 'Where did you get that hat?'

The Queen admitted years later that she had been deeply moved by the entire experience of the religious service. In 1937, as an 11-year-old, she had watched her father's crowning. Now her son, Charles, was among the 8,251 guests in the Abbey and like his mother he witnessed the coronation (Princess Anne did not attend the ceremony as she was considered too young). Prince Charles had received a special hand-painted children's invitation to his mother's coronation and watched history unfold alongside his beloved grandmother, Queen Elizabeth.

After the long procession back through London and the balcony appearances, Elizabeth had the affirmation and support of the British people and those in the wider Commonwealth. Quietly, Philip stood by her side. For him, it had been a personal triumph too. His victory against an old guard hell-bent on banning the cameras and over those who still viewed him with suspicion tasted sweet. Philip's foresight and Elizabeth's U-turn, and decision to back him, helped to change the relationship between monarch and people for the better. It laid down a marker to the courtiers not to overstep the mark with her husband too.

The Queen later discussed the funny moments of the ceremony with the Archbishop of Canterbury. She singled out one incident involving Lord Mowbray, who came down the steps from his homage bunching up his robe and tripping over it causing mothballs and pieces of ermine to fly off in all directions.

As the Queen left the chapel in the procession that would lead to the Great West Door, two verses of the National Anthem were sung. As she emerged from St Edward's Chapel, the cameras moved in closer and closer. The BBC cameraman had surreptitiously got their close-up that Churchill had been so set against.

We do not know how nervous the Queen felt upon taking such solemn oaths or upon receiving the homage of those assembled at Westminster Abbey – and, symbolically, of the nation. On that coronation day in 1953, the Queen assumed not a role to be played, but a responsibility to be discharged. She continued to do so throughout her long reign. On the day itself she later told how uncomfortable the journey to the Abbey was in the Gold Stage Coach used by George IV for his coronation.

In 2018 the Queen revealed in a BBC documentary *The Coronation* to mark the 65th anniversary of the historic ceremony just how uncomfortable the journey was for her 25-year-old self. She said: 'It's only sprung on leather [which is] not very comfortable.' Measuring 7-foot long, and weighing nearly 4 tons, it was pulled by eight horses which she states is 'not meant for travelling in at all' and only went a couple of miles an hour. When she was shown the crown again in the documentary she picked up the gem-encrusted diadem and moved it closer to her and said, 'Is it still as heavy? Yes, it is. It weighs a ton!'

Archbishop Fisher later wrote to George Barnes, Director of Television at the BBC, about the success of the eight-and-a-half-hour-long live coronation broadcast: 'You know that I am no great supporter of TV, regarding it as an extravagance, and a supreme time-waster. But I freely say that thanks to TV the Coronation Service got into countless homes and brought to the viewers a realisation of the Queen's burden, the Queen's dedication, God's presence and God's consecration, of religion and of themselves.'

That evening the newly crowned Queen made a broadcast, reflecting on the events of the day, and thanking the public for their support and promising to serve the nation.

'Throughout this memorable day I have been uplifted and sustained by the knowledge that your thoughts and prayers were with me ... As this day draws to its close, I know that my abiding memory of it will be, not only the solemnity and beauty of the ceremony, but the inspiration of your loyalty and affection. I thank you all from a full heart. God bless you all,' she said.

Due mainly to Philip's determination to get his way, the coronation was watched by 27 million people in the UK alone helping lift the new queen's subjects out of the post-war malaise. It was shared with most of the UK through the medium of television, figures seen on tiny screens in flickering black and white by groups gathered round television sets in their front rooms.

Eventually an estimated 350 million worldwide would watch the spectacular in one form or another right across the globe. Canisters of film were rushed to aeroplanes and flown to the USA, Canada, Australia and far corners of the Commonwealth nations. It was a milestone not only in history, but in the history of television.

Churchill's reservations had been shared by leading and powerful establishment figures including the Archbishop of Canterbury, the

Duke of Norfolk, senior cabinet colleagues, the Coronation Joint Committee and, indeed, initially at least, by the Queen herself. Philip had remained firm. He had shown he was not somebody to be trifled with. It was a good time to put down a marker too. But things were changing. Sir Alan Lascelles stepped down as private secretary to the monarch after 27 years of royal service on the last day of 1953, at the age of 66. He twice declined a barony, as he felt titles to be a show of self-importance, and was replaced by the Eton and Cambridge educated Sir Michael Adeane. He had been Assistant Private Secretary to George VI from 1945 to 1952 when he carried on in that post for the new queen until 1953. Adeane was old school, but he didn't have the same presence or indeed influence, as far as Philip was concerned, at least as his predecessor. Philip had grown in confidence and he was ready, now, to take on all comers.

In so many ways, Elizabeth's coronation had been a crowning glory for Prince Philip too. It had been the first great national televised event of the new Elizabethan era and it had also been the first significant victory against the palace old guard.

10: THAT LITTLE INTERLUDE

'I assign no limits to the reinforcement which this royal journey
may have brought to the health, the wisdom, the sanity
and the hopefulness of mankind.'

Sir Winston Churchill to the Queen about the
1953–1954 Commonwealth tour

Philip came tearing out of the villa, swiftly followed by a tennis racquet and a pair of shoes that were sent hurtling through the air by his infuriated wife. Moments later the Queen ran out in hot pursuit of her husband, shouting at him and telling him to get back inside. Elizabeth then grabbed her husband's arm and dragged him into the chalet in which they were staying. It was early afternoon on 7 March 1954 and the Queen and Philip were eight weeks into the mammoth tour of the Commonwealth, staying at the Metropolitan Board of Work's cottage in the picturesque foothills of the O'Shannessy Mountains in the Yarra Ranges of Victoria about 50 miles east of the city of Melbourne, Australia.

Ever the consummate professional, cinematographer Frank Bagnall, of the Commonwealth Film Unit, had already set up the equipment and tested it ahead of the pre-arranged media opportunity filming the royal couple relaxing on tour with the koalas and kangaroos in the background. The position had been signed off by palace officials for use in a film, *The Queen in Australia*, narrated by the actors Peter Finch, who had been raised in Sydney from the age of ten after being born in London, and Wilfred Thomas. The film, directed by Stanley Hawes, would eventually be played to packed cinema audiences in Australia in 1954, but if the film crew had not handled this delicate situation so diplomatically at this juncture, the entire project may have been placed in jeopardy.

The short respite adjacent to the beautiful lake had been the royal couple's only chance to relax in the Australian bush during the tour. Inevitably, government officials had meddled by stocking the local dam to ensure good fishing, should the duke wish to partake, and koalas had been brought in from other parts of Victoria so there were plenty, without the couple knowing. Elizabeth and Philip had disembarked their train at Warburton railway station on the evening of Saturday 6 March and motored to the picturesque destination in the foothills, where they were due to stay until the following Monday lunchtime. The only engagement they had scheduled for the weekend was a Christian service at St Andrew's Presbyterian Church where, sadly, none of the regular worshippers were allowed to take part and VIPs replaced them.

Loch Townsend, listed as one of the sound recordists on the film, Bagnall and Don Kennedy, who had all arrived early, were growing concerned about the loss of the natural light given that they had been kept waiting outside. 'Christ, when are they bloody well coming?' Townsend said just at the precise moment that the contretemps between the royal couple started down at the chalet. Bagnall, like any news man would, instinctively started filming. Within seconds an irate Commander Richard Colville, the Queen's press secretary, whom the media had dubbed 'The Abominable "No" Man' given that any request was invariably met with a negative response, ran towards the trio on the lawn. Colville, his chest puffed out ready for verbal combat, began by threatening the crew with immediate arrest for filming the royal disagreement. Loch Townsend stepped in and told Colville to back off and 'Calm down'.

Loch took control of the situation. 'I went up to Frank and I started unscrewing the back magazine, and he said, "What are you doing?" and I said, "Exposing the film, Frank." I said, "You may have finished using your balls, but I've still got work for mine and I'd like to keep them." I'll never forget saying that. And anyway, I unscrewed it and I took it. There was about 300 feet of film and I walked up to the house … and I said, "Commander, I have a present for you. You might like to give it to Her Majesty."'

Commander Colville's attitude immediately changed. He stopped barking his threats and orders at the film crew and was visibly relieved. He remembered his manners and gratefully accepted the package before walking back to the chalet. The typically cool Australian response to a tricky situation by Loch Townsend had pricked Colville's inherent 'pommy' pomposity*.

A few minutes later, one of the Queen's servants emerged from the chalet and brought the crew beers and sandwiches. As soon as they had finished eating the Queen stepped outside and walked over to them in order to thank them personally for their kind gesture of deleting the footage and handing over the film of the royal disagreement. Townsend recalled, 'I said who I was and introduced Don and Frank, and she said, "Oh, thank you very much. I'm sorry for that little interlude, but as you know it happens in every marriage. Now, what would you like me to do?"'

The incident would have remained private had it not been for an Australian broadcaster, Jane Holley Connors, who stumbled across the story whilst researching her philosophy doctoral thesis. Connor's extended essay on Elizabeth's post-coronation tour of Australia was titled *The Glittering Thread* and was submitted to the University of Technology, Sydney in March 1996.

It is easy from a modern 24-hour news perspective to criticise Townsend over the ease with which he handed over the film. To be fair, he knew he couldn't risk jeopardising future co-operation being withdrawn. The full-length colour film would later play to sell-out audiences around the nation.

The 'interlude', as the Queen called it, not only shows how times have changed with regard to the media, but also that Elizabeth

---

* Sir Richard Colville first went to Buckingham Palace in 1947 as press secretary to the late King George VI. He served as the Queen's press secretary until 1968. He had no experience in the newspaper or broadcasting industry, having spent his entire career in the British Navy, leaving as a commander. He was knighted in 1965 and died aged 67 in 1975.

and Philip both felt under a tremendous strain whilst on such an exhausting and important diplomatic tour, like any couple would. They were, after all, just human and would fall out with each other from time to time.

Their work schedule on that long tour was relentless since they had set off on the tour in November 1953. Not only did they have to leave their young children, Charles and Anne, behind, but from that moment on be on public display as they visited 13 countries from the West Indies, Australasia, Asia and Africa, travelling a distance of 43,618 miles, including 10,000 miles by plane, 2,000 miles by car, 2,500 by rail and the rest by sea, most of it onboard the Royal Yacht SS *Gothic*. The final leg was on the newly commissioned Royal Yacht *Britannia*. It would have taken its toll on a seasoned professional, let alone a new queen and her consort. Many of the people of the countries visited had never before seen the monarch on what was the first of 251 overseas visits the Queen carried out with Philip at her side[*].

The tour started in Bermuda 17 hours after the Queen and Philip left London because the BOAC Stratocruiser Canopus had to make a long detour to avoid a storm. After being officially welcomed at Kindley Airport by Governor Alexander Hood and Lady Hood, the royal couple were driven through cheering crowds in an open-top car through the old capital, St George's. There they visited St Peter's Church, the oldest Anglican church still in use outside the British Isles, before proceeding by Royal landau to the island's new capital, Hamilton, where Mayor E. R. Williams extended a loyal greeting to the Queen. Elizabeth and Philip then attended a garden party on the oldest self-governing colony of the old British Empire, where they met some of Bermuda's ex-servicemen, before taking a flight to Jamaica.

At Montego Bay airfield the royal couple were greeted by Governor, Sir Hugh Foot, who was decked out in a formal white

---

[*] The Duke of Edinburgh had undertaken 223 solo visits to 67 Commonwealth countries, and 385 visits to 74 other countries; an average of 12 countries per year, over the last 50 years.

uniform, who then presented them to the country's First Chief Minister, Sir Alexander Bustamante, wearing top hat and a grey morning suit. The Jamaican Constabulary formed a guard of honour for the couple who were then driven to visit the island's old capital, Spanish Town, where they were given a rapturous reception before travelling on to Sabina Park, home of the Kingston Cricket Club and the only Test cricket ground in the capital, where they were cheered by 35,000 schoolchildren. They both stood in the open-top Land Rover so that the children could see them.

In Kingston, the island's capital, the Queen addressed a joint session of the legislative assembly, and thanked the Jamaican people and the rest of her loyal subjects in the West Indies for their warm welcome. Afterwards, the couple then boarded the liner SS *Gothic*, newly refurbished especially for the trip as a temporary royal yacht, and began their passage through one of the seven wonders of the modern world, the Panama Canal, the great transoceanic waterway that joins the Pacific and the Atlantic through the Isthmus of Panama. The couple enjoyed a banquet in Panama City before leaving Balboa for the Pacific crossing. En route, in what was the most leisurely part of the entire 50,000-mile tour, the cruiser HMS *Sheffield* escorted the yacht as she crossed the equator. On board King Neptune (played by the duke's protection officer) appeared and Philip revelled in taking part in *Crossing the Line*, an initiation rite that commemorates a person's first crossing of the equator, and as a seasoned sailor, enjoyed throwing novices into the swimming pool. Wielding the barber's brush, Philip prepared Lady Pamela Mountbatten for the traditional ordeal, ably assisted by his friend Mike Parker. A great cheer went up from the watching crew when a water fight between King Neptune, the barber (Philip), and Lady Pamela, ended up in the pool. Fully clothed and soaked to the skin, Philip was the first to escape complete with his barber's apron.

As they sailed into Fijian waters a few days later, the Queen filmed a fleet of canoes rowing towards the yacht from the harbour of Suva to greet them. Local tribal chieftains from Fiji, which had been ceded to Britain in 1874, went aboard to present the Queen, whom they regarded as the highest chief, with a necklace made from whale teeth. They then formally gave permission for her to go ashore for the two-day visit.

On board HMS *Sheffield* the crew gathered on deck to give a farewell cheer to the Queen as she and Philip disembarked the SS *Gothic* by launch. Passing by the bows of HMNZS *Black Prince,* an escort cruiser from the Royal New Zealand Navy, the royal launch headed for the quayside. She was greeted by the 19th Governor, Sir Ronald Garvey, in full court uniform complete with plumed helmet, and he escorted them to accept a bouquet of welcome from the three-year-old daughter of a chieftain, who with great solemnity performed the ancient Fijian curtsey, a sign of respect for the woman the Fijians called 'Little White Queen'.

At Albert Park, named after Queen Victoria's consort Prince Albert, the royal couple received a colourful and lengthy ritual welcome of dancing from people of the 322-island group. Elizabeth, not wanting to insult her hosts, sampled the national and potent drink kava, made from the powdered roots of a yaqona tree and served in a coconut shell, which has a euphoric effect on the drinker.

A parade of chieftains then formed a queue to lay tributes at the Queen's feet, including exotic fruits such as guava, papaya and mandarins, other offerings such as turtles and toys for their children as well as Fiji's prize gift, whales teeth, before the climax of the gathering, the Meke, traditional Fijian dances, including the spear dance. As guests of honour at a banquet that evening, the couple were escorted by 200 torch-bearing runners on the way to the Grand Pacific Hotel in Suva. From the hotel veranda the couple waved to the thousands of Fijians who had gathered below as the Queen made a pledge to watch over their welfare and pray for their prosperity in the years to come. The following day they attended a service at the Anglican Cathedral in Suva and visited the Adi Cakobau School for Girls before flying to Lautoka, the second largest city in Fiji.

The Queen and the duke then left for their next destination, independent Tonga, once named The Friendly Isles by British explorer, Captain James Cook, in the 1770s. On arrival the couple were welcomed by Queen Salote Tapou as they disembarked the tender on 19 December 1953. The two countries were bound by a treaty of friendship and protection unbroken for 50 years and thousands of Tongans turned out to cheer the couple. The towering figure of Queen Salote, who had ruled over 50,000 people since she was crowned in 1918, had won British hearts six months earlier by cheerfully waving from an open carriage in the Coronation Day rain. She did her best to impress and had promised to give the royal couple the 'warmest and happiest' reception of the whole tour. She had told locals to 'open our doors and open our hearts' to the Queen and hosted a unique luncheon feast on the Mala'e that included 2,000 pigs, chickens, lobsters and yams, all washed down with coconut milk. The royal couple then boarded the launch to rejoin SS *Gothic* to sail on to New Zealand, with the warm message 'Go ye in peace.'

***

The SS *Gothic* docked in Auckland, New Zealand, known then as 'The Queen's city', on 23 December ahead of the royal couple's month-long stay. They were greeted by the Governor General Sir Willoughby Norrie and Prime Minister Sidney Holland at the quayside as huge crowds turned out to welcome their monarch and her husband despite heavy rain. It was the first-ever visit by a monarch to the distant dominion, and the first time too that Elizabeth and Philip had spent Christmas away from Britain and their children. From there, Elizabeth delivered her annual broadcast live on a midsummer's night.

The Queen spoke of how deeply impressed she was with the opportunity that the new Commonwealth presented, built on friendship, loyalty, and the desire for freedom and peace. She said that her first tour as Queen was important, because she was beginning a journey, 'To see as much as possible of the people and countries of the Commonwealth.' She added, 'At the same time, I want to show that the Crown is not merely an abstract symbol of our unity, but a personal bond between you and me.'

Margaret Lomas recalled waiting outside the Grand Hotel in Whangarei where the royal couple was staying, 'I remember the Queen's visit to Whangarei, Northland. I was about six years of age then and the Royal Party was staying at the Grand Hotel. In the evening our family walked about twenty minutes or so to the hotel and with many others chanted, 'We want the Queen, we want the Queen'. This had no response (they were most probably having dinner) so the chant changed to 'We want the duke, we want the duke.' This seemed to work as they soon appeared on the balcony to the loud cheers of the crowd. I was sitting on my father's shoulders so had a great view. I remember they looked very happy, and there was a wonderful feeling in the crowd.'

On Monday 28 December the couple took a flight to Kaikohe for a public welcome and then they were driven to Waitangi, where the 1840 treaty saw Maori chiefs retain authority over their lands, although ultimately they had ceded sovereignty to Queen Victoria. Elizabeth and Philip were greeted by representatives of the Maori people and chiefs, who repeated the pledge of allegiance made to the representatives of their ancestor, Victoria, on the same spot.

The busy schedule of events must have seemed non-stop. During the tour of New Zealand the couple visited 46 towns and cities and attended 110 separate events on both the North and the South Islands of the country. At the time New Zealand was referred to as 'Britain's larder' as Great Britain bought 70 per cent of the country's exports, nearly all was butter, cheese and meat. The couple did get some down time too; they enjoyed a brief rest at Moose Lodge, Lake Rotoiti on New Year's Day after engagements at Waitomo Caves and Karapiro Hydroelectric Power Station.

The following day, after another civic reception and lunch at Motutara Golf Course, the couple attended another significant Maori ceremony at Arawa Park, Rotorua, where they were both presented with Korowai, a Maori woven cloak and another decorated with bird feathers. In accepting the cloaks, they both agreed to become paramount chiefs, known as Ariki, an honour usually reserved exclusively for males.

It was a rare honour from the Maori people and showed that both Elizabeth and Philip were respected for the qualities of Tapu (sacredness), Mana (authority), Ihi (excellence) and Wehi (awesome power), which Maoris believed were gifts inherited from ancestors and gods. During the colourful display and singing and dancing, a little girl in a yellow dress, Esther Fawcett, emerged from the crowd and walked towards the Queen. It soon became clear she had become separated from her mother and was lost. With a minimum of fuss, the Queen urged Esther to sit at her feet as the ceremony of Maori dancing and singing continued. Eventually, mother and daughter were reunited.

The visit was not all formality. Philip decided to drive the open-top royal car when the couple went to visit the famous Autumn Lodge stud farm where the Queen, a keen racehorse owner, checked out the blood stock at the owner's invitation. Afterwards the pair returned to Moose Lodge for a short break on 4 January before the pace of the tour picked up again. They resumed the tour of North Island, travelling through towns and villages, including Stratford, where the streets bore the names of characters of Shakespeare's plays.

In total the couple travelled 1,300 miles in the royal train, with carriages that were painted red and cream. Both the Queen and Philip enjoyed travelling by train which gave them a chance to relax but also, in the more remote districts, to appear on a specially adapted platform at the back of the train to wave to impromptu crowds that had gathered. At one point, six bedridden patients were taken from the hospital to be in position at the side of a track to wave at their monarch as she passed.

In Wellington, the capital and one of the world's great deep water ports, named after Britain's famous hero of Waterloo and former prime minister, 'Greensleeves' was played at the garden party at

Government House. The Queen, wearing a soft bamboo-coloured silk dress and white hat, mingled among the VIP guests. Later she conducted a royal investiture and delivered a speech in which she spoke with pride of the New Zealanders' 'spirit of enterprise and endeavour that shines forth as ever it did in earlier times.'

The royal travellers were soon underway again. School teacher Judith Foy recalled, 'I was a young school teacher and a cub leader in Hawera. The streets chosen [for the visit] had some very unsightly buildings and the powers that be who arrange these things decided something had to be done to cover these sights from royal eyes. Every school child set about making paper flowers in red, white and blue crepe paper. These were gathered and hung on these.'

Whistle-stops in small country towns became the norm on the tour. On 15 January, Helen Tunner recalled, 'I remember when the Queen and duke visited Masterton on 15 January 1954, and drove through the grounds of Wairarapa College. I was a pupil at Wairarapa College at the time, and although it was the school holidays and summer, we were asked to don our winter uniforms, which were obviously considered tidier than our summer uniforms.'

It was reported that three out of every four citizens of New Zealand saw the royal couple and into old age many recorded the moment for posterity. After flying across the Cook Straits the couple explored the breathtaking scenery of the South Island, travelling by train. They saw the great sheep grazing country of Marlborough, and visited the communities of Nelson, Long Beach, Christchurch, Dunedin and Invercargill.

In Waipukurau the couple received a warm reception on 7 January 1954. Moira Draper, who was there at the time, recalled, 'Thousands of people from all over Central Hawke's Bay were gathered at the Railway Station in Waipukurau. A ripple of excitement swept through the crowd and heralded the arrival of the Royal Train with crimson carriages and a gleaming white roof. When the Queen and duke stepped from the train they were met by my uncle Jack McCarthy, Mayor of Waipukurau, and Aunty Tess, and then they all walked along a pathway between ropes of beautiful flowers to a dais. Uncle Jack proudly welcomed Her Majesty and His Royal Highness to his town.'

In Nelson, a city on the eastern shores of Tasman Bay, the couple worshipped together at Christ Church Cathedral in Trafalgar Street on Sunday 17 January. A huge crowd gathered outside swarmed around the royal couple as they walked down the granite steps after the service.

From Nelson the couple took a flight to Westport, a town in the West Coast region of the South Island established in 1861, for a public welcome the next day in Hokitika and then on to Greymouth by car. 'In preparation for the Royal Visit only the left-side of the 25-mile roadway was re-sealed between Hokitika and Greymouth; for some years later known locally as "Lizzie's side",' said local Bev Huston.

One eyewitness, Pat Jamieson, recalled, 'I was eleven years old and the Queen and duke were driving down High Street in Greymouth. The crowds were very thick and I wiggled to the front just as their car was passing, the Queen smiled at me and I was hooked. An instant avid royalist, I then ran alongside the car for about half a mile at which time the Duke of Edinburgh looked across and said, "If you run much further, you will burst." Well, I was just totally blown away.'

On 25 January, another eyewitness, Daphne-Anne Freeke (née Hoare) recalled the moment she caught a glimpse of the Queen and Prince Philip as a child. 'As a six-year-old, I remember journeying from Pleasant Point to Timaru with the rest of the family, in my father's old square Erskine car, and joining the crowd near the viaduct at the top of Caroline Bay, the route the Queen would be taking on her way to the official function. The town was beautifully decorated for the event and there were very large crowds of excited people all waving flags.'

In Invercargill, at the tip of the South Island, after rehearsing the speech with Philip, the Queen broadcast a message thanking New Zealand and its 'great and united people'. As the royal couple prepared to leave the country bound for Australia aboard SS *Gothic*, the Queen appeared visibly moved as she reflected on the genuine warmth of the reception that she and Philip had received.

★★★

Whatever their view of monarchy as an institution, hundreds of thousands of Sydney-siders could not resist the chance to witness history unfolding in their city. Such was the enthusiasm for the royal visit that the New South Wales Police Force estimated that more than one million people witnessed the Queen and Philip on the day they arrived on 3 February 1954, either in the Farm Cove area for the official welcome ceremony, or along the city streets later on. The *Sydney Morning Herald* added to this figure another half million in the eastern suburbs and on the northern side of the harbour, who were crowded into 'every foreshore vantage point from the Heads to the Bridge'.

This extraordinary congregation grew from a gathering of about 200 who arrived very early at Farm Cove, with the intention of sleeping out. They had become 4,000 by nightfall, with a further 2,000 camping down in Hyde Park and Martin Place, 'lying three deep across the pavement in a "cheerful and expectant mood"' according to the *Herald*, although the tabloids, which had later editions, were able to report that they were sprayed by water carts washing the roads later on and spent the rest of the night in damp rugs and blankets.

The *Sun* put the total of royal fans across the city at 60,000 with 8,000 gathered around Mrs Macquarie's Chair, several thousand more slept on boats in the harbour, and the rest dispersed throughout the inner city. The photographs of these alfresco parties show people lying cheek by jowl on a magical midsummer's eve, which was lit like fairyland by the glow of Tilley lamps and the flicker of a thousand cigarettes.

Reporters and photographers worked the streets interviewing people for human interest stories for their newspapers. One correspondent interviewed a father and son, George Gordon of

Lakemba and his six-year-old Allen, sleeping under a streetlight in William Street, in the Kings Cross area. Allen was sleeping peacefully, but his father was still wide awake when the journalist turned up. 'It's Allen's idea, so I had to be in it,' Mr Gordon said. 'We're holding a place for my other two children and my brother with his four kids. They'll be along at six a.m. with our breakfast.'

Along the foreshores onlookers watched as the restless duke prowled the deck of the royal yacht in his shorts. The actual act of landing became historic for newspapers and broadcasters alike. 'George III was on the throne when Australia's history began; the Queen's tremendous welcome this morning was the grand climax to it,' announced the ABC Radio national bulletin, 3 February.

The SS *Gothic* weighed anchor in Athol Bight, near Bradleys Head. Australia's governor general, Field Marshal Sir William Slim, and his wife Lady Slim had gone aboard at 9.30 a.m. followed by the Governor of New South Wales Lieutenant-General, Sir John Northcott, the prime minister Sir Robert Menzies and the New South Wales Premier, Joseph Cahill. Returning to shore with members of the Royal Household, they took up position on the landing pontoon with federal and state cabinet ministers, opposition leaders, and city aldermen, including the communist, Tom Wright.

Just after 10 a.m. the Queen and Prince Philip left for the shore aboard a launch and landed in Farm Cove, a tidal inlet and shallow bay in Sydney Harbour, where the 'First Fleet', led by Admiral Arthur Phillip of the Royal Navy landed in 1788. The Queen and Prince Philip's arrival was seen as a watershed moment for Australia by the media who said they could now test how far they had progressed as a modern nation. Rex Ingamells voiced this in *Royalty and Australia* when he wrote that the record of royal visits should also be seen as the record of our 'growth and advancement among the nations of the world.' He wrote that it had been 80 years before the colony had been worthy of the 'dignified compliment' of a royal visit*. By extension, a further 86 years had passed before the time was right for the ultimate reward of the presence of Queen Regnant. Reflecting the casual racism of the time, *The Herald* wrote: 'Look at us now,' said the editorial, the 'dark wilderness of the eighteenth century transformed into a light modern city, the second largest white metropolis in the Empire.'

Eventually, the Queen and Philip were welcomed ashore by the Lord Mayor of Sydney Alderman Patrick Darcy Hills who said, 'We humbly pray that Divine Providence may be pleased to safeguard Your Majesty and Your Royal Highness in your journeyings in these distant parts.' Speaking clearly and firmly from the dais at Farm Cove in the first of her many speeches in Australia, Elizabeth appeared to answer every need, 'Only 166 years ago, the first settlement was made not far from where we stand by Captain Phillip and his small band of Englishmen, and now there stands a fine city that has become famous throughout the world. In the same short space of time we have seen the rise of Australia as a great nation, taking her full share in the counsels of the British Commonwealth and of the world. I am proud indeed to be at the head of a nation that has achieved so much.' *Woman* magazine summed up the excitement of the people calling it the visit Australians would never forget. 'Ten years, even 20 years from now, we will be able to look back on this sentimental journey with pleasure and pride.' Elizabeth was dubbed, 'the girl with the golden smile.'

Elizabeth and Philip would spend the months of February and March 1954 travelling so widely across Australia that three-quarters of its population were said to have seen the monarch at least once during the tour. One highlight was the surf carnival at Bondi Beach. While they visited the federal capital Canberra, the Queen

---

* Prince Alfred, second eldest son of Queen Victoria, landed in Adelaide on 31 October 1867 becoming the first member of the British Royal Family to visit the realm. During the visit there was an attempted assassination attempt. Prince Henry, Duke of Gloucester, third son of George V, visited for an extensive 67-day tour in 1934 and later between 20 January 1945 and 10 March 1947, he became the first and only royal governor general of Australia.

opened a session of parliament dressed in her coronation robes and in Melbourne 17,000 children welcomed her to the cricket ground where legendary Australian cricketer, Sir Donald Bradman, described Philip's bowling action as 'perfect'*.

They criss-crossed Australia by plane and train, visiting the gold fields of Kalgoorlie and fruit and wine growing centres. On their visit to the town of Red Cliffs, one of several stops made on the tour, the Queen's white shoes were stained with the red dust in a local vineyard, and she was presented with enough dried fruit to last a lifetime. Before the royal couple departed on the SS *Gothic*, from Fremantle, Western Australia the Queen broadcast a farewell message, thanking the people for their 'welcome, hospitality and loyalty'.

During the Queen and Philip's eight-week tour of Australia, the royal couple had visited 57 towns and cities. The only glitch happened when the couple were in Western Australia when there was an outbreak of poliomyelitis. Prime Minister Sir Robert Menzies decided to intervene and requested that the Queen, Philip and the rest of the royal party sleep on SS *Gothic* and eat only food prepared on the ship during the last leg of the visit.

As a result, as the couple said their final goodbyes in Fremantle, there were no handshakes over fears that the royals might contract the virus. Once back on board the ship, Elizabeth and Philip moved around from port to starboard on the boat deck, waving vigorously. Little boats sailed all around them as on landing day, tooting and wailing their goodbye. And then, at the end, as Australia looked out to sea with misty eyes, the long white ship glided out through the heads into the sunset gilding the clouds on the horizon bound for Ceylon.

Sir Robert Menzies summed up the visit in an article in the *Sydney Morning Herald* he penned after the royals had left. 'It is a basic truth that for our Queen we have within us, sometimes unrealised until the moment of expression, the most profound

---

* Philip enjoyed cricket so much he would hide a radio in his top hat at Royal Ascot so he could listen to matches and became 12th Man of the Lord's Taverners, the official charity for recreational cricket and the UK's leading youth cricket and disability sports charity.

and passionate feelings of loyalty and devotion. It does not require much imagination to realise that when eight million people spontaneously pour out this feeling they are engaging in a great act of common allegiance and common joy, which brings them closer together and is one of the most powerful elements converting them from a mass of individuals to a great cohesive nation. In brief, the common devotion to the Throne is a part of the very cement of the whole social structure.' It had been an opportunity for the Queen to stamp her personality on her new Commonwealth. It had been a bold diplomatic mission that would change the perception that her subjects around the world had of her forever.

★★★

The long return journey included stopovers in the British protectorate of Ceylon (now Sri Lanka) where the Queen opened the country's parliament in stifling heat and humidity wearing her coronation robe and spoke of the 'disturbed political situation' for which she hoped with 'mutual confidence a solution would be found.' From there they sailed in the SS *Gothic* to Aden for a two-day stay in the gateway between East and West, where they disembarked their floating home housing 18,500 for the last time on 27 April. While in Aden, the Queen knighted Sir Seyid Abubakr Al Kaff, who helped bring peace to the Hadhramaut. The recipient was not happy about kneeling before the Queen, as she was a woman, until he was bluntly told that all sorts had knelt to Queen Victoria and there was no way out of it. Eventually, he knelt.

Later, the Queen and Philip went up to the RAF hospital and spoke to all the patients. Philip's questions were less conventional than his wife's. He fell behind and startled the matron by asking a patient, 'What's up with you?' On being told 'a cold' he burst out laughing and spoke so quickly to the sister who received him that she had not time to curtsy. Then they enjoyed a small lunch at Government House, where staff found them 'so easy' to serve. 'It is only the upstarts who are difficult,' recalled one.

In the afternoon, after some down time, the royal couple were received with tremendous enthusiasm in Crater, with people running beside the royal car, cheering, causing the Commissioner a few anxious moments. Nevertheless, the Queen slowed down so that the people could see her and she arrived at the garden party 20 minutes late. Prince Philip had arrived on time from Little Aden, flying his personal standard, and he was getting a little bit bored. 'Where on earth have you been?' he said as the Queen arrived.

The visit was a great success. At the garden party the Queen spoke about normal things and asked people if they had seen the latest photographs of her children. They took off on a BOAC Argonaut aircraft bound for Entebbe Airport, Uganda, in the early hours. The Sultan of Zanzibar was among many of the dignitaries to witness their arrival in Africa. One of the Queen's chief engagements was the opening of the £22 million Owen Falls Dam, the hydroelectric power station* across the White Nile near to its source at Lake Victoria. From Uganda they headed to Tobruk, the desert town known for sieges and battles in World War II. They also met King Idris of Libya who the Queen made an Honorary Knight Grand Cross of the Order of the British Empire.

The Queen and the duke were reunited with their two children Charles and Anne, who had travelled to Tobruk aboard the gleaming new royal yacht HMY *Britannia*. The family had spent six months apart. Both the Queen and Philip showed how detached they could be in public by not embracing their children with long hugs or kisses. Instead, they simply shook hands with their then five-year-old son and three-year-old daughter. The Queen later joked, 'They were terribly polite. I don't think they knew who we were at all!'

Prince Philip had little appreciation of his son's fears and inhibitions. Like many parents, the duke was inclined to poke fun at them. Of course, he made fun of his daughter Anne, too. But she was a more robust character and seemed to be able to deal with her

---

* Now known as Nalubaale Power Station

father's banter, cheerfully braving his taunts, and not taking them too seriously. In contrast Charles, who gave the impression of being totally frozen in awe of his father, gravitated to his mother, who provided him with a more sympathetic ear. Princess Anne, who was much more in tune with her father and his sense of humour, mirrored his characteristics too.

After a detour via Yarmouth to the Isle of Wight to pick up the prime minister, Sir Winston Churchill, the new yacht, with the Royal Standard and the Union Flag flying, headed towards London on 13 May, flanked by an armada of 17 Royal Navy support ships from the Home Fleet and watched over by RAF planes above. The Queen sent a message describing their meeting as a 'wonderful moment'. As the yacht came abreast of the destroyers and frigates their crews assembled on deck to give a rousing three cheers as the royal couple and their children waved back. As she neared Portsmouth the flagship of the Home Fleet, HMS *Vanguard*, was astern as the crew of the new aircraft carrier, HMS *Centaur*, waited to hail the Queen. Throughout the night the escort ships kept watch guarding the royal yacht as she progressed north to the mouth of the Thames.

On 14 May THV *Patricia*, with the Queen's uncle Prince Henry, Duke of Gloucester, aboard, waited at the mouth of the Thames to escort HMY *Britannia* the 50 miles as she made a stately progress along the river to the heart of the capital and into the pool of London, receiving salutes along the way. As RAF Spitfires flew overhead, at Woolwich Dockyard came a royal salute from a Royal Artillery Guard of Honour. Thousands cheered along the triumphant return of the young monarch and her family, while small boats sounded their sirens and factory hooters blared. A huge red and white banner hung from Tower Bridge bearing the words 'Welcome home'.

When HMY *Britannia* was safely moored, the Lord Mayor of London, Sir Seymour Howard, was rowed out to greet the Queen and Philip by Royal Navy oarsmen. A few moments later the Queen Mother and Princess Margaret, both carrying their own mink coats, arrived early to complete the family reunion when they joined the royal party on board at Tower Pier from the launch *Noor*. Philip was waiting on deck to greet them with a kiss and take them to where the Queen and the children were waiting.

The Queen shared the final leg of the journey along the river to Westminster Pier with her statesman Churchill who wore the uniform of an Elder Brother of Trinity House complete with yachting cap, an organisation chartered by the Crown in 1514 to oversee harbour pilots and aids to navigation – as he had been made an honorary Elder Brother when he was appointed First Lord of the Admiralty in 1913. She recalled, 'One saw this dirty commercial river as one came up. He (Winston) was describing it as the silver thread which runs through the history of Britain. He saw things in a very romantic and glittering way; perhaps one was looking at it in a rather too mundane way.'

Queen Elizabeth and Prince Philip's uniting mission was nearly at an end after 500 engagements across the globe. The Great Bell, Big Ben, of the Palace of Westminster Clock Tower (renamed Elizabeth Tower in 2012 to mark her Golden Jubilee) rang out as the Queen stepped on English soil again to be greeted by her aunt the Princess Royal, the Duchess of Gloucester and the Duchess of Kent. She was followed ashore by Prince Charles and Prince Philip and then the Queen Mother and Princess Margaret holding Princess Anne's hand. Once she stepped onto dry land the Queen moved forward and inspected the Guard of Honour mounted by the Third Battalion of the Grenadier Guards assembled on the Embankment. Climbing into three carriages, the Royal Family continued on to Buckingham Palace, through streets thronged with cheering, flag-waving people.

The Queen was home and her reign as British monarch and Head of the Commonwealth family of nations could begin in earnest. It had been the longest ever royal tour, lasting a marathon six months, a tour that would cement Her Majesty's position as symbolic leader of much of what was then known as the free world. Philip had dutifully played his part and had been centre stage too. He expected it to continue.

Within ten minutes of arriving home, the Queen and Philip, with their two children, appeared on the balcony. It wasn't enough for the public. After four appearances from the Queen and Philip, with the last just before 11 p.m., the crowd was only persuaded to leave once the palace floodlights were turned off. Welcoming his queen home the great orator Winston Churchill even outdid himself, saying: 'I assign no limits to the reinforcement which this royal journey may have brought to the health, the wisdom, the sanity and the hopefulness of mankind.'

The Queen was at the zenith of her popularity and it was up to Philip to keep her feet firmly on the ground. Churchill reflected on the moment years later. 'In the first years of the Queen's reign, the level of adulation, you wouldn't believe it. You really wouldn't. It could have been corroding. It would have been very easy to play to the gallery, but I took a conscious decision not to do that. Safer not to be too popular. You can't fall too far.' It was, as ever, a wise call.

11: RIFT! WHAT RIFT?

*'It is quite untrue that there is a rift between the Queen and the
Duke of Edinburgh. It's a lie.'*

Statement by Buckingham Palace, 1957

The Queen, at the age of 29 years, was beginning to find her feet
in her role as sovereign when her first prime minister Sir Winston
Churchill called time on his political career. In truth Churchill
should have retired years earlier on the grounds of his poor health;
he had been just shy of his 77th birthday when he became prime
minister for the second time in 1951. Now at 80 years of age,
the great statesman was according to his biographer, Roy Jenkins,
'Gloriously unfit for office'. Those around him knew Churchill
was not ageing well. He suffered recurring bouts of ill health and
periods of depression which led to him having to conduct state
business from his bed, with his aides and secretaries around him.
It meant the formal delivery of government policy was left to
his deputy, the quasi prime minister and Foreign Secretary, Sir
Anthony Eden, who was also the husband of his niece, Clarissa
Spencer-Churchill.

Matters reached a head in June 1953 when Sir Winston Churchill
secretly suffered a stroke. Only a few people outside his immediate
circle were made aware of the extent of his illness. Not even the
full cabinet was informed. At the time his expected successor,
Sir Anthony Eden, was recuperating in hospital in New York
after undergoing an operation. Had Eden been in better health
at the time, it is highly probable that he would have immediately

succeeded to the top job. Instead, Churchill carried on his prime ministerial duties, surprising doctors and recovering his strength over the following months. Whilst his powerful personality and oratory ability endured, Churchill had become less decisive and his ability to lead was waning.

His final prime ministerial audience with the Queen was on 9 April 1955. Despite his physical frailty, Elizabeth had developed a close bond with the formidable statesman. His fondness for both of her parents along with the shaping experience of the war, gave the pair a reservoir of memories and a common perspective, despite their five-decade age gap. His aide and confidante, Jock Colville, wrote years later that Churchill 'was madly in love with the Queen and she got more fun out of her audiences with Churchill than with any of his successors.' This appeared to be confirmed by the Queen's private secretary, Sir Alan Lascelles, who noted later, 'I could not hear what they talked about, but it was, more often than not, punctuated by peals of laughter, and Winston generally came out wiping his eyes.'

On his retirement the Queen had wanted to make Churchill a duke, the highest hereditary title of nobility that was within her personal gift, for his unstinting service to the nation. Churchill, himself the grandson and nephew of dukes – John Spencer-Churchill, 7th Duke of Marlborough and George Charles Spencer-Churchill, 8th Duke of Marlborough, who had been born at one of the most splendid ducal residences in England, Blenheim Palace – had advised her private secretary that he would refuse the honour if it were offered to him. The Nobel Prize recipient for literature for his six-volume historical study of World War II and his political speeches, who had been knighted by the Queen on 24 April 1953, said he would have been honoured, but he wanted to leave the world with the same name he was born with, Churchill.

When the Queen asked him to name his successor, as was the custom in such situations, Churchill said that should be her decision alone. The Queen, who knew what was coming, summoned the newly knighted Foreign Secretary, Sir Anthony Eden, to the palace to 'kiss hands', the constitutional term used for the formal installation of crown-appointed government ministers to their office, to become Elizabeth's second prime minister the following day.

Sir Winston Churchill's letter to his sovereign following his resignation throws a light on the importance of his role as Elizabeth's mentor during the early years of her reign. 'I have tried throughout to keep Your Majesty squarely confronted with the grave and complex problems of our time.' He wrote, 'Very soon after taking office as First Minister I realised the comprehension with which Your Majesty entered upon the august duties of a modern Sovereign and the store of knowledge, which had already been gathering by an upbringing both wise and lively. This enabled Your Majesty to understand as it seemed by instinct the relationships and the balances of the British constitution so deeply cherished by the mass of the Nation and by the strongest and most stable forces in it. I became conscious of the Royal resolve to serve as well as rule, and indeed to rule by serving.'

★★★

In his final toast to the Queen as prime minister, Churchill summed up his affection and respect for her, 'Never have the august duties which fall upon the British monarch been discharged with more devotion than in the brilliant opening to Your Majesty's reign. We thank God for the gift he has bestowed upon us and vow ourselves anew to the sacred cause, and wise and kindly way of life of which Your Majesty is the young, gleaming champion.' In response, Elizabeth sent him a handwritten letter. She wrote that, 'No other Prime Minister will be able to hold the place of my first prime minister to whom both my husband and I owe so much and for whose wise guidance during the early years of my reign I shall always be so profoundly grateful.' It was heartfelt.

Elizabeth's growing confidence in her role as monarch left Philip, whose advice she had always considered, feeling a little isolated. The Commonwealth Tour of 1953–1954 had given him a sense of purpose and the feeling that they were a team. Once they were back in Britain, however, his sense of frustration with the old court returned as he was excluded from constitutional matters. The way his wife's veritable army of courtiers embraced their monarch meant there was little room for him.

It was, however, a testing time for the Queen. With Churchill gone, she soon faced two of the most challenging crises of her reign, the first deeply personal – the furore over her sister Princess Margaret's love affair with divorcee Group Captain Peter Townsend, and her desire to marry him – and the second political, the Suez Crisis.

Firstly, Princess Margaret's love for a divorced courtier, hero Battle of Britain fighter pilot Townsend, threw up the 'love versus duty' issues that had rocked the monarchy to its foundations during the 1936 abdication crisis. Margaret had met Townsend when she was a 14-year-old and the dashing courtier was twice her age. The fighter ace had married Cecil Rosemary Pawle, a British socialite and artist, during the war on 17 July 1941 at Much Hadham, Hertfordshire, after a whirlwind two-week courtship. The couple later had two sons, Giles and Hugo. Townsend, who had brought down the first German bomber to crash in England since 1918, joined the Royal Household in 1944 under an equerries of honour scheme and he became equerry to the King. Following George VI's death in 1952 he became Comptroller of the Queen Mother's Household, and was regarded as a trusted and discreet courtier. His marriage was an unhappy one and it began to collapse, due to Townsend's prolonged absences from home. He later discovered Rosemary's affair with John de László, the youngest son of the painter Philip de László, and he was granted a decree nisi in 1952 for his wife's adultery. She later married and divorced de László and thirdly, in 1978, she wed the 5th Marquess Camden.

A tabloid newspaper reporter covering the Queen's coronation in June 1953 noticed Princess Margaret flick a piece of lint off Group Captain Townsend's jacket. It was enough to start rumours of a relationship that was to dominate newspaper headlines for many months to come. In reality by that time Princess Margaret and Townsend already had plans to marry, but her sister, in her capacity as the queen, had asked the pair to keep their relationship and plans secret for a year. Under the Royal Marriages Act of 1772, Margaret needed the monarch's permission to marry if she intended to do so before the age of 25. After that, which complicated the situation further, she needed the approval of parliament.

When news of the proposed marriage leaked to the press, it immediately made headlines around the world. As part of a compromise, Townsend was sent to Brussels to take a new position as air attaché at the British Embassy, a two-year-long posting. Margaret turned 25 in August 1955 but, by then, in an age when divorce was still scorned, parliament had already indicated it would not consent to her marriage. The princess was left with just two options: firstly, to renounce all her royal rights and privileges and become plain Mrs Peter Townsend, or, secondly, give up any idea of marrying him altogether.

The Queen Mother, a strong-willed woman with clear views on the sanctity of marriage, had backed Elizabeth's decision to refuse permission to allow Margaret to marry Townsend. As the moment approached when Margaret would be free to make her own decision, her mother urged her daughter to think very carefully about all the implications. In a letter on 9 September 1955, she wrote to Margaret, from her home in Scotland, Birkhall:

'My Darling Margaret,

I sometimes wonder whether you realise quite how much I hate having to point out the more difficult and occasionally horrid problems which arise when discussing your future. I suppose that every mother wants her child to be happy, and I know what a miserable & worrying time you are having, torn by so many difficult constitutional & moral problems. I think about it and you all the time, and because I have to talk over the horrid things does not mean that I don't suffer with you, or that one's love is any less.

Your very loving Mummy'

Princess Margaret and Peter Townsend are often portrayed as star-crossed lovers in subsequent rather romantic portrayals of their ill-fated relationship. Margaret, however, was not as helpless in the decision to abandon Townsend as the press portrayed. A letter written in 1955 showed that Margaret was determined that the decision would be hers and hers alone. Six days before her 25th birthday, Margaret wrote to Prime Minister Sir Anthony Eden spelling out her position.

'I am writing to tell you, as far as I can of any personal plans during the next few months … During the last of August and all September I shall be here at Balmoral, and I have no doubt that during this time – especially on my birthday on August 21st – the press will encourage every sort of speculation about the possibility of my marrying Group Captain Peter Townsend. I am not going to see him during this time but in October I shall be returning to London, and he will then be taking his annual leave – I do certainly hope to see him while he is there. But it is only by seeing him in this way that I feel I can properly decide whether I can marry him or not. At the end of October or early November I very much hope to be in a position to tell you and the other Commonwealth Prime Ministers what I intend to do. The Queen of course knows I am writing to you about this, but of course no one else does, and as everything is so uncertain I know you will regard it certainly as a confidence.'

Her letter is significant because it clearly shows that her love for Townsend was already waning and previous intractable belief in the match was wavering. She appears also to be assured in herself and in control of the situation. The perception was that she gave up the love of her life for duty and protocol, but this letter sets a question mark over that.

In 1955, after much soul-searching, Margaret called off her plans to marry Townsend. In a statement she said simply, 'I have been aware that, subject to my renouncing my rights of succession, it might have been possible for me to contract a civil marriage. However, mindful of the Church's teaching that Christian marriage is indissoluble, and conscious of my duty to the Commonwealth, I have resolved to put these considerations before any others.' She continued: 'I have reached this decision entirely alone, and in doing so I have been strengthened by the unfailing support and devotion of Group Captain Townsend.'

Margaret's decision not to wed was welcomed by the Church of England and Commonwealth leaders. The Archbishop of Canterbury, Dr Geoffrey Fisher, said: 'What a wonderful person the Holy Spirit is.' Fleet Street's newspaper editors felt that the princess had been bullied by the establishment to put her royal duty before love.

Five years later, in 1960, she married the flamboyant photographer, Antony Armstrong-Jones, who was later ennobled and became the Earl of Snowdon. The couple had two children, David, later the 2nd Earl of Snowdon, and Lady Sarah Chatto. The marriage ended in 1978 on the grounds that they had been living apart for two years, meaning that Margaret became the first senior member of the Royal Family to divorce since six-times married Tudor king, Henry VIII. Townsend married 20-year-old Marie-Luce Jamagne, a Belgian national he had met the previous year, in 1958.

They had three children, Isabelle, Marie-France and Pierre. Their younger daughter, Isabelle Townsend, became a Ralph Lauren model in the late 1980s and early 1990s. Isabelle Townsend and her family renovated and lived at Le Moulin de la Tuilerie in Gif-sur-Yvette, where the Duke and Duchess of Windsor had once lived. Townsend died of stomach cancer in 1995, in Saint-Léger-en-Yvelines, France. He was 80 years old.

***

The Suez Crisis was, in global political terms, the first major setback of Elizabeth's reign. Shrouded in secrecy, British involvement was a calamity, and although she was not actually pulling the strings, it still happened on her watch. Accounts in popular culture suggest Elizabeth had reservations about the way her Eden-led government handled the affair and that she was even hoodwinked by Eden who kept her in the dark on the detail, a point that, historically, remains a matter of dispute. What is known, however, is that Eden did meet with the Queen during the crisis, but neither of them have ever given a public account of their privileged conversations.

What the Queen knew about the invasion, much less her opinion of it, is not known. Historians have said Eden failed to brief her fully on the strategy. Others claim, as the monarch, she had access to all Suez documents through her daily boxes. Regardless, it appears Elizabeth was not happy with the plan. Eden later claimed that the Queen did not voice any disapproval, but he added, 'Nor would I claim that she was pro-Suez.' Elizabeth's long-time courtier, Lord Charteris, put it much more bluntly: 'I think the Queen believed Eden was mad.'

The crisis unfolded on 29 October 1956 when Israeli forces, in a provocative act of war, invaded Egypt and pushed their combat troops toward the Suez Canal after Egypt's president, Gamal Abdel Nasser, had nationalised the key waterway that effectively controlled two-thirds of the oil used by Europe. Nasser intended to use its revenues to finance the construction of the Aswan Dam to control flooding and drought in the region. The United States and Britain had offered him a financial grant to start construction, but Nasser was also weighing up a counter offer from the Soviet Union. This was, of course, at the height of the Cold War and the US and UK were both outraged over his double-dealings with communists.

The military action against Nasser was part of a three-way collusion under the Sèvres Protocol, a top-secret signed agreement, where it was agreed that the Israelis would invade Egypt first, thus providing Britain and France with an alibi, and they would send in troops moments later to back up the Israelis under the guise of a peacekeeping force. Eden ordered all evidence of the plot to be destroyed. But the details did leak, and the impact was catastrophic, threatening to bring the Soviet Union into play and damaging the British relationship with the United States. The US President, Dwight Eisenhower, was furious that he had been blindsided by so-called allies, Britain and France. 'I've just never seen great powers make such a complete mess and botch of things,' he said at the time. 'I think that Britain and France have made a terrible mistake.' What followed was humiliating for the two European nations, with President Eisenhower leading the diplomatic moves against the invasion by increasing pressure on the International Monetary Fund (IMF) to withhold any loans to Britain until Eden agreed to a ceasefire in Egypt.

It left Eden boxed in. In the end, humbled and embarrassed, he had no choice but to bow to the US demands. Eden continued to insist, officially at least, that he had only sent in British troops to keep the peace. Along with the French and Israeli governments the British were forced to withdraw their troops in late 1956 and early 1957 as Nasser and Egypt emerged victorious. In a speech he said the British had been humiliated. 'They brought a fleet here to Port Said and what happened?' he said. 'We defeated them. They came out demoralised, they came out embarrassed, and now all they can do is insult us,' he added. 'When they call us names we feel we're important. Our papers aren't able to insult their queen and their prime minister. Well we can insult them, of course we can. Remember the insults written on the walls at Port Said. Remember those words. Should we let them hear the words you wrote on those walls? You said, "Your queen is a what?"' He then laughed as the enthusiastic crowd shouted in unison, 'A bitch!' in response.

Eden was horrified that news of the secret deal with France and Israel had been put on paper and for good reason; any physical proof of his clearly underhand collusion in what was an illegal invasion was political dynamite. 'Oh my God,' he is understood to have said when told his representatives had signed a written agreement. 'I never expected anything to be signed!'

On 9 January 1957 Eden, who had been prime minister for just one year and 279 days, fell on his sword. He had gambled his political career and lost. Although initially he had been a popular leader, his decision to use armed intervention over Suez after a secret back-door deal was the beginning of the end for him. It would be a decision that would haunt him and seriously damage his reputation and legacy. Eden's poor health was given as the official reason for his abrupt resignation and departure.

It is true that Eden had undergone a series of operations to correct a gall bladder condition in 1953. The opinion of four doctors – signed by Sir Horace Evans, Sir Gordon Gordon-Taylor, Dr Thomas Hunt and Dr Ralph Southward and issued to the press – was that he was unfit to govern. His physicians said his health would, 'no longer enable him to sustain the heavy burdens inseparable from the office of prime minister.' After their written medical opinion was made public, Eden announced, 'I do not feel that it is right for me to continue in the office as the Queen's First Minister knowing that I shall be unable to do my full duty by my Sovereign and the country.'

The rapid deterioration in his health coincided with the slide in trust in his government amid the embarrassing fallout over Suez. On political grounds alone there were plenty of reasons for Eden to quit. For one thing, according to the Queen's private secretary, Martin Charteris, she did not trust Eden and it seems she had good reason. His Suez policy had been attacked by senior figures in his own party as well as the majority of members of other political parties. The demoralising end to the crisis seriously wounded British credibility and standing on the world stage as a military player and power. It dismayed those who had initially praised its inception and led to widespread criticism over the financial consequences of the blocking of the Suez Canal. Not only had it breached and damaged Anglo-American relations, as well as Britain's position in the United Nations and the Commonwealth, it had a serious impact on the UK economy. The following day, 10 January, another Old Etonian, Harold Macmillan, a pragmatic politician and protégé of Sir Winston Churchill, accepted the Queen's offer to become her third prime minister at the age of 62, as Eden went into the political wilderness.

Eden's sympathetic official biographer, D. R. Thorpe, described the Suez Crisis as 'a truly tragic end to his premiership, and one that came to assume a disproportionate importance in any assessment of his career.' Yet even in retirement, Eden continued to insist that there had been no collusion with Israel and France and that no such agreement had ever existed. Despite revelations that put the Anglo-French-Israeli 'collusion' over Suez beyond doubt, Eden doggedly stuck by his story that Britain had only entered the affray to preserve the peace and that officially he had no prior knowledge of Israel's war plans.

The Queen created the title, the Earl of Avon, for Eden in 1961 together with the subsidiary title Viscount Eden of Royal Leamington Spa in the County of Warwick. When Eden died in 1977 an obituary in *The Times* declared he was, 'The last Prime Minister to believe Britain was a great power and the first to confront a crisis which proved she was not.'*

With the Queen preoccupied with serious matters of state, Philip busied himself by continuing to carve out a role for himself. He established the Duke of Edinburgh's Award (as previously mentioned), but he still felt he lacked direction and purpose. It gnawed away at him, however, and worried him; he knew he needed a fresh challenge. As a naval officer he was used to being away from

---

* He could hold this line honourably only in the absence of the Sèvres Protocol. The other two copies didn't surface until after his death. David Ben-Gurion, the primary national founder of the State of Israel and its first prime minister, died in 1981, leaving Shimon Peres the guardian of the Sèvres Protocol. In 1996, as prime minister, Peres permitted its release in response to a request by a documentary film team after getting the agreement of the French and British governments. The film crew found only a faded photocopy preserved in a sealed envelope in a safe at the Ben-Gurion Archives in Sde Boker, the retirement home of Israel's first prime minister. Apparently Ben-Gurion's original was lost. The secret document had long ago served its and his purpose. By getting the parties to sign the Sèvres Protocol, Ben-Gurion had opened the way for a military victory that transformed the perception of Israel. The Suez conflict was a disaster for Britain, but the Sinai campaign was a triumph for Israel, giving it, until June 1967, a decade of quiet on its troubled Egyptian border.

loved ones for months at a time. He loved life on the open seas and the sense of freedom it afforded him. He was itching to put HMY *Britannia* through her paces. At 32, Philip felt a yearning for his old life as a naval officer and jumped at the chance to test out the new HMY *Britannia Royal* when it was suggested that he be the 'Queen's representative' and make a solo voyage to open the Olympic Games in Melbourne, the first Olympic Games held in the Southern Hemisphere.

★★★

When the Queen and Prince Philip visited Australia in 1954 they were shown preparations for the Olympics and she accepted an invitation to become patron of the games. But even then it was clear that her schedule, and the backlog of requests for her to officiate at various events, would not allow her to make another visit to Australia so soon after the long tour. Philip's mission was structured into a tour of New Guinea and other nearby islands, including Manus Island. His adventure took him to far-flung parts of the Commonwealth including Malaya, New Zealand, Ceylon, Gambia, Antarctica, the Falkland Islands, South Georgia, Tristan da Cunha, Ascension Island and St Helena and the Galapagos Islands on what would be his longest trip aboard HMY *Britannia*, 40,000 miles in 140 days from October 1956 to February 1957.

Philip had sailed with a small personal staff, including his private secretary, Mike Parker, whom he had appointed to his personal staff when he and Elizabeth had taken up residence at Clarence House. The duke took him completely under his wing and introduced him to many of his friends. He made him a member of the Thursday Club, a very exclusive luncheon party of men with bright ideas. Sometimes at night the pair would slip out of the palace for an evening with other royal acquaintances. The royal staff soon got used to these expeditions. 'Murgatroyd and Winterbottom,' they would say, 'have popped out for a stroll.' He eventually became

Philip's private secretary, but they were more friends than a master and servant. After one boozy night out, the pair were so late getting back to Clarence House, where Philip and Elizabeth were living at the time, that they had to climb over the locked gates.

For the people of Melbourne hosting the Olympics was a landmark moment in their city's history. They promised the greatest show on earth. More than 100,000 people packed into the Melbourne Cricket Ground on 22 November 1956 to witness the spectacle. The huge crowd roared its appreciation after Philip, resplendent in his Royal Navy uniform, was driven into the stadium in an open-top Rolls-Royce, to officially open the games. It coincided with his ninth wedding anniversary and it was undoubtedly a testing time for the pair's relationship. Their only reliable communication during Philip's lengthy period away was by telegram, letter and the occasional difficult-to-hear and long-distance telephone conversation.

Philip's extended absence from the Queen's side soon became the subject of gossip and speculation. His tour had started just as the Suez Crisis was being played out but because the purpose of the tour was a first-ever royal visit to a number of Commonwealth countries, the Queen supported it. In her 1956 Christmas broadcast she referred to his absence from her side and why, 'Whilst my husband cannot be at home on Christmas Day, I could not wish for a better reason than that he should be travelling in other parts of the Commonwealth.'

Fleet Street's editors were not satisfied with the veracity of the story the palace was putting out. They, and the proprietors, were no longer as deferential towards the Royal Family as before the war. A juicy scandal meant increased sales. Rather than reporting what Philip was actually doing, the newspapers created the impression that his voyage was a pleasure cruise. There were pages upon pages of speculation about the fragility of the royal marriage too. So by the time the royal yacht docked at Gibraltar in February 1957 on its last leg, the duke remained on board instead of flying home as he was intending on joining the Queen on a state visit to Portugal

and had arranged to join her there instead. The *Sunday Pictorial**
slammed Philip for being a bad father because he didn't rush home
to see his wife and children.

Matters were made worse by an article published in an American
newspaper, *The Baltimore Sun,* that further fuelled the flames of
controversy with allegations of a romantic liaison involving Philip
under the salacious headline: 'Queen, Duke in Rift Over Party
Girl'. The gossip-mongers had a field day. Some speculated that
the unnamed party girl referred to in the article was actress Pat
Kirkwood, a beautiful musical comedy star. Rumours about her
and Philip having an affair had first surfaced as early as 1948, when
Princess Elizabeth was eight months pregnant with Charles. Pat,
then the highest-paid star on the London stage, was the girlfriend
of society photographer Baron Nahum, the duke's friend and a
member of the Thursday Club in Soho, which Philip regularly
attended for a boys' night out.

Philip was incandescent with rage over the cruel and
unsubstantiated reports.'He was very, very angry and deeply hurt,'
said his friend Mike Parker.The Queen was equally dismayed, and,
surprisingly, given her instinctive caution broke the unwritten
rule that royalty never answers back and authorised her press
secretary, Commander Colville, to issue an official and complete
denial.

Just as Colville was preparing to release the statement word
reached the palace of a crisis in the marriage of Philip's right-hand
man, Commander Mike Parker. To make matters worse for both
men, as the press were digging into a crisis in the royal marriage,
Eileen, Parker's wife, decided to sue for divorce while her husband
was away on duty with Philip. Parker immediately resigned and flew
back from Gibraltar to London Airport where he was greeted by a
pack of reporters demanding a comment from him. At the back of
the crowd, he spotted his old palace sparring partner, Commander
Colville. At first, Parker thought the courtier had come to offer

---

* Now known as the *Sunday Mirror*

155

support and solidarity in his hour of need. In fact his reason for being there was the complete opposite. 'I've just come to let you know that from now on you're on your own,' Colville told him and abruptly left. To Parker it confirmed everything he thought of the ruthless aides at Buckingham Palace, that once you were gone, you were gone.

Despite his resignation, Parker remained on close terms with both his former employers, corresponded regularly with them and always called in at Buckingham Palace when he was in London. He was courteous and helpful to royal biographers and journalists, although he never lost an understandably jaundiced attitude towards some members of the press. When one popular London paper asked him to name his sum for an interview to mark Philip's 80th birthday, his response was 'They can't afford me because I simply don't trust the bastards'.

The collapse of Mike and Eileen Parker's marriage gave Fleet Street the perfect starting point. In the court circles of the time, a separated and soon-to-be divorced courtier was deemed newsworthy. The press was not going to stop there. Reports hinted that the breakdown of the Parkers' relationship mirrored that of the Queen and Philip's with reports suggesting that the royal marriage was under intense strain too.

Commander Colville felt he had no choice but to react to the speculation fearing it was out of control and needed to be stamped on. He went to the Queen and asked if he could issue a statement to quell the stories about the state of her marriage. A week after Mike Parker's resignation, Colville issued the unequivocal palace statement. It read, 'It is quite untrue that there is any rift between the Queen and the Duke.'

It was a decisive move but it failed to stop the story of a crisis in the royal marriage going global. The Associated Press reported in 1957 that Parker's resignation had rocked court circles. 'Parker's marital troubles set off rumours of a rift between Prince Philip and Queen Elizabeth II. Buckingham Palace denied the rumours. A leading British newspaper said early this week Buckingham Palace

156

officials were worried about "detailed evidence" that might emerge in a Parker divorce case.'

Eileen Parker, later revealed that the Queen and Philip had not wanted Mike to quit and had asked him to remain in his post. Eileen was granted her divorce in London on 28 February 1958 on the grounds of Mike's adultery, naming Mrs Mary Alexandra Thompson as his mistress.

In her 1982 book *Step Aside for Royalty*, Mrs Parker wrote: 'I learned that both Prince Philip and the Queen had tried to dissuade Mike from resigning.' She claimed she had not intended their split to go public while Mike was away on duty with Prince Philip but her lawyer, Meryn Lewis, had issued a statement without consulting her to journalist Rex North of the *Sunday Pictorial*.

By now it didn't make any difference what anyone said in a bid to clarify matters. Thanks to the press tongues were wagging about Philip's alleged sexual transgressions. The Queen and Philip did their best to rise above the speculation but the rumours continued. What the reporters did not know, of course, is that the duke, a romantic at heart, had sent his wife white roses to mark their ninth wedding anniversary and did his best to be in regular contact with her and the children while he was away. The press had the story they wanted and were determined to run with it.

The People, a big-selling British Sunday newspaper at the time (which was edited by the irrepressible Harry Ainsworth, who had increased circulation from 250,000 per issue to a staggering five million during his 32-year editorship from 1925 to 1957), in one article advised Elizabeth to promote Philip to prince consort. 'It was one way of keeping him busy at home,' the journalist wrote. The commentary in the newspaper argued that, otherwise, the duke was 'a man without a real job … until he is given one, he will always be tempted to seek out for himself a real job of work and go off on extended goodwill trips around the Commonwealth.'

In February 1957 the Queen joined Philip on board HMY *Britannia* as she sailed up the River Tagus into the heart of Lisbon, Portugal's capital, where they enjoyed two days together before starting a state visit hosted by President Craveiro Lopes and First Lady Berta Ribeiro. The pair put on a perfect display of unity at an official welcome at the Black Horse Square and at other events including a tour of the Jerónimos Monastery.

A few days later on 28 February, at a lunch held at the Mansion House hosted by the Lord Mayor of London, Lieutenant-Colonel Sir George James Cullum Welchat, attended by the prime minister, Harold Macmillan, as well as Lord Mountbatten to mark his return to London, Philip made no mention of the stories in the press. He was even accompanied by his pilloried outgoing private secretary Mike Parker and his equerry, Squadron Leader Henry Chinnery. It was his first major public engagement since the Queen had conferred on him the title, 'HRH The Prince Philip, Duke of Edinburgh.'

'I find it rather difficult to realise that I've been around the world and covered nearly 40,000 miles since the 15 October last year. Now it would be quite easy to claim that this was all part of some deep-laid scheme but I'm afraid, I have to admit, that it all came about because I was asked to start off the Olympic Games in Melbourne where I made if I may say so the best speech of my life which is exactly five words.' The tour, said the duke, naturally involved the personal sacrifice of being separated from his wife and children. There are some things, he said, for which personal sacrifice is worthwhile, and he said he believed the British Commonwealth is one of those.

He went on, 'This Commonwealth of which every member is so proud came in to existence because people made sacrifices and offered their service to it. Now it has been handed to us and if we don't make sacrifices for it we shall have nothing to hand onto those who come after us and would have lost something of much greater value than just a grand conception.

'On Saturday, 16 February, four months almost to the day after I left home, the Queen flew out to Portugal and we enjoyed two days there together before paying a state visit to that country and then followed three hectic but wonderful days when the friendliness and enthusiasm of the Portuguese people knew no bounds. And then as you know this adventure ended where it began at London Airport with a very happy family reunion,' he said pointedly. The publicity the trip had attracted was rather less happy. An obedient and deferential press was from now on a thing of the past, something the duke acknowledged, 'The media is a professional intruder, you can't complain about it.'

Years later, Pat Kirkwood spoke of her encounter with Philip that one evening, after a performance in the musical *Starlight Roof* at the London Hippodrome. She said his friend Baron had taken Philip and an equerry to her dressing room. The foursome then went out to dinner at Les Ambassadeurs Club in Hamilton Place, one of the capital's most exclusive and distinguished gambling clubs. Afterwards, they carried on to the Milroy Club, a favourite venue of Princess Margaret, nearby for some music and dancing. According to Pat, the prince wouldn't let her sit down, dancing with her to whatever the band played. They stayed out until dawn and had scrambled eggs at Baron's Mayfair flat. Pat insisted that the only time she had met Philip again was at theatrical command performances. After she died in 2007, her fourth husband Peter Knight announced that, at her request, he would one day give 'correspondence' between Pat and the Duke of Edinburgh to Prince Philip's official biographer. It would prove that there was no illicit relationship, he said. This didn't explain, however, why she and the prince were corresponding with each other at all.

At the time Pat Kirkwood categorically denied an affair and is understood to have asked Philip to make a statement supporting her denial. The actress gave her friend, writer Michael Thornton, a letter between Philip and herself, and said that in it Philip replied: 'Short of starting libel proceedings, there is absolutely nothing to be done. Invasion of privacy, invention, and false quotations are the bane of our existence.'

Of the incident, Thornton said Pat Kirkwood had later told a journalist friend, 'A lady is not normally expected to defend her honour. It is the gentleman who should do that. I would have had a happier and easier life if Prince Philip, instead of coming uninvited to my dressing room, had gone home to his pregnant wife on the night in question.'

12: BADGE OF BASTARDY

'What upsets me is the prince's almost brutal attitude to the Queen over all this.'

Harold Macmillan's entry in his personal diary
over Philip's stance over his surname

On 1 August 1959, a decade after the birth of their daughter, Princess Anne, Elizabeth and Philip issued a statement that they were expecting their third child. The birth of the baby would be historic too, as it would be the first born to a reigning monarch since 1857, when Queen Victoria delivered her youngest child, Princess Beatrice. The joyful news, however, was tainted because both parents knew it would open wounds, and once again raise past issues about the child's surname. Philip believed the matter of his children not using his surname had never been resolved properly. This time, an emboldened duke was happy to take on all comers and he was more determined than ever to win the argument for his name to be recognised and used by his children. He also had a wily ally in the form of his uncle Lord Mountbatten who, like Philip, had been affronted by the Queen's last ruling on the matter.

By now the decorated war hero, Lord Mountbatten, had risen to become Chief of the Defence Staff, having served with distinction in the Royal Navy during World War II as Chief of Combined Operations and ultimately Supreme Allied Commander, South East Asia Command. His role as the last Viceroy of India, as well as its first governor general from 12 February1947 to 21 June 1948, had given him more sway in political circles too. Inspite of all his significant achievements and obvious merits he was still viewed by the establishment with suspicion. The Queen Mother, for one, was wary of his power and the mastery with which he used it and long established courtiers feared he was the driving force behind Philip's apparent obsession to modernise the monarchy. Senior figures at court, such as Sir Michael Adeane, the private secretary to the Queen, felt Her Majesty should keep her cousin, Lord Mountbatten, at arm's length.

Once again the senior courtiers feared that Dickie wanted to push what was seen as his minor branch of the Royal Family centre stage and with him pulling strings to secure greater influence. Lord Mountbatten, like his nephew, wanted Philip and Elizabeth's children to bear the Mountbatten name in some form, thus raising him up to the top level of society, as he saw himself as the *paterfamilias* of the Royal Family.

Philip's previous attempts to ensure his children had his surname had fallen on deaf ears. Thanks in no small part to an unlikely champion, an English lawyer and amateur constitutional expert, Edward Iwi, this was about to change. Mr Iwi was obsessed with the detail of English law and for decades he had bombarded British establishment figures with letters listing corrections to the legal system. He regularly penned contributions to the letters column of *The Times* newspaper in which his articles exposed what he regarded as serious errors in English law and new legislation. Despite the high quality of his arguments his letters were often initially dismissed, only to be proved to be right on subsequent more detailed examination. In Mr Iwi, Lord Mountbatten and Philip had unearthed a gifted and persistent champion.

***

On 10 August 1959, Lord Mountbatten and Mr Iwi secretly met to discuss the situation regarding the legitimate surname of Elizabeth and Philip's children and descendants. Mr Iwi made a note in his personal diary chronicling what had happened that evening. The lawyer had a proposal that he felt would be accepted by the

Queen, a new hyphenated so-called double-barrelled surname, 'Mountbatten-Windsor'. Mountbatten loved the idea and told his new-found friend to pursue it.

Once he had the green light, Mr Iwi kicked off the campaign with a letter in September 1959, which is now filed in the National Archives at Kew, to Prime Minster Harold Macmillan in which he set out his grave concerns. 'When the new baby is born, as matters now stand it will bear the "Badge of bastardy" namely, its mother's maiden name. As far as I know, it will be the first legitimate child to be so born. You will recall that Windsor was the Queen's maiden name and on marriage she took her husband's surname of Mountbatten. Prince Charles and Princess Anne were born with the surname Mountbatten.'

What followed next was another bitter fight over what the baby should be called which engulfed the Prime Minister, the Lord Chancellor Lord Kilmuir and Buckingham Palace. It even triggered an official inquiry into the history of the royal name, which resulted in a bizarre conclusion that at one point a family called 'Guelph' had been occupying the British throne for 170 years. The previously unknown and artificial family names of 'Windsor and Mountbatten' were only adopted at the height of anti-German feeling at the end of World War I.

Lord Kilmuir warned Macmillan that Iwi should not be ignored but had to be stopped as he had already shown himself to the authorities as something of a constitutional expert, 'This is in very bad taste. Iwi must be silenced... he might go quietly.' Sir George Coldstream, Lord Kilmuir's private secretary, advised the Prime Minister to tell Iwi 'in friendly terms to keep his mouth shut'. 'The trouble with Iwi is that he usually puts his finger on an awkward question. You will no doubt recall that Iwi has on several occasions been proved right and on at least one of these occasions he could have caused the government great embarrassment. I refer to the unfortunate mistake by which Princess Arthur of Connaught was named as a Counsellor of State in 1944. Iwi spotted the error but was good enough to keep quiet about it. [He should be told] in friendly terms to keep his mouth shut.'

Macmillan's main line of argument, that Iwi had been wrong to suggest that the Royal Family had a surname, was flawed. It was true that the Tudors and Stuarts had surnames but their female sovereigns had not taken their husbands' names on marriage – 'Mary Tudor remained Mary Tudor and neither Queen Anne nor her children bore the name Oldenburg.' He went on, 'You are quite wrong in stating that Windsor was the surname of Her Majesty before marriage or that Mountbatten was ever the surname of Prince Charles or Princess Anne. Moreover, even if you were right about this, I could not think that the surname Windsor could be other than a distinction or that there is anything ignominious in bearing the name of a great house derived through a female ancestor.'

This failed to silence the determined Iwi. He responded to Macmillan on 17 November 1959: 'No one is infallible. If the royal family has never possessed a surname or a family name, then the Proclamation of 1917 substituting Windsor for Guelph would never have been necessary.' Iwi refused to go quietly. Indeed, within weeks he had won the support of a powerful voice, the Bishop of Carlisle, Thomas Bloomer. The bishop himself had attracted press coverage when in a Sunday sermon he preached that he did not like the idea of any child 'born in wedlock' being deprived of the right and privilege of every legitimate child. He refrained from mentioning the 'bastard' word.

In Iwi's letter to Macmillan of 17 November 1959 he informed the Prime Minister that he had 'Strong conscientious feelings against allowing a legitimate child to be born with its mother's maiden surname or family name. I have reason to believe that many right-thinking people share my view.'

Macmillan and his advisers were not to know which other 'right-thinking people' shared Iwi's view. Not everyone took the issue seriously. One senior civil servant has added to the file, 'Not to be confused with the Browne-Windsors.' But the Prime Minister and the crown certainly did take it seriously. Others such as barrister Sir George Coldstream, who served as Permanent Secretary to the Lord Chancellor's Department and Clerk of the Crown in Chancery at the time, took it a little too seriously. 'One is sorely tempted to cane him for being so cheeky.'

The discussion of the name had reduced the pregnant Queen to tears, according to the deputy prime minister R. A. Butler. Prime Minister Macmillan was concerned and noted in his private diary, 'What upsets me is the prince's almost brutal attitude to the Queen over all this.' Once again she faced a choice between a man whom she loved and who had given up so much for her sake and the Windsor dynasty to which she was devoted and born to serve.

There were further exchanges between Macmillan and Iwi with no resolution. Then in January 1960, when the Prime Minister was on an official visit to South Africa, he received a telegram from "RAB" Butler* who was standing in for him as prime minister. Rab reported to Macmillan that at his first audience with the Queen she had advised him that she had 'absolutely set her heart' on a change to the Royal surname. 'Lord Mountbatten ever interested in such matters, may possibly have had something to do with it,' Butler noted. The correspondence shows that the struggle had already been raging for three months before the Queen raised the matter.

The entire Whitehall machine suddenly went into reverse. On 8 February 1960, just 11 days before the birth of Prince Andrew, the Queen made a new declaration saying that she had adopted 'Mountbatten-Windsor' as the name for all her descendants who did not enjoy the title of His or Her Royal Highness. Iwi explained in an article in the *New Law Journal* and elsewhere that it would remain a 'hidden or latent' surname to be used by any of the Queen's children, should they lose their titles, and passed on to their descendants and utilised by them when the use of a surname becomes necessary.

Lord Kilmuir wrote to Lord Mountbatten and informed Prince Philip that, after a lengthy inquiry, it was deemed that Mr Iwi had

---

* Richard Austen Butler was generally known as R. A. Butler and familiarly known from his initials as Rab.

reached the right conclusion as set out in his article in the *Law Journal*. As for the Queen, when Rab Butler conveyed the news to Macmillan, her prime minister, 'it took a great load from my mind'.

The Queen's statement in the *London Gazette* did not mean that the Windsor dynasty was over and the name would change – that could only happen with an Act of Parliament. It was the perfect compromise, as far as Philip was concerned; as a family, the royals from that moment would be known as 'Mountbatten-Windsor'. The Labour-supporting *Daily Herald* newspaper* was in no doubt that it was a victory for Philip. Its front page headline trumpeted: 'PHILIP WINS FIGHT FOR THE ROYAL MOUNTBATTENS'. The name change would only apply to certain descendants of the Queen. Iwi was vindicated; Philip and his uncle Dickie were jubilant.

The day after the Queen's statement Iwi, according to his personal diary, was invited to Lord Mountbatten's home. At his host's request he slipped in through a side door to avoid undue attention. Once safely inside Iwi enjoyed a celebratory drink with Mountbatten. The two men, who had worked so hard to achieve this result, were joined by none other than an ecstatic Prince Philip and all three raised a glass in triumph.

---

* First published in 1912 the *Herald* underwent several changes of management before ceasing publication in 1964, when it was relaunched as *The Sun*, in its pre-Rupert Murdoch form.

13: A MAN IN THE MASK

*'All we know is that Ward and Prince Philip knew each other
because he sketched Philip several times.'*

Lord Andrew Lloyd-Webber, 2017

It was a story that just kept on giving as far as the press were
concerned. The fall of John Profumo, the war minister in Harold
Macmillan's Conservative government, and the inquiries and
courtroom battles associated with it, had everything. It was a
sordid tale of sex and high-end politics at a time of dramatically
changing social attitudes. Add to this the paranoia of the Cold
War and it was a newspaper editor's dream. If it had just been
about sex it would have been bad enough for Macmillan's
shaky government, but it was much worse than the man the
press dubbed SuperMac could have imagined. 'I was forced to
spend a great deal of today over a silly scrape (women this time,
thank God, not boys),' the Prime Minister wrote in his diary for
15 March 1963. But this 'scrape' was going to get a lot more
serious. It would involve MI5 and the KGB – as the Soviet
Union's London-based naval attaché was having sex with the
same showgirl as his minister Profumo – with events spiralling
out of control so much that it would lead to a loss of confidence
in Macmillan's authority, that was already on the slide downwards,
and his resignation.

The political crisis unravelled after his war minister, the
Harrow School and Oxford University educated John Profumo (a
quintessential High Tory, who was married to the film star, Valerie

Hobson), had a sexual relationship with 19-year-old aspiring model, Christine Keeler, in 1961. When Profumo, who moved effortlessly in the highest echelons of society, was exposed he then made matters much worse by lying about his indiscretions to the House of Commons. Miss Keeler, who lived with her mother, Julie, in a converted railway carriage near a gravel pit at Wraysbury in Berkshire, was an intimate friend of society osteopath Stephen Ward, who was an acquaintance of Prince Philip as well as a member of the infamous Thursday Club, like the duke. Ward, who treated the rich and famous in London, was also close to Philip's first cousin and close confidante, David Mountbatten, the 3rd Marquis of Milford Haven.

Twice-married Milford Haven, who was a wartime Royal Navy officer who was decorated during World War II and awarded the Distinguished Service Cross, was known to host parties for discreet friends at his flat in Grosvenor Square at which the evening would begin with cards, followed by the arrival of women. Ward was often among the guests and sometimes brought some of the women too. When Milford Haven died from a heart attack in 1970, he was just 50.

Stephen Ward arranged for Keeler to move into his Wimple Mews flat in London and the two struck up a close but apparently non-sexual relationship. She accompanied him to a number of risqué parties where he introduced her to wealthy and high-profile individuals. At this time, Keeler had a brief affair with John Profumo, after the pair met at a party at Lord Astor's estate, Cliveden House, in Berkshire. It later emerged that Keeler, who was sexually promiscuous, was also intimate with Soviet naval attaché, Captain Yevgeny Ivanov. When this became known it sparked security fears among politicians and the public alike as it was at the height of the Cold War.

Keeler's affair with Profumo only became public after clashes between jazz singer Aloysius 'Lucky' Gordon and jazz promoter Johnny Edgecombe, who both competed fiercely for Keeler's affections, resulted in a violent fight at the London Flamingo Club in 1962, which was reported in the newspapers. Keeler, who had been having sex with Edgecombe too, ended their relationship.

Edgecombe, however, refused to accept being dumped by Keeler and turned up at Ward's flat where she was staying. He fired five shots into the front door, further pushing Keeler into the public spotlight when police were called to investigate the incident. After that, Keeler was catapulted into the public eye, and she naively began to speak about previous sexual dalliances with both John Profumo and Ivanov, as well as her friendship with Ward.

Initially John Profumo felt he could front out the claims. It was his word against a young woman with a suspect reputation and he felt he would be believed. He addressed the matter in a speech in which he told MPs in the House of Commons that there was 'no impropriety whatsoever' in the way he conducted his relationship with Miss Keeler. With mounting pressure, however, Profumo capitulated and later admitted to the affair with Keeler, which forced his resignation from both government and parliament. It didn't stop there and there were further far-reaching implications. Stephen Ward was later put on trial for living off the earnings of prostitution, and for procuring a girl under 21 years old in relation to his friendships with Keeler and her friend Mandy Rice-Davies, to which he pleaded not guilty.

To fund his legal expenses, Ward decided to put some of his artwork up for sale, including his excellent portraits of Prince Philip, Princess Margaret, and her husband Lord Snowdon. These portraits of members of the Royal Family were part of a series, assigned to Ward by a magazine. There is no further firm evidence tying Prince Philip or Princess Margaret to the scandal that has emerged in the decades since.

Tragically, Ward took an overdose on 30 July 1963, which turned out to be the day before the verdict in his trial was returned. He died a few days later on 3 August*.

---

* Keeler was convicted on charges of perjury after she accused former lover Gordon of assault but later withdrew her accusation. She was sentenced to nine months in prison. Profumo devoted the remainder of his life to charity work. He was appointed a Commander of the Order of the British Empire (CBE) in 1975, and received the honour at a Buckingham Palace ceremony from the Queen, signalling his return to respectability. He died in 2006 aged 91.

Years later it emerged Ward had been the scapegoat in an elaborate establishment conspiracy by influential figures who were terrified that he would expose Profumo before he was forced to admit his lies. The British secret intelligence services had been aware of Profumo's affair with Keeler and her links to Russian spy Ivanov long before the minister's statement to the House of Commons. Ward had also been approached by MI5 and had been appointed a mysterious 'handler' who went by the name of Woods. At the time Ward believed he was helping his country and the security services in their operation to set up a honey trap for Yevgeny Ivanov and had agreed to cooperate with them.

According to the acclaimed investigative journalist Tom Mangold in BBC documentary *Keeler, Profumo, Ward and Me* (screened February 2020), Ivanov was a Soviet spy who was friendly with Ward and had also slept with Keeler. Despite the fact that Ward was trying to turn him into a double agent, his friendship with Ivanov was genuine. In his own naive way, Ward was working for the good of the country. But the government came to view Ward as a threat and liability fearing that he was going to expose Profumo and trigger a national security crisis. On 27 March 1963 a meeting between the home secretary, Henry Brooke, the chief constable of the Metropolitan police, Sir Joseph Simpson, and the head of the security service, Roger Hollis, was held to discuss what action could be taken against Ward. After the meeting the police tapped Ward's phone and stationed officers outside his practice, causing high society friends to abandon him. In May a desperate Ward rang Macmillan's office demanding a meeting.

A memorandum, in the National Archives, reveals that Macmillan's private secretary, Sir Timothy Bligh, was so concerned by the phone call that he rushed from his office to parliament to brief the Prime Minister and also consulted Simpson, who told him that an arrest was imminent. The timing of this memorandum is crucial, as it came in the period between Profumo's lie in parliament and his confession in early June when the government knew that Ward was the smoking gun who needed to be silenced.

At Stephen Ward's trial at the Old Bailey, the judge, Sir Archie Marshall, directed the jury to convict the osteopath on the grounds that none of his friends had come forward to support him. MI5 remained silent when they could have saved him by confirming that he had worked for them at a time when they wanted help in getting Ivanov to defect. Hollis should have informed the prosecution, which was wrongly accusing Ward of fantasising about his security service links, or at the very least arranged for a witness to confirm that he had given the state some service.

Some two months earlier, Macmillan had asked the Master of the Rolls, Lord Denning, to conduct a judicial inquiry into the circumstances leading to the resignation of Profumo. The Denning Report was to be published in September 1963. Its main role was to publicly crucify Stephen Ward, while effectively clearing the Minister for War for a peccadillo. Ward discovered, too late, that he had been set up. He knew what verdict the jury would return the next day and had no doubt what a hostile judge would do to him so he took an overdose of sleeping tablets and died later in hospital.

Hundreds queued to buy a copy of the report when it was released. But there were few revelations; those were squirrelled away into secret files. Denning did criticise the government for failing to deal with the affair more quickly, but concluded that national security had not been compromised. To the disappointment of the public, he failed to identify the man who, naked except for a mask, had served at Ward's dinner parties, the so-called 'man in a mask'.

Extracts from a transcript of a telephone interview for the BBC Home Service with Harold Macmillan by Jack 'Peter' Hardiman Scott – then BBC political correspondent (and later one of its finest political editors) – on 26 September 1963 in the National Archives about the then recently published Denning Report on the Profumo Affair show the Prime Minister's thinking and that he still felt he could cling on to power. It reads:

SCOTT: Yes, it's not a question – I agree there – of integrity at all. But perhaps the fact that you did fail in this instance may lead some people to regard Lord Denning's remark about ministerial responsibility as begging the question of competence. Is this the kind of occasion, in your judgement as prime minister, Sir, that you think calls for any ministerial resignation?

MACMILLAN: No, Sir – not at all. I have defended myself in the House of Commons, and my Ministers, and I am prepared to do so again. As I say, I think the broad judgement of the country before Lord Denning's report only confirms what I had already said – is that most people think – have a sort of feeling of sympathy for our having been treated in this way, rather than of blame for having fallen victim to deceit.

SCOTT: I feel now I must come to the effect of this report on your own future, Sir. You have made it plain in the past that you would see the Profumo affair through. I am sure your Party and the country is interested to know what you will do now. Once this debate is over in Parliament, might not in fact this be another occasion for the outbreak of the leadership controversy all over again?

MACMILLAN: Well, the leadership controversy is nothing to do with the Profumo report. It starts, it's natural, after – in a position – of this political position as to what is the best way of our winning the next election; and I've said over and over again – I'll tell you again – when I come to make my decision, I shall have only one thing in mind: what is best for the country and for the Conservative Party. It'll have nothing to do with

Profumo, which doesn't seem to me to be relevant to it at all. It'll be simply: is it best for the Party and the country that I should go on, or not? I have naturally thought a great deal about it, and when I make my decision I shall not hesitate to make it quite clear.

SCOTT: I was in fact going to put the question quite straight: how does this report affect your leading the Party at the general election? You say it doesn't, Sir?

MACMILLAN: No. The considerations were long before that and are quite separate from that. They are whether at this point, having had, as I say, seventeen years in office in war and peace, and seven years as prime minister, I should now lead the Party to another election, or whether I would do better in everybody's interests to hand it on to somebody else. That's my decision, and I will make it on exactly the same basis as I have tried to make all my decisions: what's the right thing to do?

Right or not, people lost confidence in Macmillan and his government. After weeks of indecision over whether to stay on and lead the Tory party into the next election, he resigned on 10 October 1963 citing ill health as the reason for his departure. He then entered the King Edward VII Hospital because of the prostatic obstruction which had afflicted him. Four days after his resignation announcement came a handwritten note from the Queen: 'My dear Prime Minister, I have just returned this morning from Scotland and I send you this small "reviver" with all my good wishes for a speedy and complete recovery, and I hope it will make you feel much better. Yours sincerely, Elizabeth R'.

★★★

Macmillan, who in 1957 famously told a Tory rally: 'Most of our people have never had it so good,' was out, replaced as prime minster by another Old Etonian, the 14th Earl of Home. It was unacceptable for a prime minister to sit in the House of Lords, so Home disclaimed his hereditary peerage and successfully stood for election to parliament as Sir Alec Douglas-Home. Labour, led by Harold Wilson, narrowly won the 1964 general election with an overall majority of just four seats. The Profumo affair, that challenged the established order as never before, had clearly had a devastating impact on trust in the old ways and the establishment, that included the monarchy and those charged with privately protecting it.

Stephen Ward's association with Prince Philip through the Thursday Club and the fact the osteopath, who was also an acclaimed artist, had sketched the duke's portrait several times, was enough to excite the newspapers and worried the security services. Despite Philip's association with the Profumo Affair being at most peripheral, it didn't stop the satirical magazine *Private Eye* linking Philip with Ward and dubbing the royal 'The Man in the Mask', the mystery figure referred to in Denning's report who served drinks at Ward's parties wearing only a skimpy apron. There is no evidence that this is true whatsoever and it infuriated those close to the duke.

What is true, however, is that Philip's acquaintance with some of the key figures involved in the Profumo scandal attracted the attention of MI5 when investigative journalists started digging into the possible role of Philip in the affair. Veteran journalist Clive Irving explained how he was involved in investigating the affair when he was working for London's respected *Sunday Times* and how MI5 became interested in his work. Mr Irving wrote in the *Daily Beast*, 'When the scandal broke I led a team from the Insight investigative unit at the London *Sunday Times*. For many weeks we had been trying to make sense of the labyrinth of interests trapped in the affair, reaching from picaresque Soho to the upper reaches of the security services.'

Mr Irving soon began looking at the Thursday Club, that Philip attended, and that counted Christine Keeler's friend Stephen Ward among its members. He continued, 'One of our reporters discovered that members of the Thursday Club had a favourite place for carousing, the studios of a professional portrait artist named Felix Topolski. Topolski was gregarious and famous for ripe gossip and, he told our reporter, he was happy to talk – in fact, he wanted to brag about knowing many of the people in Stephen Ward's orbit. With one exception: "I can't discuss Prince Philip."

'Naturally, we got interested in Philip. But nobody else was talking about him, either, and since our focus was mainly political, pursuing a widespread cover-up to establish what Macmillan knew and when he knew it, we dropped that titillating strand of the story. However, somebody knew we had talked to Topolski.' Irving explained, 'I had a phone call from a "Mr Shaw". He explained that he worked for MI5 and said he would be obliged if, together with two colleagues, I could meet him the following day at a hotel near the St James's Park Tube station. Nothing to be alarmed about, just a matter of courtesy.' Mr Irving went on to say how he and his two colleagues met Mr Shaw, flanked by two assistants, who seemed to know about every interview the journalists had conducted in their investigation.

There are six Profumo Affair files in the National Archives at Kew, in south-west London, but only five of them are open for public inspection. The bulging sixth, file 1/4140, containing the highly sensitive information, is closed and will remain so until at least the year 2046. The unseen documents, which were deemed so sensitive even the head of MI5 was banned from reading them at the time, have at least escaped the shredder. The Cabinet Office confirmed in January 2014 – more than 50 years after Ward's conviction after the seven-day trial – that the Denning Inquiry papers had been selected for permanent preservation. Supporters of Ward believe that the secret documents may help to exonerate him and reveal the names of other ministers and members of high society embroiled in the scandal. For years Mandy Rice-Davies was active in attempting to clear Stephen Ward's name. She fought an eventually successful battle against the National Archives, which were so determined to aid and abet the Profumo cover-up. The trial of Stephen Ward was a disgraceful event. There can be no justification, other than a cringing regard for the reputation of a long-gone establishment, for the National Archives to withhold papers evidencing this miscarriage of justice.

Whether any mention of Prince Philip is contained in the remaining secret file is unknown. Friends of the Royal Family are understandably outraged that his name is repeatedly linked with the scandal without any evidence. 'It's quite appalling,' said one senior member of the Royal Household. 'I am sure the duke would want those secret files made public so we can see who really is being protected and he would be vindicated.'

The Ward case and government cover-up fascinated composer and impresario Lord Lloyd-Webber so much he wrote a musical about it. Unfortunately for him the musical *Stephen Ward* flopped and closed after a West End run of less than four months in March 2014. But nevertheless, he firmly believes the contents of the file are 'explosive'. Why is he so certain? 'I can only say my source is totally reliable – it couldn't be more reliable,' he said in September 2017. 'Of course, the person in question has not released any details to me, but is at a very high level indeed.'

In the Upper House, Lord Lloyd-Webber, a Conservative peer since 1997 – rose to his feet in June 2013 and said, 'What concerns me is the fact that these files will be closed for a staggering 83 years [and] this gives rise to an awful lot of unhealthy speculation about who might be the individuals named within the files.' Later Lord Lloyd-Webber again called for the secret file to be made public: 'We could speculate for ever about who and what is in this file, but that is so dangerous. Goodness knows where it could lead. The problem is it makes everyone wonder who on earth it could be who needs that level of protection for that length of time. I can't believe that if I'd been involved, someone like me would receive protection like this.'

So could Prince Philip really be mentioned in the secret files? 'All we know is that Ward and Philip knew each other because he sketched Philip several times,' said Lord Lloyd-Webber. Interestingly, however, we also know that a mystery figure arrived and bought for cash all the Ward pictures of members of the Royal Family at an exhibition that took place before Ward's trial to raise money for his legal fees. To this day nobody knows who it was.

14: INTO THE RED

'We go into the red next year. I shall probably have to give up polo.'

Philip's remark on the US show *Meet the Press* on Royal finances, 1969

Standing at the foot of the steps outside St Paul's Cathedral, Prince Philip, dressed in Royal Navy uniform, saluted the coffin, draped in the Union Flag, of the great statesman, Sir Winston Churchill. At the duke's side, dressed in black, the Queen looked solemn as she held the order of service. Behind them stood the Queen Mother and Prince Charles. Queen Elizabeth had taken the decision to break protocol for her former prime minister, honouring the late wartime leader who had died, aged 90, six days earlier on 24 January 1965.

The reigning monarch usually arrives last and leaves first for such events. But at Churchill's state funeral on 30 January 1965 the Queen put such etiquette aside and arrived before his widow, Lady Clementine, and his immediate family and before Sir Winston's coffin was in the church. Churchill's grandson, Sir Nicholas Soames, said the Queen's 'sweet gesture' had meant a lot to him and his family. He said, 'It is absolutely exceptional for the Queen to grant precedence to anyone. To arrive before the coffin and before my grandfather was a beautiful and touching gesture.'

***

The funeral marked the end of an era and a new beginning for Britain. It was the 'Swinging Sixties' – a time of change, of The

Beatles, women's liberation, the pill, playwrights, satirists and directors dramatising hot-button issues, and social revolution. Class barriers and sexual prejudice were being dismantled and fashion and music seemed to change the vibe of the nation almost overnight.

The Queen sent a personal message of condolence to Churchill's widow, Lady Clementine. It read, 'The whole world is the poorer by the loss of his many-sided genius, while the survival of this country and the sister nations of the Commonwealth, in the face of the greatest danger that has ever threatened them, will be a perpetual memorial to his leadership, his vision, and his indomitable courage.' It was a heartfelt tribute to the great man for whom she had deep respect and affection.

A seismic change was sweeping the nation and the social expectations of the British people were changing too. The monarchy seen 12 years earlier, with the coronation of the Queen, as representing something at the heart of the British psyche but with a new queen also being the dawn of a new Elizabethan age, was beginning to look outdated, still locked in its old traditions, almost Edwardian and out of step with the new mood of change. Traditional values were under attack by a hypercritical youth who packaged the Royal Family as the embodiment of those outmoded ways of so-called 'Colonel Blimps' and the age of Empire. This was the age of the Vietnam War, of violent street protests and student demonstrations; the monarchy was seen as out of touch and there were even calls for it to be abolished.

The hugely respected Hugh Gaitskell, Labour leader since 1955, had died suddenly in 1963 just when he appeared to be on the verge of leading his party back into power, and had been replaced by the wily Harold Wilson. Labour had been out of office since 1951 and in the end, that last point almost certainly swung the election. The slogan '13 wasted years' was hammered home again and again, and resonated with the electorate who believed times were changing. Many middle-class voters felt that the Tory old guard who had propelled an Eton-educated earl into Downing Street could not possibly represent them and their aspirations.

Wilson was a decidedly different character to those who had served the Queen before. Her first Labour premier, many MPs, even his own, saw him as shifty and a politician without principle. Senior figures in his cabinet were hostile to the institution of monarchy too, but he was not. With his everyman appeal, quirky personality, the straight-talking, pipe-smoking intellectual Wilson was to become a favourite with the monarch over time.

Having a more relaxed demeanour than her previous high-born prime ministers, he was much closer to her own age too (just ten years her senior), which helped them strike up a cordial relationship*.

From a lower middle-class background as well as being her first Labour Party prime minister she welcomed and respected his sage advice. A grammar school boy, he went on to read Modern History at Jesus College, Oxford, graduated in PPE (Philosophy, Politics and Economics) with an outstanding first class Bachelor of Arts degree, with alphas on every paper in the final examinations, and a series of major academic awards. He continued in academia, becoming one of the youngest Oxford dons of the century at the age of 21. He was a lecturer in Economic History at New College from 1937, and a research fellow at University College.

When the war broke out in 1939 he was drafted into civil service in the war cabinet, then as head of statistics and economics at the Ministry of Fuel and Power. In 1945, he was elected to the House of Commons for the Labour Party. Two years later, at the age of 31, he was appointed as President of the Board of Trade, making him the youngest cabinet member in Britain since 1792. It was clear he was destined for the top. From 1955 to 1961 he served as chancellor in the Shadow Cabinet (a political group in the British government formed by members of the minority party to examine

---

* In the years since his turn in office, Wilson has long been presumed to have been one of the Queen's favourites. The *New Statesman* actually referred to Wilson as 'the working man's Melbourne' (a reference to Victoria's avuncular prime minister of 1837–1841)! When the Postmaster General, Anthony Wedgwood Benn (later recycled as Tony Benn) proposed issuing postage stamps without the Queen's head on them, Wilson vetoed the idea.

the actions of the Cabinet and offer alternatives), then as Shadow Foreign Secretary from 1961 to 1963 before becoming Labour leader and eventually prime minister.

Wilson enjoyed what he referred to as 'relaxed intimacy' with the Queen. Following their first meeting, she took the rare step of inviting him to stay for drinks, and he was reportedly allowed to smoke his famous straight billiard pipe during their audiences too[*]. For Wilson's part, he was enormously proud of his close association with the Queen and even kept a photo of the two of them on his wall.

His wife's increasing confidence in her ability to fulfil her constitutional role and the success and warmth of her close working relationship with her new prime minister, Wilson, meant Philip felt increasingly isolated. Elizabeth no longer always turned to him first for advice; he was no longer her primary adviser. Given her status he always knew this moment would come but it meant he began to feel like a spare part at court. But he refused to wait in line.

Sensing his moment Philip, always a modernist at heart, was ready to seize the reins in trying to breathe new life into the institution of monarchy. By now in his mid-forties, the duke was the first to appreciate just how out of step the monarchy as an institution had begun to appear, particularly in the eyes of the younger generation. His work not only with the Duke of Edinburgh's Award Scheme, but with organisations like London Youth, his first charity patronage in 1947, meant he was perfectly placed to hear feedback on the ground. He started again to examine the outmoded practices of the palace and what he discovered infuriated him. He insisted royalty and staff no longer had their meals cooked in separate kitchens

---

[*] Some claimed Wilson's pipe smoking was affectation and in private he preferred to smoke cigars. Lord Donoughue, who as Bernard Donoughue was a senior aide to Wilson between 1974 and 1976, conceded that he often used the pipe in his hand as a prop to give him more time to think of an answer to a difficult question. 'He didn't smoke it much in private,' he said. 'It was not always lit because he had to put it away in his pocket. If he was being interviewed or questioned, the moment he was asked a difficult question he would take out his lighter and light the pipe to give him time to think of an answer.'

at the palace, saving huge amounts of money and waste. It was only when Philip questioned the custom of servants leaving a new bottle of whisky by the Queen's bed every night that the reason was revealed. Queen Victoria had once asked for Scotch whisky to combat a cold, and the order had never been rescinded.

He felt the situation was serious enough to raise his concerns with the Queen and bluntly warned that unless the monarchy she led took proactive steps to modernise and embrace the age the institution they both served would be vulnerable. While some senior courtiers were vehemently opposed at the time, Philip felt it was essential that the Royal Family was more accessible to the public to help boost their popularity. Philip believed the traditionalist, still wedded to the past, approach was actually doing harm to the institution. Philip was determined that the monarchy benefit from the new vibe for change and set out to reboot the ancient institution so that it appeared more relevant to a less deferential public and remained in step with the societal revolution.

He was open to new ideas, even off the wall ones. With the mass interest in outer space – after Soviet cosmonaut Yuri Gagarin became the first human in space on 12 April 1961, making a 108-minute orbital flight in his Vostok 1 spacecraft – Philip, a keen pilot, became obsessed with the subject. He even started subscribing to the *Flying Saucer Review* saying publicly, 'There are many reasons to believe that they [UFOs] exist.*'

Attempting to modernise the monarchy inevitably came with its own pitfalls, presenting new challenges and dangers. As the sixties

---

* According to biographer Philip Eade he even sent his equerry, Sir (Beresford) Peter Horsley, 'to meet an extraterrestrial humanoid at a house in Ealing.' Eade wrote, 'A number of witnesses were invited to Buckingham Palace to discuss their experiences, as Horsley later explained in a 1997 memoir, to "put them on the spot" and to test their honesty in the presence of royalty, a method as effective as any truth serum.' Horsley was on the prince's staff from 1952 to 1955 before rising to the lofty rank of Air Marshal in the RAF. Lord Mountbatten had similar interests. In a biography by Philip Ziegler in 1985, he wrote that Mountbatten had admittedly odd ideas about the origins of mysterious phenomenon. In 1955 Lord Mountbatten investigated a UFO in the grounds of his Broadlands Estates in Romsey, Hampshire.

swung, age-old rituals such as Trooping the Colour were starting to look tired and outdated and as a result so did the institution itself. Philip sensed the mood, instinctively realising that monarchy and the Royal Family who represented the institution, were beginning to feel separate from a new exciting spirit that was revitalising post-war Britain. He argued unless the monarchy as an institution embraced the change it would be left behind and be regarded as an irrelevance.

Throughout the 1950s Philip had been a lone voice at court. He was the one person at the heart of monarchy who was seen as an innovator alive to new ideas. He wanted the Windsor Dynasty to reflect that modern face. A man of his time, he embraced new technology and set out to identify himself with scientific advancement and industrial achievements. He was fascinated by new gadgets and was the first person in Buckingham Palace to put computers in his office. He more than anyone encouraged the Queen and her advisers to re-engage with a modern Britain in transition. One medium above all presented the royals with that opportunity, television. He saw the advantages of speaking directly to the public, bypassing what he saw as the sneering press who he had by now grown to detest. His loathing for the press was best summed up in comments like, 'You have mosquitoes. I have the press,' as he joked to the matron of a Caribbean hospital in 1966.

Philip's use of television was interpreted as a significant step towards modernising the Royal Family. Philip became the first member of the Royal Family to give an interview on television in a *Panorama* programme broadcast on 29 May 1961. The duke was interviewed by broadcaster Richard Dimbleby, talking about the Commonwealth Technical Training Week. As patron of the initiative, Philip, who was usually only glimpsed on ceremonial occasions as the Queen's consort, emphasised the need to encourage the training of skilled workers for the modern labour force. The interview was on an uncontroversial subject, and Dimbleby's tone was respectful throughout, but it was still remarkable as the first time a member of the Royal Family had been questioned on camera.

Television had overtaken the radio to become the dominant means of mass communication. By 1960, nearly three-quarters of the population had television, and by the end of the sixties, nearly 95 per cent. Television had become a universal habit with the population and he felt failing to embrace it was a mistake. He had urged Elizabeth to deliver her first televised Christmas message, broadcast from Sandringham in 1957 – something that has since become a fixture in many people's Christmas Day celebrations and her own truly personal message to her people.

Philip has always been known for his schoolboy sense of humour. Knowing his wife was racked with nerves ahead of recording her first-ever televised Christmas message in 1957, he decided to act. Courtiers have described the screams of laughter from the monarch when her husband ran up and down the hallways brandishing a pair of false teeth to the delight of her and their children. Philip sent a message to her through the director saying, 'Tell her to remember the wailing and gnashing of teeth.'

Ronald Allison, the Queen's press secretary from 1973 to 1978, said, 'Prince Philip was very much holding her hand through all of this.' His comments were echoed by Christina Aldridge, the daughter of Peter Dimmock CBE, who had produced it for the BBC. Christine said, 'The Queen was rather nervous and Prince Philip would also have known that she was rather nervous, so he stood behind the camera and made encouraging faces, ridiculous faces, which encouraged her to relax and smile.'

If the Royal Family weren't approachable, or at least perceived to be so, why should the people show them respect any longer? The duke believed that the Royal Family could no longer expect the same degree of affection unless they were putting in the hours to earn such devotion. He had been pressing for years for the monarchy to present itself in a more dynamic way to the people to show its importance and worth to the nation and felt the Royal Family had to re-engage with the people or become an irrelevance. One national disaster, and the way that the Queen showed her emotional side in reacting to it, went some way to reconnecting her with her people.

In October 1966 tragedy hit the coal-mining village of Aberfan in South Wales, when a colliery spoil tip located directly above the village slid downhill. The devastating event resulted in the death of 144 people, 116 of whom were children. After the final victim was recovered from the debris, the Queen and Prince Philip travelled to pay their respects to the deceased and their loved ones. It was later reported that waiting eight days to visit was one of the monarch's biggest regrets, but she appeared visibly moved as she walked around the site of the tragedy with her husband. It affected her very deeply and was one of the few occasions where she shed a tear in public.

The Queen had not gone sooner because she thought she would be a distraction and she feared they might miss some poor child who might have been found under the wreckage. 'I think she felt in hindsight that she might have gone there a little earlier. It was a sort of lesson for us that you need to show sympathy and to be there on the spot, which I think people craved from her,' said Sir William Heseltine, who was working in the royal press office at the time of the tragedy, before being elevated to her private secretary. But it was the fact that she had let her guard down, and cried a little, that made the desperate locals and the nation warm to her.

In one television interview in 1968 on *Face the Press* on Tyne Tees Television/ITV, Philip said, 'Instead of having to fend off too close a scrutiny in an attempt to try and live a normal life, it is now possible not to go on the offensive but to try and make contact and try and create a kind of two-way relationship.' Philip, perhaps more quickly than anyone in the Royal Family and Royal Household, had recognised that the royals could not stay hidden away in that metaphorical gilded tower forever and they had to get out and communicate with the public. And, in his view, this was the time to do it.

Senior Buckingham Palace courtiers were by now growing increasingly concerned about an apathy felt towards the institution of monarchy in Australia and New Zealand in particular. After the success of the Queen's first Commonwealth tour – which reached fever pitch on the Australian leg of the trip – many felt the links between Britain and its former colonies were assured. However when the Queen returned to Australia in 1963, nine years later, on a less formal tour than before, the love affair with the royals seemed to have cooled. Outspoken critics said the British government's drive to get closer to its European neighbours in the European Economic Community was at the expense of its old Commonwealth ties. Support for the monarchy had reduced and there were growing calls for Australia and New Zealand to become independent republics. The Queen and her advisers needed to respond.

The Queen was open to suggestions and when Philip saw an opportunity to put his theories to the test he grabbed it with both hands. Lord Mountbatten's son-in-law, Lord Brabourne, was a television producer and in 1968 he asked Philip if he could make a so-called 'fly on the wall' documentary about the Royal Family. Inspired by the idea, Philip championed the project to film inside the palace and show the royals carrying out their everyday lives. He also chaired the committee to explore the idea.

The Queen's more cautious courtiers tried to convince her that the public would lose respect for the Royal Family and monarchy if they saw them as television characters in some kind of soap opera. They advised her that once you invited the cameras in they would be hungry for more. There was a conflict, two visions of monarchy. It boiled down to – stay as you are relying on looking backwards and doing what you've done well in the past, or adapt Philip's vision and change because if you don't you die.

Philip's influence was in the ascendency. By 1968 the Queen Mother was approaching 70 and was no longer the power she was, the old Queen Mary and the traditionalist Churchill were both dead. Lord Brabourne suggested such a film would be a good way of introducing the public to the then 20-year-old Prince Charles, ahead of his investiture as Prince of Wales. The concept behind the documentary was to soften and modernise the royal image. Members of the Royal Family, including the Queen, were reportedly dubious about the idea from the start. But she eventually agreed to support her husband this time, feeling Philip's vision had caught the spirit of a new Britain. Her press secretary, Sir William Heseltine, backed the idea too and felt Philip was right to endorse a new approach to public relations. Cameras were allowed into the palace for the first time, thus letting 'in daylight upon magic' something writer, Walter Bagehot, had warned against when writing about the future of the monarchy during Queen Victoria's reign in his book, *The English Constitution* (1867).

The Mountbatten camp had won the day and filming began in 1968. Richard Cawston, the chief of the BBC Documentary unit, was put in charge of shooting the royals at work and play. For months, he shot 43 hours of unscripted material at Buckingham Palace, Windsor Castle, on the royal yacht, the royal train, and even at the Queen's beloved Balmoral Castle in Scotland. Understandably, the Royal Family had a difficult time adjusting to the presence of the crew in their personal space.

Peter Conradi wrote in his 2012 book, *Great Survivors: How Monarchy Made it into the Twenty-First Century*, that during a film day at Balmoral, Philip snapped at the crew, 'Get away from the Queen with your bloody cameras!' While the documentary was meant to show the human side of the monarchy, its narration carried an official tone. The voice-over, read by English actor and broadcaster Michael Flanders, ruminated on the importance of the crown to the country in an ostentatious manner such as, 'Monarchy does not lie in the power it gives to the sovereign, but in the power it denies to anyone else.'

The finished film, that took 18 months to make, claimed to show a year in the life of the Royal Family. The Queen was featured tirelessly working and making small talk with world leaders like American President Richard Nixon. During his state visit, she is filmed asking him, 'World problems are so complex, aren't they, now?' To which Nixon replied, 'I was thinking how really much more complex they are than when we last met in 1957.' There were also some charming scenes, like one in which the Queen takes her youngest son, Prince Edward, to a sweet shop, paying for his treats herself even though the monarch was thought never to carry cash*.

Philip was pleased with the way his family was portrayed as a genuinely sporty family. Charles was shown waterskiing and fishing, Philip flew an aeroplane and the Queen drove her own car surprisingly fast. But there was a number of awful moments, according to critics. At one point Philip describes an instance when George VI took out his rage with a pruning knife on a rhododendron bush, screaming curse words while hacking it to bits. 'He had very odd habits. Sometimes I thought he was mad.' This did not go down well with the Queen and traditionalists. On another occasion Elizabeth joked, 'How do you keep a regally straight face when a footman tells you: "Your Majesty, your next audience is with a gorilla?" It was an official visitor, but he looked just like a gorilla.' Such casual racism didn't go down well either.

***

Philip was shown a rough cut of the film by Cawston before showing it to the Queen. 'We were all a little bit nervous of showing it to the Queen because we had no idea what she would make of it,' the film's editor Michael Bradsell said to the Smithsonian channel in a 2017 special. 'She was a little critical of the film in the sense she thought it was too long, but Dick Cawston, the director, persuaded her that two hours was not a minute too long.' He was right. A few clips were released before the broadcast but only in black and white. When it finally aired on the BBC it was a major ratings smash with more than 37 million viewers in Britain alone and a PR success too with public support swinging back behind the Royal Family.

'They were criticised for being stuffy, and not letting anybody know what they were doing, and my brother-in-law helped do up a film, and now people say, "Ah, of course, the rot set in when the

---

* Apart from the ironed note she gives after a Sunday church service

film was made,"' royal cousin Lady Pamela Hicks and daughter of Lord Mountbatten said. 'You can't do right; it's catch-22.'

On 21 June 1969 two-thirds of the British population watched history being made on their television sets as the documentary, *Royal Family,* was aired. At the time it was seen as a masterstroke of public relations, showing the people what went on behind palace doors and enabling them to see their queen and her family as they really are. With the benefit of hindsight, since then, many have criticised the project as an act of folly. They said by allowing the cameras to film their private lives, the Royal Family effectively justified the intrusive journalism that followed and the rise of the paparazzi. 'I never liked the idea of *Royal Family.* I thought it was a rotten idea,' said Princess Anne, according to an account in the 2015 book, *Queen Elizabeth II and the Royal Family.* 'The attention which had been brought upon one, ever since one was a child, you just didn't need any more.' On reflection, the Queen and the Royal Family – with the exception of Philip – didn't like the film. The Queen and her advisers felt that being seen as normal rather than being a positive was a dangerous negative. She took the decision that the film should never be shown again. In fact, she did relent on the ruling and it was shown only once more in full, in 1977.

In 2011, Buckingham Palace gave the National Portrait Gallery a 90-second clip of the breakfast scene during the Diamond Jubilee celebration. This footage somehow found its way onto YouTube where it has been viewed more than 500,000 times. Buckingham Palace allowed a few more brief clips to be included in the 2011 documentary, *The Duke at 90,* too. In January 2021 the full 90-minute documentary, which had Crown copyright, was leaked to the public and uploaded to YouTube after being kept out of sight in the BBC archives for years. In 1972, Buckingham Palace reportedly ordered the fly-on-the-wall film to be locked away and it has never been seen in full since, until it appeared on the internet out of the blue. The BBC swiftly sought to have it removed from the web and it was taken offline citing breach of copyright, but the corporation refused to comment further.

Prince Philip's drive to modernise the institution of monarchy was bold and essential. Under the Queen's stewardship the institution was in danger of becoming irrelevant, and drifting too far from the people it is supposed to serve. The *Royal Family* documentary film is the embodiment of Philip's influence. Perhaps, however, there was one thing that he didn't foresee.

Publicity is, after all, a double-edged sword. Philip didn't expect Fleet Street newspaper editors to believe what amounted to a sugar-coated advertisement for the institution without wanting to know more. It was the start of the royal media industry, with an inquisitive press feeling they now had a right to pry further and criticise the Royal Family as they had already invaded their own privacy. From the moment the film was aired publicly the royals became fair game for the tabloids, in a way they had never been before.

Another comment made by the duke in the same year, 1969, attracted even more newspaper column inches and even a political backlash too. The monarchy's detractors felt there was a secret scheme behind Buckingham Palace's sudden interest in raising the public profile of the Queen and her immediate family; the need for more cash.

During an official tour of North America, Prince Philip delivered an example of his 'dontopedalogy', putting his foot in his mouth, by apparently unwittingly shining a public spotlight on a subject both the palace and Wilson's Labour government would have wanted to remain in the dark, the mystery of royal finances. In an interview on NBC's *Meet the Press* Philip announced that the monarchy was broke or about to be so: 'We go into the red next year, now, inevitably if nothing happens we shall have to – I don't know, we may have to move into smaller premises. For instance, we had a small yacht which we had to sell, and I shall have to give up polo fairly soon.'

What Prince Philip said was essentially correct, but his comments caused uproar in the media and among the wider public. Negative headlines followed from a cynical Fleet Street, whose commentators said Philip had let down his country. After all, a rich and privileged man complaining about having to give up an expensive hobby such as playing polo was not well received with the general public. A group of dockers in a pub in Bermondsey, London penned a sarcastic letter in which they offered to club together to buy the duke a polo pony. Barbara Castle, First Secretary of State and Secretary of State for Employment and Productivity in Wilson's Cabinet, and the Labour Party's so-called 'Red Queen', pointed out to the Prime Minister, Harold Wilson, that there was a widespread lack of sympathy from the public for Philip's cries of poverty, especially when the comments were made by the husband of, 'One of the richest women in the world.' She had a point.

15: SONS AND DAUGHTER

'We grew up singing on the way to and from barbecues.'

Princess Anne on her childhood

A week after the *Royal Family* documentary had aired the public were served another television first. On 1 July 1969 a UK audience of 19 million, just short of a third of the country, tuned in to watch as the Queen installed her 20-year-old son, Prince Charles, as the Prince of Wales at Caernarfon Castle, the medieval fortress in Gwynedd, north-west Wales at the mouth of the River Seiont. Philip, the proud father, watched from his vantage point among the 4,000 VIP guests as Prince Charles swore to be the Queen's 'liege man of life and limb' during the colourful ceremony, just as the duke had done at his wife's coronation 16 years earlier.

Charles had in fact been made the Prince of Wales when he was nine years old when his mother had issued the Letters Patent, published on 26 July 1958. At the time she said an investiture would be held when she felt her eldest son would fully appreciate its significance. The prince was invested with the Insignia of his Principality and the Earldom of Chester: a sword, coronet, mantle, gold ring and gold rod. The footage shows that the prince was a little awkward, perhaps overawed by the spectacle, with him centre stage. He acquitted himself manfully as he gave his formal response. 'I, Charles, Prince of Wales, do become your liege man of life and limb and of earthly worship and faith and truth I will bear unto you to live and die against all manner of folks.'

The event, again with Philip pulling the strings behind the scenes, had been a carefully choreographed spectacle brilliantly arranged by Lord Snowdon, Princess Margaret's husband. With a colourful mix of old and new, the investiture was modelled on the previous one arranged for Prince Charles's great-uncle, David (later King Edward VIII and Duke of Windsor), again at Caernarfon Castle, on the 13 July 1911, when he too was sworn in as the Prince of Wales. Lord Snowdon, however, ensured that this time there would be more than a nod to the epoch and towards the future.

On the eve of the ceremony Charles boarded the Royal Train, used to convey senior members of the British Royal Family, along with his parents, bound for North Wales. All three of them knew that this pageant had to win over the public and were hoping for a positive response from the people. They had no choice but to trust in the stringent security already put in place by the police and the army. Welsh nationalist fanatics had formed what they called the Free Wales Army and their actions had put them on the radar of the British security service, MI5. A wake-up call came when an RAF warrant officer was seriously injured in an incident they had planned. A few days later the same gang planted a bomb that destroyed the Temple of Peace in Cardiff. Another bomb was found in the lost-luggage department of the railway station. Trying to maximise publicity, police received word anonymously that Prince Charles had been placed on their target list. It left the 20-year-old heir to the throne understandably uneasy about the investiture ceremony.

After completing four terms at Trinity College, Cambridge, Prince Philip believed it was important that Charles be sent to study at the University College of Wales in Aberystwyth in order to master the Welsh language ahead of his investiture. Charles had excelled at Trinity College, gaining an upper second class in his Part One examinations in 1968, and was enjoying his academic life. He joked, 'The tables will now be turned and I will be envisaged as a princely swot!' The switch of colleges was a political decision rather than simply a cultural one. Philip felt that if his son completed a period of academic study in Welsh it might help quell the surge in the revival of nationalism in Scotland and Wales.

Just before his departure to the Welsh college, Prince Charles recorded his first-ever radio interview for the BBC Radio 4 *Today* show on 1 March 1969. The interviewer, Jack de Manio, talked about the prince's student theatrics as part of the 'Revolution' revue at Cambridge and Charles also did his impressive *Goon Show* impersonation, but he was also asked about his attitude towards the apparent hostility towards him in Wales. He answered frankly, saying, 'It would be unnatural, I think, if one didn't feel any apprehension about it. One always wonders what's going to happen. As long as I don't get covered in too much egg and tomato I'll be all right. But I don't blame people demonstrating like that. They've never seen me before. They don't know what I'm like. I've hardly been to Wales, and you can't really expect people to be overzealous about the fact of having a so-called English prince to come amongst them.'

Prince Philip insisted that Charles's stint in Wales must go ahead regardless, as to cancel the university term in Wales would have been a public-relations disaster for both the government and for the prince himself. The Queen and prime minister, Harold Wilson, agreed with Philip, and felt to pull Charles out would be perceived as weakness and worse be seen as bowing to extremist terrorist threats.

Upon his arrival at Pantycelyn Hall, where he would share accommodation with 250 other students, Charles was met by a 500-strong cheering crowd, that left him 'deeply touched'. In fact, the students were not at all antagonistic towards him and embraced him as one of their own. In the end Charles thoroughly enjoyed his time at the university and acknowledged later that he was treated very kindly in Aberystwyth. Charles wrote to a friend, 'If I have learned anything during the last eight weeks, it's been about Wales. They feel so strongly about Wales as a nation, and it means something to them, and they are depressed by what might happen to it if they don't try and preserve the language and the culture, which is unique and special to Wales, and if something is unique and special, I see it as well worth preserving."*

★★★

More bomb threats came within days of his instalment as the Prince of Wales. Charles was driven through Cardiff in an open carriage on his way to the castle past cheering crowds. As the guests and choir sang 'God Bless the Prince of Wales', he was conducted to the dais and knelt before the Queen wearing a robe by royal warrant holders Ede & Ravenscroft whose skilled tailors had crafted it from hand-woven purple velvet lined with ermine, and finished it with an ermine cape and collar fully lined with white silk, similar to the robe made for the previous Prince of Wales, including original solid gold clasps.

He would later write that he found it profoundly moving when he placed his hands between his mother's and spoke the oath of allegiance. The Queen then presented the prince to the crowd at Eagle Gate and at the lower ward to the sound of magnificent fanfares. After that he was again paraded through the streets before retiring aboard the royal yacht at Holyhead for a well-deserved dinner, an emotionally exhausted but very happy prince. Buoyed by the experience, the prince noted, 'As long as I do not take myself too seriously I should not be too badly off.'

The next day the newly installed Prince of Wales set off alone to undertake a week of solo engagements around the principality. He recalled being 'utterly amazed' by the positive reaction he received. As the tour progressed into England, the crowds grew even bigger. At the end of it, Charles arrived exhausted but elated at Windsor Castle. He retired to write up his diary, noting the silence after the day's cheers and applause, reflecting that he had much to live up to and expressing the hope that he could provide constructive help

---

* Years later he said the time he spent studying there had left him with his fondest memories of the time he spent in the principality. He recalled with pleasure the 'memorable times spent exploring mid-Wales during my term at Aberystwyth University' where he learned 'something about the principality and its ancient language, folklore, myths and history'.

for Wales. If the young man was looking for praise from his mother and father he would be disappointed. That was not their style. Philip didn't like being praised and wasn't one for giving it either.

Charles's sensitive nature as a child did not exactly sit well with his alpha male father. Worried his son would be seen as weak and vulnerable, Philip deliberately set about attempting to toughen him up, an attitude that undoubtedly may be frowned upon today. He believed and practised so-called 'Authoritarian Parenting'. They have many rules and very high standards. Many of these rules are in place to exert control over a child's behaviour or activities, and children are expected to follow these rules from a young age. Such parents seldom show warmth towards their children. This is how Charles grew to see his father.

But in his defence Philip was concerned by signs that Charles, aware of his status, was being overindulged by those around him, not least the Queen Mother. He felt it was his fatherly duty to introduce some 'tough love' to counteract the spoiling. The duke is also said to have made personal remarks and relied on sarcasm when dealing with Charles. When Charles would sit with his parents during teatime, it wasn't exactly quality happy family time. 'Somehow even those contacts were lacking in warmth,' Martin Charteris, the Queen's former adviser, explained. He added, 'The Queen is not good at showing affection either.' They simply weren't a touchy feely family. There were lighter moments with his mother but they backfired. When Charles was four years old, the Queen did set out to teach her son horseback riding, but unfortunately Charles, he said, found the whole idea of taking off scared him stiff.

Philip's no-nonsense approach to life extended to his choice of school for his son. The duke seemed to be of the attitude, 'What is good enough for me, is good enough for him.' But he seemed to totally disregard Charles's character and sensitivities. The two were like chalk and cheese. The boisterous Philip excelled at sports and outdoors endeavours as a child while Charles, although still an accomplished sportsman, was more reserved and sensitive as a boy who preferred the comfort of his nanny's company. While the structure of royal life meant it wasn't unusual for the children and the duke to live fairly separate existences, the decisions Philip made over Charles's education contributed to their relationship remaining stilted from adolescence into adulthood. They undoubtedly loved one another, but just did not show it openly.

Philip showed his love for his son through action. His determination that Charles went to these hardy boarding schools, rather than Eton College, has since been deemed an error of judgement by some, including the Queen, the late Queen Mother and even Charles himself. In Jonathan Dimbleby's excellent authorised biography of Charles*, the duke is quoted saying, 'Children may be indulged at home, but school is expected to be a spartan and disciplined experience in the process of developing into self-controlled, considerate and independent adults.' This was a bad mistake.

***

It seems strange to say, give her status as monarch, but Elizabeth was powerless to intervene over her son's education for fear of upsetting the family dynamic. For after her ascension the Queen made it clear that she would defer to her husband over their children's education. Philip, blinded by his desire for his son to mirror his boisterous and robust nature, missed Charles's other attributes and selected the wrong school for him. He failed to recognise that Charles's character meant he would not flourish at a school like Philip's alma mater Gordonstoun where the duke had been in his element. Later in life Charles described his time at Gordonstoun, where he was mercilessly bullied by his peers, as 'hell on earth' – he viewed it as an incarceration.

Eton College, where the Queen Mother wanted him to go, would have been a far better choice for his character. The Queen Mother, who viewed Charles as her favourite grandchild, tried to sway his parents' choice of schooling because she rightly predicted attending Gordonstoun would bring him misery.

---

* *The Prince of Wales, A Biography*, Little, Brown and Company, 1994

Previously unpublished letters written to her daughter reveal that the old queen pleaded for the sensitive Charles not to be sent to Gordonstoun, the remote Scottish boarding school he hated and later described as 'Colditz in kilts'. 'I have been thinking such a lot about Charles,' she wrote in a missive dated 23 May 1961 and addressed to 'My Darling Lilibet'.

'I suppose that he will be taking his entrance exam for Eton soon. I do hope he passes because it might be the ideal school for one of his character and temperament. However good Gordonstoun is, it is miles and miles away and he might as well be at school abroad.' She added, 'All your friends' sons are at Eton and it is so important to be able to grow up with people you will be with later in life. And so nice and so important when boys are growing up that you and Philip can see him during school days and keep in touch with what is happening. He would be terribly cut off and lonely in the far north. I do hope you don't mind my writing my thoughts on this subject, but I have been thinking and worrying about it all (possibly without cause).'

The Queen Mother knew she had cause, but Prince Philip was adamant that his firstborn would attend his own alma mater. The duke was adamant that Eton College was far too close to Windsor and the prince would be 'harassed by the media'* there.

Elizabeth and Philip saw their children only after breakfast and after teatime. This certainly doesn't sound good, but it doesn't mean that they were dreadful people. 'She had been brought up in that style herself,' author Robert Lacey, the historical adviser for Netflix's *The Crown*, and author of *The Crown: The Inside History*, explained to *Town & Country*, referring to the formality of the parent/child relationship and the relative lack of daily contact she and Philip had with their two older children in particular.

---

* William Shawcross reproduced the correspondence in his book *Counting One's Blessings*.

He further added that the Queen thought it best to have nannies raise her children while she was travelling, rather than bring them along. In contrast, the Queen Mother knew how to nurture him. I think the key to their relationship is that she saw in him the same sort of insecurity she saw in her husband George VI. In other words, she knew Charles needed to be given a lot of support and to be bolstered emotionally, which is what she did very well, rather better than his parents.

Charles took every opportunity to escape Gordonstoun and visit the Queen Mother at her Scottish home, Birkhall. Once there, in his book *Charles: A Biography* Anthony Holden says, 'The Queen Mother listened to Charles's plaintive outpourings about his loneliness, his homesickness, the impossibility of blending into school like other boys.' 'She provided a much-needed shoulder to cry on,' respected royal writer and the Queen Mother's biographer Hugo Vickers wrote in *Elizabeth: The Queen Mother.* 'You must remember that, when the Queen was away on her tour of the Commonwealth, from November 1953 until May 1954, the Queen Mother was really Prince Charles and Princess Anne's guardian. They were very young then and they would share weekends at Royal Lodge in Windsor Great Park, and they spent a long Christmas holiday together at Sandringham. I think it was then that Charles in particular bonded with his grandmother.'

They had a completely mutual adoration. Their sense of humour was the same, they enjoyed the same activities and the Queen Mother instilled a love of culture in him, taking him to the ballet when he was very young and walking him through the corridors of Windsor Castle explaining all the paintings. Until her death she kept a boyhood photo of Charles on her desk and her letters about him radiate affection. 'Charles is a great love of mine. He is such a darling,' she says in one, later telling the Queen, 'He is intensely affectionate. I'm sure that he will always be a very loving and enjoyable child.'

Her personal letters to the prince are perhaps the most doting. She is thrilled when he sends her flowers after an appendix operation in 1964, saying, 'My darling Charles, I can't tell you how touched and delighted I was.' He in return tried to make light of his misery. Even when down he would joke about the masters and teachers and his own inadequacies. On his attempt to learn the trumpet he recalled, 'I can hear the music teacher now… she would put down her violin and we would all stop and she would shout, she had a heavy German accent and somehow that made her more agonised, "Ach! Zoze trumpets! Ach! Zoze trumpets! Stawp zoze trumpets!" So I gave up my trumpet.'

Mostly his memories of the place filled him with dread. 'I hate coming back here and leaving everyone at home… I hardly get any sleep at the House because I snore and get hit on the head the whole time. It is absolute hell,' he noted about boarding at Gordonstoun, in a private letter of 9 February 1963. One incident to this day irritates him, by the severity and unfairness of its consequences. It is the so-called 'Cherry Brandy incident'*. When Charles arrived, his housemaster warned the other boys that to be caught bullying the heir to the throne would risk expulsion. This had, unsurprisingly, the opposite effect. Charles was picked on at once, 'maliciously, cruelly and without respite'. A prince, let alone an insecure prince, would have found it hard enough to befriend his peers. 'Even to open a conversation with the heir to the throne was to court humiliation, to face the charge of "sucking up" and to hear the collective "slurping" noises that denoted a toady and a sycophant,' Dimbleby observed in his book *The Prince of Wales*.

The prince took this thuggery on the chin, without complaint. He was far too proud to let it show. But privately he was miserable, and hated returning. Charles wrote in a letter home in 1963, describing the tough time he was having, 'The people in my

---

* On a sailing trip to the Isle of Lewis, a cinema visit to see a Jayne Mansfield film had to be diverted to the local pub because of excessive public attention. Never having entered licensed premises before, Charles was startled to be asked by a barman what he would have. The choice of a cherry brandy — he was 14 — brought the world down around his ears because also in the bar was a freelance journalist who transmitted this innocent fact to the waiting world.

Prince Philip of Greece and Denmark aged five. He was born in Mon Repos on the Greek island of Corfu on 10 June 1921.

Prince Philip of Greece and Denmark was a star pupil at Gordonstoun School. He is pictured checking the spikes of his running shoes before taking part in an inter-schools sports day in Edinburgh, Scotland in 1935.

Buckingham Palace announced the engagement of Princess Elizabeth and Lieutenant Philip Mountbatten RN in July 1947, when the couple were 21 and 26, respectively.

Princess Elizabeth and the newly ennobled Philip, Duke of Edinburgh wave to the crowds from the Buckingham Palace balcony on their wedding day, 20 November 1947. They are pictured with King George VI, Princess Margaret, Queen Elizabeth (later Queen Mother) and Queen Mary.

Picture Credit: Keystone Press/Alamy Stock Photo

Family guy. Prince Philip and the Queen pictured with their four children
Prince Charles, 17, Princess Anne, 15, Prince Andrew, 5, and Prince Edward, 1 in 1965.

Picture Credit: Arthur J. Edwards MBE/Shutterstock

Charles, Prince of Wales, Admiral of the Fleet, Louis Mountbatten, 1st Earl Mountbatten
of Burma, and Prince Philip, Duke of Edinburgh at a polo match in 1977. Lord Louis, who
was murdered by the IRA on 27 August 1979, was a beloved mentor to both
Charles and Philip.

Picture Credit Arthur J. Edwards MBE

The Duke of Edinburgh took up the sport of carriage driving after quitting polo at the age of 50. He went on to become an international class carriage driver and in the 1982 World Championships in Holland Prince Philip finished sixth overall out of 39 entries.

Picture Credit Arthur J. Edwards MBE

Prince Philip pictured in May 1995 as he opened a new £25million Warner Stand at Lord's cricket ground wearing his gold MCC tie. The Duke joked that people were about to 'see the world's most experienced plaque-unvieler.'

Picture Credit Arthur J. Edwards MBE

Ever the gentleman, Prince Philip supports the Queen's arm as she alights her carriage in Islamabad, during the State visit to Pakistan in 1997.

Picture Credit: George Edmondson/Jobson Media

The Queen at the opening of one of the UK's biggest veterans' housing projects in October 2019, at Haig Housing Trust's estate in Morden. She described Prince Philip as her 'strength and stay' at a banquet to mark their Golden wedding anniversary in November 1997.

Picture Credit Arthur J. Edwards MBE

The Duke of Edinburgh meets the Manchester 2002 Commonwealth Games Mascot.

Picture Credit Arthur J. Edwards MBE

The Queen and Prince Philip join U.S. President George W. Bush and the First Lady Laura Bush at the White House in Washington D.C. on 7 May 2007 for a state visit to mark the 400th Anniversary of the Jamestown settlement. The other state visits to the USA were, in October 1957 (President Eisenhower), in July 1976 for the US Bicentennial (President Ford), and in May 1991 (President Bush). They also made an official visit to the West Coast of America in February/March 1983.

Picture Credit Arthur J. Edwards MBE

Always a joker, Prince Philip always seemed to be able to make the Queen smile at formal occasions, as they left the traditional Maundy service at York Minster in April 2012.

Picture Credit Arthur J. Edwards MBE

Prince Philip, Duke of Edinburgh, at Epsom racecourse on 1 June 2013 for the Derby Festival. The Queen is one of Britain's biggest thoroughbred owners and breeders and her interest in the turf is legendary. Philip does not share her interest in the sport and often used to go to the back of the box and work quietly on his papers.

Prince Philip enjoys a close relationship with his grandchildren. He is pictured at the Epsom Derby race meeting in the Royal Box chatting with Princess Eugenie of York in 2013.

The Queen and Prince Philip smiling at the crowds as they drive though Windsor, standing in an open top car to mark Her Majesty's 90th birthday in 2016.

The Duke and Duchess of Cambridge pictured during a walkabout in Stockholm, Sweden in January 2018. They have embraced the role of future King and Queen.

The Duke and Duchess of Sussex were all smiles for the cameras on their final Royal tour to Nyanga township near Cape Town, South Africa in September 2019 prior to their decision to quit the royal family and the crisis talks at Sandringham.

Picture Credit: Arthur J. Edwards MBE

At 99, the Duke of Edinburgh made a rare public appearance for the short ceremony in the Windsor Castle quadrangle on 22 July 2020. The Assistant Colonel Commandant, Major General Tom Copinger-Symes (pictured), gave the salute, telling him: 'All Riflemen, whether serving or retired would like to thank you for 67 years of continuous service, support and leadership to the Rifles and to our forming and antecedent regiments.'

Picture Credit: Arthur J. Edwards MBE

Prince Philip smiles as he emerges into the sunlight of the Windsor Castle quadrangle after he had been living in COVID lockdown isolation with the Queen, 22 July 2020. He was handing over his role as Colonel-in-Chief of The Rifles to his daughter-in-law, the Duchess of Cornwall.

dormitory are foul. Goodness, they are horrid. I don't know how anybody could be so foul.' To be sent to one of the toughest schools in Britain was a ghastly mistake.

'A prison sentence,' was how Charles later described it. It was 'like penal servitude,' agreed William Boyd, the bestselling novelist and screenwriter and a Gordonstoun contemporary of Charles. 'I happen to know, from his own lips, that Prince Charles utterly detested it.' 'He was bullied,' recalled Ross Benson, the late *Daily Mail* correspondent, who was also a contemporary. 'He was crushingly lonely for most of his time there. The wonder is that he survived with his sanity intact.'

The prince was not entirely abandoned. Two cousins, Norton Knatchbull (now 3rd Earl Mountbatten and estranged husband of Philip's close friend Penny) and Prince Welf of Hanover*, were sent there ahead of Charles's arrival to help smooth the way for the future king. But their presence did little to shield Charles from the misery that lay ahead – for in preparation for the 13-year-old prince's arrival, a new set of rules had been hurriedly imposed on the previously libertarian school's regime.

Smoking was suddenly a caning offence where formerly there had been no corporal punishment. Drinking, while not previously condoned, now carried the threat of expulsion. The changes had nothing whatsoever to do with the prince, but Charles was blamed for their imposition – and he was to pay a heavy price. For the school was filled with toughs. 'Had their parents not been rich enough to pay the fees – a third higher than those at Eton – these pupils would probably have ended their educational careers in prison rather than at a public school,' reflected Benson.

His father did not see it. So Charles struggled dutifully on, head held high and said nothing. To be fair the Duke of Edinburgh had had a happy time at the school in the 1930s and admonished his son in letters urging him to be more resourceful. 'This did not

---

* Prince Welf of Hanover, first cousin and friend of Prince Charles at Gordonstoun, died early, aged 33, in January 1981 from a cerebral hemorrhage.

help.* As Charles grew older, and his peers became more mature, his school environment began to improve. His school life was still not to his liking, but nor was it all hell.

At 17, Charles was given a break from the numbing Scottish regimen with two terms at the Australian outback school, Timbertop. It helped him grow as a person. 'I took him out there a boy,' said his acting equerry, David Checketts, 'and brought back a man.' Charles's return to Gordonstoun was triumphant, first being appointed head of house, then Guardian (head boy) of the school. 'In many ways,' summed up Ross Benson. 'Charles was worthy of that responsibility placed upon him. He was honest, honourable and hardworking. If his judgement was sometimes flawed, he erred only on the side of compassion. Along the way, however, he had to acquire a hard veneer of self-absorption to protect the vulnerability that had been such a mark of his young character – but was now, forever, lost from sight.'

In a BBC interview in the 2002 four-part series *Queen & Country*, the Princess Royal hit back at her elder brother's apparent criticism of Philip and the Queen and their lack of parenting skills. Some commentator had gone so far as to suggest that Elizabeth had been an 'uncaring mother'. The princess insisted that the Royal Family was essentially a happy one**.

Instead of aligning herself with Charles – whose biographer Jonathan Dimbleby, in his 1994 book about the Prince of Wales, was told by the prince that the Queen spent only an hour and a half a day with him when he was a child and suggested that she lacked warmth – Anne defended their mother as a loving parent. She disagreed with

---

* Jonathan Dimbleby wrote in his authorised biography of Charles.

** In 2002 in a controversial examination of Her Majesty by the respected writer Graham Turner in the *Daily Telegraph* the Queen was portrayed as a distant mother who failed to provide her children with firm guidance. An unnamed private secretary was quoted as saying that the Royal Family would have been in a far better state had the Queen 'taken half as much trouble about the rearing of her children as she has about the breeding of her horses'. Turner also quoted the former Dean of Windsor, Michael Mann, who recalled how Anne herself came to see him before her second marriage and complained that she had been unable to talk to her mother about it.

Charles's recollections that he felt 'emotionally estranged' from his parents and all his life had yearned for a different kind of affection that they'd been 'unable or unwilling to offer'. He is quoted as saying that the people who raised him were not his parents, but 'inevitably the nursery staff.' In her 2005 book, *The Firm*, Penny Junor went further saying that Philip did not show much affection towards his son. Ms Junor wrote: 'The Duke of Edinburgh was and is a bully, and was sparing in his affection.' She claimed Philip was 'rough' with his son and 'frequently reduced the boy to tears' causing 'irretrievable damage' to the father/son relationship.

Of course he always had the unwavering love and support of his grandmother, the Queen Mother, who doted on him. She wrote many loving letters to her 'Darling Charles' from his birth and throughout his adulthood. One, sent on 11 May 1969 from HMY *Britannia* shows her deep feeling for him.

'My Darling Charles
… Everyone loves you, & is proud of you, and I absolutely know that you will be able to do wonderful things for this country, not only in leadership, but by being your own kind hearted, loving and intelligent & funny self!
Lots of love darling Charles from your very devoted Granny'

Princess Anne, always close to Philip, didn't get drawn into the 'parenting' controversy but painted a very different picture of her mother and father. 'Judging by some families,' she said, 'I think we are all on pretty good speaking terms after all this time, and that's no mean achievement for quite a lot of families. I think we all enjoy each other's company,' she said. Dubbing the Royal Family a 'happy unit' in which they all got along, she explained that, as children, she and Charles may not have been too demanding of their mother's time because they recognised 'her (Elizabeth's) unique position as, you know, ruler of the country and all.' They may have been just young children, but, according to Anne, they seemed to have a pretty good idea of what the monarchy entailed – including travel.

She added, 'I don't believe any of us for a second thought she didn't care for us in exactly the same way as any other mother did.'

By the mid-1960s being Queen may not have exactly been old hat, but Elizabeth had become more comfortable in her role and what it entailed. She had learned to manage her time and to ensure she left space for family too. Unlike the awkward meals she once shared with Charles when he was a boy, Elizabeth spent time cycling and chasing her two younger children through the palace and even along the long corridors. Once a week, Edward and Andrew's nanny was given the night off and Elizabeth would take over; that never happened when Charles and Anne were small.

The Queen began to refer to Mabel's night off as her favourite night of the week. She enjoyed putting the boys to bed and even 'happily got up in the night' when they would awake and need soothing before falling back to sleep. She was certainly a more hands-on parent than she was the first time around. Sadly, though, there is no rewind and do it over again when it comes to raising children.

When pressed Philip clearly didn't want to get drawn on the subject of his parenting. Lady Georgina Kennard (d. 28 April 2011), a distant cousin of the Queen and one of her oldest friends, had already jumped to both Elizabeth and Philip's defence at the time. They were hurt by the way Charles aired his feelings publicly. All that Philip would say on the record was that they did the best they could as parents. Lady Kennard went further and, recorded in the Dimbleby biography, said their best wasn't so bad. Philip, she insisted, was a 'wonderful parent. He played with his children, he read them stories, he took them fishing, he was very involved.'

Anne was close to her father. After she was born, he allegedly told everyone, 'It's the sweetest girl.' He encouraged her boisterous behaviour as a youngster, which might explain her strong and opinionated personality. She was much more a chip off his old block than his more sensitive son. Like the Queen Philip had more time for his younger sons, Andrew, Duke of York and Edward, Earl of Wessex and developed close and loving relationships with them. Philip admired Andrew's 'macho action-man image' but the duke has not held back from criticising his son's apparent transgressions and was furious at the way Andrew had allowed the Royal Family to be tainted by the sordid Epstein affair*.

Philip and Prince Edward, his youngest child, always shared a unique bond. Before giving birth to Edward, the Queen spent some time perusing women's magazines and read of the advantages of fathers being present for the birth of their children. Philip agreed and held her hand as Edward was born on 10 March 1964 and in doing so became the first royal father in modern history to be present for the birth of his baby. Typically, he lightened the mood in the delivery room (a bathroom at Buckingham Palace) saying: 'Only a week ago, General de Gaulle was having a bath in this room.' The Queen was thrilled to be a mother for the fourth time. 'What fun it is to have a baby in the house again,' she is reported as saying. Philip and Elizabeth were able to spend a lot more time with their younger children, Andrew and Edward, than they had been able to with both Charles and Anne at the outset of her long reign. With the large age gap it was almost as if they had a new young family.

Edward's quiet nature and that of his wife Sophie, whom he wed at St George's Chapel, Windsor on 19 June 1999 when they became the Earl and Countess of Wessex, proved invaluable to both the Queen and Philip in their latter years. He admired Edward's quiet resilience, as an efficient figure who just got on with his projects not seeking attention or praise from newspaper headlines. Edward's portrait was the only one in his father's study and he is expected to inherit his father's title. Technically, the title of Duke of Edinburgh would be

---

* Prince Andrew was ordered to move his private office from Buckingham Palace in 2019 amid continuing fallout over his former friendship with the deceased sex offender Jeffrey Epstein. The Queen authorised his eviction and forced him to quit royal duties. Billionaire Epstein died in jail from what authorities ruled a suicide while awaiting child sex trafficking charges in New York.

returned to the crown after Philip's death, but senior sources have confirmed the title is intended for Prince Edward. Never personally ambitious, Edward took on the lead role in the Duke of Edinburgh's Awards on his father's retirement. As time passes he will take on even more of the roles once held by Prince Philip.

Sophie formed a close relationship with her mother-in-law too, addressing her affectionately as 'Mama'. In 2015 the Queen hosted a reception to celebrate the patronages and affiliations of the Earl and Countess at Buckingham Palace – a pretty special honour for the pair.

Whether the Queen ever made much effort to temper her husband's behaviour with Charles is doubtful: she is a woman who believes firmly in letting a man be head of the family. During holidays – Christmas and the New Year at Sandringham, Easter at Windsor and most of the summer holidays at Balmoral – the whole family would play football, with the diminutive Queen acting as goalkeeper. 'Nothing has the same meaning and soul-refreshing quality that Balmoral can provide,' Charles noted after returning to Cambridge University for his final year in 1969. He wasn't always a devoted student. He preferred the outdoors to musty old libraries. 'Any excuse to escape from Cambridge and plod across ploughed fields instead of stagnating in lecture rooms is enormously welcome,' he noted after he went shooting while at university in January 1969.

There would also be endless picnics. 'We grew up singing on the way to and from barbecues,' recalled Anne*. 'Mostly First World War songs – we have quite a repertoire of those.' The Queen was always a very competent singer. 'I think we were very lucky as a family to be able to do so much together. We all appreciated that time.' Charles, perhaps, had a different perception that allowed the negative to outweigh the positive.

But negative stories still persist despite Anne's positive spin. Respected *Daily Telegraph* writer Graham Turner, who spent 18

---

* From Ingrid Seward's book *My Husband and I: The Inside Story of 70 Years of the Royal Marriage*

months compiling a unique biography with the help of senior palace courtiers past and present, revealed in 2002 that one former senior aide told him that Elizabeth and Philip were deeply upset with the way they treated Charles in particular. They discussed the 'desperation they felt about their relationship with their children.' Elizabeth implored her husband, 'Where did we go wrong?' and 'What can I do now?' Of course they are the kind of questions that just about break your heart into pieces. Turner claimed boldly that the Queen still feels 'the most tremendous guilt' over the fact that her work, though no fault of her own, so often took her away from her firstborn children.

When another retired but unnamed courtier was asked by Turner to give his opinion on the Queen's role as a mother, he replied in earnest, 'Utterly, utterly lacking, I'm afraid.' To make matters worse, the Queen's perceived failure as a parent has also called her rulership into question. By not showing Charles the royal ropes, the courtier thinks she even 'made the future of the monarchy less secure.' Those are heavy charges, for sure.

Years later during an interview with Alan Titchmarsh for an ITV documentary to mark the duke's 90th birthday in 2017, Philip was very defensive when asked about his parenting.

'I spoke to Princess Royal last week and she tells me you're the best reader of bedtime stories,' enthused Titchmarsh, trying to engage him.

'What?' Philip gasped. 'I don't remember it.'

Titchmarsh replied, 'How important was fatherhood compared with being the Queen's consort? Was that a role you were conscious of fulfilling?'

'No, I was a father,' Philip snapped back. 'Are you a father? Well, do *you* think about it?'

16: IN FOR THE KILL

'We are not going to be able to survive on this limited planet if the population keeps on growing there isn't going to be anything left.'

Perched precariously on the top of an elephant, seated in a howdah and armed with double barrel .458 Winchester magnum calibre rifles, made by the English firm Holland and Holland, the hunting party went in for the kill. It took just a single 'kill shot' from Philip's gun to slay the desperate beast. Moments later, the Queen, and her husband stood beside the body of the slain tiger in the Ranthambore National Park, Rajasthan, India for what was for them an awkward group photograph with their proud hosts, the Maharaja and Maharani of Jaipur, Sawai Man Singh II and Gayatri Devi. Their friends' extended family squeezed into the shot too, clearly thrilled to be standing alongside the VIP British guests and the dead trophy tiger.

In the past those who organised tiger hunts legitimised them by highlighting the threat posed by the beasts in India, when they regularly terrorised villages, leading to entire districts having to be evacuated, as the beasts killed hundreds of people every year. Just a sighting of a tiger could completely stop work on a public road for weeks. The distribution of the mail, at the height of the British Raj in the 1920s when more than 100,000 wild tigers lived in Asia, would be suspended due to tiger activities. By 26 January 1961, however, the time of the royal visit, the attitude to such pursuits had changed dramatically. Tiger hunts, in the new India, led by its first prime minister, Jawaharlal Nehru, were viewed as a cruel indulgence for the elite from a bygone age. Indeed, Nehru rejected Buckingham Palace's request for a live calf to be used as bait during the tiger hunt, but he did not veto it taking place. Killing a calf was deemed more morally and, possibly, politically reprehensible than shooting tigers for sport, even by a statesman as perspicacious as Nehru*.

Despite the tiger still being seen as a menace in India at the time, it was also a very desirable trophy in the early 1960s. But times had changed and angry protests were voiced in both the British and Indian press and politicians attacked the Duke of Edinburgh for accepting the Maharaja's invitation, which the prince described as an 'honour'. On the same excursion Philip killed a crocodile as well as six mountain sheep. For this shoot buffalo was used as bait and the Maharajah, now the titular ruler of the princely state, had been very clear about the main purpose of the visit, for Philip to kill a tiger.

A colourful character, who had ruled the region from 1922 to 1949 when it was acceded to the Dominion of India, the Maharaja had three wives at the same time and also enjoyed a brief romance with married Lady Ursula Manners, an English socialite who served as a maid of honour to the Queen at the coronation of George VI and Queen Elizabeth in 1937. He was not accustomed to his offers of hospitality being refused. Philip, like the tiger he was destined to kill, was cornered.

At this time Philip was behind the scenes quietly in the process of establishing the World Wildlife Fund, which would be announced in a media fanfare when founded four months later. The Queen, the duke and their hosts waited in the howdah while 200 beaters scoured the jungle below. Finally, on their third outing, the duke bagged the tigress who was, it transpired lame, just as it was time for the royal party to return to Delhi.

Given that Philip had made powerful speeches supporting conservationism the press questioned the ethics of him taking part before they learned that he had actually killed a tiger. In typically

209

robust style, to one question, he replied indignantly, 'Of course I plan to shoot a tiger if possible, why not?' The controversy rumbled on for some time with some commentators in the UK outraged not because the tiger had been killed but because of the particular bait, a buffalo, that had been used.

The outraged protesters didn't care about the past when the Queen's grandfather George V, who shot 39 tigers and 4 bears when he visited Nepal in 1911, happily posed alongside his collection of dead trophies. A decade later, photographs showed his son and heir, the Prince of Wales, on another equally bloody hunting trip to Nepal. That was then, this was a very different now. The Queen did not get physically involved in the actual killing of the beast. Instead, she happily shot films on her cine camera of the birds and other wildlife from her vantage point in a howdah on top of an elephant. A story in *Time* magazine reported that Fleet Street's editors were determined to label the duke Britain's biggest hypocrite for making speeches about saving endangered species while blasting them to death for fun.

Given the abuse he had received from the British press, Philip faced a dilemma a week later when the royal couple returned to the region in February 1961 for a state visit to Nepal at the invitation of the young and ambitious, King Mahendra. Mahendra, who had been busy reforming his country by removing the bureaucratic system and improving the political system to make it more representative, had been on the throne just under five years. He saw the state visit by the Queen to his country as a vehicle to reaffirm his authority and the prestige of the Nepalese monarchy. Unfortunately for Philip that meant among the many activities the king had arranged in Philip and the Queen's honour was a tiger shoot that would take place in the Chitwan National Park, about 110 miles from the capital Kathmandu. The king had mustered a magnificent army of 327 elephants for sole purpose of bagging one tiger and prepared a set, an area of white canvas into which a tiger had been driven by beaters. Apparently tigers having never seen white canvas before, would not attempt to break out of the compound. The area selected for the hunt, the king assured Philip, was one where the population had always lived in fear of marauding tigers.

It was such an elaborate occasion Philip knew he would need a very good reason to decline firing his rifle to bag another trophy without causing deep offence to his host. The duke cannily emerged from his tent with a huge bandage on his trigger finger and told the king he was incapable of using his painfully infected finger to shoot his rifle. The king, who had attended the first WWF meeting in Switzerland, was no fool and graciously accepted Philip's reason for not using his rifle, knowing that the duke would have no qualms about shooting a tiger had the British press, eager for a story, not been in tow.

The Pathé newsreel commentary that chronicled the tiger hunt in a short film about the royal visit simply reported, 'As the Duke had a whitlow on his trigger figure the tiger was not royally slain,' nor was it even shot by the Foreign Secretary, who was at the time Old Etonian, Alec Douglas-Home, 14th Earl of Home, who 'had an off day.' Instead it was Rear Admiral Sir Christopher Bonham-Carter, then Treasurer to Prince Philip, and another Old Etonian, Sir Michael Adeane, the Queen's private secretary, who put 'an end to the beast' and were credited with the trophy kill of the 8 feet 8 inches long tigress. It was the perfect compromise, King Mahendra had fulfilled the time honoured obligation as the host and provided the royal party with a tiger to shoot and Philip had avoided actually doing the deed.

There was, however, more hunting to come for the royal party. The next prey was a rhinoceros, but once again Philip did not fire a shot. The English journalist, author and broadcaster Bernard Levin, described by his paper as 'the most famous journalist of his day' wrote about the absurdity of the incident in *Uneasy Lies the Head* published in *The Times*, 23 January 1989. 'I recall an amazingly ridiculous campaign against him [the Duke of Edinburgh] because, on a visit to India, [Levin's error it was actually in Nepal] he was invited to go tiger-shooting, such an invitation is a great honour there, and after a few days of the newspapers back home yelling and screaming and jumping up and down, he had to pretend that he had a whitlow on his trigger-finger and so couldn't shoot anything, not even a tabloid journalist.'

Two months later, on 29 April 1961, Philip joined forces with Prince Bernhard of Lippe-Biesterfeld, the controversial, jet-setting consort of Queen Julianna of the Netherlands, and father of the future Queen Beatrix[*] to pledge they would give up big game hunting in a bid to send a message to the world that it was important to protect the world's dwindling endangered species of wildlife.

The two royal consorts, along with a small group of passionate European intellectuals – Sir Peter Scott, Julian Huxley, Edward Max Nicholson, Victor Stolan and Guy Mountfort – used their fame and position to create the World Wildlife Fund. Its mission statement was set out in the 'Morges Manifesto.' The 'international declaration' read, 'We must save the world's wildlife. All over the world vast numbers of fine and harmless creatures are losing their lives, or their home, in an orgy of thoughtless and needless destruction.'

This simple act laid the foundations for the World Wildlife Fund for Nature, an NGO that has grown into the world's largest and most respected independent wildlife conservation organisation. More than 50 years on, its black and white logo of a panda is a well-known household symbol in many countries. The organisation has won the backing of more than five million people throughout the world, and has raised billions to fight the cause of saving endangered species.

This was Philip at his pioneering best. A visionary cause he could throw all his energies behind and blaze the trail for future generations. He attributed his initial interest in conservation to a medium-format camera, a Hasselblad with a 250mm/f4.0 lens, that

---

[*] He belonged to the princely House of Lippe and was a nephew of the Principality of Lippe's last sovereign Leopold IV and a member of the Reiter-SS, a mounted unit of the SS. He had joined the Nazi party before the war. He later also joined the National Socialist Motor Corps.

he purchased when he went to the equestrian events of the 1956 Olympics*. He became obsessed with photography, he recalled, when he began to use the camera seriously on the long voyage home from the Melbourne Summer Olympics to photograph the birds he saw from the deck of HMY *Britannia*. His amateur interest in bird-watching led naturally to meeting bird conservationists and renowned ornithologists, and, as he put it, 'Almost before I could tell the difference between a Bewick and a Whooper, Peter Scott got me involved in the formation of the World Wildlife Fund.'

Philip was hooked and conservation became a lifelong passion. He became the WWF's first joint president, a position he held until 1982. He also became a prolific writer on the environment too, as well as on technological, equestrian and animal subjects. His books include *Selected Speeches 1948–1955* (1957); *Birds from Britannia* (1962); *Down to Earth* (1988); and *Survival or Extinction: A Christian Attitude to the Environment* (1989). *Down to Earth* was even translated and published in Japanese.

Philip also founded Australia's first-ever environmental organisation, the Australian Conservation Foundation, which is today Australia's most prominent such organisation. Years later the duke explained that he had to work out his role 'by trial and error'. He said in a BBC interview**, 'There was no precedent. If I asked somebody, "What do you expect me to do?" they all looked blank. They had no idea, nobody had much idea.'

It was a cause he could throw himself into and he did. In many ways ahead of his time in environmental conservation, many of the natural disasters caused by the degradation of nature Philip foresaw have sadly came true. During speeches and interviews he was more than happy to open up about his passion for conservation and happy too to risk being criticised by the media for venturing into political areas. In 1981, in a rare interview with *60 Minutes Australia* as President of the WWF on board *Britannia*, he was asked about

---

* Held separately from the rest of the events in Stockholm in June 1956

** With Fiona Bruce in June 2011

avoiding politics when discussing conservation issues. He said, 'It's almost impossible to avoid politics if you open your mouth at all, short of saying rhubarb because practically every issue is political in the sense that it's a public interest. There's a big difference between what is political and what is party political and I don't think that conservation is party political.'

He bought into the conservationist philosophy, believing himself to be somebody who tried to avoid the human species disturbing the balance of nature on the planet more than necessary. 'If we've got this extraordinary diversity on this globe it seems awfully silly for us to destroy it,' Philip said. 'All these other creatures have an equal right to exist here, we have no prior rights to the earth than anybody else and if they're here let's give them a chance to survive.'

Philip believed the world's out of control growth of human population rates was by far the biggest challenge to nature conservation and believed that 'voluntary family limitation' was the only way to tackle it. On a visit to the remote Solomon Islands in 1982 he said, when he was told that the annual population growth was 5 per cent, 'They must be out of their minds.' 'The duke invariably spoke his mind, sometimes not necessarily with a high degree of tact,' his cousin, Countess Patricia Mountbatten, noted. 'But on the other hand, I think that people have come to expect that of him, and they really rather enjoy it and they think, how nice to hear somebody actually say what they think.' Philip, unlike his son, the Prince of Wales, did not see himself as some form of 'green' crusader. He went on, 'I think that there's a difference between being concerned for the conservation of nature and being a bunny hugger or people who simply love animals. People can't get their heads round the idea of a species surviving, you know, they're more concerned about how you treat a donkey in Sicily or something,' he said.

Philip identified that one serious problem with getting a global solution to conservation was that every country had its distinct problems and used different solutions and ideas to resolve them. His big idea was to work through the Commonwealth Secretariat, an organisation that represented a huge land mass across the world, to achieve greater connectivity among nations when dealing with conservation. 'The amount that is spent on conservation is peanuts,' he told *60 Minutes Australia* reporter, Ray Martin, in 1981, the year he was invited to become President of WWF International, a position he held until 1996 when he became President Emeritus.

Through his association with the WWF, now the World Wide Fund for Nature, he visited WWF projects in over 40 countries on five continents. His extensive travels to remote areas and the briefings he received when he was there, gave him great insight into the problems facing the natural world. He believed that for conservation to be successful it was necessary to take into consideration that mankind could only be relied upon to do anything consistently if he believed it was in his own interest. 'He (man) may have occasional fits of conscience and moral rectitude but otherwise his actions are governed by self-interest. It follows then that whatever the moral reasons for conservation it will only be achieved by the inducement of profit or pleasure.'[*]

The Duke of Edinburgh argued passionately that the ignorance and neglect of mankind towards the destruction of all wild animals would certainly bring devastating changes to our existence on this planet as we know it today. 'The trouble is that everything in nature is completely interdependent. Tinker with one part of it and the repercussions ripple out in all directions,' he said. Philip also identified the sheer weight of numbers of the human population, its habitations, machinery and ruthless exploitation of the living and organic resources of the earth as crucial; together these are changing our whole environment. He stressed humanity could not go on ignoring the awkward consequences and the most 'direct and menacing' threat of pollution caused by mankind and overpopulation. 'Pollution is a direct outcome of man's ruthless exploitation of the earth's resources. Experience shows that the growth of successful organic populations is eventually balanced by

[*]   World Wildlife Fund: British National Appeal Banquet, London (1962)

the destruction of its own habitat. The vast man-made deserts show that the human population started this process long ago,' he said in 1970.

A common theme running through all Philip's speeches on conservation was that the situation could be controlled and even reversed if world leaders co-operated on a scale and intensity beyond anything achieved before. 'I realise that there are any number of vital causes to be fought for, I sympathise with people who work up a passionate concern about the all too many examples of inhumanity, injustice, and unfairness, but behind all this hangs a really deadly cloud.' He feared unless world powers had a joined-up approach to conservationism the process of destroying the natural environment would gather speed and momentum. 'If we fail to cope with this challenge, all the other problems will pale into insignificance,' he warned as early as 1970. 'If we are to exercise our responsibilities so that all life can continue on earth, they must have a moral and philosophical basis.'

The duke stressed self-interest, economic profit and absolute materialism are no longer enough. 'A threat to any part of the environment is a threat to the whole environment, but we must have a basis of assessment of these threats, not so that we can establish a priority of fears, but so that we can make a positive contribution to improvement and ultimate survival,' he said. He was not afraid of upsetting anyone in this global quest for enlightenment, even his hosts. 'Your country is one of the most notorious centres of trading in endangered species in the world,' he said after accepting a conservation award in Thailand in 1991.

He argued that although change in saving the planet and its wildlife was a slow process it had to start somewhere and in time would make an impact if the population persisted. 'Whatever happens, don't give up and don't despair' Results may not be immediately apparent, but you may have touched a receptive chord without knowing it. Even the most unsympathetic and unenlightened politician, industrialist or bureaucrat begins to take notice when a lot of people write about the same subject. The quality of life to be enjoyed or the existence to be survived by our children and future generations is in our hands now,' Philip told the World Wildlife Fund Congress in London in 1970.

He went on, 'Looked at in that light it may well turn out that money spent on proper pollution control, urban and rural planning and the control of exploitation of wild stocks of plants or animals on land and in the sea, is the less expensive alternative in the long run... The conservation of nature, the proper care for the human environment and a general concern for the long-term future of the whole of our planet are absolutely vital if future generations are to have a chance to enjoy their existence on this earth'.

Philip was an active and influential environmental activist extraordinaire throughout his long life. He used an LPG-powered taxi cab around London to attend engagements, often unrecognised. Had it not been for people like him the world could possibly have been in a worse situation, as far as the environment is concerned, today. There is no doubt that Prince Philip has influenced the thinking of many people particularly those in the field of conservation and protection of the environment. It is a passion shared by his eldest son Charles, the Prince of Wales who not only actively campaigns directly or indirectly but practises what he preaches as well.

Philip's passion for conservationism led him to found ARC – Alliance of Regions and Conservations – in 1986, the 25th anniversary of WWF. The WWF International conference was held in Assisi, the home of St Francis, the patron saint of wild animals. The plan had been for a secular conference but Philip thought it would be a good idea to take advantage of the venue to get the major religions to take an interest in the conservation of nature. At Assisi five religious leaders [representing Buddhism, Christianity, Hinduism, Islam and Judaism] agreed that they had a responsibility and then he asked each of them to describe the attitude of their religion to the natural environment. He said: 'We don't want to be ecumenical; we don't want a paper that has been agreed by everybody. Instead we want each of you to say what is relevant

217

to you and your tradition.' The purpose of the Assisi meeting was really to say to the religions: If you think this is important then tell us what you think but don't try and get it agreed with everybody else. 'The result is that the religions now communicate with each other on the subject of what they are doing for the conservation of nature, not about their religious dogma.' Philip said with pride.

'The interesting thing is that after the Assisi meeting there was a press conference and inevitably somebody said "what are you going to do next?" We said we didn't know... so we [the religious leaders and conservationists] sat down afterwards and talked about it. And what we all said was that main thing is that we don't want to burden the whole thing with a new body and its inevitable administration,' he said. Asked if he had been influenced personally by the religious people he had met through his involvement with WWF or ARC, he said he had been born and brought up a Christian and did not see the point in looking for anything else. 'I've often discussed the various philosophies with people of other religions. It's an interesting discussion.'

As president of WWF and later WWF International his work took him all over the world where he witnessed first-hand the urgency of conservation: from the forests of Malaysia to polluted lakes in Scandinavia. 'The curious difficulty when I became president of WWF,' he reflected, 'was that the increase in public donations was going up and we couldn't spend it as fast as it was coming in.'

At the age of 82 in 2003 he reflected in interview, 'The world population 60 years ago was just over two billion and it is now more than six billion. This huge increase – an explosion really – has probably done more harm to the environment than anything else. We take up a lot of room; we use a lot of resources, we harvest and don't replant; we exploit wild fish; we exploit wild forests. Another big change is how we protect the environment. The National Parks in America for instance are now looked at as protecting the natural environment, but when they were started in the 1930s they weren't that at all. They were parks for people. Now what we're looking at are protected areas for resident species, which is slightly different. It's a positive change that they're there but it's a negative change that they are needed at all.'

Did he see a solution? 'When you start talking about the human population some people think that you want to control it. I don't want to control it: I want people to control it themselves for their own good reasons. Those reasons may be put to them by their religions, by their scientific understanding or simply because of their intelligence. But we are not going to be able to survive on this limited planet if the population keeps on growing: there isn't going to be anything left,' he said.

He may have been a passionate wildlife conservationist but Philip's vision never extended to being a fanatical environmentalist. He always took a more pragmatic approach to nature, especially when dealing with matters closer to home. Indeed his position as Ranger of Windsor Great Park, which he took on in 1952, occasionally brought him into conflict with what he derogatorily described as 'tree huggers' who were hell-bent on trying to stop him ordering the cutting down ancient limes and oaks. The controversy arose when Philip said he wanted to fell a stand of ancient limes, up to a dozen, which he described as 'a few decrepit old things' in a BBC documentary series, *The Queen's Castle*. Philip was filmed touring the grounds of Windsor in a Land Rover. Berating the Crown Estate, which has to be consulted on decisions, he remarks: 'There is a circle of limes which I want to take down, which … they want to keep. I can't understand why. When Queen Anne's drive was damaged by wind and one thing and another, I came to the conclusion that the only thing for it, was to replant it. Well, we were taking some of them down and the tree huggers from Newbury bypass, they descended on us some time ago and made the most appalling fuss to the extent that it's been almost impossible to take down dead trees. Or even to remove dead branches. All hell broke loose amongst the tree huggers and all the people who thought we were destroying the oak trees. I mean can you imagine, a few decrepit old things, and a few that were planted you imagine, in the wrong place? It seemed absolutely crazy not to straighten it out and, as I say, we planted one thousand oaks. So what's wrong with that?'

The problem was, as far as the 'tree huggers' were concerned, that the 400-year-old trees were home to some of the rarest insects to be found in the UK. Add to that the rekindled controversy of 1995 when, in his capacity as Ranger of Windsor Great Park, Philip ordered 63 mature oaks be cut down, prompting calls for the Royal Family to be stripped of its crown immunity from prosecution. It meant Philip could ignore the provisions of the Wildlife and Countryside Act and not comply with legislation relating to sites of special scientific interest.

Environmentalists were furious at Philip's dismissive remarks. Matt Shardlow, conservation director of Buglife, The Invertebrate Conservation Trust, spoke out against him publicly. He told the Independent in April 2009 that, 'Damage to this internationally important habitat would be a serious crime if done by any other landowner.' Dead wood from the limes, he pointed out, provided a unique breeding ground for insects including the woodwasp soldier-fly (*Xylomya maculata*), the cranefly (*Ctenophora ornata*) and the stag beetle (*Lucanus cerusis*). The wood was also very important for rare fungi, mosses and lichens associated with decaying timber, he insisted. Philip would not budge. Eventually, the Queen intervened and turned to one of the Prince of Wales's friends, Professor Ian Swingland, a wildlife expert, who she hoped could help to resolve the issue after, as she put it, 'a certain gentleman' decided to chop down the trees regardless.

Prince Charles loved his Highgrove estate in Tetbury, Gloucestershire, which he purchased, with Camilla's encouragement, back in 1980. Ever since the prince has set about transforming the 25-acre estate into his sanctuary. It includes his beautiful, eclectic garden, where he insists on applying his principles which are strictly organic, along with neighbouring Home Farm, Tetbury. In August 2020, Clarence House announced the Prince of Wales was to leave his organic farm and not renew the lease after 35 years, as he accepted that he would not be able to dedicate the same amount of time to it when he is one day king. Instead it was revealed that he would focus on his commitment to organic farming at the Sandringham Estate and Windsor.

For years Philip was at odds with his eldest son, Charles, and the duke publicly challenged the benefits of organic farming. He backed the Genetically Modified industry by playing down fears about the products. In an interview for *The Times* newspaper in 2000 Philip said: 'Do not let us forget we have been genetically modifying animals and plants ever since people started selective breeding.' The introduction of foreign pests, such as the grey squirrel, had done more damage to the environment than genetically modified crops would ever cause, he argued. 'People are worried about genetically modified organisms getting into the environment. What people forget is that the introduction of exotic species, such as, for instance, the introduction of the grey squirrel into this country, is going to do or has done far more damage than a genetically modified piece of potato.'

The Prince of Wales, from his own exhaustive research, believes that genetic engineering takes man into the realms that belong to 'God and God alone'. Reflecting on the 2000 Reith Lectures, Charles said: 'Part of the problem is the prevailing approach that seeks to reduce the natural world, including ourselves, to the level of nothing more than a mechanical process.' He went on, 'I happen to believe that if a fraction of the money currently being invested in developing genetically manipulated crops were applied to understanding and improving traditional systems of agriculture, which have stood the all-important test of time, the results would be remarkable.'

In a television interview a few years later in May 2008, Philip again questioned the value of the organic agricultural system that his son so passionately espouses. 'Organic farming is not an absolute certainty that is quite as useful as it sounds,' Philip said in the ITV1 documentary, *The Duke: A Portrait of Prince Philip.* 'You have got to be emotionally committed to it,' he told the legendary Trinidadian–British newsreader and journalist Sir Trevor

McDonald. 'But if you stand back and be open minded about it, it is quite difficult to really find where it has been a real benefit. It's interesting now that it isn't ridiculed to the same degree. I think people are beginning to realise that some of the chickens are coming home to roost and settle heavily in the genetically modified trees.'

As he took Sir Trevor on a tour of the Queen's Sandringham estate, the duke talked openly about conservation, animal welfare and soaring food prices. 'The food prices are going up – everyone thinks it's to do with not enough food, but it's really that demand is too great, too many people,' he said. The fact that in 2017 Philip was happy to let Charles take over the Home Farms at Sandringham and Windsor shows there has been a rapprochement between the two men on the subject. 'They didn't see eye to eye on this for years but it is interesting that the duke now respects the work the Prince of Wales has done in this field. The prince often writes to his father when he is away on overseas tours, it is a way they share ideas,' said a current member of the Royal Household.

For all his visionary work on protected endangered species and wildlife the media, to his immense frustration, would always undermine his achievements and refer to the tiger hunts he joined in India and Nepal in the early 1960s. The media feel him bagging a tiger has left the stench of hypocrisy. When asked about this 'contradiction' by Nicholas Owen, the then ITV royal correspondent (from 1994 until 2000) Philip's demeanour suddenly turned and he treated the widely respected reporter and broadcaster as if he was some lowly serf from a bygone era for having the temerity to even ask the perfectly legitimate question. Clearly irritated by Owen's impertinence, Philip responded, 'I only shot *one* tiger, and it happened to be lame at the time anyway. I imagine you weren't even born then anyway, so what do you know about it?' The interview, conducted in a train carriage, ended abruptly and Owen admitted that the rest of the journey was more than a little awkward when their paths crossed afterwards. 'He's famous for the occasional acid aside, and I've had one or two of those from him.' After *that* interview Philip's attitude towards the reporter changed. In an interview with *Country Life* magazine in December 2016, Owen said, only half-jokingly, 'Sometimes he wasn't very keen to see me, and I was very wary of seeing him.'

17: TABU MAN

'He left Tanna to go to England as a messenger. Once there, he married the Queen. Prince Philip is the spirit of the garden.'

Chief Siko Nathuan of Yaohnanen village, Tanna, Vanuatu

In the village of Yaohnanen, 6 kilometres south-east of the main town, Lenakel, on the tiny island of Tanna, one of 82 in the archipelago of Vanuatu stretching 1,300 kilometres across the South Pacific, the Kastom people worship Prince Philip as a Divine Being. Locals, known as the Cargo Cult, believe Philip is the son of their ancestral mountain god, Tabu Man. For them he is a deeply spiritual figure, a human who possesses qualities and powers that make him sacred, but it is more complex than simple worship.

The closest the duke came to visiting the remote community, who live deep among the moist broadleaf tropical rainforests, where the temperatures can reach near 90°F and it rains significantly for up to ten days a month, was in 1974. HMY *Britannia* had docked at Port Vila during a royal visit to Vanuatu, then known as the New Hebrides, as part of a tour of the Commonwealth. While Philip was in the capital, he was approached and given a symbolic white pig by a Tanna man. Philip was not then aware of the cult that worshipped him, but when it was brought to his attention several years later by John Champion, the British Resident Commissioner in the New Hebrides, he took it very seriously. Mr Champion suggested that the prince should consider sending the tribal leaders a signed photograph of himself.

The prince took Champion's advice and ever since 1978, messages and gifts have flowed between Buckingham Palace and Tanna. The villagers responded by sending him a traditional pig-killing club called a *nal-nal*. In compliance with their request, Philip sent a photograph of himself posing with the club. Another photograph was sent in 2000. All three photographs were kept by Chief Jack Naiva, who died in 2009, and they became cherished icons on Tanna[*].

The late Chief Naiva's grandson, Siko Nathuan, now chief of the village, explained that his people believe Philip is a physical representation of the ancient warrior leader returning home with his wife, Queen Elizabeth. According to their beliefs, Philip ruled England with the help of the Queen and was very supportive of traditional ways of life.

They believe that out of Mount Yasur, one of the most active volcanoes in the region, came the world, life and Prince Philip. The chief explained, 'Once upon a time there were two women. They were sitting when this volcano came. They had intercourse. Prince Philip came. Then they were sent back. That's how we know about Prince Philip. He left Tanna to go to England as a messenger. Once there he married the Queen. Prince Philip is the spirit of the garden.'

According to the prophecy Philip would return to Tanna on his 89th birthday. Ahead of the date, 8 June 2010, the entire village prepared for the homecoming. Chief Siko Nathuan became the custodian of the village stories, the myths and legends that have defined the belief system of the cult in 2009 when his grandfather died. 'Everyone in the Pacific says that Prince Philip is from England or Greece, but our grandfathers carved the club and sent it off to him with a message saying, "If you're from Tanna hold this club and take a picture so that everyone who sees the picture will know that you are from Tanna."' Showing the photo to reporters from France 24 in 2010, he continued, 'This is the club he is holding. It has been

---

[*]   Philip also sent a letter of condolence to his son when Chief Jack died.

carved here and sent to him. You can see it in this photo.' They truly believed it was time for him to come back and they would now 'open the door' for his arrival.

The late Chief Jack had been one of the paddlers of a traditional war canoe which greeted the HMY *Britannia* in 1974. He was quoted as saying: 'I saw him standing on the deck in his white uniform. I knew then that he was the true messiah.' In the village a shrine – a Union Flag draped over framed photographs of the Queen's consort – in honour of the duke takes pride of place. It is still the custom for villagers in Yaohnanen and Yakel to gather every evening, drink kava, and pray to Philip, asking him to increase the production of their crops in the garden, or to give them the sun, or rain. Indeed it is believed up to half of Tanna's more than 30,000 people are followers of the Cargo Cult, which began early last century.

In 2007 the makers of the Channel 4 documentary *Meet the Natives* arranged for a delegation of five islanders to meet Prince Philip at Windsor Castle in Berkshire. Before the meeting, there was some trepidation in anthropological circles. 'In one slip of his tongue, he would after all be capable of shaking their entire religion to its foundations and the Duke is not, let's face it, a man renowned for tact,' *The Independent* newspaper reported.

As it happened the meeting passed off without incident. Since then, however, a rivalry has developed between Yaohnanen and another nearby village Ikunala. Yappa, village chief of Ikunala, was one of the Tanna delegation sent to Windsor Castle to meet Philip. 'On top of the building there was a flag and we were standing inside the house. Everywhere inside there was gold. When I met Philip I was happy and I nearly cried because it was a prophecy from my grandfather and my father. This man was their friend but they were never able to see him, but I met him on their behalf and I am very glad I did.'

Many believe that Philip's retirement from public life triggered a tropical cyclone that hit the island in 2015. Author and journalist Matthew Baylis, who lived among the villagers while writing a book about the experience, said the cyclone could indicate the duke had reached a higher ' sacred status'. They told him that they saw Philip living in a palace, surrounded by guards, and travelling in a car with darkened windows, as evidence of his taboo status. 'So they may well see his withdrawal from public duties as connected to that, having attained some higher rung of taboo, sacred status. Equally, they might think he is preparing to come "back" to Tanna, in some form, spiritually or bodily.'

Philip never did visit the island.

18: SILVER LININGS

*'If I am asked what I think about family life after 25 years of marriage,
I can answer with equal simplicity and conviction, I am for it.'*

The Queen, November 1972

The Pulitzer Prize winning *New York Times* foreign correspondent,
Richard Gray Eder, was not overly impressed by what he witnessed,
given the blasé tone of his copy. 'The sentiments were often
overstated, and ranged from affection to mawkishness, from respect
to irreverence,' he wrote when reporting on the celebrations
to mark the Queen and Philip's silver wedding anniversary in
November 1972. The front page headline in his newspaper, which
accompanied a photograph of a smiling Queen and Philip wearing
a top hat, was more positive, when it said, 'Queen is hailed on 25th
anniversary'. Londoners may not have been riveted by the events,
Eder observed, but he conceded that they clearly enjoyed them,
turning out in good sized crowds. His 'special' report for the top-
selling American newspaper concluded, 'The family life of Queen
Elizabeth, who is 46 years old, and Prince Philip, who is 51, has
shed all traces of royal fear and replaced it with a kind of royal
coziness.'

It's true that to the people the Royal Family had come to
feel like a snug old armchair in the corner by the early 1970s. It
didn't really represent the shiny new age, but it was familiar and
it was just something that seemed to always be present. It was
comfortable and certainly no one in the UK was serious about
throwing it out, at least for now. The same could be said about

Elizabeth and Philip's marriage. From the public's perspective the couple's silver wedding anniversary marked a moment to look back and reflect, for both them, and for the country. The Queen, Prince Philip, Prince Charles and Princess Anne* rode in an open carriage through Trafalgar Square, past Nelson's Column and along the Strand and Fleet Street, past St Paul's Cathedral and on to the Guildhall for a celebratory lunch hosted by the Lord Mayor. Once inside, surrounded by the Gothic grandeur of the Great Hall, Lord Mais, the mayor, the first peer to be elected to that office, addressed the assembled VIP guests. 'Families throughout Great Britain have been able to identify with the unity and happiness of the Royal Family,' he said. Both the Conservative prime minister, Ted Heath, and the Labour Party leader, Harold Wilson, at this time Leader of the Opposition after his party lost the 1970 General Election in June, said much the same thing in the House of Commons earlier, as did practically all the Fleet Street editorial writers and commentators.

Queen Elizabeth, who found Ted Heath very heavy weather when dealing with him on a one to one basis, partly because of his patent lack of interest in the Commonwealth, began her remarks after lunch with a take-off of her own stiff speaking style. 'I think everybody really will concede that on this, of all days, I should begin my speech with the words "My husband and I,"' she said, using the formula she was often parodied as saying. The VIP guests laughed at the appropriate pause in her speech. Her delivery was warmer, less stilted than usual throughout the address. She even made a very mild joke. 'When the Bishop was asked what he thought about sin,' she said, 'he replied with simple conviction that he was against it.' She went on, 'If I am asked what I think about family life, after twenty-five years of marriage, I can answer with equal simplicity and conviction, I am for it.'

The royal couple's jovial mood continued on a walkabout around the Barbican Centre which followed, with the Queen,

---

* Prince Andrew and Prince Edward were viewed as too young to take part.

Philip, Charles and Anne mingling freely among the crowd. 'How long have you been married?' Philip asked one couple in the crowd of well-wishers. 'Eleven years,' they responded in unison. 'The first twelve years are the worst,' he then assured them, grinning cheerfully. 'After that it's all downhill.'

Earlier, at Westminster Abbey, a fanfare of trumpets heralded the arrival of the Queen and the Royal Family. A smattering of European royalty, as well as a hundred couples who had married on the same day as the Queen and Philip, were among the congregation already seated in the nave as the Sovereign's official bodyguard, the Honourable Corps of Gentlemen at Arms – bedecked in their splendid uniforms of Dragoon Guards officers of the 1840s with a skirted red coat with Garter blue velvet cuffs and facings embroidered with the Tudor royal badge of the portcullis, and helmets with white swan feather plumes – marched slowly ahead of the Royal Party.

After the Queen, wearing a pale blue outfit, and Philip, had taken their places, the Dean, The Very Reverend, Eric Symes Abbott, stepped forward and gave thanks 'for the blessings which have come to each and all of us through their marriage and their lives of service.' Several lessons were read and two hymns sung. Passionate musician Prime Minister Ted Heath (who had won an Organ Scholarship after being educated at Chatham House Grammar School, Ramsgate to Balliol College, Oxford) stood amid his cabinet ministers, singing 'Praise My Soul the King of Heaven' with gusto. It was undoubtedly a positive time for the Queen and the monarchy in Britain in terms of popularity. Philip too, after a rocky few years in his relationship with the press, seemed to have been accepted by the Fourth Estate, warts and all, as a force for good.

The Queen's Christmas Broadcast that year included scenes from the celebrations to mark their milestone anniversary. 'My whole family has been deeply touched by the affection you have shown to us when we celebrated our Silver Wedding and we are especially grateful to the many thousands who have written to us and sent us messages and presents,' she said. 'One of the great Christian ideals is a happy and lasting marriage between man and wife, but no marriage can hope to succeed without a deliberate effort to be tolerant and understanding. This doesn't come easily to individuals and it certainly doesn't come naturally to communities or nations.' The Queen also made reference to the terrible violence in Northern Ireland, and preparations for Britain to join the European Economic Community (EEC) the forerunner to the European Union. Britain was changing and she and Prince Philip knew the monarchy had to embrace that change or suffer the consequences.

The following year Elizabeth and Philip saw their daughter, Princess Anne, then 23, wed fellow equestrian, Captain Mark Phillips, of 1st The Queen's Dragoon Guards, at Westminster Abbey on 14 November 1973. The wedding took place just days ahead of their 26th anniversary. Philip adored his feisty, single-minded daughter; she was everything he wanted in a child. He would tell jokes about the horse-loving princess, saying, 'If it doesn't fart or eat hay, she isn't interested.' It seemed, however, Captain Phillips, who had caught Anne's eye, was the exception. She said he looked like 'an Adonis' on a horse and Anne was smitten. Despite the physical attraction for one another, the pair later realised that sadly they did not have very much in common, apart from horses. Princess Anne appeared to be smarter and more sharp-witted than her husband. Her brother Charles, who was unhappy about the match as he did not think that Captain Phillips was worthy of his sister, cruelly christened his new brother-in-law 'Fog' – because he regarded him as a little dense and thick, just like a pea-souper. Even Prince Andrew and Prince Edward used to joke about the unfortunate Mark. 'Let's see how long it is before Foggy talks about a horse' they would say – and they would time him to the second.

Hundreds of thousands of loyal royal fans turned out on the streets to cheer the newly-weds and a further 500 million tuned into the coverage of the marriage on television around the world. For Philip one aspect of the wedding was particularly significant.

After proudly walking his beloved daughter down the aisle, and handing her over to her husband, the notable moment came for the newly-weds to sign the register at the Abbey, just after the couple had exchanged vows. As Anne signed the register she logged her surname as 'Mountbatten-Windsor' making it the first time the name that Philip had fought so hard over was recognised in this way.

The much-derided Captain Phillips was soon to show his mettle and that he was not as wet as his sneering brothers-in-law liked to portray him, when he was at the centre of one of the most dramatic and dangerous incidents ever involving a senior member of the Royal Family. Just four months after their wedding, at around 8 p.m. on 20 March 1974, Princess Anne and her husband were being driven home towards Buckingham Palace after attending a charity film screening. Princess Anne's lady-in-waiting, Rowena Brassey, sat across from the couple in the back of a maroon Rolls-Royce limousine, marked with the royal insignia. In the passenger seat rode Anne's personal protection officer, Inspector James Beaton of Scotland Yard's Special Operations Royalty Protection branch, SO14.

As chauffeur Alexander Callender drove down the Mall, a white Ford Escort suddenly overtook the royal car at speed and forced him to stop about 200 yards away from the palace. Inspector Beaton, then 31, at first assumed that the man was a disgruntled driver and stepped out to block him, getting shot in his right shoulder in the process. In fact the man was Ian Ball, who was armed, and had hatched a plan to kidnap Princess Anne and demand the Queen pay £2 million ransom, which he wanted to be delivered to him in £5 sterling notes.

Inspector Beaton placed himself in the line of fire between Ball and the princess, who remained, as instructed, inside the car, and tried to return fire but his aim had been affected and his gun jammed. Ball then shot Beaton again and progressed to the rear door.

Anne and Mark did their best to hold the door shut. Then as Anne's lady-in-waiting crawled out of the door on the passenger side, Beaton jumped back between the couple and their assailant, who shot into the car. Beaton's hand deflected the bullet. Ball then shot him a third time, causing a wound that forced Beaton out of the car and onto the ground. The driver, Callender, stepped out and confronted the gunman but Ball shot him in the chest and Callender fell back into the car. Then Ball grabbed Anne's forearm as her husband dragged her back by the waist. Her dress ripped, splitting down the back. In response to one of Ball's pleas, Princess Anne retorted, 'Not bloody likely.'

'I was frightened, I won't mind admitting it,' Mark said later. The scariest part, he remembered, was feeling like a caged animal when police officers started arriving. Then 'the rescue was so near, but so far' as constables hesitated to advance on an armed man so near the princess. Police Constable Michael Hills assumed the conflict was over a car accident and approached Ball who shot him in the stomach. Before collapsing he radioed his station. Ron Russell, the former boxer, saw Ball attack the officer and stepped in along with *Daily Mail* journalist Brian McConnell, who pleaded with Ball to put the gun down and was shot for his troubles. Seconds later Russell punched Ball in the back of the head as police officers began to arrive. Ball ran off but was eventually arrested by Peter Edmonds, a temporary detective constable, who had chased him. The following day headlines around the world reviewed the night's events: *Princess Anne Escapes Assassin; Lone Gunman Charged in Royal Kidnap Plot; Security Increases Around Prince Charles; Witnesses Describe Panic on the Mall; Queen is Horrified at Attack on Princess.*

Home Secretary Roy Jenkins ordered an investigative report for the Prime Minister and told the press that the investigation needed to remain 'broadly confidential'. Scotland Yard and Buckingham Palace refused to comment on specific details of the attack. Newspaper reports claimed Ball was mentally ill and suggested the kidnap plot must have been the work of a wider network of criminals. Royal protection on the Home Secretary's orders was stepped up but the palace released a statement saying that the Royal Family 'had no intention of living in bullet-proof cages.'

Ball's statement to court on 4 April read, 'I would like to say that I did it because I wished to draw attention to the lack of facilities for treating mental illness under the National Health Service.' He pleaded guilty to attempted murder and kidnapping and was sentenced to a life term in a mental health facility. The Queen later awarded the George Cross, Britain's highest civilian award for courage, to Inspector Beaton and bravery honours to PC Hills, Ron Russell, PC Edmonds, John Brian McConnell and Alexander Callender. In a 2006 interview, Ron Russell recalled the Queen told him, 'The medal is from the Queen of England, the thank you is from Anne's mother.' Philip was privately deeply concerned but publicly, typically, he made light of it. 'If the man had succeeded in abducting Anne, she would have given him a hell of a time while in captivity,' he said.

The incident again meant the British royals were world news in what was to become a decade when Elizabeth cemented her role as The People's Queen. It started slowly with murmurings of hostility to any big 1977 Silver Jubilee celebrations. Palace officials, trying to gauge the mood, had been cautious in their planning. It was the era of punk rock and a loud disaffected youth movement snarled their protest against the establishment and the nation. They vented their anger at monarchy and criticised money being spent on the festivities. If the royals wanted a party, they should put their hands in their own pockets came the message. Punks claimed the Jubilee was akin to fascism. Testament to that was that the song *God Save The Queen* by the Sex Pistols, released at the time, was widely banned, including by the BBC. The punks had their anthem and famously the band performed it on 7 June, sailing down the Thames mocking the Queen's Thames River procession planned for two days later. It ended in chaos.

The Queen's only ambition for her Silver Jubilee was to meet as many people as possible. It was a watershed moment last achieved by her grandfather George V in 1935 shortly before his death. She studied her grandparents' schedules and wanted to mirror them. Philip urged his wife to use the milestone to travel the length and breadth of the country. He felt certain the more she was seen, the more the momentum would grow. He got his wish when the Queen arrived in Glasgow on the 17 May. Philip's idea was to transform their walkabouts into 'talk-abouts', which left many Glaswegians with personal memories after meeting the royal couple. Their approach was noticeably less formal as they worked the 60,000 crowd. A girl of 15, from Queenslie, took a photo of Philip on her new Polaroid instant camera. He waited for the picture to develop – and when she showed it to him, he replied, 'That's beautiful.'

One couple, Mary and Albert Currie, of Napier Terrace, Govan had been scheduled to meet the Queen. They and their three children were waiting at the door when the royals arrived. On the living-room table was a pot of tea, a plate of salmon sandwiches and bone china that had been bought especially for them. They did not have time to stay but thanked them for their hospitality. 'They were very nice and warm people,' Mrs Currie told reporters afterwards.

Later the couple went to Hampden Park, as they had done in 1953, then to the Kelvingrove galleries. There Philip chatted to cleaners, who had put in two hours' overtime to make sure the place was looking its best. As he passed them, he ran his finger along a chair and told them: 'You have got it clean!' They ended the day with a Royal Variety Show at the King's Theatre, where the stars included Frankie Howerd and Dolly Parton.

The Queen and Philip had arrived the previous day on Platform 11 at a flag-bedecked Central Station and, outside, clambered onto the horse-drawn Scottish State Coach, ahead of a Jubilee procession formed by the Household Cavalry. Their first stop was Glasgow Cathedral, followed by George Square. 'The couple were three minutes late in arriving at George Square, but everyone knew they were on their way as more than 6,000 people flooded down George Street to get to the square before the procession and get a second look at the Jubilee Queen,' the city's *Evening Times* newspaper reported. The Scottish visit kick-started the celebrations and from then on the detractors' voices started to fade into the background.

On the big day 7 June, a national holiday, Britain was in full celebratory mood with 12,000 street parties and a London parade watched by millions on television. The spirit of the moment was captured as the Queen arrived at St Paul's Cathedral, as a regal distant figure in a golden coach. She was resplendent in an impeccably elegant, tailored Hardy Amies ensemble in a striking shade of pink, complemented by Simone Mirman's inventive hat with stylised flower-heads hanging from 803 silk stems. Inside world leaders, including United States President Jimmy Carter, and Prime Minister James Callaghan as well as all of the living former prime ministers, Harold Macmillan, The Lord Home of the Hirsel, Sir Harold Wilson and Edward Heath, waited to honour her service.

Afterwards the Queen walked among the people packed together outside the Cathedral. She was the picture of happiness. 'Everybody quite happy?' she asked one set of cheering spectators who had clearly suffered waiting outside for hours in the indifferent weather. Then, before they answered, the Queen replied for herself. 'I am.' Then later: 'What a lovely day, we are so lucky.'

The Queen then caught ten-year-old Lynette Woods. 'Where are you from?' she asked. 'From Deptford, Your Majesty,' said Lynette in a proper South London accent. 'Oh, I shall be down to see you on Thursday. Are you going to be waving your flag then?' Her Majesty asked. 'All our school's going to be there, and me dad's got the afternoon off,' the youngster declared. The Queen beamed and her smile remained every step along her 35-minute walkabout from the Cathedral to the special luncheon at Guildhall hosted by the Lord Mayor, Peter Vanneck. At the reception that followed the Queen made an address of great significance. In it she concluded, 'When I was 21, I pledged my life to the service of our people and asked for God's help to make good that vow. Although that vow was made in my salad days, when I was green in judgement, I do not regret nor retract one word of it.' Elizabeth II was now, without doubt, the 'People's Queen'.

Earlier, 100,000 people crammed together outside Buckingham Palace and in unison shouted, 'We want the Queen. We want the

Queen'. The slow chanting turned into rapturous applause and cheers when Elizabeth and Philip, followed by the senior members of the Royal Family, at last appeared on the palace balcony, smiling and waving, and acknowledged the crowd. The Silver Jubilee colour was in evidence everywhere. There was an impressive procession of 400 Silver Ghost Rolls-Royce cars before the Queen at Windsor and the London Underground's planned Fleet line, coloured silver on the Tube map, was renamed the Jubilee Line. 'We have come here because we love you,' said an office girl. 'I can feel it and it means so much to me,' said the Queen.

Streets and villages up and down the country threw elaborate parties for all their residents, and many streets strung bunting (the little flags were usually modelled after the Union Flag) from rooftop to rooftop. In addition to parties, many streets decorated motor vehicles as historical events from Britain's past, and drove them about town, organising their very own parades. In London alone there were over 4,000 organised parties for individual streets and neighbourhoods. Throughout the entire day, onlookers were greeted by the Queen many times as she made several appearances for pictures from the balcony of Buckingham Palace.

On 9 June, the Queen and Philip made a Royal Progress trip via boat up the River Thames from Greenwich to Lambeth, in a re-enactment of the famous progresses taken by Queen Elizabeth I. On the trip, the Queen officially opened the South Bank Jubilee Gardens, one of numerous places named after the festivities. In the evening, she presided over a fireworks display and was taken subsequently by a procession of lighted carriages to Buckingham Palace, where she greeted onlookers yet again from her balcony.

Philip's masterplan to re-engage monarchy with the people, not for the first time, had worked a treat.

19: 'A SENSELESS ACT'

'His infectious enthusiasm, his sheer capacity for hard work,
his wit made him an irresistible leader among men.'

The Prince of Wales's tribute to Lord Mountbatten,
20 December 1979

Thomas McMahon, one of the Provisional IRA's most experienced
bomb-makers, had slipped onto the unguarded boat *Shadow V*
undetected in the dead of night and attached a radio-controlled
23 kilogram incendiary device. The deadly explosive was set to be
detonated by remote control at 11.39 a.m. the next day, 27 August
1979, when the boat was about 200 yards from the harbour.

The terrorist attack happened at the height of The Troubles,
as Northern Ireland's sectarian strife came to be known. Lord
Mountbatten's family regularly holidayed at his summer home
Classiebawn Castle in Mullaghmore, a small seaside village
between Bundoran, County Donegal, and Sligo. The village was
only 12 miles away from the border with Northern Ireland and
an IRA hotspot. Despite security advice and warnings from the
Garda, Mountbatten, who had been staying at his family castle,
went ahead with his plan to go lobster potting and tuna fishing
aboard the boat. Incredibly Mountbatten, who lost his legs in the
blast, was pulled out of the water alive, but died of his injuries.
The other fatalities were his twin grandson, Nicholas, aged
14, and local boy Paul Maxwell, who was 15 and was earning
pocket money as a boat hand. Another passenger, Dowager Lady
Brabourne, then aged 83, died the day after the attack. Timothy

Knatchbull, Mountbatten's other grandson, was badly injured in the blast.

The Queen, who as supreme command authority of the British Armed Forces was also targeted as a so-called 'legitimate' by the IRA, was told of the assassination of her second cousin at her summer residence, Balmoral Castle. At the time Prince Philip was away in France on route to Normandy from Cherbourg where he was scheduled to take part in an international equestrian event. The British Embassy contacted the gendarmerie nationale about Lord Mountbatten's death and an officer was despatched to intercept Philip's car and tell him of the murder of his uncle and other members of his family. Prince Charles was in Iceland where he was on a private holiday. When Charles was told of his great-uncle's assassination, he recalled, 'My heart literally sank and I felt sick in the pit of my tummy. A mixture of desperate emotion swept over me, agony, disbelief, a kind of wretched numbness closely followed by a fierce and violent determination to see that something was done about the IRA.'

The murder of Mountbatten came at what was already a very difficult time for the Queen. Three months earlier, in May 1979, Margaret Thatcher had become Elizabeth's first female prime minister and had ousted the incumbent Labour government led by Prime Minister James Callaghan with a parliamentary majority of 43 seats. It is often cited that the two women, born only five months apart but with very different views on society, had a frosty relationship from the start. The Queen reportedly had anxieties about her divided nation during the Thatcher years. Between March 1984 and March 1985, more than half the country's 187,000 miners left work in what was the biggest industrial dispute in post-war Britain in an attempt to prevent mines from closing. Bernard Ingham, Thatcher's former press secretary, claimed she was 'extremely respectful of the monarchy' and perhaps 'too punctual' when it came to her weekly audience. Whenever Mrs Thatcher went to see the Queen, she would always arrive a quarter of an hour too early and every week the Queen let her wait for 15 minutes.

Shortly before Mountbatten's murder, the Queen and Mrs Thatcher had publicly clashed when the monarch overrode her UK prime minister and insisted on attending the Commonwealth Heads of Government Meeting in Lusaka. Once there the Queen, as Head of the Commonwealth, was welcomed by thousands of Zambians, as Mrs Thatcher moved towards recognition of the Zimbabwe Rhodesian government of Prime Minister Abel T. Muzorewa. Her Majesty had shaken hands with a line of dignitaries, including the Zambian President, Kenneth D. Kaunda. Joshua Nkomo, the Zambian-based joint leader of the Patriotic Front guerrilla alliance, refused to go to the airport because of references to him in Britain as a 'terrorist leader'.

Mrs Thatcher had earlier expressed grave concern about the prospect of the Queen's safety during her visit and had jumped the gun by announcing in a Downing Street press statement that, for security reasons, the Queen should not attend the meeting, without prior consultation with senior officials at Buckingham Palace. Within 24 hours the press secretary to the Queen, a career diplomat as well as an author of political thrillers and non-fiction, Michael Shea, issued his own statement, in which he said, after consultation with the Queen, that she had 'every intention' of going. The Queen had never been to Zambia and felt its President, Kenneth Kaunda, also known as KK, needed her support. Not for the first time her judgement was proved to be right. During the summit, the Queen, as Head of the Commonwealth, played an important diplomatic and conciliatory role, resulting in Britain agreeing to new Rhodesian elections under a new constitution. Reflecting on the incident years later, Kenneth Kaunda said, 'At the Lusaka meeting in 1979, she played a very vital role. The Queen is an outstanding diplomat; that's how she gets things done.'

Despite tensions between the Queen and Mrs Thatcher, both Philip and the Queen Mother warmed to the Conservative leader and were encouraged by her unflinching patriotism. Philip, during the height of the 1981 economic recession, famously remarked, 'Everybody was saying we must have more leisure. Now they are complaining they are unemployed.' The Queen Mother, according to respected royal biographer, Kenneth Rose, spoke of a lovely day spent visiting little churches near Aylesbury, which is located near the country residence at the disposal of British prime ministers. In an entry of Mr Rose's diary dated 20 July 1982, he noted, 'Lunch with the Queen Mother at Clarence House. She describes going to see Ramsay MacDonald at Chequers. "He took us to see some of the little churches in the neighbourhood. Now darling Mrs Thatcher would never do that! But then she has other great qualities such as PATRIOTISM – that's what we want!"' In 1989, he revealed, the Queen Mother also expressed, 'Strong admiration for Mrs Thatcher's determination to concede no sovereignty to the EEC.'

The private conversation, that was published following Mr Rose's death in 2014, also revealed that the Queen Mother was of a Eurosceptic nature, a political position her son-in-law Philip agreed with too. This appeared to be confirmed on 29 June 2016, during a visit to the Ignite Trust Youth Centre in Harrow, Greater London, where he met a group of former gang members who described him as 'cool' because he understood issues facing modern youths; the enthusiastic way he greeted former defence chief, Lord Guthrie, spoke volumes. Guthrie had made headlines in the media when he switched sides to the pro 'Leave' campaign in the European Union Referendum, citing the fact that he was fearful of the prospect of a European army and the impact it would have upon Britain's defence. I watched as Philip enthusiastically shook the field marshall's hand and congratulated him on the wisdom of his decision. Even though he did not vote, there was little doubt what side of the argument Philip was on.

As the Queen asked for more information about Lord Mountbatten's assassination, she was also informed of the devastating news that the IRA had also ambushed and murdered 18 British soldiers at Warrenpoint. The IRA's successful guerrilla attack at Warrenpoint, also known as the Narrow Water ambush, along with the attack on Mountbatten and his family members, marked the highest death toll suffered by the Army on a single day in The Troubles. The IRA admitted carrying out the bombing, issuing a cold statement saying it was designed to, 'Bring to the attention of the English people the continuing occupation of our country.'

At the time of the explosion that killed Mountbatten, the bomb-maker, McMahon, was already 70 miles away and had been taken into police custody. By chance he and a second man, gravedigger Francis McGirl, then aged 24, had been stopped at a checkpoint after he had laid the explosive. But McMahon, then 31, had retained tiny green flakes of paint from Lord Mountbatten's boat and traces of nitroglycerine on his clothes. He and McGirl were eventually charged with Mountbatten's murder.

The coffins of Lord Mountbatten, the Dowager Lady Brabourne and young Nicholas Knatchbull were flown back to the UK from Northern Ireland and arrived at Eastleigh Airport, Southampton before being taken on to Broadlands by hearse. Lord Mountbatten's coffin was subsequently taken to Romsey Abbey, where members of the Broadlands staff carried out a day and night vigil for two days. From there Lord Mountbatten's coffin was taken to The Queen's Chapel at St James's Palace, where over 25,000 people filed past to show their respects to the royal cousin and wartime hero.

Understandably, Prince Charles was grief-stricken and deeply affected by the murder of his beloved great-uncle, the man he would later describe as, 'The grandfather I never had.' At the time of his mentor's murder Prince Charles said that, 'It made me want to die too.' Mountbatten was paramount in his development from boy to man in almost every area. They wrote long and meaningful letters to one another, and Dickie became his most trusted mentor, filling the void left by Charles's more complicated relationship with his father, Philip. There was nothing Charles couldn't share with Mountbatten, from affairs of the heart to advice on matters of state to his military career, that the old man didn't seem to have a handle on. Dickie had always been there for him, just like his beloved grandmother, Queen Elizabeth, the Queen Mother.

The IRA had robbed Charles, the future king, of his wisest adviser. The prince felt at a total loss without him. Dickie had not always been kind, but brutally honest. He once went ballistic over what he saw as Prince Charles's behavioural traits like his great-uncle, King Edward VIII. Dickie had sent Charles a scathing letter after the prince suddenly, and rather rudely, changed his holiday plans, which led to much more work for others who had been busy preparing for his arrival. Dickie bluntly told Charles that his behaviour was totally indefensible. He wrote to Charles, 'I see all the same irresponsibility and frivolity coming out. You must not become like your great-uncle David (the family name for Edward VIII, the Duke of Windsor) – think what happened to him.'

Years later, in May 2015, Charles addressed an audience in the nearby town of Sligo before making a visit to the area of the assassination of Mountbatten. 'At the time I could not imagine how we would come to terms with the anguish of such a deep loss,' he said. 'Through this dreadful experience I now understand in a profound way the agonies borne by others on these islands of whatever faith or political persuasion.'

Philip, privately angry and emotional, was determined to remain silent about the murder of the man who had done so much to shape his life's journey. Dressed in his Admiral of the Fleet Royal Navy Ceremonial Day Dress for the sombre occasion, he chose not to speak at either the funeral or the memorial service to his beloved uncle, leaving his eldest son, Charles, to address the congregation. On 5 September Britain bade a final farewell to one of the last of its storybook heroes, who had been granted the rare honour of a ceremonial funeral. 'Kings, queens, princes and dukes from all corners of Europe, representatives of the Commonwealth, comrades in two world wars and friends of many nationalities, more than 2,000 people in all, joined the royal family beneath the ancient Gothic arches of Westminster Abbey for an hour-long service full of sadness and splendour,' wrote the London correspondent of the *New York Times*.

Tens of thousands of others, many of them wearing black, stood silently along the broad avenues of central London as the body of the

79-year-old sailor and statesman was borne from St James's Palace to the Abbey on a gun carriage. The cocked hat of an admiral of the fleet, his sword of honour and his gold stick were laid on top of the earl's coffin that was draped by the Union Flag. Lord Mountbatten's horse, Dolly, was led near the head of the parade with the admiral's boots reversed in the stirrups, a symbol of a fallen leader.

The official pall bearers, who walked alongside his coffin, were among the most senior military figures of the day as they paid the ultimate tribute to the only man other than the king to hold rank in all three military services. They were Admiral of the Fleet Sir Edward Ashmore, First Sea Lord 1974–1977; General Sir Robert Ford, Adjutant-General 1978–1981; Admiral John T. 'Chick' Hayward, USA Admiral; Admiral Robert L. Pereira, Indian Chief of Naval Staff 1979–1982; Lieutenant-General Sir John Richards, Commandant-General HM Royal Marines 1977–1981; Marshal of the RAF Sir William Dickson, the first Chief of the Defence Staff in 1959, being Mountbatten's predecessor; Général Alain de Boissieu, Chief of Staff of the French Army 1971–1975, the son-in-law of Général Charles de Gaulle; and Rear Admiral Chit Hlaing, formerly Commander-in-Chief of Myanmar (Burma) Navy. Philip and Charles were among those who walked behind the coffin.

The Tenor Bell tolled for 38 minutes before the service, while the cortège made its way slowly to the Abbey. As it entered the Great West Door a fanfare of trumpets was sounded. The Prince of Wales, also wearing Royal Navy uniform then read the lesson, from Psalm 107, 'They that go down to the sea in ships, that do business in great waters; These see the works of the Lord, and his wonders in the deep. For he commandeth, and raiseth the stormy wind, which lifteth up the waves thereof.' He looked lost, but he held his composure.

He was 'so rare a person,' said the Most Rev. Dr Donald Coggan, Archbishop of Canterbury, of the man whom Queen Elizabeth II, his cousin, called 'Uncle Dickie,' whom Queen Victoria held at his christening, who fought in the North Sea during World War I and in Europe and Asia during World War II, who eased the birth of an independent India as the last British Viceroy on the subcontinent and who shaped the post-war British military command. The Archbishop said that Lord Mountbatten would long be remembered for 'his outstanding gifts: high enthusiasm and liberality of spirit; his integrity and flair for leadership; his lifelong devotion to the Royal Navy; his courage and sense of companionship in times of war; his dedication to the cause of freedom and justice; his service to the peoples of Southeast Asia and to India at a critical period in her history.'

That afternoon, Lord Mountbatten's body was taken by special train to Romsey station, 87 miles south-west of London, for the final time. He was buried in the south transept of its twelfth-century abbey. Mountbatten was laid to rest, exactly as he had requested, facing out to sea, only a few miles from his beloved country estate, Broadlands. His plaque is much less wordy than the one unveiled at Westminster Abbey by his nephew Philip on 14 February 1985*. This one reads simply: 'Admiral of the Fleet, Earl Mountbatten of Burma, 1900–1979, In Honour Bound.'

The day after the pomp, pageantry and solemnity of the ceremonial funeral, the *Daily Mail* newspaper front page featured a photograph of a grieving Prince Charles at the moment he wiped a tear from his eye at the funeral, under the banner headline 'The Last Goodbye'. The same day the Mountbatten family held the funeral of Nicholas and Doreen at the local parish church in Mersham, Kent close to the Brabournes' family home, Newhouse. That service was private, but Prince Philip attended. His cousin, Patricia,

---

* Just inside the West door of Westminster Abbey, at the base of a pillar, is a memorial brass to the Earl and Countess Mountbatten of Burma. This was unveiled by the Duke of Edinburgh on 14 February 1985 and is by designer Christopher Ironside. The Belgian fossil marble slab is inlaid with brass and stainless steel. It shows facing profile portraits of the Earl and his wife and ribbons give the various honours they held with badges, insignia and emblems of organisations or services they were involved with. The inscription reads: Admiral of the Fleet THE EARL MOUNTBATTEN OF BURMA THE COUNTESS MOUNTBATTEN OF BURMA with the respective dates 1900–1979 and 1901–1960 given below.

and her husband John were unable to attend due to being in hospital. The service was led by the Archbishop of Canterbury, Dr Donald Coggan, who had baptised Nicholas.

On 20 December, the same year, the Prince of Wales, paid another touching tribute to his great-uncle during his address at the memorial service at St Paul's Cathedral, London. In front of 2,000 people, Charles didn't hold back. He lashed out at, 'The kind of subhuman extremist that blows people up when he feels like it.' He also spoke of Lord Mountbatten as having, ' A constantly active brain which was never allowed a moment's rest.'

Charles continued: 'There was always a new challenge to be overcome, fresh projects to be set in motion, more opposition to be defeated, all of which were pursued with a relentless and almost irresistible single-mindedness of purpose. Although he could certainly be ruthless with people when the occasion demanded, his infectious enthusiasm, his sheer capacity for hard work, his wit made him an irresistible leader among men.'

The IRA bomber, McMahon, was charged with the Mountbatten murders after Garda found traces of the chemicals used to make the deadly bomb on his clothes. He served the majority of his sentence in Portlaoise Prison where he and others staged a failed escape attempt in 1985. Three years later, he fired a shot from a gun he had smuggled into a holding cell in the Four Courts in Dublin. He later claimed he had turned his back on the IRA. There was insufficient evidence to place McGirl at the fishing village of Mullaghmore. He was acquitted and he died in 1995.

McMahon, who has never apologised for the killings or for the pain caused to the victims' families, was released from jail in August 1998 as part of the Good Friday peace agreement. He remains a Sinn Féin member actively involved in his local community. He lives with his wife Rose in a hillside bungalow in Lisanisk, close to the market town of Carrickmacross in County Monaghan. His two sons have grown up and he is believed to work as a carpenter from his home, which is decorated with some of the landscapes he painted during his years in jail.

Gerry Adams, Sinn Féin's spokesman, said of Mountbatten's death at the time of the Queen's historic visit to Ireland in June 2012, 'The IRA gave clear reasons for the execution.' He went on, 'I think it is unfortunate that anyone has to be killed, but the furore created by Mountbatten's death showed up the hypocritical attitude of the media establishment. As a member of the House of Lords, Mountbatten was an emotional figure in both British and Irish politics. What the IRA did to him is what Mountbatten had been doing all his life to other people; and with his war record I don't think he could have objected to dying in what was clearly a war situation. He knew the danger involved in coming to this country.'

The Queen, with Philip at her side, was forced to put aside sad memories of the murder of her cousin the Earl of Mountbatten by the IRA on the Irish visit and to shake the hand of Martin McGuinness, the commander understood to have ordered Mountbatten's killing.

Philip, not one for wearing his heart on his sleeve, kept his counsel over the murder of his beloved uncle who had played such a pivotal role in the shaping of his life's journey. The only comment he made was revealed later in a poignant reply to a letter of condolences from actor Lionel Jeffries, who starred in 1960s films *Murder Ahoy!*, *Camelot* and *Chitty Chitty Bang Bang*. Penned on Balmoral Castle letter-headed paper on 13 September 1979 Philip wrote of his uncle's murder, 'Let us hope that the great wave of revulsion against this senseless act of terrorism may yet help to bring a change of heart in those who believe that violence and brutality are the only solutions to their problems,' signing it, 'Yours Sincerely Philip.'

Perhaps, even more poignant was the simple floral tribute, a wreath of hydrangeas, lilies and roses, left on the grass outside Westminster Abbey. The inscription read, 'In loving memory from Philip and Lilibet.' It was heartfelt.

20: AFFAIRS OF THE HEART

'Good God, woman! Have you ever stopped to think that for years I've not moved anywhere without a policeman accompanying me? How the hell could I have got away with anything like that?'

Philip's angry response to a journalist who asked about rumours of his infidelity

The unkempt father of four wandered freely along the corridors of Buckingham Palace in the dead of night unchecked. He then proceeded to help himself to a bottle from the Prince of Wales's personal collection of wine. He was a little unsteady on his feet and reeked of stale alcohol as he had been drinking earlier, but he couldn't resist drinking some more. He was desperate to go to the toilet but couldn't find one, so he urinated in the royal corgis' bowl of food. The unemployed painter and decorator from Islington, north London, later claimed, when questioned by police about the incident, that had he wandered 'willy-nilly' around the corridors at 7 a.m. on 9 July 1982, before finally walking into the Queen's bedroom, pitching up at her bedside, pulling back the curtains of her four-poster and then waking a shocked monarch from her sleep. His name was Michael Fagan, the unlikely booze-loving perpetrator of the biggest royal security breach of the twentieth century.

'It was a double bed but a single room, definitely, she was sleeping in there on her own,' he told writer Emily Dugan. 'Her nightie was one of those Liberty prints and it was down to her knees.' Somehow the hapless intruder had scaled the barbed-wire-topped, 14-foot wall of Buckingham Palace and shinned up a drainpipe before entering the palace and wandering around via King George V's multi-million pound private stamp collection. He did trigger the security alarm twice but instead of investigating the police on duty simply turned it off as they assumed the warnings were technical errors, rather than a real intruder. Later it prompted an outcry over security and the then Home Secretary, Willie Whitelaw, offered his resignation to the Queen, which she refused.

It was reported in the newspapers at the time that the Queen coolly had a long conversation with Fagan to stall him while security was summoned. It didn't happen like that. 'What are you doing here?' the then 56-year-old Queen said before running out of the room. 'She went past me and ran out of the room; her little bare feet running across the floor,' he told the reporter from *The Independent on Sunday* in February 2012.

When, finally, the Queen managed to summon help, it came in the form of an unarmed footman, Paul Whybrew, who stood watch until the police came. Fagan recalled: 'The footman came and said, "Cor, fucking hell mate, you look like you need a drink." His name was Whybrew, which is a funny name for someone offering you a drink, innit? He took me to the Queen's pantry, across the landing, where I presume she cooks her baked beans and toast and whatever and takes a bottle of Famous Grouse from the shelf and pours me a glass of whisky.'

Mr Whybrew, known as 'Tall Paul' on account that he is 6 feet 4 inches tall, had a starring role in the London 2012 short James Bond film for the Olympic Games, alongside the Queen and 007 actor Daniel Craig. In court the account slightly differed. It emerged that Fagan was finally cornered in a pantry near the Queen's bedroom by footman Mr Whybrew. Mr Whybrew, who had been at the palace for six years at the time, said in a statement that Fagan kept insisting that he wanted to talk to the Queen and calling her, 'My queen'. He added: 'I tried to keep him calm and he said he was all right. He said it was urgent and tried to pass me but I got in his way. I also noticed his breath smelled of alcohol. I laughed and tried to be casual and friendly and said: "How did you get here?" He replied: "I just want to talk to her."' To stall for time, Mr Whybrew told him, 'All right but let her get dressed first.'

Mr Whybrew said Fagan appeared not to be coherent or rational and seemed very tense. That's when the footman asked him if he would like a drink, and then PC Robert Roberts arrived in the pantry to find Fagan sitting on the sideboard, swinging his feet and drinking a whisky. Fagan said, on the night of his arrest, that it was not the first time he had managed to elude security and sneak into the palace. A month earlier he admitted that he had broken in and managed to spend most of the night inside before leaving, again undetected, in the early hours. Fagan climbed in through the bedroom window of palace maid, Sarah Carter, who ran straight to security to report the incident. When they found nobody in her room they placated her but the investigating officer thought she had imagined it. The gross lack of diligence left Fagan free to explore the corridors of the palace undisturbed.

Days after the first and undetected break-in Fagan was arrested for the theft of a car and he was sent to Brixton prison, but released on bail. The next day, however, Fagan headed to Buckingham Palace for the second time. When questioned later he could not explain why he did it. 'Something just got into my head,' he said, claiming it all stemmed from him putting too many magic mushrooms, containing psilocybin, the substance that causes a hallucinogenic effect, in his soup five months earlier.

A Home Office inquiry later discovered that the security breach had been the direct result of, 'serious errors and omissions' by the Scotland Yard police officers on duty at the palace. Home Secretary, Willie Whitelaw, whose offer of resignation was rejected by the Queen, later told MPs when he addressed the House of Commons, 'The basic cause of the breakdown of security was a failure by police to respond efficiently and urgently.'

The day after the court verdict was handed down, *The Sun* newspaper's front page splash declared that the decision to clear Fagan of the charge of burgling Buckingham Palace was 'BONKERS!', after an Old Bailey jury took just 22 minutes to acquit him. He had told the court that a 'little voice' in his head had ordered him to break into the palace twice, to prove that the Queen's security was slapdash. 'In my opinion I have done the Queen a favour,' Fagan said, claiming that he had exposed vital flaws in the monarch's security system. In his evidence, the arresting police officer, PC Robert Roberts, said, as he grabbed the intruder to lead him away, he became very abusive and told him his name was Rudolph Hess, the former Deputy Führer to Adolf Hitler and a leading Nazi. It transpired that Fagan was not charged with entering the Queen's bedroom, which happened during his second Buckingham Palace escapade, because the Director of Public Prosecutions said that no criminal offence was committed.

Once the news had played out in the media, the press raked over the fine detail of the case that had inadvertently been revealed. They inevitably focused on the fact that the Queen and Prince Philip, according to what Fagan told the court, apparently didn't share a bed and slept in separate rooms. Such an arrangement seemed odd to the average working class or middle-class couple of the time, who routinely slept in the same bed as their life partners. Royal commentators later explained that such sleeping arrangements were part of a long-standing tradition among the British upper classes. It prompted the tabloid press to question, where was Prince Philip? Why was he not on hand to come to his wife's rescue? Indeed the fact that the royal couple did not appear to share a bedroom caused more comment than the fact that a man could wander off the street into the sovereign's bedroom without challenge.

In his 2004 book, *Philip & Elizabeth: Portrait of a Marriage*, Gyles Brandreth told a different story, and claimed that the newspapers, and Fagan, had got it wrong, 'I am able to tell you that, customarily, when sleeping under the same roof, the Queen and Prince Philip do share the same bed,' he asserted a little over confidently. 'It just happened that on the morning of Fagan's intrusion, Philip had a crack-of-dawn start for an out-of-town official engagement and so spent the night in his own quarters.' This may have been true, but it did not tell the whole story.

Even as a young married couple Elizabeth and Philip arranged to have separate bedrooms, with an interconnecting door between the two. The Princess Elizabeth was once left in an embarrassing position when the couple lived at Clarence House. The duke's valet, James MacDonald, was surprised after discovering Elizabeth in her husband's bed one morning wearing her silk nightgown. Philip was unfazed when his man-servant walked in and was naked. Writing in his biography of Philip, *Young Prince Philip: His Turbulent Early Life*, author Philip Eade revealed that in the early years Elizabeth and Philip did, 'Enjoy the visitation rituals which that system involves'.

Lady Pamela Hicks, Philip's first cousin and former lady-in-waiting to the Queen, perhaps much better placed to really know the couple than Gyles Brandreth, explained that, 'In England, the upper class always have had separate bedrooms. You don't want to be bothered with snoring or someone flinging a leg around. Then when you are feeling cosy you share your room sometimes. It is lovely to be able to choose.'

For Prince Philip duty, and leading by example, ranked high on his list of importance. Gyles Brandreth, a former Conservative MP, may well have had excellent access to the duke and his team and used it very well in the writing of his tome. He wrote, 'I think we can take it as read that the Queen has been faithful throughout her married life. There are those who persist in believing that Prince Andrew's natural father was the Queen's racing manager, Henry Porchester, 7th Earl of Carnarvon, suggesting the conception occurred at some point between 20 January and 30 April 1959 when Philip was away on another of his long sea voyages in the *Britannia*. It does not seem to bother these gossips that the dates don't stack up. After all, Prince Andrew was born on 19 February 1960, a happy by-product of the Queen and Philip's post-*Britannia* reunion.'

Philip never denied that he had girlfriends before he married. He certainly had dates with women when he was on leave during the war. In the hit TV Netflix drama *The Crown,* however, Philip and his married private secretary, Mike Parker, are shown cavorting with bare-breasted women during an official tour of the Commonwealth. The episode, first broadcast in 2017, culminated in a letter written by Commander Parker, in which he suggests Philip's solo tour of Australia and the South Pacific in 1956–1957 was a 'five-month stag night' with 'whores in every port'. As a result, in the drama, Commander Parker not only loses his job, but is divorced by his wife Eileen. It is almost entirely false, and the events featured did not happen. Commander Parker's son, Michael, denounced the series as 'rubbish', and insisted his late father was not a philanderer. He said the family were keeping the episode a secret from the woman at the centre of the storyline, their mother, Eileen who was 94.

'I can't believe they've portrayed my father like this,' said Mr Parker, 73, from his home in Hampshire. 'He was an honourable man and looked after Philip very well.' There is no evidence, he said, that the tour was a 's★★g-fest. It would have been very unlike my father.'

That said, it would have been odd if he had not played the field when he was free to do so. Philip was, understandably, always sensitive to persistent unproven claims that he committed adultery. Publicly, he brushed it off, but privately, the rumours irritated him for years. There is no hard evidence that the duke was unfaithful to the Queen. He has, however, been labelled a ladies' man over the years and been accused of being overfamiliar with a number of beautiful women. Philip's association with the British stage actress, singer and dancer, Pat Kirkwood, in the 1930s and early 1940s, perhaps caused the most public controversy.

Given that Philip was five years Elizabeth's senior and he met her when she was only 13, it was not only inevitable that he would date other women of his own age, but healthy. Cobina Wright, an American actress, met Philip when they were both 17 and they hit it off straight away. The pair enjoyed a summer romance and Philip fell hopelessly in love with her. There was even talk of marriage between them, but she didn't feel quite as strongly as he did and the two of them drifted apart naturally. Within weeks Philip met another beauty who stole his heart, Osla Benning, a stunning Canadian debutante. The duke dated Osla briefly after a mutual friend set them up on a blind date. The pair would enjoy intimate weekends together at Philip's Uncle Dickie's estate Broadlands, but again the relationship soon fizzled out. While Philip was on Navy leave in Australia he reportedly romanced society beauties Sue Other-Gee and Sandra Jacques, the latter of which was said to be 'a very full love affair'.

It was not, however, these youthful and pre-marital liaisons that raised eyebrows among the old guard at the palace, but persistent rumours that Philip was involved in illicit liaisons after he wed Elizabeth. There is a long list of beautiful women with whom Philip is alleged to have had enjoyed intimate relationships, although no evidence has ever emerged that any of these developed into full-blown affairs.

The women Philip was closely associated with included Florence-born Lady Saunders, the wife of the English theatre impresario Sir Peter Saunders, who was noted for his production of the long-running murder mystery play *The Mousetrap,* written by Agatha Christie. Lady Saunders was better known as Katie Boyle. Other glamorous women linked to Philip included the actresses Merle Oberon and Anna Massey.

Another woman with whom the duke was romantically linked was Hélène Cordet, formerly Hélène Foufounis. The pair had become friends as children. They spent holidays together at Hélène's parents' villa in Le Touquet, France. When Cordet first married, when she was 20 and Prince Phillip was 16, he walked her down the aisle. The pair remained close and she had two children while separated from her first husband, Max and Louise. Hélène, who became the hostess of the BBC variety show *Café Continental*, refused to reveal who their father was. So when Philip elected to become godfather to both in a giant leap some assumed that it must be him. Despite this, Hélène allowed the paternity of her children to remain a mystery, though one of her sons, Max, has flatly denied that Philip is his father.

More serious than claims of fanciful flirtations with actresses and dancers, perhaps, were the whispers that Philip had become a little too well acquainted with wives of senior palace courtiers or the wives of his friends. Among those he was romantically linked with was the hot-tempered novelist Daphne du Maurier, who was 14 years his senior and the author of the 1938 book *Rebecca*. She also penned *Jamaica Inn* and a short story that inspired film director Sir Alfred Hitchcock's classic *The Birds* and was married to Lieutenant-General Sir Frederick Arthur Montague 'Boy' Browning, former Comptroller of the Royal Household. Boy Browning was a close colleague of Philip's uncle Lord Mountbatten during World War II and was asked to work for the Royal Family on his return home. Du Maurier, whose husband died in 1965, is said to have had a fluid sexuality and enjoyed affairs with both men and women. An archive of informal photographs of Philip and the Royal Family emerged from her estate after she died in 1989.

One photograph shows a youthful Elizabeth sitting on a blanket eating sandwiches next to her husband, dressed in country attire. Others include Elizabeth and Philip on board Daphne's husband's yacht and the Queen Mother sitting on a picnic blanket with the writer. Shortly before the wedding, Philip went to stay with Daphne in Cornwall. Their relationship was 'emotionally intimate' though not sexual but, at the end of the weekend, he told her: 'I don't want to go back, I want to stay with you.' Du Maurier told him not to be silly: 'Your country needs you.'

Another woman linked to Philip was Philippa de Pass, Lady-of-the-Bedchamber to the Queen and wife of the duke's Royal Navy friend and shooting companion Lieutenant Commander Robert de Pass, who lived in a seventeenth-century Grade I listed house on the Petworth House estate in West Sussex, where the duke was a regular and welcome guest. He was even alleged to have enjoyed an intimate friendship with Sarah Ferguson's glamorous mother, Susan Barrantes and of being too close to the Queen's cousin, Princess Alexandra.

Philip always brushed away these stories with feigned indifference, punctuated by the occasional exasperated denial. Wearily he has pointed out: 'I have had a detective in my company night and day since 1947' – a reference to his police bodyguard who always accompanies him. So, of course, did his son, Charles, who conducted a long affair with married Camilla Parker Bowles, and Princess Diana, who 'loved and adored' Major James Hewitt. Diana also enjoyed intimate affairs with others, including married art dealer Oliver Hoare. Philip's daughter Princess Anne too had an affair with the equerry to the Queen Tim Laurence, who she later married, when married to Captain Mark Phillips. She also even enjoyed an affair with her married Scotland Yard personal protection officer, Peter Cross, in the early eighties. Scotland Yard removed Cross from royal duties but Anne continued to see him and used the pseudonym Mrs Wallis when she wanted to contact him, potentially a reference to Wallis Simpson. After their alleged affair was exposed, Anne stopped seeing Mr Cross, whose marriage ended in divorce. He ended up selling his story to the *News of the World*. So Philip's claims that having a bodyguard proved he was faithful don't prove anything.

One passionate relationship Philip shared that did raise eyebrows at court was with the beautiful Sacha, Duchess of Abercorn, the wife of the James, the 5th Duke of Abercorn, who was Lord Steward of the Royal Household between 2001–2009. Sacha – Alexandra Anastasia Hamilton (d. 10 December 2018 aged 72) – was related to Russia's Romanov dynasty and the British Royal Family, and admitted to author Gyles Brandreth that she shared a 'highly charged chemistry' with Philip, who was 25 years her senior.

She told Brandreth for his book, 'Our friendship was very close. The heart came into it in a big way. There's a hugely potent chemical reaction in him. It's a highly charged chemistry. We were close because we understood one another. He felt he could trust me and I felt I could trust him. It was a passionate friendship, but the passion was in the ideas. It was certainly not a full relationship. I did not go to bed with him, although, it probably looked like that to the world.'

Sacha was a passionate woman driven by her social responsibility, who went on to establish The Pushkin Trust, which promotes creative writing in schools and is named after her Russian ancestor, the writer Alexander Pushkin. When asked whether she thought Philip had slept with any of his girlfriends she said, 'I doubt it very much. No, I'm sure not... But he's a human being. Who knows? I don't. Unless you are in the room with a lighted candle, who knows?'

Royal biographer Sarah Bradford, Viscountess Bangor, had no doubts; pulling no punches, she labelled Philip an adulterer in her 2011 book *Elizabeth II: Her Life in Our Times*, although in truth she had precious little evidence for her claims. 'The Duke of Edinburgh has had affairs, full-blown affairs and more than one,' she wrote. 'He has affairs and the queen accepts it. I think she thinks that's how men are. He's never been one for chasing actresses,' she continued. 'His interest is quite different. The women he goes for are always younger than him, usually beautiful, and highly aristocratic.'

The Queen, however, appears to always have had faith in her marriage and confidence in the intimacy she shared with Philip. The couple were regular weekend guests at Broadlands, Lord Mountbatten's estate, where they spent their honeymoon. Staff noted that only one of the two bedrooms in their suite was ever slept in. 'They were like a pair of teenagers,' recalled Chief Petty Officer William Evans, who was head of Mountbatten's personal staff and witnessed how sexually playful Philip and Elizabeth were together. Evans recalled that he saw one encounter between the couple on the staircase at Broadlands, when an amorous Philip couldn't wait to chase his wife into their bedroom.

Evans went on, 'The Queen had a look of panic on her face that wasn't really panic at all, if you know what I mean – she was loving it, and Philip knew that. He was enjoying himself, and he wouldn't stop, but just kept pinching her bottom all the way to the top, and it's a lot of stairs. I wondered whether they ever behaved like that at Buckingham Palace.' What was even more telling, Evans thought, was they were this sexually boisterous 15 years into their marriage at a time when they had already had three of their four children. 'But this is how they were. Whenever they came to stay they always had lots of fun together. She always looked at him with a glint in her eyes,' the former servant said.

What is not in doubt, however, is that throughout his life Philip always enjoyed the company of beautiful women, and in later life, he preferred them to be several years younger than him. An excellent dancer, he was a regular on the dance floor tripping the light fantastic rhythmically at the Royal Yacht Squadron Ball during Cowes with Penny Romsey, the wife of his cousin, the then Lord Brabourne. Onlookers observed that the pair were both very relaxed, laughing, flirting, neither seemed concerned what anyone might say. There is no doubt Penny and Philip enjoy a close relationship.

Her lively mind, as well as her beauty, had turned this former meat-trader's daughter into a central figure at the heart of royal life. She was often at Windsor Castle at weekends, telling both Philip and the Queen about what was going on in the outside world. The Queen was said to be relaxed about the friendship and the three of them at times sat and watched television together in the evenings.

Penny, a butcher's daughter, found herself living the dream when she married into a scion of the Royal Family. She was chatelaine of a vast and historic country house set in 6,000 acres. For although Penny Brabourne's father had left school at 15 years old and become a butcher, like his father and grandfather before him, he died a wealthy man, having founded the hugely successful Angus Steakhouse chain of restaurants which he eventually sold for several million pounds. Penny, the restaurant tycoon's only daughter, had the appearance of a fashion model. Tall, slender, blonde and beautiful Penny developed an intimate friendship with Philip. She shared his passion for carriage driving. Philip explained, 'I had been playing polo and I decided to give up at the age of 50,' he said. 'I was looking around to see what next, you know, what was available. I thought to myself we have got horses and carriages, so I borrowed four horses from the stables and took them to Norfolk and practised.'

He went on, 'The second competition I entered was the European championship. I came in not quite last, but very nearly.'

Philip and Penny's shared enjoyment of the exhilarating sport enabled them to develop their close friendship. They refused to let media speculation about the possibly intimate nature of their relationship interfere in their lives or limit the time they spent alone in each other's company. Indeed, it is said that Penny's enthusiasm for the sport of carriage driving was crucial in keeping Philip's hands on the reins into his 90s, when most people would have given up. Penny and Philip were regular competitors at the Royal Windsor Horse Show. Their humorous repartee and flirtatious affection for each other was obvious. The Queen, often sitting just feet away, was always relieved to see her sometimes cantankerous husband looking so relaxed and contented.

The Queen was always aware of, and accepted, Philip's penchant for beautiful and often younger women. After all, the duke never made a secret of it. His flirtatious nature kept him young at heart, his close circle said. Princess Alexandra of the Hellenes said of her cousin, Philip: 'He liked blondes, brunettes and redheads. He was very impartial.' Elizabeth never felt the need to question her husband's loyalty and support for her. 'She [the Queen] was worldly enough too, to accept that some men may have certain needs and that doesn't mean they love their wives any the less,' she said. The duke's cherished relationship with Penny, out of all his intimate extramarital friendships, was by far the most abiding. He spent many weekends away with her carriage driving over the country. She was a regular guest at the weekend house parties he holds at secluded Wood Farm on the Sandringham Estate in Norfolk.

The 'Penny Romsey situation', as palace courtiers would privately refer to it, first emerged in public after details of a rambling telephone conversation between Penny and Philip were leaked to the press by an electronic eavesdropper. In the conversation the pair were overheard discussing some of the Royal Family's most private and pressing issues: from Charles and Diana's divorce to Camilla Parker Bowles. Even the Queen Mother's hip operation was discussed by the couple. From the nature of the conversation their relationship was clearly a warm one and it was obvious that he valued her insight. At one point in the conversation, however, she handed the phone over to her husband, Norton Knatchbull, thus rather destroying any illusion of a clandestine affair.

After the so-called 'Squidgygate' and 'Camillagate' scandals, when telephone conversations between Diana, Princess of Wales and her friend James Gilbey, and another between Prince Charles and his mistress Camilla Parker Bowles, were intercepted and then leaked to the press, the media inevitably dubbed it 'Dukegate'. Philip was understandably irritated over the breach to both his and Penny's privacy.

Ever since 1975, when Norton first introduced his girlfriend, the then Penny Eastwood, to Prince Charles, with whom he was at school, and then Philip, she has always been a popular figure at the heart of the Royal Family. She was a natural young woman, outgoing but not brash or flirtatious. Philip immediately found the combination of her beauty, humour and intelligence irresistible.

Even towards the end of his life when he is unable to do much carriage driving, they found their mutual love of painting watercolours another good reason to spend quality time together. One critic said of his work, 'Exactly what you'd expect, totally direct, no hanging about.'

The Queen was always very relaxed about Penny and her husband. She would shrug her shoulders and says, 'Philip likes to have her around.' For his part Philip didn't feel he had anything to feel guilty about and frankly didn't give a damn what anyone, least of all the press, thought, as long as his behaviour did not humiliate his wife.

Over the years Elizabeth was known to be irritated by the talk of her husband's flirtations. She had grown to accept that he took a lot of 'amusing' in his younger days. In the autumn of his life that was less of an issue for her. What mattered to the Queen was that his love and his loyalty as far as she was concerned was always unquestioning.

Penny's life continued much the same, even though her husband did leave her, and decided to quit Britain to conduct a serious affair with his fashion designer girlfriend, Lady Nuttall, in the Bahamas. That relationship didn't work out as he had hoped and he returned to Broadlands, but moved into a cottage on the estate. Penny continued to be a frequent guest of the Queen and Philip at Windsor Castle. She would also spend time alone with the duke at Wood Farm on the Sandringham estate. There is no doubt that Penny adored Philip and she had a special place in his heart.

Penny's late mother-in-law, Patricia Mountbatten, commented[*], 'Philip is a man who enjoys the company of attractive, intelligent younger women. Nothing wrong in that. He's always had somebody there, sharing one or other of his particular pursuits. He has special friends, like Penny. But I am quite sure, quite sure, absolutely certain, he has never been unfaithful to the Queen.'

---

[*]   To Gyles Brandreth, in his 2004 book *Philip and Elizabeth: Portrait of a Marriage*

21: CHINESE WHISPERS

'If you stay here much longer you will go back slitty eyed.'

Prince Philip's remark to student Simon
Kirby on the state visit to China, 1986

The two hours they spent together was much longer than the fastidious Chinese Communist leader Deng Xiaoping had scheduled in his busy diary. But the meeting, conducted through an interpreter, turned out to be more small talk than substance. Deng and the Queen sat next to each other in the Joint Happiness Garden as he reminisced about the time he had spent in Europe as a young man. She smiled as he recalled how he twice climbed the Eiffel Tower in Paris in the hope that he could see London, but told her on both occasions it was too cloudy. The Queen, wearing regal purple, didn't dismiss the absurd notion out of hand, but simply responded with typical diplomacy, 'I'd think that would be rather difficult, it's quite a long way.'

Elizabeth and Philip also met Deng's top two aides, Communist Party General Secretary, Hu Yaobang, and China's Premier, Zhao Ziyang, with much of the time taken up with what a spokesman for the royal party, Michael Shea, termed, 'gossipy conversation'.

'How is your sister, Princess Margaret?' the General Secretary asked at one point. 'She is very well, thank you,' the Queen replied. Nor did she bat an eyelid when the ageing Communist leader spat into a spittoon that was placed by his seat. Philip did not show such tact, letting out a loud guffaw each time he did it.

The historic meeting was designed to help cement diplomatic and economic relations between the two great trading nations now that the biggest political obstacle between them, Hong Kong, had been removed with the deal two years earlier to return the British colony to China in 1997. The state visit, from 12 to 18 October 1986, was therefore seen as one of the most important royal tours the Queen had ever undertaken, a critical diplomatic mission, coming so soon after those testing negotiations.

Underlying the pleasantries was a major Chinese effort to portray the disputes between China and Britain over Hong Kong as a thing of the past, and to try to deflect British attention away from controversies over how much democracy it should allow in Hong Kong over the next 11 years before China took over. 'With the successful solution of the Hong Kong question, our duty now is to develop the friendly relations between our two countries. It is in this context that I wish you the warmest of welcomes,' Deng told the Queen.

Having schmoozed the most senior Chinese government officials, the Queen and Prince Philip then went to see the country's top tourist attraction, the Great Wall of China at Badaling, the most visited section of the fortification, approximately 80 kilometres north-west of urban Beijing, in Yanqing District. Back home in the UK viewers watched the Queen become the first-ever British monarch to walk along it, due to the first-ever satellite transmission from the site of the seventh-century BC defensive wall. At the time it was seen as a great technological, broadcasting achievement. The BBC had over 120 staff in China for the special broadcasts, including one of its best known broadcasters and journalists, Sue Lawley, who anchored the shows and then would hand over to the then BBC Royal Correspondent, the urbane and immaculately attired Michael Cole.

The Queen, along with Philip, decided to carry on and climb to a much higher level than had been mapped out for them, perhaps partly to send a message to Fleet Street editors back home, who had published unsubstantiated rumours that suggested she had heart trouble, that they were off the mark. Once at the top of the climb, Elizabeth and Prince Philip joined Foreign Secretary Sir Geoffrey

Howe, who was so excited that he couldn't help playing at being a tourist by turning the camera around and taking a few photographs himself. On the way back down, the Chinese officials pointed out every step to the Queen, as they were desperate to prevent her taking a tumble and avoid a diplomatic incident.

The British diplomats and Chinese officials had painstakingly prepared a series of cultural engagements in four other Chinese cities, including visits to places where foreign leaders rarely went then. They including Xi'an, the capital of Shaanxi Province, which was one of the oldest cities and the capital of China's two greatest ruling empires, the Han and the Tang dynasties. It was there that the Queen inspected a very unique guard of honour: 8,000 ancient clay warriors called the Terracotta Army, standing alongside each other in battle formation. Created 2,200 years earlier, and only unearthed in 1972, the warriors – all standing 5 foot 11 inches tall, and each with a unique face – were made on the orders of the first Chinese Emperor, Qin Shi Huang. Although he was an effective leader he had also inspired such widespread hatred and fear throughout his life he knew his enemies would seek him out, even beyond the grave. The clay army of warriors was created to protect him in his tomb.

What happened next, however, was to remain a source of extreme irritation for Prince Philip throughout his life. Fleet Street newspaper reporters, who were assigned to cover the tour, did their best, in his view, to wreck the important diplomatic mission by blowing one of his off-the-cuff remarks out of all proportion. Philip, not for the first time, looked to blame the messenger, not himself.

Back in the UK the BBC *News*, unsure of the authenticity of the story and even more unsure of its sources, took the decision to run a story reporting that during the tour Prince Philip, 'May have walked into a small problem.' Newsreader, Nicholas Witchell, who would later became the long-serving BBC Royal Correspondent, said on air, 'The royal press secretary, Michael Shea, has had to deny that certain remarks that were attributed to the prince were intended in any way to be insulting to the Chinese people.' It emerged, said the seasoned journalist, that Philip had spoken to a British student who claimed the prince had said a few things about Peking that the BBC described as 'rather less than flattering'.

The unfortunate student in question was Simon Kirby, a 21-year-old Chinese language student from Edinburgh University, who was based in China on an 18-month exchange. He had spent ten minutes in the company of the duke and the Queen during a visit at Xi'an's Xibei University. No journalists were present but Alan Hamilton heard about the comment from another student afterwards. Hamilton, of *The Times,* who was covering the engagement on a pool basis for the rest of the Fleet Street newspaper reporters, noted that the duke had not been over flattering about China. 'The duke was very outspoken and said Beijing was not very nice,' Simon Kirby told him. Hamilton was then hurried back from the engagement to the media bus, along with colleague Tom Corby of the Press Association, with the kernel of a story.

When the experienced correspondent returned to the waiting press bus he began to offload his notes as the pool system requires as they headed to the airport to take a flight to Kunming in Yunnan province. When he got to relating the exchange between Prince Philip and the student, *Sun* royal reporter Harry Arnold, dubbed 'the Jack Russell of Fleet Street' for his countless scoops and noted for his sharp Savile Row suits, instinctively knew it was a much bigger story. Arnold was desperate for more detail that Hamilton simply couldn't provide. 'Harry was determined to get every spit and cough, and, with the agreement of the others, told the bus driver to stop the bus at the nearest hotel so he could make some calls. When we got there he and the reporter from the *Evening Standard* got off the bus and we waited for them,' said his colleague *Sun* photographer, Arthur Edwards MBE, who was there.

'Alan Hamilton fortunately had noted the name of the student who had spoken to Philip and Harry tracked down the student by phone. This was in the days before mobile phones and we were in the middle of nowhere. How he did it, I just don't know, but he found the student, spoke to him on the phone and what he told him was sensational and made headlines around the world. We used to have a saying, "Sometimes it is words, sometimes it is pictures,"; this time it was all about the words and Harry showed what a brilliant reporter he was,' said Arthur.

The unsuspecting student, Kirby, from Leamington Spa, came to the phone and Harry used his finely honed interview skills to glean exactly what Philip had said. Kirby revealed he'd told the duke that he liked studying there, but added that he didn't live with Chinese students, to which the duke replied, 'So they [the Chinese] don't want to mix with the barbarians.' The duke went on to describe China's capital city Beijing as 'ghastly' and asked Kirby how long he had been studying Chinese at the university. Kirby then told the journalist Philip's response to his reply. 'He said to me, "If you stay here much longer you'll be slitty eyed."' Even Harry, an experienced hack, was shocked, so he checked the precise words again. He knew this was going to run and run. In mitigation, Kirby added that the Queen had said she thought the Forbidden City was fascinating. Harry then raced back to the bus to share the spoils of his telephone chat. As far as the press was concerned this could be whipped up into a full-scale diplomatic row and was a dream start.

Even though the royal rota pool reporters, Hamilton and Corby, had been elsewhere when the exchange between Philip and the student happened, *Daily Mirror* photographer Doreen Spooner was on the spot. Immediately afterwards Spooner, the first noted female photographer working on Fleet Street, 'didn't think' before she spoke. 'I said to Philip, "I don't think you should have said that, do you?" Philip agreed, "No, I don't think I should."' Ms Spooner, however, probably wisely decided to keep quiet as the furore unfolded and let the reporters do their job, not wanting the sourcing of controversial quotes to rest on her shoulders.

Years later Harry Arnold told me how the story unfolded shortly before his death from liver cancer on 9 November 2014 aged 73. 'This conversation should have been obtained from a pool position but the reporter was missing from that position. The trip to China was one which had been planned probably for decades and it was ruined by one stupid remark by the Duke of Edinburgh and it's all very well to blame the press for it but it was an official tour, he was on duty, he knows that his words are reported wherever he goes.'

Within hours it exploded into a major diplomatic incident. Dame Ann Leslie, the chain-smoking, multi-award-winning *Daily Mail* journalist, was overheard talking to her editor, Sir David English, who was digging down into the detail of the story before he published. He wanted to know the reliability of the source. 'I don't doubt the veracity of Harry Arnold,' Ann insisted. When the royal press secretary, Michael Shea, got wind of the story he tried to shut it down pleading with the journalists on tour not to create a diplomatic incident by reporting the remark. 'Surely *The Times*, of all people, are not going to use this?' he implored Alan Hamilton, who had after all started the ball rolling. 'Most certainly,' Hamilton replied, 'but not until paragraph 14.' The broadsheet newspapers prided themselves in not getting over excited on such matters and left the scandals to the tabloids. But Hamilton had grossly misjudged the mood of the people. By now the media was in a flat spin and this was a global story.

Harry Arnold, rightly, felt like the cock of the walk. So he should; his tenacity had unearthed a cracking story and a major blunder by the duke. When the press party reached Kunming he told the *Sun* photographer, Arthur Edwards, to commandeer one of only six phones in the media centre, so he could file his story via the copytakers, while he talked to his news editor, Tom Petrie, in London on another. Before Harry could finish briefing the story down the line Mr Petrie cut him short, 'I know all about it Harry, it's all in the *Evening Standard*,' he said, pricking the reporter's bubble. In the adrenalin rush of nailing the scoop, Harry had forgotten that the *Evening Standard*'s shrewd correspondent, Lynda Murdin, (d. April 2011, aged 61) had shadowed his every move. She filed her copy via the copy-takers in London immediately from the information she had gleaned from overhearing Harry questioning the student on the phone, without seeking confirmation from Buckingham Palace press secretary, Michael Shea.

The time difference between Beijing and London was in the evening paper's favour and its editor, John Leese, decided to 'publish and be damned' and just ran the story. When it appeared first in the *Evening Standard* all hell broke out among the press. Shea dismissed it as 'trivial' but didn't deny that the words 'slitty-eyed' had been used. He said it was nothing more than a 'happy, jokey, private conversation' but Fleet Street, particularly the tabloids, were having none of it.

Then a flustered Mr Shea seemed to make matters worse when the press questioned him further. Harry Arnold said, 'When he finally acknowledged that the words "slitty eyes" were used he then insisted that Philip in using them was, "In no way disparaging of the Chinese people."' Wearing what was described as a pained expression, Mr Shea said: 'It's a well-known physiological fact that people in different parts of the world have eyes that are differently shaped. My eyes are round.'

A little deflated by the *Evening Standard* being first to print the story, Harry Arnold's inner 'Jack Russell' came to the fore. He was as determined to keep the story rolling as the palace and Foreign & Commonwealth Office were to shut it down. 'This story has legs,' he said, very long legs as it turned out. 'Philip Gets It All Wong,' screamed the front page of *The Sun*, illustrated with a photo of Philip retouched so as to give him darting Fu Manchu eyebrows and eyelids. Harry Arnold's copy read, 'Prince Philip torpedoed the royal visit to China.'

The Sun wasn't the only newspaper to revel in Philip's discomfort. They all had a field day. China's leading English-language newspaper, *China Daily*, described the duke's remarks as 'foot in mouth disease' while the *Daily Mirror* dubbed him 'The Great Wally of China'. Perhaps the most sophisticated headline was in the *Daily Mail*, which asked the question, 'Does Britain Need a Terracotta Duke?' Under it was a photograph of a grim-faced-looking Queen inspecting the Terracotta warriors guarding the imperial tomb of the Chin Dynasty emperor, near Xi'an, and a strapline which read, 'They're tall, dignified, ceremonial and above everything else, they are silent.' To add insult to injury, there was also a cartoon of the Queen's husband with a gag over his mouth.

The state-controlled Chinese press had largely ignored the remarks. Arthur Edwards recalled that the Chinese officials monitoring the tour were most worried about the controversy being reported on *Voice of America* which had a powerful influence on public opinion across the world. It wasn't. That said it has since gone down in history as one of Philip's most indelicate remarks and a huge diplomatic blunder.

The next day, 16 October, in Kunming, the capital and largest city of Yunnan province, the Queen and Philip were driven in a black Mercedes-Benz past enormous crowds of well-wishers. Their route took them from Wujiaba Airport to the Green Lake Park area of the city, where officials had organised for the streets to be widened and repaved for the event. Street lights topped with white swans, many of which still stand today, were also installed in anticipation of the royal visit. The Queen, however, had a face like thunder. 'The Queen was so angry she could barely look at the duke. Her expression hardly changed. You could hardly get a shot of the Queen smiling if you tried. They wouldn't look at each other,' said Harry Arnold. Arthur Edwards sent a particularly glum-looking photograph of the Queen to his picture desk at *The Sun*. 'We carried another headline saying, "Queen Velly Velly Angry",' said Harry, 'I mean it was just a terrible time for the duke and he suffered a lot of criticism as a result.'

Buckingham Palace and the Foreign & Commonwealth Office continued to persist with the line that Philip's remark was simply, 'jocular'. It caused the British Ambassador, Sir Richard Evans, a considerable headache. Sir Richard also attempted to pass it off as good-humoured banter, but the Magdalen College, Oxford-educated diplomat, who had initialled the historic Sino-British Joint Declaration on 26 September 1984, was very unhappy. 'British diplomats will have to walk on eggshells for the next few weeks, in readiness for a possible face-saving retaliation,' reported the conservative-leaning *Daily Telegraph*.

Documents released from the Foreign & Commonwealth Office in 2016, shared under the Freedom of Information Act, revealed how the student, Simon Kirby, who divulged what Philip had said to him, tried to make amends, with a personal plea to the unimpressed ambassador. 'Please be assured that I was in no way guided by anti-Royal sentiments, I am certainly not some kind of Communist nutter. I would like to convey my regrets to you for being the cause of such embarrassment to you and to the royal tour,' he wrote to Sir Richard. 'It was unfortunate for me that I was singled out and I have since suffered the consequences.' Sir Richard replied rather curtly, 'I of course accept what you say about the frame of mind in which you spoke to the journalists. I now regard the incident as closed.'

The day after the gaffe, Philip, during a visit to Kunming's ancient Huating Temple, appeared nonplussed by the growing media storm, and seemed happy to blame the student for his indiscretion rather than himself for his inappropriate comments. He told the waiting press that the Edinburgh student involved had been 'rather tactless' in divulging the details of the private conversation they had had to a journalist. The furore seemed to irritate Philip years later when the subject came up during an awkward interview with broadcaster Fiona Bruce for a BBC documentary to mark his 90th birthday. Prince Philip shifted in his seat and looked uncomfortable as he insisted the media outcry was disproportionate. He said: 'I'd forgotten about it. But for one particular reporter who overheard it, it wouldn't have come out. What's more, the Chinese weren't worried about it, so why should anyone else?' In truth privately his Chinese hosts felt the remarks appeared to be at best both tactless and ill-timed.

That said perhaps the Queen and the diplomats should have cautioned Philip about speaking his mind. They had fair warning. Just days earlier the duke spoke at the celebrations for the World Wildlife Fund's 25th anniversary, on 26 September 1986, with a convocation of leaders from different faith traditions in Assisi, Italy. 'If it has got four legs and it is not a chair, if it has got two wings and it flies but is not an aeroplane, and if it swims and it is not a submarine, the Cantonese will eat it,' he joked. He didn't apologise for that statement either.

22: 'DEAREST PA'

*'If invited, I will always do my utmost to help you and Charles
to the best of my ability, but I am quite ready to concede that
I have no talents as a marriage counsellor!!!'*

Prince Philip in a letter to Princess Diana at
the height of her marriage crisis

It wasn't until Lady Diana Spencer spent a weekend at the Queen's
Balmoral estate as the guest of the Prince of Wales, in September
1980, that news of their fledgling romance was shared with the rest
of the world. On 8 September, *The Sun* newspaper proclaimed on
its front page, 'He's in Love Again, Lady Di is the new girlfriend
for Charles.' It was the first time Diana had been called 'Lady Di'
in the press.

Arthur Edwards, *The Sun* royal photographer, had taken
a picture of Lady Diana in July at a polo match in which the
Prince of Wales had been playing. Arthur had vaguely recognised
her and the gold 'D' hanging around her neck, and had taken
some pictures for his files, just in case he needed to verify who
she was. At Balmoral, Harry had spotted Diana again, this time
at Charles's side, while he was on assignment, photographing
Prince Charles fishing by the River Dee. He quickly figured out
this was the same girl from the polo match in July, and pulled
the picture out of his file to check. He knew instantly he had his
major scoop.

Once his eldest son Prince Charles's relationship with Lady
Diana was out of the bag, Prince Philip became concerned by what

he saw as the unruly behaviour of the photographers and reporters outside her London apartment. After all the innocent aristocrat was 19 at the time and had voiced concerns about the attention she was receiving and said she felt 'under siege'. Prince Philip felt sure something decisive must be done to protect her, and fast.

Lady Diana had first met Charles, when she was 16 in November 1977, when he was dating her older sister, Lady Sarah, and the heir apparent attended a grouse shooting party at Althorp, the Spencer family estate. Charles's relationship with Sarah fizzled out after she reportedly shared the story of her royal romance with two reporters, and admitted to having an eating disorder. She was reported as saying she'd had 'thousands of boyfriends' and apparently told them she would not marry the prince, 'If he were the dustman or the King of England.' Shortly afterwards Charles saw the article and told her, 'You've just done something incredibly stupid.'

Charles and Diana met again three years later, in July 1980, when they were both invited to a weekend barbecue at Philip de Pass's house in Sussex. 'I was asked to stay with some friends in Sussex and they said, "Oh, the Prince of Wales is staying," and I thought, "I hadn't seen him in ages,"' Diana told her speech coach on a tape that was later used for the Channel 4 documentary *Diana: In Her Own Words*. She added, 'He'd just broken up with his girlfriend and his friend Mountbatten had just been killed. I said it would be nice to see him. I was so unimpressed. I sat there and this man walked in and I thought, "Well, I am quite impressed this time round." It was different.' According to Diana, the prince appeared to be taken by her too. She said in the tapes, 'He was all over me.' Adding, 'We were talking about Mountbatten and his girlfriend and I said, "You must be so lonely." I said, "It's pathetic watching you walking up the aisle with Mountbatten's coffin in front, ghastly, you need someone beside you." Whereupon he leapt upon me and started kissing me and I thought, "Urgh, this is not what people do." And he was all over me for the rest of the evening, following me around like a puppy.'

Diana also spoke of how difficult she found those early days of dating the prince. 'He wasn't consistent with his courting abilities. He'd ring me every day for a week, then wouldn't speak to me for three weeks. Very odd. I thought, "Fine. Well, he knows where I am if he wants me." The thrill when he used to ring up was so immense and intense. It would drive the other three girls in my flat crazy.'

Prince Philip, who along with the Queen, was keen for the Prince of Wales to marry a suitable bride and, in time, to produce an heir. Given that Charles was approaching 32, the duke decided to write to his eldest son about it, stressing that he felt the prince should either propose marriage to Lady Diana or let her go. It was a warm, affectionate and encouraging letter from father to son, not an abrupt order, as some critics of the duke have interpreted it to be. Contrary to popular belief, Charles did *not* blame his father for what some viewed as effectively forcing him into an ill-conceived marriage to Lady Diana.

'They chased me everywhere,' recalled Diana, on the tapes recorded years later by Peter Settelen, British actor and voice coach. 'We are talking thirty of them.' The princess received no practical support from Charles, the police or from media advisers at Buckingham Palace. Charles, of course, felt duty bound to try to protect his new girlfriend, but he was, effectively, powerless to do so. He didn't need a letter from his father to remind him of his responsibilities as a gentleman.

'It was measured and sensitive,' said Lady Pamela Hicks, who claimed to have read the letter her cousin Philip sent to Charles. Some unfairly use this as evidence that Charles felt he was 'bullied into marriage' by his parents and claim that Philip said he could go back to his mistress, Camilla, if things didn't work out. But that is not fair or true, and Charles did not feel that.

In reality, Charles felt once the power of the press machine gathered momentum, he had could see no way out but to marry Lady Diana. He explained to a close friend years later, 'To have withdrawn [from the marriage], as you can no doubt imagine, would have been cataclysmic. Hence I was permanently between the devil and the deep blue sea.*' 'Things were very different in those days,' Charles explained [to close friends]. 'The power and influence of the media driving matters towards an engagement and wedding were unstoppable.' Charles was right of course. The so-called Fourth Estate was all powerful and the tabloid editors drove the royal romance story because it sold newspapers. If Charles blamed anyone for what turned out to be a disastrous marriage, it was a hostile media, 'Aided and abetted by somebody rather close to me [Diana]', who he believed, towards the end of their marriage, 'Lived hand to mouth with the press'.

The bottom line was that Charles and Diana were not a compatible couple. The so-called 'fairy-tale' marriage, was doomed from the start, and the prince knew it. The couple shared that infamous and deeply awkward engagement interview when they were asked about love. 'I had a long time to think about it, because I knew the pressure was on both of us. And, um... it wasn't a difficult decision in the end. It was what was wanted,' Diana said, adding quickly, 'It's what I wanted.' Asked if they were in love, Charles followed up Diana's quick 'of course' with that infamous and damning line, 'Whatever "in love" means.' They were words that would be repeated on air, in books and in newspapers time and again and established the *parti pris* narrative of an uncaring older husband, who wilfully wrecked the life of the pure young woman who was devoted to him.

Even before the relationship disintegrated, Charles was deeply unsure of Diana's suitability as his wife at the time and after a few meetings believed they were totally incompatible. He told his close circle of friends, 'I desperately wanted to get out of the wedding in 1981 when during the engagement I discovered just how awful the prospects were, having had no chance whatsoever to get to know Diana beforehand.' Charles was, of course, when referring to the 'awful' prospects, speaking of Diana's bulimia and her mood swings

---

★   Taken from *Charles at 70: Thoughts, Hopes and Dreams* by this author.

and temper, which he found impossible to deal with. Despite barely knowing each other, the die was cast. Charles was not the only one to have second thoughts. Diana told her sisters, Lady Jane and Lady Sarah, just days before the wedding that she didn't think she could marry Charles because he was still besotted with Camilla Parker Bowles.

Despite all his misgivings, Charles proposed to Lady Diana on 3 February 1981. The couple had dated mostly through phone calls in those early days, with sources saying they only met 13 times before Charles went on to propose. 'It was like a call to duty, really,' Diana said later. In reality, neither Charles nor Diana was actually in love with the other, although both may well have been enamoured with the idea of it. In all honesty, this was effectively the last of the great arranged royal marriages.

The wedding, described by the Archbishop of Canterbury, Robert Runcie, as the 'stuff of which fairy tales are made', went ahead on 29 July 1981. But there would be no, 'Happy ever after' for this marital union as their relationship, sadly, descended into acrimony and adultery, which, ultimately, led to divorce on 28 August 1996, when Diana received a lump sum settlement of £17 million, as well as £400,000 per year.

Prince Philip's relationship with Charles was, at times, so strained that they resorted to only communicating by writing one another letters. 'Of course they loved each other,' said one senior member of the Royal Household. 'They kissed each other when they met, but only within a short time the mood would change and they would fundamentally disagree about big issues.' To a bystander, however, these discussions may have looked quite heated, even volatile. 'They were both passionate people who were extremely passionate about their beliefs. That didn't make them enemies, it just meant that they disagreed,' the senior figure pointed out.

Philip, however, somehow used to curb his overzealous temper with just one word or look from his wife. When they stayed in hotel suites on state visits, while the Queen was in one room being attended to by staff, Philip might be while the Queen was in one room being attended to by staff, Philip might be in another room ranting, because he couldn't get the television to work so he could watch the news. The Queen would just ignore it.

Even when he was on holiday on the beautiful, windswept Balmoral estate, a place that Queen Victoria found to be, 'A breath of freedom and peace, and to make one forget the world and its "sad turmoils",' Philip could lose it; tranquillity and the duke never sat well together. If Philip overstepped the mark, a raised eyebrow from his wife or a timely cough could be enough to silence him. On one such occasion the monarch was awoken by his swearing at his police protection officer who insisted on accompanying him, as instructed by his superior officer, while he was on the Balmoral estate. The disagreement took place directly below the Queen's window at just before 5.30 a.m. Restless, Philip was not enamoured with the idea of being assigned the bodyguard to watch over him while he was on holiday and on the royal estate. 'I am on fucking holiday, I don't need you with me. Now bugger off!' he shouted.

An experienced personal protection officer, like the duke, he did not suffer fools gladly. He had been assigned to do a job and he was damn well going to do it. After all the Commissioner of Scotland Yard was his boss, not Philip. He simply removed the keys from the Range Rover and started walking off. The act of defiance sent the duke into an apoplectic rage.

'Where the hell do you think you are going with my fucking keys?' By now Philip was puce with rage but the officer was unmoved; he was completely in the right. Ignoring the duke he started to head back to the police control unit, keys in hand, to inform his superior officer of the duke's failure to engage with the security he had been assigned.

In the Highlands the Queen is usually woken by the sound of her personal piper, *Piobair an Bhàn Righ* in Scottish Gaelic, not the rantings of her irate husband berating an officer who was simply doing his job and not in a position to answer back. Unfortunately, the altercation had taken place directly below the Queen's bedroom window and thus within earshot. She was not amused.

'Philip,' she said, opening and leaning out of her window, 'what on earth is the matter with you?'

At that point all went quiet.

Philip knew he was in the wrong. Without apologising he persuaded the police officer to get in the car. 'Get in, get in man,' he said, before the pair sped off quickly with the duke at the wheel. As the Land Rover Discovery 4x4 disappeared from view, the Queen snapped her window shut and tranquillity returned to the castle, at least for a few hours, whilst Philip went deer stalking, his protection officer in tow a few yards behind as he was assigned to be.

Like any couple Elizabeth and Philip had their fair share of spousal disagreements. In private Philip lost his temper and dismissed his wife as a 'bloody fool' on numerous occasions. Despite her position he was never afraid of telling her if he felt she had got something wrong. Her Majesty, of course, was perfectly capable of standing up for herself, but his bluntness sometimes helped her shape her own thoughts and even her decisions. Sometimes his volatile nature took its toll.

She once even refused to come out of her State Room on the Royal Yacht *Britannia* after a disagreement with the duke, telling her then private secretary Martin, later Lord Charteris, that she would not move an inch from the locked room until Philip's foul mood had subsided and she didn't care how long it took.

'Prince Philip is the only man in the world who treats the Queen simply as another human being. He's the only man who can. Strange as it may seem, I believe she values that,' Martin Charteris said. Possibly, but only after it had all calmed down.

The Queen might have been his monarch but on domestic matters Philip was – with the exception of the debate over the surname their children would take that caused a serious schism between them – the head of the family. As Lady Pamela Hicks, Philip's cousin said, 'Prince Philip has always been the head of the family privately which is what the Queen wants because she thought it was the natural state of things. Don't forget we are talking about a generation, two, three generations ago when we all thought like that.'

The year of Charles and Diana's wedding was a momentous one for Her Majesty and a great start to an eventful but largely positive decade. The Queen's first granddaughter was born when Princess Anne gave birth to her daughter Zara Phillips on 15 May 1981. Like her brother Peter, Zara did not have a royal title as their parents were said to have refused offers of one. In 1982 Prince William was born on 21 June, the next in direct line to the throne; and Elizabeth and Philip would see their son Andrew return home a hero following the Falklands War. He flew a Navy helicopter close behind the carrier HMS *Invincible* as Argentine jets screamed in to attack. His nerve-racking job was to make the missiles swerve towards the helicopter instead of the ship.

The Queen's third grandson Prince Harry was born on 15 September 1984 to Charles and Diana and the summer of 1986 saw yet another royal wedding when Prince Andrew, Duke of York, married Sarah Ferguson on 23 July 1986. The future of the monarchy looked secure. But behind the scenes all three marriages of her children were in serious trouble. Philip, who personally liked Diana, did all he could do to help.

But the 1990s proved to be one of the most testing decades of Elizabeth's long and illustrious reign. The year 1992 in particular was trying for the Queen as her children's marriages unravelled and the separations played out in the pages of an unforgiving tabloid press. It ended with Windsor Castle being severely damaged by fire which broke out on 20 Nov 1992 and was finally extinguished on 21 Nov 1992, threatening one of the world's greatest collections of art. The Queen and her second son, Prince Andrew, the Duke of York, helped to rescue priceless works from the royal residence, as fire brigades from five counties fought the flames. It took 250 firefighters 15 hours and 1.5 million gallons of water to put the blaze out. One hundred rooms were damaged in the fire, which was started by a spotlight shining on a curtain.

An intense public debate was sparked about whether the taxpayer should foot the bill for repairs, as the British government and not the Royal Family owned the castle. But the Queen agreed to meet

70 per cent of the costs, and opened Buckingham Palace to the public to generate extra funds. The £40-million restoration took five years and was completed in November 1997. Elizabeth dubbed 1992 her 'annus horribilis'.

In the address Elizabeth delivered to mark the 40th anniversary of her accession on 24 November 1992, at the Guildhall, she acknowledged that some of the criticism levelled at her family and the institution should be heard. Magnanimously, the Queen conceded, 'No institution, city, monarchy, whatever, should expect to be free from the scrutiny of those who give it their loyalty and support, not to mention those who don't.'

The Queen Mother wrote a letter, on 3 February 1993, in a bid to encourage her daughter:

'My Darling Lilibet,
How can I ever thank you enough for my heavenly weeks at Sandringham. I do hope that you feel rested and relaxed after all the ghastly happenings of last (& this) year. I do think that you have been marvellous, & so does everybody.

        Very much love from your grateful and hopping lame, Mummy'

Sadly, more troubles followed for the Queen and Philip. The death of Diana, Princess of Wales, in a car crash, just a year after her divorce from Charles was finalised, forced the Queen, for the sake of the monarchy, to show the world a side of herself that had not been seen before. Elizabeth's first instinct, advised by Philip, was to keep her young grandsons, William and Harry, at Balmoral away from the prying eyes of the press and the public. It led to her and the Royal Family facing a public backlash for being stand-offish. Elizabeth responded by bravely moving herself from the margin to the very centre of the unfolding tragic drama.

In a heartfelt televised address to the nation, on 5 September 1997, everyone saw Elizabeth as a vulnerable grandmother, showing her concern, love and protection for her two grandsons who had tragically just lost their mother. 'I, for one,' the Queen said in her live broadcast, 'believe that there are lessons to be drawn from [Diana's] life and from the extraordinary and moving reaction to her death.' It showed Her Majesty's grasp of the magnitude of the situation. She had to act and she did so decisively and proved as good as her word. It was a groundbreaking moment, that changed the opinions of many who, until then, had been criticising her and the royals for their coldness.

Philip, who provided much-needed stability for his traumatised grandsons, took them walking, horse riding and fishing on the estate every day, anything to occupy them and stop them dwelling on the tragic loss of their mother. As far as the Queen, Philip, and their father, Charles, were concerned the two boys had to be their priority. When the Queen was told by a member of the crowd outside the palace, 'Look after the boys,' when she did a walkabout almost in silence as she returned to London, Philip snapped back defensively, 'That's what we have been doing.'

Indeed, it later emerged that Philip launched a fierce tirade at Downing Street aides during a conference call between London and Balmoral after a disagreement with Prime Minister Tony Blair over the arrangements for the funeral. As the spin doctors from Downing Street came to Buckingham Palace and started to discuss what roles Harry and William should play in the funeral, Philip told them over the speaker phone from Balmoral to, 'Fuck off!'" The incident was witnessed by Anti Hunter, who worked for Mr Blair and who later married Adam Boulton. She confirmed, "I can remember, it sends a tingle up my back."

Philip later sided with Blair and his son, Charles, and saw the sense in the two boys taking part. Prince William, who had been reluctant to do so and later admitted it has been one of the hardest things he had ever had to do, agreed to take part but only if his grandfather walked beside him. In 2017 Prince Harry, who had previously said walking behind her coffin aged 12 was something

---

* *Tony's Ten Years: Memoirs of the Blair Administration* by Sky's political editor Adam Boulton, 2008

no child 'should be asked to do', said on reflection that he was "glad to have been part of the day."*

Charles, sources said at the time, was consumed with guilt that he had contributed to Diana's unhappiness. In so doing he had also disappointed the Queen, the Queen Mother, his father, Philip, and his sons as well as the British people. He found a rare moment of solace in a letter he received from his normally critical father, who wrote that he felt Charles had displayed the 'fortitude of a saint' by putting up with Diana. Critics of Diana said that she was difficult within the marriage and during their subsequent separation, but others continued to blame Charles for their break-up, due to his prolonged affair with Camilla.

Few outside royal circles are aware how hard the Duke of Edinburgh worked during the breakdown of Diana's marriage to Charles. Philip actually enjoyed a good rapport with Diana at the start. Claims that she 'hated' Philip are not true. Their relationship had begun well too. The two would chat at functions and he helped her conquer her innate shyness. As Charles and Diana's marriage began to fail, Philip tried to help, writing to his daughter-in-law in warm and encouraging correspondence, signing off with the word, 'Pa'. He repeatedly questioned his eldest son's affair with Camilla, and said he was silly to risk everything for his mistress.

'Diana showed me some of the correspondence between the two of them. They were very warm and genuine,' said Diana's personal protection officer at the time, Inspector Ken Wharfe. 'There was nothing aggressive in the letters, the duke was encouraging and praising her. All the talk that Diana hated the Duke of Edinburgh is wide of the mark, certainly not when I was with her,' said the officer who retired as her bodyguard in 1993 after eight years guarding her.

Even after the formal separation of the Prince and Princess of Wales in November 1992, Philip continued to try to heal the divisions and save the failing marriage or to at least find a solution

---

* Prince Harry told BBC documentary "Diana, 7 Days" in 2017

that would not damage the institution. In a letter from the duke to Diana, made public at the High Court in London during the inquest into her death, Philip told Diana that he and the Queen disapproved of Charles's affair.

Prince Philip wrote, 'Charles was silly to risk everything with Camilla for a man in his position. We never dreamt he might feel like leaving you for her. I cannot imagine anyone in their right mind leaving you for Camilla. Such a prospect never even entered our heads.' He reassured her, adding, 'I will always do my utmost to help you and Charles to the best of my ability.' The letter was signed off, 'With fondest love, Pa.'

In June 1992, Diana wrote back:

'Dearest Pa,
I was so pleased to receive your letter, and particularly so, to read, that you are desperately anxious to help. I am very grateful to you for sending me such an honest and heartfelt letter. I hope you will read mine in the same spirit.

With fondest love, from Diana'

Four days later, Philip replied by sending a signed typewritten letter, 'Thank you for taking the time to respond to my letter. I hope this means that we can continue to make use of this form of communication, since there appears to be very little other opportunity to exchange views.'

Four days after that, just before her 31st birthday, Diana replied:

'Dear Pa,
Thank you for responding to my long letter so speedily. I agree this form of communication does seem to be the only effective one in the present situation, but at least it's a start, and I am grateful for it. I hope you don't find this letter over-long, but I was so immensely relieved to receive such a thoughtful letter as the one you sent me, showing such obvious willingness to help.

My fondest love, Diana'

On 7 July Philip replied, 'I can only repeat what I have said before. If invited, I will always do my utmost to help you and Charles to the best of my ability. But I am quite ready to concede that I have no talent as a marriage counsellor!!!'

Diana's response was affectionate, even playful,

'Dearest Pa,
I was particularly touched by your most recent letter, which proved to me, if I did not already know it, that you really do care. You are very modest about your marriage guidance skills, and I disagree with you! The last letter of yours showed great understanding and tact, and I hope to be able to draw on your advice in the months ahead, whatever they may bring.'

Around two weeks later, a dinner was organised at Spencer House to celebrate the Queen's 40th anniversary as monarch. Diana knew she would not only be seeing her estranged husband that evening, but Prince Philip and the Queen too. The evening before the event Diana wrote to Philip,

'Dearest Pa,
I would like you to know how much I admire you for the marvellous way in which you have tried to come to terms with this intensely difficult family problem.
                                                        With much love, Diana'

By now the correspondence between the duke and Diana was well established. The next exchange came after Philip had returned from Balmoral in September, when he told Diana, 'You will be relieved to see that this letter is rather shorter than usual!' On 30 September, after a trip to Cornwall, Diana replied,

'Dearest Pa,
Thank you again for taking the trouble to write and keep up our dialogue. It is good that our letters are getting shorter. Perhaps it means that you and I are getting to understand each other.'

Although the precise details of all the letters are not available, the theme of Philip's missives was that Charles was wrong to have returned to Camilla, but that Diana, too, was wrong to have taken other lovers. As the letters went to and fro, he asked her to reflect on why her husband had returned to his old flame. Eventually, it proved too much for the emotional princess, who was struggling to cope with the break-up. Unable to take personal criticism, she decided she no longer wanted to hear from her father-in-law.

Diana's butler Paul Burrell later commented that 'Prince Philip probably did more to save the marriage than Prince Charles, and his intentions were honourable, even if he wore steelworkers' gloves for a situation that required kid mittens.'

But Simone Simmons, Diana's healer, told a different story. According to her, there were other letters from the duke that were written in quite a different tone.

Philip denied this and issued a statement through his office saying so. He regarded the suggestion that he used derogatory terms to describe Diana as a 'gross misrepresentation of his relations with his daughter-in-law and hurtful to his grandsons'. When Philip feels that his advice is being ignored, he reverts to the cold man he is frequently portrayed as being.

For her part, Diana had made the fatal mistake of alienating him and continued to do so, particularly with her infamous BBC *Panorama* interview. The relationship which he had tried so hard to establish with her was at an end. He now regarded her as 'a loose cannon'.

The full weight of his displeasure was evident when he proposed that, as well as losing her HRH rank, Diana should be downgraded from Princess of Wales to Duchess of Cornwall on the basis that if she wanted out, she was out. Philip had said his piece and made up his mind. He refused to have anything more to do with Diana, and on the rare occasions she appeared at Windsor Castle with Princes William and Harry, he would make himself disappear.

On the flip side Philip did send letters to Diana which apparently made her 'boil with anger' when he criticised her behaviour towards her husband. Philip also made it clear neither he nor the Queen would support Diana having new romantic relationships of her own, writing, 'We do not approve of either of you having lovers.'

The missives, sent in 1994 and 1995, again came to light at Diana's inquest, when her confidante, Simone Simmons, spoke about them. Miss Simmons told the inquest, 'Diana read one out to me because she was absolutely furious and she was actually imitating the voice of the Duke of Edinburgh.' When asked if the duke had made, 'cruel and disparaging observations' about the princess's conduct, Ms Simmons replied 'yes'. She agreed the letters had been 'extremely derogatory'. Ms Simmons also believed the princess was targeted by the security services, MI6, as she apparently planned to release a document exposing British companies' links with landmines. Added to this was the somewhat tarnished testimony given by the princess's butler, Paul Burrell, who alleged that Philip made 'unpleasant and nasty' comments about Diana.

As a result, Philip came under increasing media pressure to testify at the inquest after Ms Simmons' account, not least because a central thread of the case was Mohamed Al Fayed's persistent, but patently absurd, allegations that his son, Dodi, and the princess were victims of a murder plot instigated by Philip himself to prevent the pair of them getting married and having children. The coroner, Lord Justice Scott Baker, ultimately decided against calling the duke to give evidence. He said most of the letters contained 'highly personal' material, 'As you would expect in any family correspondence concerning the breakdown of a marriage'. That detail did not contain any unpleasantness and it would be inappropriate for its private nature to be released into the public domain, he said. So the versions they saw were heavily censored and were mostly the 'top and tail' of each letter. Nevertheless, the extracts did give a rare, first-hand insight into what was happening at the time of the marriage crisis and Philip's proactive role in seeking to resolve it.

Mr Al Fayed persisted with his vendetta against Prince Philip. He was called to give evidence on 18 February 2008 and, as with every passing moment, his testimony got more and more bizarre, if it hadn't have been so sad it would have been comical. It ended, predictably, with a vile and unsubstantiated rant against the duke. It was well known, he continued, that Prince Philip was a racist. Dodi was a different religion, 'Naturally tanned, curly hair and they will not accept that he will have anything to do with the future king'. The duke 'grew up with the Nazis', Fayed said, and was brought up by an auntie 'who married Hitler's general'. He added: 'This is the guy who is now in charge and manipulating everything and can do anything. They are still living in the eighteenth or nineteenth century.' With a flourish, Al Fayed produced a newspaper article from a folder in front of him and jabbed at a photograph on the page. He told the jury it showed Prince Philip walking with one of Hitler's generals when he was 15 years old. 'You think someone like that, growing up with the Nazis, accept my son? There is no way. This is the proof again. Time to send him back to Germany or from where he came from.'

Then Al Fayed dropped a mischievous nugget of misinformation. 'You want to have his original name?' he asked the court. 'It ends with Frankenstein,' (which is is of course nonsense, we know he was a member of the Danish-German House of Schleswig-Holstein-Sonderburg-Glücksburg). 'Well, it sounds like Frankenstein,' added Al Fayed. 'So who was the MI6 assassin who carried out the murder?' he was asked. That was James Andanson, the so-called paparazzi and 'secret agent' in the infamous white Fiat Uno that was seen in the tunnel that night. Why, then, with all the might and power of the Royal Family and MI6 behind the plot, would the murderous assassin choose one of the world's lightest and least powerful cars (a 'clapped out one at that', the coroner interjected) and take his dog with him? That was his own car, Mr Al Fayed said, and he simply chose to use it that night.

Calm and assured, Richard Horwell QC, a leading silk in inquest, who was counsel for the Commissioner of the Metropolitan Police, then asked the tycoon how it would have been possible for a murder plot to be put into action with just minutes to spare. 'The first that the establishment could have known of the pregnancy and the engagement was this telephone call. No one else was telephoned. They have moments to put this conspiracy into action, Al Fayed. Prince Philip has to be told, Prince Philip has to issue the order to MI6, MI5, the French security services, CIA, the ambulance service, the French doctors, the French scientists, James Andanson and his dog, all have to come together within a matter of moments, Mr Al Fayed, to kill Diana and Dodi.'

Mr Horwell, QC, paused for a moment, allowing a period of calm to fall on the courtroom after Fayed's bluff and bluster. Then the commanding advocate embraced the moment, 'You have not even permitted this woman to have dignity in death, have you, Mr Al Fayed?' Slowly but surely he then dissected Fayed's preposterous claims, making the tycoon's theories look more and more fanciful. It was a classic case of giving someone enough rope to hang themselves. It undid months of work by Al Fayed's brilliant barrister, Michael Mansfield, QC, who had chipped away at the edges, raising unanswered questions and pointing out issues that had not been properly investigated. At that moment, it was clear the game was up. Until then it had seemed possible that there might be enough doubts for jurors to go for an open verdict on the grounds that there were so many unanswered questions. The plain fact, however, is that after years of multi-million pound inquiries by police in Britain and France as well as Al Fayed's own one-sided investigators, not a scrap of direct evidence ever emerged to support his conspiracy theories.

Amid the vast cast of characters involved in the supposed plot, not a single person – from ambulance workers to policemen and statesmen – broke ranks to reveal the scale of the crime. Some named by Al Fayed were not even there. Diana's brother-in-law, Lord Fellowes, who was married to her sister, Lady Jane, then the Queen's private secretary, was said to have been in Paris that night, masterminding the assassination plot from the British embassy's communications centre. This was, of course, complete nonsense, as he was in Norfolk that evening and went to an entertainment by Mr John Mortimer in Burnham Market Church.

Faced with the reality of a very weak case, even Al Fayed's legal team, under a professional duty to only make serious allegations against people with sufficient evidence, were forced to abandon the central planks of the tycoon's murder conspiracy plot. Of course, they clung to the claim that Philip created such a climate of hostility towards Diana that, like the four knights who killed the Archbishop of Canterbury, Saint Thomas Becket – on 29 December 1170 after Henry II complained 'Who will rid me of this troublesome priest?' – rogue MI6 officers must have taken matters into their own hands and tried to frighten or injure the couple. There was, of course, not a single shred of evidence to support that either. It was pure fantasy.

Outside the court, Al Fayed did not halt his invective. Asked by the BBC's unruffled royal correspondent Peter Hunt whether he was lying, Al Fayed shot back: 'You work for MI6, you idiot.' Al Fayed was sounding more deluded with every utterance and his PR team tried to keep reporters at bay. The tycoon, who had after all provided the car, the driver and the security for Diana and his son that day, had his day in court. It was certainly unforgettable for all concerned, but ultimately it was the day the conspiracy theories surrounding Diana's death were exposed as nonsense.

After 22 hours of deliberation, spread over four days, following a hearing lasting six months, the inquest jury of six women and five men returned a 9–2 majority verdict that Diana and Dodi had been unlawfully killed by a combination of the driving of their Mercedes by their chauffeur, Henri Paul, and the driving of following vehicles carrying the posse of paparazzi photographers. Philip had done nothing wrong. He had said nothing wrong either. His good name and character had been dragged through the mud. The final ruling rightly put an end to the outrageous allegations made against him.

23: PARTING TEARS

'Britannia is the one place I can truly relax.'

The Queen

'Yak, yak, yak,' he bellowed at the top of his voice in the direction of his wife from the deck of HMY *Britannia* in Belize. Doing her best to ignore Philip's impertinence, the Queen dutifully said her goodbyes to her hosts. Nobody else would have got away with it, nor, perhaps, should they have. A little startled, the governor general of the tiny Commonwealth realm, Sir Colville Young, and his wife, Lady Norma Young, with the Queen at the quayside, looked up, at first not knowing if the irritable royal was joking or not. It was the duke at his best (or worst, depending on your standpoint) taking his irreverent behaviour to a new level. When she went aboard the Queen was not best pleased.

It had been an exhausting schedule, and the couple were only half way through the two-week tour on 24 February 1994, having completed visits to Dominica, Anguilla, Guyana and now Belize in Central America. They had packed in a lot, including being guests of honour at luncheon at the San Ignacio Resort Hotel and a visit to Mayan ruins at Cahal Pech in the village of Succotz in the Cayo District, where they had been received enthusiastically.

A restricted Foreign Office 'Telno' from British Commissioner for Belize David Mackilligin stated, 'A happy, incident free, well organised visit. The link with the Crown reinvigorated. Media coverage, extensive and mostly rapturous.' He went on, 'I had expected a sour editorial on a republican theme from the black consciousness anti-colonial newspaper *Amandala* that restricted the editorial to a "tiny" report on the front page with the "least attractive photograph they could find." They even reproduced a report in September in Jamaica's *Daily Gleaner* headed, "Keating [then Australian PM] tells Queen Australia no longer wants her.'" Mackilligin concluded, 'On the evidence on this visit Belize is unlikely to follow Mr Keating's lead.' Intriguingly, for some reason the next six lines of section 4 of the restricted memo had been redacted*.

By the time HMY *Britannia,* docked in the harbour, the ocean-loving sailor in Philip had got the better of him. He ignored all the niceties, strode ahead of his wife and went aboard, excited by the prospect of a week at sea aboard. First stop was Jamaica and from there the royal couple would sail on to the Commonwealth of the Bahamas nestling within the Lucayan Archipelago of the West Indies for further official visits. Both overseas royal visits were hailed as great successes in the FCO restricted reports. 'People admired the fact that HM the Queen had gone ahead with it [the visit] despite the recent injury to her wrist.' The memo by British High Commissioner of the Bahamas, Brian Attewell, also noted that, 'Possible protests discussed in Telno 45 did not materialise.' The visit to the Bahamas was incident free too, apart from, 'A few Rastafarians popped up once or twice but were kept on the sidelines.' It concluded, 'Republican views attract little support at present.'

This royal voyage was one of the last great adventures aboard HMY *Britannia* for Philip and Elizabeth. The yacht really showed her worth too in March 1995 during the state visit to Nelson Mandela's hopeful Rainbow nation, South Africa. She made a

---

* Years later, in 1999, David Mackilligin, by then the former British Commissioner for Belize, called on the then Conservative leader, William Hague, to order an ethics committee of inquiry into the conduct of party Treasurer, Michael Ashcroft. Mr Ashcroft, a major donor to the Conservatives over many years, was accused of pressuring the Tory government in 1994 to protect his tax exemptions in Belize where he had substantial business interests.

spectacular entrance sailing into Cape Town harbour, surrounded by a flotilla of small pleasure craft*. A 21-gun salute boomed out across Cape Town Harbour as the Queen was greeted by South Africa's first black president, Nelson Mandela, at the Victoria and Alfred Waterfront. He was flanked by his deputy presidents, Thabo Mbeki, and F. W. de Klerk, as well as Archbishop Desmond Tutu. The Queen and President Mandela inspected a 96-man naval guard of honour, against the backdrop of Table Mountain, before the two South African anthems, 'Nkosi Sikelel' iAfrika' (God Bless Africa) and the old Afrikaans anthem 'Die Stem' (The Voice), were played. Throughout, President Mandela was accompanied by his grand-niece, 26-year-old Rochelle Mtirara.

A despatch from British High Commissioner Sir Anthony Reeve about the six-day visit wrote of the 'highly successful' visit to six of the nine new provinces. 'All races turned out in large numbers to meet the Royal Couple.' He stressed, 'Much welcome emphasis by senior South Africans on the Commonwealth which is perceived as setting the seal on South Africa's re-integration.' Then the senior diplomat focused on the importance of the royal yacht. 'The inclusion in the programme of commercial events, and the subsequent use of *Britannia* for this purpose, was particularly helpful.'

In a longer despatch to Foreign Secretary Douglas Hurd, in John Major's government, which signalled the yacht's demise, Sir Anthony wrote, '*Britannia* provided a spectacular arrival for the royal party at Cape Town harbour on the morning of 20 March. *Britannia* was also present at Durban for the final leg of the tour, which included the Queen's State Banquet.' He noted that the South Africans had wanted the visit to reflect their new country but the president's office, 'Gave very little indication of their own preferences until very late in the day' but said Mandela's personal involvement on the official days the tour had help cut through the bureaucracy and made the visit an overwhelming success. It

---

* The Queen and Philip had actually arrived separately the previous day at Cape Town Airport before being transferred to the yacht for the stage-managed official arrival.

was one of the Queen's most important visits, along with those she made to China and Russia.

***

Philip played it straight in Russia in 1994 when he so easily could have gone off-piste. The Queen became the first British monarch to have set foot on their soil. (In 1908, Edward VII got as far as sailing into Russian waters for lunch with the Tsar.) Philip, in 1967 in the *Soviet Times*, said, 'I would like to go to Russia very much – although the bastards murdered half my family.' The royal couple visited the capital city, Moscow, and St Petersburg. At the Kremlin, they exchanged gifts with Russian President Boris Yeltsin, who presented the Queen with previously unseen photographs of her and Philip's Tsarist relatives who were murdered by the Bolsheviks in 1917. With Philip present, they discussed problems of corruption and violence facing the new so-called democratic Russia, and she listened as Yeltsin told her how difficult he felt it would be to establish a proper, functioning government given the volatile economic and political situation in his country. The state visit was one of the most significant episodes in relations between post-Communist Russia and Great Britain. Years later, in 2007, Philip donated DNA as part of an investigation into identifying human remains found in a field in Yekaterinburg, Russia, believed to belong to the Romanovs, the Russian royal family executed by Communist revolutionaries under Yakov Yurovsky in Yekaterinburg on the night of 16-17 July 1918. (Philip is a grand-nephew of the last Tsarina, Alexandra, and a great-great-grandson of Tsar Nicholas I.) Princess Alice, Philip's mother, tried to save the Tsar's daughters Princesses Olga, Maria, Tatiana and Anastasia by bringing them to England in the aftermath of the Leninist coup and the Tsar's abdication. She wrote to Lloyd George asking if he could do something so that she could have the girls and look after them. She knew she could not save the Tsarevich Alexei, as he was the heir. 'The answer was no it would not be possible. Which we all thought was very hard,' said Lady Pamela Hicks, Philip's cousin.

***

The Cape Town Journal, under a banner headline 'Britain's Queen Comes Bearing a Gift: Acceptance', reported that, 'The Queen did not mix with crowds and hug children, as does the Princess of Wales, her daughter-in-law. In fact, she had hardly any contact with the large crowds greeting her at the pier, at Parliament and later in black townships, just a few waves of a gloved hand during her strictly monitored strolls and drives. But this did not quell the enthusiasm.'

At Langa township, near Cape Town, however, the enthusiasm of the crowds alarmed the Queen's security so much they cut short the visit as people surged past them, as they tried to catch a glimpse of the royal entourage. 'If most of the people at the Cape Town pier were whites, royal-watchers interested in the thrill of catching a glimpse of a monarch, the most moving greeting was at Queen Elizabeth's first visit to a black township,' the *Journal*'s correspondent reported. 'In Khayelitsha, just near Cape Town's airport, a sea of squalid, rusted corrugated-iron shacks with little sanitation or electricity, she was greeted with cheers, chants and waves.'

Philip was on deck to greet the guest of honour, President Mandela, for a state banquet on board in 1995. 'Ah, Your Royal Highness, how are you?' said the president, who was the last guest to board. Inside, the Queen mingled with ease among her guests, telling them, 'You don't have to stand in a line' as 'Snaps', the nickname for the yacht's official photographer, captured the shot of the Queen, Philip and President Mandela together, before rushing off to process and print it so that it could be signed by both the Queen and Prince Philip, without the recipient knowing, in time for him to leave.

Britannia, that night as on other state banquets, was like a show at one of London's top West End theatre productions, and everyone had a part to play. The set was changed after dinner with the tables and chairs removed so that 200 after-dinner guests could come aboard and mingle in the royal dining room. For a state banquet everyone has to help out: palace staff, *Britannia* stewards but also stokers, electricians and engineers found themselves serving drinks or washing up. They volunteered to help all evening, for which they received the tiny sum of 45 pence for the privilege.

The Queen had developed a close relationship with President Mandela since they met for the first time in 1991 at a reception in Zimbabwe for Commonwealth leaders. The meeting was captured on film and shown in the 1992 BBC documentary *Elizabeth R.* Mandela was there representing the African National Congress (ANC) as an observer after being released from jail in 1990, amid growing domestic and international pressure, and with fears of a racial civil war, by the then president, F.W. de Klerk. Mr Mandela had spent 27 years in prison, split between Robben Island, Pollsmoor Prison and Victor Verster Prison, and was poised to become the first black President of South Africa.

The Queen broke precedent and invited Mandela to join them at the banquet and the chemistry between them was instant. South Africa's first non-racial elections were held in April 1994, resulting in Mr Mandela's historic election as president. One of his first acts was to return South Africa to the Commonwealth of Nations. In 1961, during the apartheid era, the country had decided to leave the organisation when it was ruled that racial equality was a condition of membership.

The friendship between President Mandela and the Queen was an enduring one. He famously referred to Her Majesty as 'My friend Elizabeth'. She returned the compliment and, in correspondence between the two, she signed off, 'Your sincere friend, Elizabeth'. He gave her a hand-painted silk scarf to mark South Africa's return to the Commonwealth after the apartheid years, something that she still cherishes to this day.

The two leaders would meet many times, including during his state visit to the UK in 1996 when the president was her guest at Buckingham Palace. Among the honours the Queen bestowed upon Mr Mandela was the Order of Merit, a special award for great achievement. When he died in 2013 the Queen led tributes to the great man. Speaking of his legacy she said, 'He worked tirelessly for the good of his country, and his legacy is the peaceful South Africa we see today.' She said she remembered him, 'with great warmth'.

HMY *Britannia*'s final voyage, after the handover of Hong Kong to China in July 1997, was to bring the Prince of Wales and the former British Governor of Hong Kong, Chris Patten, and his family, home from the British colony. She was the 83rd royal yacht since the restoration of the monarchy in 1660 during the reign of King Charles II and the second to be called '*Britannia*'. A letter written on behalf of the Queen showed how Elizabeth privately lobbied the Cabinet Office to push for a replacement yacht. Shortly after the then prime minister, John Major, made the announcement, a senior Buckingham Palace official, Sir Kenneth Scott, the former British Ambassador to Yugoslavia and at the time the Queen's Deputy Private Secretary, wrote to the Cabinet Office detailing how the Queen 'would very much welcome' a new yacht. It was a carefully couched letter that called for the ultimate discretion and acknowledged that the Queen's lobbying would be unpopular with the public if it came to light. Dated 5 May 1995, the letter read, 'I have deliberately taken a back seat in recent correspondence, since the question of whether there should be a replacement yacht is very much one for the government and since the last thing I would like to see is a newspaper headline saying, "Queen Demands New Yacht." At the same time I hope it is clear to all concerned that this reticence on the part of the palace now (sic) way implies that Her Majesty is not deeply interested in the subject; on the contrary, the Queen would naturally very much welcome it if a way could be found of making available for the nation in the twenty-first century the kind of service which Britannia has provided for the last 43 years.'

On 10 December 1996, Lord Ashbourne rose in the House of Lords to try and convince the Upper Chamber that HMY *Britannia* should be replaced. 'We have spoken to and corresponded with a number of Cabinet Ministers with an interest in the yacht and have pointed out to them the merits of the vessel and the importance to the country of replacing the present yacht ... We see the Royal Yacht as a national yacht, which is both a status symbol for Britain and, indeed, a symbol of British excellence. There are not many things we do better than anyone else in the world, but ceremonial is one.' He went on, 'If Her Majesty wished to use the yacht privately, say for the Western Isles cruise which has historically taken place after Cowes each year, the Palace would be charged for those events. Thus one might end up with a vessel largely funded by public money, with a contribution from the Palace for non-governmental royal use, where appropriate.'

In his speech he quoted one-time US Ambassador to Britain Henry E. Catto Jnr (in office 17 May 1989 to 13 March 1991) who wrote on 27 July 1994: 'I remember my farewell call on the Queen, as I left my post as Ambassador to the Court of St James. We chatted about a number of things, *Britannia*, included. Jokingly, I told her if the day ever came when there were parliamentary hearings to decide whether or not to build a new *Britannia*, I would be glad to come and testify. For a foreigner, I have had a unique experience with the grand old vessel. I know what she has done for Britain, and for the world for that matter. In a time of increasing public ugliness, of ethnic strife, of endless drabness, *Britannia* is a point of light and beauty, a symbol of British greatness, in which I, for one, am still a believer.'

It was, sadly, a case of too little, too late. The decommissioning was signed off by Prime Minister Blair and the ceremony in Portsmouth on 11 December 1997 was inevitably an emotional event. All the senior royals were there, with one notable exception, Queen Elizabeth the Queen Mother, who preferred not to take part. This was where the Queen had enjoyed so many family moments – not just with her own family, but with her 'family of nations'.

She once described a trip on the HMY *Britannia* from Portsmouth the long way round to Aberdeen as her only holiday of the year. Rear Admiral Sir Robert Woodard said that when he went to see the Queen on being appointed Flag Officer Royal Yachts, as *Britannia*'s captain was known, in 1990, she asked him, Would it be helpful, if she were to offer her own thoughts on the role of the Yacht? The Queen said of the yacht, which carried the Royal Family on 968 official voyages: '*Britannia* is the one place I can truly relax.'

Sir Robert said the Queen said at their meeting, 'People who know us at all know that Buckingham Palace is the office,' she began, 'Windsor Castle is for weekends and the occasional State thing and Sandringham and Balmoral are for holidays. Well, they aren't what I would call holidays. For example, there are 90 people coming to stay with us at Balmoral this summer. The only holiday I get every year is from Portsmouth the long way round to Aberdeen on the Royal Yacht, when I can get up when I like and wear what I like and be completely free. And if you as Flag Officer Royal Yachts can produce the Royal Yacht for my summer holidays, that's all I ask.'

Britannia was the closest they had ever come to creating their own home away from the palaces, castles and country estates the Queen had inherited through 40 previous monarchs going back to William the Conquerer. The Queen has steadied the nation with her unwavering strength and stoicism and is regarded worldwide as the epitome of a true leader. That's not to say the monarch is without emotion. Although incredibly infrequent, the Queen has been seen to cry in public on occasion: at a visit to the site of the Aberfan tragedy in 1966, at the Field of Remembrance at Westminster Abbey in 2002 when she took her late mother's role, in 2016 when she became visibly emotional during a moving service for the fallen soldiers of the Duke of Lancaster regiment (having unveiled a statue in memory of members of the regiment who have died since it was formed) in 2006 and in 2019 she was seen wiping away a tear during the Remembrance Sunday service at the Cenotaph as Britain fell silent to honour our war heroes.

It's not surprising given the deeply personal memories of her time on *Britannia* that the Queen, in a scarlet coat and hat, shed a tear when she attended the decommissioning of the royal yacht. Overcome with emotion, she was seen wiping her eyes with her black gloves as she stood with her husband and eldest son, both in their ceremonial Royal Navy uniforms.

Britannia had a special place in Philip's heart too. He said of the royal yacht: 'She is special for a number of reasons. Almost every previous sovereign has been responsible for building a church, a castle, a palace or just a house. William the Conqueror built the Tower of London, Edward I built the Welsh castles, Edward IV built St George's Chapel at Windsor and Edward VII built Sandringham. The only comparable structure built in the present reign is *Britannia*.'

Philip and Elizabeth could try their own ideas and choose everything from the paint colour to the carpets with the help of architect and interior designer Sir Hugh Casson. The couple took their inspiration from the modernist movement sweeping through the UK following the 1951 Festival of Britain, curated by Sir Hugh. So furnishings were stripped back while chairs and tables bore the unmistakable imprint of streamlined mid-century design.

Aboard, informality would go a long way – but it had its limits. John Gorton, former prime minister of Australia, later recalled one beach barbecue with the family during a 1970 tour of Australia, when the royal party decided it was time for a swim. 'Princess Anne was thrown in and then Prince Philip,' he said. 'I was sitting next to Her Majesty and I was just about to throw her in but I looked at her and something about the way she looked at me told me that perhaps I shouldn't. In the end, the Queen was the only one who stayed dry.' As both a ship and a royal residence, *Britannia* was unique. There was no other palace in which the Royal Family would seat their guests on cheap wicker chairs (purchased by Prince Philip during a Hong Kong stopover in 1959) just as there was no other Royal Navy ship in which orders were delivered in complete silence and by hand.

It was assumed that the Royal Family blamed the Labour Party for the demise of *Britannia*. In the mid-nineties a substantial refit was required. Shortly before the 1997 election, the Conservative government announced that it would build a new yacht with a budget of £60 million. But it had failed to follow a political golden rule, that major undertakings involving the crown require cross-party agreement. Blair's New Labour was not consulted and duly opposed the idea, which thus became an election issue. Not surprisingly, on being elected a few months later, the Labour government declined to commission a new yacht.

Philip felt the decision to save £60 million was short-sighted and believed it did lasting damage to the global standing of the United Kingdom. What's more there were many more nautical miles left in her and with a few tweaks *Britannia* could have been seaworthy for many more years. It was not as if the Royal Family were misusing the yacht for lavish junkets, as a private craft. It was, as Philip and his son Charles both felt strongly, part of the process of trying to represent Britain abroad, 'entirely motivated by a desperate desire to put the "Great back into Great Britain",' as the Prince of Wales put it. Philip, who said the decision to decommission the yacht 'saddened' him, was adamant this was the wrong decision, too. In a forthright interview to mark his 90th birthday, he said as much: 'She should have had her steam turbines taken out and diesel engines put in. She was as sound as a bell and she could have gone on for another fifty years,' he said.

Many in the Royal Family and the Household still feel aggrieved by the decision and that the blame for the demise of the royal yacht lies with Sir John Major and his Conservative government. Sir John said in his autobiography that he was a supporter of a new royal yacht but that Kenneth Clarke, then chancellor of the exchequer, blocked any moves to replace it. By failing to show clear leadership Major allowed the issue to drift unguided for two and a half years. It was so ineptly handled that it became a political football at the election. The reaction of the Labour Party was hardly surprising and virtually sealed the fate of a possible new royal yacht before it could become the focus of a more reasoned and bipartisan discussion.

The yacht held a special place in both Philip and Elizabeth's hearts, since the day she launched her with a bottle of Empire wine on the Clyde, back in April 1953. The Prince of Wales, who shared his parents' fondness for the yacht, wrote, 'There was a kind of exasperated sadness experienced by all and sundry.' He also noted that American officials did not understand the decision to decommission 'the dear yacht'.

Britannia's pulling power, after all, was the stuff of legend. The yacht gave the Queen time to recharge fully, instead of charging around in jets from one engagement to the next. But it was more than that. It was what this ocean-going palace could achieve for the greater good that interested the prince. 'It really did have great convening power,' I said during a conversation between the author and the Prince of Wales for his book, *Charles at Seventy: Thoughts, Hopes and Dreams,* 'and helped raise billions' for the UK economy, referring – like the former foreign secretary, Boris Johnson – to the clear 'soft power' benefits of such a yacht. 'Sadly, the Treasury did not seem to think so,' Charles told me. 'What's more, the Royal Navy didn't want to pay to staff it, either,' he added. 'Blair and Brown … and the Treasury simply wouldn't have it, so there we are,' he said, with an air of resignation in his voice. He wasn't being controversial, just stating a fact.

Britannia's pulling power was the stuff of legend. Presidents, billionaires, bankers and ambassadors couldn't resist an invite – even if a member of the Royal Family was not on board. On one occasion in 1993 when she staged a trade day in what was then known as Bombay* contracts worth an incredible £1 billion were signed. When she was due in any port, particularly when carrying the Queen and Prince Philip or the Prince of Wales, the British Ambassador was suddenly the most popular person in the entire country.

At the decommissioning ceremony in Portsmouth after her 44-year service, the emotion of the occasion got the better of the Queen who openly wept. Clearly it was a decision that caused her great hurt. Even Tony Blair, whose new Labour government decommissioned the yacht, admitted they had got it wrong. Blair later said. 'I think if it had happened five years into my time [as prime minister], I would have just said "no".' Many key figures believe post-Brexit a new royal yacht would be a huge boost to British overseas trade. Lord Jones of Birmingham, who as Digby Jones ran

---

* The City has been officially known as Mumbai since 1995 when it was renamed by the far-right regional party Shiv Sena, an ally of the Bharatiya Janata Party.

the CBI for six years from 2000 to 2006 and later served in Gordon Brown's government as a minister, said a £100 million replacement could be funded by a 'three-way split' between businesses, taxpayers and the National Lottery.

Lord Jones added, 'I was Minister of State for Trade. I got round ninety-odd countries, banging the drum for British business, brand Britain. And I can tell you the Royal *Britannia* moored in a harbour, asking big decision makers on board [offers] the atmosphere of something that no other country has got – the British Royal Family.

'I don't care what the politically correct "Liberal-ati" from Metropolitan Islington say, believe me it sells around the world like very few other things.'

★★★

Much to both Charles's and Philip's irritation, the old lady HMY *Britannia* is now a tourist attraction docked in Edinburgh, something lamented by the man who will be the only British king since Charles II not to have a royal yacht. He has never forgiven the politicians for making it an election issue.

Philip's vision for a new royal yacht, which was mooted again by Boris Johnson's government in 2020, was for a floating trade platform for Britain with a secondary role within the Royal Navy. 'It would need to have a dual role as a training ship or a command ship,' he said. 'We used *Britannia* to help trade, for exhibitions and so on. It'd be fine for "invisibles" but you couldn't go down a completely commercial route. I don't think we'd want Mr Fayed hiring the royal yacht to promote Harrods, do you?'

The duke always blamed Sir John Major, his chancellor Norman Lamont and Defence Secretary Michael Portillo for dithering until the opportunity was lost. He told Gyles Brandreth: 'Major was blocked by Lamont and didn't get the Opposition on board. And then Portillo got involved and made a complete bollocks of it. Absolutely idiotic.'

24: THE GAFFER OF INDIA (AND OTHER INDISCRETIONS)

'Dontopedalogy is the science of opening your mouth and putting your foot in it, a science which I have practised for a good many years.'

Philip told the General Dental Council,
quoted in *Time* in 1960

Prince Philip's remarks were, for the most part, regarded as harmless fun. On other occasions, however, with the media doing their utmost to stoke the fire of controversy, they led to a furious backlash and criticism. The duke himself felt it came with the territory, and even joked about his ability to put his foot in it, saying he suffered from 'Dontopedalogy', that he described as the science of opening your mouth and putting your foot in it. 'It's my custom to say something flattering to begin with so I shall be excused if I put my foot in it later on,' the duke said in 1956. Indeed, he became so well practised at the so-called gaffes that bestselling books of collections of his riskier comments have been published.

Eleven years after his infamous 'slitty eyes' comment in China (covered extensively in Chapter 21, *Chinese Whispers*), he was at it again on another important state visit to India. This time Philip queried the death toll of the Amritsar massacre as he and the Queen made a sensitive visit to the city on 14 October 1997. British estimates put it at 379, while Indian estimates are in the thousands. I was among the accredited journalists covering that visit. Except for police and press, Jallianwala Bagh park was empty when the Queen and Philip walked with their entourage as well as officials from the Indian government. The Queen and Philip then solemnly laid a wreath at the obelisk commemorating the atrocity, then walked out again as briskly as they walked in. It was brief, and appeared if anything perfunctory, but the relatives of those who were gunned down and died in the massacre said the visit was 'a sufficient act of atonement'.

When the then *Daily Telegraph* correspondent, Robert Hardman (who would go on to produce a series of acclaimed royal documentaries and books later in his career), returned to the group of reporters, who were huddled together in a fixed point viewing position organised by the British Embassy, with his pool report to share, our eyes lit up. As we scribbled Philip's words verbatim in our notebooks we knew a big story was brewing. For Philip had, perhaps, atoned a little less than some might wish. As he was leaving, he stopped abruptly at a plaque that recorded an official toll of the 'martyred'. It read, 'This place is saturated with the blood of about two thousand Hindus, Sikhs and Muslims who were martyred in a non-violent struggle.' Philip stared quizzically at the plaque for a moment or two before making a conscious decision to speak. This was not an ill-thought-out 'off-the-cuff' remark. 'Two thousand? It wasn't, was it?' he said, within earshot of Robert Hardman. Clearly confident of his facts, Philip went on, 'That's wrong. I was in the navy with Dyer's son. That's a bit exaggerated. It must include the wounded.'

Philip may well have had his facts right. A martyr, after all, is a person who is killed because of their religious or other beliefs and records show at least 379 unarmed Indian civilians died and over 1,200 others were injured on 13 April 1919, when Acting Brigadier General Reginald Dyer ordered troops of the British Indian Army to fire their rifles and the massacre followed*.

---

* Brigadier General Dyer was lauded for his actions by some in Britain, and indeed became a hero among many of those who were directly benefiting from the British Raj, such as members of the House of Lords. He was, however, widely denounced and criticised in the House of Commons, whose July 1920 committee of investigation censured him. Responses polarised both the British and Indian peoples.

Philip's pedantic questioning of the number of fatalities undoubtedly spoiled what was a hugely successful day which had been marked by enthusiastic crowds and a rapturous welcome at the Golden Temple, also known as Harmandir Sahib, meaning 'abode of God', a gurdwara in Amritsar which is the pre-eminent spiritual site of Sikhism and where the couple were given a phantasmagorical tour. It was the part of the trip that her host, Indian prime minister I. K. Gujral, had advised the Queen to skip, but it was the first time the tour really came alive.

The backdrop of the 1997 visit was no less controversial. Hours before the Queen and Philip landed in New Delhi, Prime Minister Gujral reportedly told a meeting of Egyptian intellectuals in Cairo that Britain was a 'third rate power'. Gujral was said to be livid at the then British foreign secretary Robin Cook for suggesting during a visit to Pakistan that Britain might mediate between India and Pakistan on the Kashmir issue, and used the 'third-rate power' phrase first mentioned by Lord Curzon, who had said in 1901, 'As long as we rule India, we are the greatest power in the world. If we lose it we shall straightaway drop to a third rate power.'

***

Up until that point the royal couple had mostly seen vacant streets where there were a few limp Union Flags interspersed with Indian flags and an occasional gaggle of schoolchildren. But Amritsar was different. It seemed that every schoolchild in the city with a population of 884,000 was on the streets waving flags, and there were golden streamers everywhere. The exuberant atmosphere masked a more complicated reality. Earlier a demonstration in the city against the Queen's visit ended in a baton charge by police, with injuries and a number of arrests.

At the Golden Temple, spiritually the most significant shrine in Sikhism, a few miles down the road, a very different scene awaited them. It was a confection of white marble and gold leaf, with a lake full of carp where on ordinary days believers immerse themselves. The place was crammed with the faithful in gorgeous Sikh costume, with swords and shields and daggers; sages with long grey beards; and nuns and monks all in white, associated with peace. It was fantastically exotic. The Queen and the duke were propelled through the Akal Takht shrine, almost destroyed by army tanks during the siege of 1984. It was organised Indian chaos, but the royal couple were clearly thrilled by the experience and when they left they were laden with gifts. Gurchan Singh Tora, president of Sikhism's ruling body, said: 'The Queen's visit will send the message around the world that peace prevails in the Golden Temple.' Perhaps it was no wonder that the secular but Hindu-dominated Indian government was so wary about the purpose of the royal visit.

The following day, inevitably, it was not the hugely successful visit to the Golden Temple that dominated the headlines in the British newspapers, but Philip's ill-advised remark questioning the number of 'martyrs' at the Amritsar massacre. The *Daily Express* pulled no punches and dismissed Philip as a blundering fool with the headline 'The Gaffer of India'.

Rarely, however, has Philip been forced to apologise for his gaffes. His attitude towards such slip-ups was always 'like it or lump it' or to blame the press for overplaying and twisting his words. But on 10 August 1999 during a routine engagement his ill-advised comments caused another storm after the British Indian community became the latest group to be offended by one of his off-the-cuff remarks. During a walkabout, as he toured the hi-tech Racal-MESL electronics factory in Edinburgh, Philip remarked that a fuse box bursting with wires looked 'as if it was put in by an Indian' prompting immediate condemnation. Kumar Murshid, chairman of the National Assembly Against Racism, said the prince's comments were disgraceful. 'This sort of thing is of great concern to us because people expect the Royal Family to set an example,' he said.

This time the Queen's advisers felt Philip had gone too far and took action. Within hours Buckingham Palace had issued an apology.

'The Duke of Edinburgh regrets any offence which may have been caused. With hindsight he accepts that what were intended as light-hearted comments were inappropriate,' a statement said.

The official statement did little to assuage the anger prompted by the remark. 'If anyone else had said it I'm sure the repercussions for them would be far more severe than for him,' said a spokesman for the Scottish National Party. 'He needs to respect other races and cultures far more than he does. Once again Prince Philip misses the target with what he thought was a jovial aside and offends more people than he entertained,' said Scottish Tory deputy home affairs spokeswoman Lyndsay McIntosh. 'It is just another example of him going about with his foot in his mouth,' said Liberal Democrat MSP George Lyon.

It had only been a matter of weeks since the prince provoked similar offence when he asked a group of profoundly deaf children if they had lost their hearing listening to a Caribbean band that was obviously not to his taste. In Scotland, he had commiserated with students for being unfortunate enough to be studying in Glasgow. Four years earlier, he had asked a Scottish driving instructor: 'How do you keep the natives off the booze long enough to get them through the test?'

He was never afraid to take his insensitivities abroad. In Germany, he offended Helmut Kohl, who served as Chancellor of West Germany and then Germany from 1982 to 1998, by addressing him by Hitler's Nazi title, *Reichskanzler*. Kohl's repost came some years later in 2014. In his bestselling book *Legacy: The Kohl Protocols*, he described the duke as a 'blockhead' and criticised the behaviour. His comment was revealed in more than 600 hours of taped conversations Mr Kohl held with a journalist, Heribert Schwan, lined up to help ghostwrite his memoirs but which he later tried to ban from print.

Philip has described Hungarians as 'pot-bellied' and pretended to be amazed that a student trekking in Papua New Guinea had managed to do so without being eaten by cannibals. Brazil, also, would apparently be a paradise were it not for the Brazilians. Given the duke's propensity to speak his mind the newspapers soon had plenty of material. In 1969 he said to Welsh singer Tom Jones [later Sir Tom] after the *Royal Variety Performance*, 'What do you gargle with – pebbles?' He added the following day: 'It is very difficult at all to see how it is possible to become immensely valuable by singing what I think are the most hideous songs.' Another favourite, that he first used in Canada in 1969, was, 'I declare this thing open, whatever it is.'

For some, his rude comments are merely more grist to an all too familiar mill. Phil Dampier, author of the bestseller *Prince Philip: Wise Words and Golden Gaffes*, believes people should accept the duke at face value and see him as a national treasure rather than be outraged. Phil said 'I've heard some of the duke's classic gaffes travelling around the world with the royals in recent years. I remember in 2002 in Cairns, Australia where he said to an aboriginal leader, "Do you still throw spears at each other?" I'll always remember the look on the guy's face, he was smiling, he was happy and then all of a sudden his face just fell and I knew instantly that Philip had done one of his infamous gaffes.'

But Phil thinks the duke should not be condemned for his straight-talking, as he is a man of his time. 'In my view he is a national treasure. The Queen has had a very successful reign and he must take a great deal of credit for it. A lot of people admire him and respect him. Yes, some people think some of the politically incorrect comments are outdated but most people feel he has done a fantastic job. It hasn't been easy, but he has given a great deal of service and support to the Queen.'

It would be easy to turn the duke into a caricature of the deep-thinking visionary that he is. It would be wrong if his gaffes, whilst noteworthy when taken out of context, were all he was remembered for. But his humour helps one understand his complex character. He knows he is being rude, and frankly he likes being controversial. It is partly that devil-may-care attitude that makes him an attractive figure. My personal favourite came after a banquet in Brazil, when the president of the National Bowling

Club made a short speech in Portuguese. Realising that Prince Philip did not understand it, he made an effort to summon up his entire English vocabulary when presenting the emblem of the club to the prince and said, 'Balls, you know.' The prince graciously replied, 'And balls to you, sir. '

25: GOLDEN AGE

'The Duke of Edinburgh has made an invaluable contribution
to my life over these past 50 years.'

From the Queen's Golden Jubilee speech
at the Guildhall in June 2002

They were the powerful triumvirate at the heart of the monarchy, never illustrated more clearly or visually than in the famous photograph of all three, taken to celebrate the Queen Mother's 80th birthday. The 'royal sisterhood' of the Queen, Queen Mother and Princess Margaret was impenetrable. The monarch, especially in the early years of her reign, relied on their counsel more than any other. Philip avoided challenging them, knowing it would be fruitless. Although, one to one, he got on well enough with Margaret, despite her reputation of being difficult, demanding and impolite, he often clashed with his mother-in-law, Queen Elizabeth, the Queen Mother as she viewed him as someone who defied her authority as family matriarch.

While the Queen Mother was old-fashioned and traditional with her approaches, Philip was progressive and a moderniser. Their disagreements continued throughout her long life, especially with regard to the direction the Royal Family and institution of monarchy was going. There was a definite want of empathy between the two. From the early years of the Queen's reign they were involved in a kind of tug-of-war for the new monarch's ear which the Queen found trying. After all, the Queen Mother was only 51 when she was forced to step down as Queen Consort on the untimely death of King George VI and felt she had been cut off in her prime. She loved to remind people that she had been the last Empress of India and believed it was her duty to put on a show in return for the fabulous privileges she enjoyed. She had grown to cherish the position of Queen Consort that had been thrust upon her and grown into the challenge only for it to be suddenly and cruelly taken from her just when she had mastered and was embracing the role.

Ever since he was suggested as a suitor for her eldest daughter the Queen Mother had viewed Philip with suspicion. She felt, especially in the early years of her daughter's reign, that he wielded too much influence over Elizabeth. One on one, Philip was more than happy to position himself as his wife's most senior adviser, but when the Queen invited her mother and sister to jointly discuss an idea and they had reached a consensus Philip felt it pointless to question it, at least openly.

From the day of Princess Margaret's birth her older sister, then four, assumed a protective attitude that continued until her death. 'Lilibet' as Princess Margaret pronounced her sister's name, a nickname which stuck, and 'Margot' as Princess Margaret became known within the family, shared the same nursery at the top of 145 Piccadilly. In later life, when it came to Princess Margaret's affairs of the heart her sister, by now the Queen, was almost always sympathetic. She felt keenly for her during the romance with Group Captain Peter Townsend. But she despaired of her sister's affair later with the landscape gardener Roddy Llewellyn. She never received him at any of her palaces. The matter was discussed between the Queen and James Callaghan, the then prime minister. As the princess's behaviour led to calls for her to be struck off the Civil List and lead a private life, the Queen objected. Afterwards the Queen shared her sister's disappointment that there were to be no other great loves. In her middle years Margaret devoted herself more to public engagements that cut her sister's workload.

The Queen's protective attitude continued, especially during the bouts of ill health that plagued Margaret towards the end of her life.

When Margaret turned 60, Elizabeth awarded her sister the Royal Victorian Chain, a decoration instituted in 1902 by King Edward VII as a personal award of the monarch. It ranks above the Royal Victorian Order, which marked the esteem and affection in which she was held. At the time, other than her own mother, the Queen Mother, she was the only member of the British Royal Family to have received the honour. Her Majesty, however, conferred the honour on her husband, The Duke of Edinburgh, in 2007*.

Princess Margaret and Queen Elizabeth, the Queen Mother, didn't always see eye to eye, and in fact had a somewhat strained relationship, especially during Margaret's adulthood. She relates how she wanted to marry the divorced courtier Peter Townsend, who had comforted her after her father's death. When Margaret realised she would have to give up her royal status to marry a divorcee, she backed out. But she spent one final weekend with Peter Townsend. When Margaret returned to Clarence House, Queen Elizabeth, the Queen Mother, who was due to keep an evening engagement at the University of London, simply set off for this, unconcerned that her daughter would be having dinner alone on a tray. It was just part of her character. She could be cruel to the 'little people' in private, because, I think, she despised them; she was smelted with class prejudice. She hated classlessness and confided to Woodrow Wyatt, 'It's so unreal.' According to her equerry Colin Burgess, she wondered why people were always thrusting babies at her to kiss. She mimicked the voice of a former servant who had come to visit her. She mocked people who pronounced 'Ma'am' wrongly; it is supposed to rhyme with spam, not harm.

Margaret gave as good as she got, however. The princess was frequently rude to her mother in front of staff, which meant she was not always popular with them, as they were devoted to the old queen. She would question her mother's dress sense and get increasingly irritated that drinks before lunch, which were famed

---

* King Carl XVI Gustaf of Sweden, Princess Beatrix of the Netherlands, and King Juan Carlos I of Spain were among other recipients.

for their potency, would drag on for up to an hour. The control of the television set at Royal Lodge was another cause of irritation between them. Margaret would simply switch it to another channel on the remote without a word if she was bored with what the Queen Mother was watching.

'Those weekends at Royal Lodge were always fun, despite the bouts of bickering between the Queen Mother and Princess Margaret, who at times had a slightly strained relationship,' wrote Margaret's long-term friend and lady-in-waiting, the charming Lady Anne Glenconner. Lady Anne went on, 'One would do things like open all the windows, only for the other to go around shutting them. Or one would suggest an idea and the other would dismiss it immediately.' When she noted that Margaret had looked upset at her sister's coronation, Lady Anne wrote that Margaret replied, 'Of course I looked sad, Anne. I had just lost my beloved father and, really, I had just lost my sister, because she was going to be so busy and had already moved to Buckingham Palace, so it was just me and the Queen Mother.'

The Queen Mother and Margaret, however, despite their differences, were together a tremendous source of strength to the Queen, throughout her long reign, part of her private support system. Suddenly, within weeks of each other they were gone, and the Queen was bereft. First, just three days after the 50th anniversary of Elizabeth's ascension to the throne, the Queen's sister, Princess Margaret, died at 6.30 a.m. on 9 February 2002. After developing cardiac problems during the night, Margaret was driven from Kensington Palace to King Edward VII's Hospital, London. Sadly, there was nothing the doctors there could do apart from make the princess comfortable in her final hours. She passed away following her third stroke, with her children, Lord Linley (later 2nd Earl Snowdon) and Lady Sarah Chatto, at her side.

Princess Margaret's death, at the age of 71, was not unexpected, but it was still a devastating blow for the Queen Mother, whose own health was giving the Queen cause for serious concern. Six weeks later, on 30 March, the Queen Mother, who had been suffering with a bad cough and a chest infection in the preceding days, died peacefully in her sleep at Royal Lodge. The Queen was at her bedside when she died at 3.15 p.m. at the age of 101 and 238 days old, the longest-living member of the Royal Family in British history at the time of her death*. Buckingham Palace released a heartfelt statement. It read, 'The Queen, with the greatest sadness, has asked for the following announcement to be made immediately: her beloved mother, Queen Elizabeth, died peacefully in her sleep this afternoon at Royal Lodge, Windsor. Members of the royal family have been informed.'

A huge outpouring of grief followed from the public. The Prince of Wales said at her ceremonial funeral on 9 April 2002 in Westminster Abbey, 'For me, she meant everything. And I had dreaded, dreaded, this moment, along with, I know, countless others. Somehow I never thought it would come. She seemed gloriously unstoppable and, since I was a child, I adored her.'

It was a devastating way for Elizabeth to start her Golden Jubilee year, which was, after all, planned to be one of tumultuous celebration. Recognising her deep sadness, the Queen's people reacted with a warm outpouring of genuine affection towards the monarch. On 2 May the Queen embarked on her nationwide Golden Jubilee tour at Falmouth, on the coast of Cornwall in south-west England, to the sound of a 21-gun salute and rousing cheers from flag-waving children. The salute was from the frigate, HMS *Cornwall,* and signalled her arrival at the first engagement of her tour, which was at the new but not yet completed National Maritime Museum. On display was the *Bluebottle*, a Dragon class racing dinghy that had been given to the Queen and Prince Philip as a wedding gift.

Among the 3,000 people waiting to greet the couple was Sir Robert Woodard, Cornwall's Deputy Lieutenant and the last Admiral to captain the by now decommissioned HMY *Britannia*.

---

* Her last surviving sister-in-law, Princess Alice, Duchess of Gloucester, exceeded that, and died aged 102 on 29 October 2004.

'Terribly sad,' he noted about the Queen's arrival by royal train. 'Quite wrong. There is only one way to arrive in Falmouth, and that's aboard HMY *Britannia*. But if the Queen leaves here full of joy and happiness, then it sets the tone for the rest of the tour,' he said. In that respect, Falmouth was right on course. Pleasure boats crammed with sightseers applauded as the Queen launched a new lifeboat and then followed as she was given a brief floating tour of the harbour aboard the £1.4 million vessel. There was more cheering, flag-waving and flower-giving as the royal couple, Elizabeth and Philip, disembarked at the Prince of Wales Pier, the foundation stone of which was laid by her grandfather, King George V, and headed for a celebration of Cornish gardens at Trelissick.

At Truro Cathedral she celebrated the diocese's 125th anniversary with a 'Cornish lunch' of chicken, new potatoes and vegetables, served with a Cornish white wine. Philip opted for a bottle of Bishop Bill's Special Brew – a beer brewed by the local brewery Skinners to celebrate the cathedral's anniversary, and named after the Bishop of Truro, Bill Ind. 'I shall never be a saint,' said the bishop, 'but having a beer named after you is something.' As the royal couple waved goodbye to Truro they were presented with a hamper of Cornish foods. 'Blimey,' said Philip, pointing to a pasty. 'Look at that. It's enormous!'

'Yes,' replied the bishop, 'you can eat it on the train.'

'It would feed a family,' retorted the prince.

Next stops on the West Country tour were visits to Exeter, Taunton, Wells and Bath where the crowds were large and enthusiasm infectious. The couple then criss-crossed the nation from June to early August travelling as widely as possible across England, Scotland, Wales and Northern Ireland.

The focal point of the celebrations was the Golden Jubilee weekend between 1 to 4 June 2002, when a crowd of over one million people converged on Buckingham Palace for fireworks and fanfare. Street parties and parades across the country marked the jubilee which hit a high note with an evening pop concert in the grounds of Buckingham Palace, featuring superstar acts including the former Beatle, Sir Paul McCartney, Latino singer Ricky Martin, and soul diva Aretha Franklin. The monarch and other royals were joined by 12,000 guests and the concert was televised around the world. The enduring image will be of the rock group Queen's lead guitarist, Brian May, playing 'God Save the Queen' from the palace rooftop.

London was festooned in Union Flags and pictures of the Queen as locals gathered for parties which echoed similar events held for the Silver Jubilee 25 years before. While numbers were smaller and attitudes less reverential than in 1977, the response to the jubilee heartened the Royal Family. Thousands of people waving flags lined the streets of Windsor, site of Windsor Castle, the royal residence just west of London, to watch a parade march past Her Majesty.

The Queen, wearing a green suit and hat, smiled and waved as bands and other acts filed past her. The head of state was due to light the last of nearly 2,000 beacons stretching from Land's End to John O'Groats and from Antarctica to Zambia to celebrate her reign and then watch 3 tonnes of fireworks being set off from the roof of Buckingham palace. Three balcony appearances and more than a million voices raised in a thunderous rendition of the National Anthem crowned the amazing celebrations.

The magnificent climax to the Golden Jubilee weekend followed the pomp and pageantry of the Queen's ceremonial procession to St Paul's for a national service of thanksgiving and the rhythmic riot of colour that was the Festival in The Mall. It was the Queen on the balcony to watch a fly-past of 27 aircraft that most excited the crowd. The highlight – Concorde flying low with nine RAF Red Arrow Hawk jets streaming red, white and blue smoke over the palace roof – brought cheers so loud the roar of the engines was barely audible.

The Queen said she was both 'overwhelmed and deeply moved' by the public's response to her jubilee and made clear how vital the support of her family had been during her 50-year reign. In a speech at Guildhall, with Tony Blair in the audience, she spoke of the strength she drew from her husband and children. 'The Duke of Edinburgh has made an invaluable contribution to my life over these past 50 years, as he has to so many charities and organisations,' she said, as guests applauded. 'We both of us have a special place in our hearts for our children. I want to express my admiration for the Prince of Wales and for all he has achieved for this country. Our children, and all my family, have given me such love and unstinting help over the years and especially in recent months,' she added, referring to the recent deaths of her mother and sister.

At a time of national hopes for England's World Cup squad, as well as pride in the monarchy, the Queen joked, 'I am more than conscious at the moment of the importance of football. Although this weekend comes about half way through my jubilee year, as far as we are concerned it bears no relation to a rest at half-time. However, I am very glad that the 50th anniversary of my accession is giving so many people all over this country and in the Commonwealth an excuse to celebrate and enjoy themselves.'

Beautiful weather favoured the ceremonial procession. This was only the third occasion on which the Queen had used the Gold State Coach, which transported her to her coronation and during her Silver Jubilee procession. The sun glinted off the coach as it left the palace to cheers from a flag-waving crowd so vast that The Mall resembled a shimmering great red, white and blue ticker-tape parade. Prince Charles was behind on horseback in full ceremonial Royal Navy uniform, as was the Princess Royal in the uniform of Gold Stick-in-Waiting. Flanking them were the Household Cavalry in plumes and gleaming breastplates. Other senior members of the Royal Family preceded the Queen in carriages: Prince William, Prince Harry, the Duke of York and Princess Beatrice in the first; the Earl and Countess of Wessex accompanying Princess Eugenie, 12, in the second, and the Princess Royal's family in the third.

Thirty-five lesser members, the so-called 'minor royals', had been taken, somewhat unceremoniously, to St Paul's in a motor coach operated by a company appropriately called Windsorian. A 41-gun salute began in Green Park, one for every minute of the journey to the Cathedral. The Queen was carried on a wave of music for the two-and-a-half miles as a 3,000-strong choir with orchestras soared through *Progress for the Queen*, a composition beginning with a rousing 'Zadok the Priest' and weaving together 'Men of Harlech', 'Scotland the Brave', 'Oh Danny Boy' and other national songs. At Temple Bar the coach halted for the Queen to perform the ancient ceremony of touching the historic Pearl Sword, proffered by the Lord Mayor Sir James Oliver and symbolic of the Queen's authority in the City of London. A 61-gun salute from the Tower of London heralded her arrival in the City.

At St Paul's, before a 2,500-strong congregation, including senior politicians and 47 members of the Royal Family, the Archbishop of Canterbury, Dr George Carey, praised the steadfastness and abiding constancy of the monarch. He said that the bond between the sovereign and her people had grown 'stronger and deeper with the passage of time.' By the time the Queen emerged from the service, for her first official ride in her new twin-turbocharged, 6.75-litre V8 engine state Bentley, modified from the Arnage R, police officers were in shirtsleeves.

During lunch at Guildhall, Prime Minister Tony Blair echoed Dr Carey's praise. 'We know that you are, without falter or hesitation, totally committed to serving us, the British people,' he said. 'Whatever the vicissitudes of your own life, whatever dramas or crises are played out around you, no one ever doubts that commitment to serving Britain.'

A 'river of gold' then paved the Queen's journey up The Mall as 400 children waving gold streamers ran alongside the open-topped Range Rover carrying the Queen and Prince Philip to the royal box on the Queen Victoria Memorial. It was from there that they watched the Festival on The Mall parade. Other members of the Royal Family were already seated, with the Duke of York filming the spectacle with a small digital video camera.

It had taken the Prince of Wales and his sons almost half an hour to walk from St James's Palace to their seats as they stopped and chatted to spectators along the way. The choir, now swollen to 8,000 after the arrival of 5,000 gospel singers, belted out 'Consider

Yourself One of Us', from the musical *Oliver*. The crowd joined in as the Queen took her seat and waved. Old police cars, ambulances and fire engines took part in a services procession representing people who have served the community. It included proud Chelsea Pensioners, some in electric buggies. Four thousand children, with a rainbow of wishes from children around the Commonwealth and accompanied by dancers from New Zealand, Australia, India, and elsewhere provided the main basis of the final parade. A huge embroidery made up of flags from the Commonwealth was unveiled from the palace balcony.

It was then that the Royal Family made the first palace balcony appearance. The Queen and Prince Philip emerged first and took the applause before being joined by other senior members of the family. The Queen smiled and looked up as the first of the 27 aircraft flew over, running just over half an hour behind schedule due to the parades overrunning. Elizabeth's smile broadened as Concorde and the Red Arrows completed what had been a truly memorable day. The cheers and singing continued until, for the third and final time, the balcony doors closed on an historic occasion. The celebrations brought a wave of nostalgia across the country as people reflected over the five decades Elizabeth had reigned and also deepened affection for her. A poll in the *Mail on Sunday* said the Queen was the most respected figure in Britain, showing that her popularity had recovered strongly from the negative reaction to her apparent coldness after the death of Princess Diana in 1997.

26: WINDING DOWN

'It's better to get out before you reach the sell-by date.'

Prince Philip in an interview with
Fiona Bruce for the BBC, 2011

Despite his fearsome reputation, Prince Philip was always self-effacing when asked to talk about himself. Any discussion of his accomplishments always made him feel uncomfortable. In a BBC interview to mark his 90th birthday, he was asked by the interviewer if he was proud of his achievements. The duke looked genuinely puzzled at the question. 'No, that's asking too much,' he said. So what of his successes? 'Who cares what I think about it, that's ridiculous,' he said. His son, Prince Edward, Earl of Wessex, put his father's rather irascible response down to his modesty. 'My father, plain and simply, is very modest about himself and doesn't believe in talking about himself. One of his best pieces of advice he gives to everybody is to talk about everything else, don't talk about yourself. Nobody is interested in you.'

During the fraught television interview with BBC *News* anchor Fiona Bruce Philip admitted he did not want to take part in the documentary to commemorate his 90th birthday. The interviewer's courageous attempts to delve into Philip's private thoughts and private life, were given curt treatment. Persistent and cool throughout, Ms Bruce did manage to extract one key phrase from him, which made the headlines the next day. 'I reckon I've done my bit so I want to enjoy myself a bit now, with less responsibility, less frantic rushing about, less preparation, less trying to think of something to say. On top of that your [my] memory's going, I can't remember names and things,' he admitted. 'It's better to get out before you reach the sell-by date.' Philip also said he would be 'winding down' and reducing his workload too.

In the months after his remark there was little evidence of that. He not only carried out hundreds of public duties but even made a two-day solo trip to Toronto, where he was presented with the highest rank of the Order of Canada as well as awarding new regimental colours to the Third Battalion of the Royal Canadian Regiment. He also performed scores of private functions that were not recorded on any official list.

Although it didn't happen immediately, it was the first serious indication that Philip intended to one day step down from royal duties and retire from public life. He had recognised his frailties and made sure others, including his family and the senior courtiers of the Royal Household, were aware of them too. But first there was the little matter of the Queen's Diamond Jubilee, celebrating the milestone of 60 years on the throne.

Philip had hoped to be at his wife's side throughout all the scheduled celebrations, but the frailties he had warned of finally began to show. During the weekend the nation united to pay tribute to the Queen, and also to Philip, doctors stepped in to prevent him taking a further active part. When the Queen cautiously climbed the steps of St Paul's Cathedral on 5 June 2012, without her partner of 64 years at her side, she gave the outward appearance of frailty too. As the Queen progressed, slowly, followed by Prince Charles and his wife, Camilla, and the rest of the senior Royal Family, that abiding air of implacable confidence seemed to have escaped her. She was now Britain's oldest ever monarch and was there for the Diamond Jubilee Service of Thanksgiving, held in her honour. It had been an exhausting weekend for her, complete with pomp, pageantry and tumultuous celebration and it had clearly taken its toll.

In the streets outside, the loyal Union-Flag-waving well-wishers kept on coming. By dawn, thousands had already gathered at the nation's cathedral to stand patiently behind steel police barriers. One woman said she had got up at 3.30 a.m. to travel to the historic event from her home in Essex. 'My children wanted to watch it on television, but I told them the atmosphere would be so different if we were there,' she said. It was the right call. Inside, senior members of the government, the Opposition and representatives from around the UK and the Commonwealth heard Dr Rowan Williams, the Archbishop of Canterbury, praise Her Majesty's 'lifelong dedication'.

The Queen, however, seemed preoccupied, even a little pensive. She could be forgiven as her husband and stalwart, Philip, was not by her side. Instead, he was recovering at King Edward VII's Hospital in London a few miles away, where he was being treated for a bladder infection. Elizabeth was understandably worried, but, characteristically, she carried on.

Four days of Diamond Jubilee celebratory events eventually culminated in an appearance by the Queen on the Buckingham Palace balcony in front of a huge, cheering crowd. There was also a fly-past by World War II aircraft, and the Royal Air Force Red Arrows capped it off perfectly. Significantly, however, this was not witnessed by the usual extended Royal Family appearing at their palace vantage point. This time it was just the core family, the *New Royal Family*. The sovereign was joined by just five family members: the Prince of Wales, the Duchess of Cornwall, the Duke and Duchess of Cambridge and Prince Harry. This was clearly a conscious decision, and was the shape of things to come.

Prince Philip's absence that June day was a catalyst for a major shake-up in thinking at the heart of the Royal Family. Senior palace insiders remarked privately that it had simply looked wrong for the then 86-year-old monarch to be entering St Paul's Cathedral for a celebration of her own life in the complete absence of a male family member at her side as a supporter. It is a role that Charles might have been expected to take on, but his responsibilities to his wife, the Duchess of Cornwall, created a delicate quandary for him.

The service was the culmination of a glorious weekend of celebrations. The Thames River Pageant, in freezing rain, had contributed to the worsening of Philip's health as he had stood on the deck of the royal barge for the duration, refusing to sit in one of the rather gaudy gilded thrones provided for them. As Philip chose not to sit, so too did the Queen. Despite this, the duke had seemed like he was having the time of his life; resplendent in his ceremonial Royal Navy uniform, he appeared on top form.

As the party had rolled on, news emerged that, on the advice of his doctors, the duke would have to miss the Jubilee concert, organised by singer Gary Barlow of the pop group Take That, and had even been hospitalised. Among the media, there was a mood of genuine concern. Fortunately, on cue, Prince Charles stepped up to the mark and left his mother visibly moved by his kind, warm and sometimes emotional speech in praise of her at the close of concert. The Prince's opening word, 'Mummy', earned him rapturous cheers from the crowd. She beamed back, looking every inch the diamond Queen when she arrived on stage, adorned with Swarovski crystals, in an elegant cocktail dress of gold lamé, designed by Angela Kelly, under a dark cape, with sweeping trimmings of antique gold lace and deep olive.

Mother and son, accompanied by the Duchess of Cornwall, had minutes earlier made their way down to the stage encircling the Queen Victoria Memorial to a standing ovation. Celebrities, including Kylie Minogue and Cheryl Cole, jostled to stand as close to the royal party as possible. There was no jostling by the pop knights, Sir Paul McCartney, Sir Tom Jones and Sir Elton John, who had all been guaranteed prime positions close to the monarch at the finale. Prince Charles warmed his audience up by making a joke about the terrible weather for Sunday's river pageant, 'If I may say so, thank God it turned out fine!' It was when he made a poignant reference to the Duke of Edinburgh, in hospital just a few miles away, that Her Majesty's stiff upper lip for once appeared to weaken, if only for a moment. He went on, 'Your Majesty, millions, we are told, dream of having tea with you. Quite a lot nearly had a picnic with you in the garden of Buckingham Palace. The only sad thing about this evening is that my father could not be here with us because, unfortunately, he was taken unwell. But, ladies and gentlemen, if we shout loud enough he might just hear us in hospital and get better.'

Spontaneous cheers and applause broke out. The prince spoke for everyone when he added, 'Your Majesty, a Diamond Jubilee is a unique and special event. Some of us have had the joy of celebrating three jubilees with you. And I have the medals to prove it. And we are now celebrating the life and service of a very special person over the last 60 years. I was three when my grandfather George VI died and suddenly, unexpectedly, you and my father's lives were irrevocably changed when you were only 25. So as a nation this is our opportunity to thank you and my father for always being there for us. For inspiring us with your selfless duty and service, and for making us proud to be British.' Then turning to his mother, Charles paid tribute to 'The life and service of a very special person'.

It was a timely and brilliant performance by the heir to the throne. That gloss, that had so pleased the cheering masses, won all the plaudits in the newspapers the next day. In the palace corridors of power, however, the absence of the Duke of Edinburgh and his ill health the next day had focused minds. Philip was blessed with a remarkably robust constitution. No chances were ever taken with his health. It was abundantly clear to everyone, including the Queen herself, that it was no longer reasonable to expect him to keep up the same pace as he approached his century. There would inevitably be more occasions when the duke would not be in his usual place a few paces behind his wife.

It will not be an easy transition, but, in the course of celebrating what a magnificent service the two had given to their country, it had become obvious to everyone that it was time to allow them to step back, if only slightly. Philip refused to let his wife down and was reluctant to cut down on his busy schedule of private engagements. Indeed, if he had cut back as he suggested he would, there was no real evidence of it in the months following the Diamond Jubilee.

However, another hospitalisation for Philip — and the Queen's concern about his workload — accelerated her plans to hand over some responsibility to Charles. Together with his wife — the now fully accepted Duchess of Cornwall — his brothers Andrew and Edward, and the next generation of William, Kate and Harry, he began to ease the pressure on the Queen and her dutiful husband by taking on more of the royal duties. There has been talk of Charles adopting a 'Shadow King' role, enabling his mother to spend more time with her husband privately.

'There is no question of Her Majesty abdicating her responsibilities,' one senior member of the Royal Household explained. 'It's more about sharing the workload and being more selective of the duties she undertakes. Her Majesty and the Duke of Edinburgh worked tirelessly throughout the Diamond Jubilee. Perhaps too much was expected of them.'

The aide went on, 'The Queen is remarkably fit, but she appreciates that when she is on duty the Duke, as her liege man, believes it is his duty to be at her side. The difficulty is persuading him that any of his sons can step in for him to accompany Her Majesty and that that would be acceptable. If the Duke does not agree to that, the only solution is for Her Majesty to do fewer engagements and for the younger members of the family to represent her at the others.'

The younger generation had already acquitted themselves well during the London Olympics of 2012, when they appeared in Team GB T-shirts to shout encouragement to our athletes. Now they would become far more visible. Despite his PR slip in Las Vegas, royal advisers believed Prince Harry, too, had a key role to play. His improving reputation would survive the exposure. Successful Jubilee visits to Jamaica and Brazil in 2012, followed by an equally positive USA tour in 2013, confirmed his star quality as a roving royal. He may be a maverick but, like his late mother Diana, he certainly has the wow factor.

But the Queen's subtle move to take a step back in 2013 undoubtedly had deeper and more far-reaching consequences for Prince William – still serving as an RAF search and rescue pilot for the first half of 2013 – and his pregnant wife. It meant, too, he would have to rethink any ideas for a longer-term military career in order to instead become a full-time royal to fill the void. When Philip was taken ill and hospitalised again a few weeks later – forced to spend six days in Aberdeen Royal Infirmary while on his annual Balmoral holiday – the Queen took the opportunity to discuss how to handle this important reshaping of the monarchy with her heir Prince Charles.

The transition was imperceptibly gradual, tightly managed. Even if they come across as a little dull, the British like their Royal Family to appear calm, composed and in control at all times. The Queen backed it up with real action too. The palace revealed she was poised to quit long-haul overseas travel so that she could 'pace herself' for her future role as monarch.

Coming just weeks after the Queen was herself hospitalised, suffering from gastroenteritis, it showed her determination to manage her workload appropriately going forward. The decision to send Charles to Sri Lanka and represent her at the high-level meeting was also a canny move. He would be expected to step in whenever the Queen needed him to represent her on future long-haul trips, just like he and other royals had done during the Diamond Jubilee year. It seemed that not only had the Diamond Jubilee celebrations, when she had taken centre stage, been a crowning moment, but also it might perhaps have been her final great public display of pomp and pageantry. Now it was time to give the next generation their chance, and, for Charles, there was no better place to showcase his skills than at the Commonwealth meeting.

The Commonwealth has been one of the great successes of Her Majesty's reign. It is not an organisation on a mission – as Her Majesty has said. Instead, it offers its 2.1 billion people the unique opportunity to work together to achieve solutions to a wide range of problems. It is, she is proud to say, a major force for change. With a combination of quiet modesty, wisdom and experience, she has been central to holding the association together for over 60 years and taking it forward. It is central to her role as a modern monarch and, close sources say, she believes it is at the heart of the new Royal Family. Yes, she wants Charles to take his position at its head, but she also believes the next generation of William, Kate and Harry has a vital role to play here too.

That said, with Prince Charles poised to take on a 'Shadow King' role, it is for the younger generation to take up the torch, particularly when it comes to the Commonwealth and international diplomacy, which after all is at the core of what modern monarchy is all about. In the Jubilee year, it had been a team effort – particularly when it came to representing the Queen abroad. The Duke and Duchess of Cambridge visited Malaysia, Singapore, the Solomon Islands and the tiny island of Tuvalu. Prince Harry, who was on his first solo trip on behalf of the Queen, went to Belize, Jamaica and the Bahamas.

The extended Royal Family did their bit too. The Duke of York went to India, while the Princess Royal toured Mozambique and Zambia. Her Majesty's first cousin the Duke of Gloucester went to the British Virgin Islands and Malta, and the Duke of Kent took in the Falkland Islands and Uganda, while the Earl and Countess of Wessex journeyed to the Caribbean, visiting Antigua and Barbuda, Barbados, Grenada, Montserrat, St Kitts and Nevis, St Lucia, St Vincent and the Grenadines and Trinidad and Tobago, with an extra visit to Gibraltar.

Her Majesty, in organising who went where, was sending another clear message – the Commonwealth really mattered to her. Under her stewardship, the Commonwealth has grown into a voluntary association of 54 independent countries, spanning six continents – about 30 per cent of the world's population, with half of those under 25 years of age. She calls it the original worldwide web. The Royal Family's future long-term involvement with the Commonwealth in an official capacity is, therefore, a delicate subject. Some within the organisation have argued that one of the central reasons for the success of 'the family of nations' has been the personal involvement of the Queen. She has been, and continues to be, the talismanic figure at the heart of it all. She knows most of the nations' leaders personally, and many of them are now old friends.

The Queen and Philip have been inspirational servants to the nation, an example to all. After more than 60 years at the helm of the monarchy, few can remember a time without Elizabeth II as sovereign. There is a quiet, irrational belief among us all that the Queen will just go on and on indefinitely. Both Elizabeth and her consort, Philip, are realists and have acknowledged that their advancing years will inevitably force them to slow down. There is no question of the sovereign abdicating like the Dutch Queen Beatrix, who stepped down in favour of her son in 2013. Clearly, however, as she approached her 90th year, the Queen set the wheels in motion for the significant adjustments that needed to be made.

Prince William explained his dilemma in 2011. 'For the grandchildren, it's a bit difficult for us to say, "Take it easy" when she's so much older than us, and has done so much more. We do hint at taking some things off her, but she won't have anything of it. She's so dedicated and really determined to finish everything she started.' He went on, 'She'll want to hand over knowing she's done everything she possibly could to help, and that she's got no regrets and no unfinished business; that she's done everything she can for the country and that she's not let anyone down – she minds an awful lot about that.'

In an interview in the same year Prince William's brother, Harry – who would later on in adulthood escape the gilded 'royal cage' and abandon Britain in favour of a freer life on the west coast of the US with his wife, Meghan – admitted that his grandmother's heavy workload concerned him. 'Regardless of whether my grandfather seems to be doing his own thing, sort of wandering off like a fish down the river, the fact that he's there, personally, I don't think that she could do it without him,' he said.

Princes William and Harry's first cousin, Peter Phillips, Queen Elizabeth and Philip's eldest grandchild, agreed with them. 'You have got to remember his age, both of their ages. If occasionally there is the odd engagement cancelled, it shouldn't come as such a surprise,' he said, on 6 June 2013, the day his grandfather was taken to an exclusive Harley Street London Clinic for a procedure. When it comes to health, the Royal Family traditionally maintains a 'Keep calm and carry on' attitude. Like Philip himself, none of them believe in making a fuss.

Earlier on the same day, Philip had been at a garden party attended by 8,000 guests at Buckingham Palace and spent the afternoon cracking jokes with guests. In his top hat and morning suit, he looked dapper as always, defying his great age. He could pass for a man ten years younger. Towards the end of the party, he quietly slipped away from the event unnoticed, and left at around 5.30 p.m. He changed and was driven by his Scotland Yard personal protection officer to the medical appointment at the private London clinic, two and half miles away in Harley Street via Park Lane.

Buckingham Palace did not issue a statement until the duke was safely inside the clinic and the procedure complete. It read, 'The results will now be analysed. At this early stage he is progressing satisfactorily. Further updates will continue to be issued when appropriate.' When pressed, one senior member of the Royal Household did not mince his words: 'Look, what do you expect. He's old.' There was cause for concern, for a man of Philip's age to be operated on under general anaesthetic was worrying enough, and this latest bout of ill health for the Royal Family patriarch had far-reaching implications.

As ever, the Queen put duty first. She was understandably concerned about him, but decided to go ahead with her scheduled engagements anyway, without him at her side, at the BBC's new £1 billion headquarters at Broadcasting House. Hundreds gathered outside cheering loudly as the Queen's car arrived at 11.10 a.m. Elizabeth even pulled a surprise of her own when two BBC journalists, Julian Worricker and Sophie Long, who were presenting live on the BBC *News* channel, suddenly realised the sovereign was right behind them. After discovering they had a special observer, the pair acknowledged

Her Majesty's presence with a nod of the head in an unscripted, light-hearted moment before continuing the broadcast.

The Queen, who was wearing a powder-blue coat and hat, then broadcast a short live address from the BBC in the UK and around the globe via the BBC World Service referring to a previous visit to Broadcasting House with Philip shortly before her coronation 60 years before. It was to be her only mention of her husband. BBC Trust chairman, Lord Patten, and BBC director general, Lord Hall, who made a short address in which he wished the duke a speedy recovery, escorted her throughout the visit.

She began the tour by visiting Radio 1 and meeting hosts including Nick Grimshaw, Trevor Nelson and Sara Cox, before being led to the station's well-known Live Lounge to watch a performance by The Script. At the end, she chatted briefly to lead singer Danny O'Donoghue, then a judge on BBC1 show *The Voice*. When the Queen learned he was playing the Glastonbury festival, she joked, 'The place you get covered in mud?' The singer replied with a laugh, 'You've got to bring good wellies.'

Her next destination was the third floor where Fran Unsworth, acting director of News, introduced her to several BBC Radio 4 staff, including *Today* presenter John Humphrys. She joined another *Today* presenter, James Naughtie, and Sian Williams, live on Radio 4 where she gave an address to declare the BBC's new home open, saying, 'I hope this new building will serve you well for the future and I am delighted to declare it open today.' Afterwards, she met TV presenters, Huw Edwards and Sophie Raworth, at the start of a tour of the BBC newsroom, followed by other big names including David Dimbleby and Sir Bruce Forsyth. When veteran BBC radio presenter, John Humphrys, asked her about her husband's condition, she responded sharply, 'I've no idea, he's only just gone in.'

He added, 'He looked on awfully good form yesterday.'

Giving nothing away, the Queen responded, 'Did he?' She paused for a breath before adding, 'That's because he's not ill.' Hers was a consummate performance by the consummate professional, but the question had irked her.

On his 92nd birthday, three days later on 10 June, the Queen arrived at the clinic carrying a birthday card, with 'HRH The Duke of Edinburgh' written on the envelope. He had been too tired to accept any visitors since the exploratory operation had taken place, but nothing could keep his wife of 65 years away. Over the next few days, the rest of his close family went to see him. The Prince of Wales left smiling and, when asked about his father's health, replied, 'Much better.'

After this hospitalisation there was growing concern within the family about Philip's workload. Behind-the-scenes plans for a subtle handing over of more of the monarch's responsibility to the Prince of Wales were under way. There was growing confidence too in the next generation of royals. On 22 July 2013 the Queen and the Royal Family celebrated the arrival of Prince George, at the Lindo Wing of St Mary's Hospital, Paddington, London. Official notification of the prince's birth was announced on an easel at Buckingham Palace. The following day the waiting crowds and the world's press saw their first glimpse of the new prince outside the hospital. Prince William joked: 'He's got her looks, thankfully,' while Kate replied: 'No, no, I'm not sure about that.'

In October, Prince George's christening brought together four generations of royals for the first time since 1894. The Queen and three future kings – Prince Charles, Prince William and Prince George – were photographed together after the intimate ceremony. George, just three months old, sat contentedly in his proud father's arms wearing the magnificent replica of the 172-year-old Honiton lace and white satin christening gown. His sister, Princess Charlotte, fourth in line to the throne, was born on 2 May 2015 and the Cambridges' third child, Prince Louis on 23 April 2018.

★★★

Another significant milestone came in 2013 when the Queen announced she would not attend a Commonwealth Heads of Government Meeting (CHOGM) – for the first time in over

40 years – in November the same year, and ask Prince Charles to represent her instead. Coming just weeks after the Queen was herself taken to hospital suffering from gastroenteritis, it showed how important it was for the Queen to manage her workload appropriately.

The Queen's decision to ask the Prince of Wales to take her place at CHOGM in Sri Lanka and thus to represent her at the high-level meeting was also a decisive act. From that moment, Charles, supported by Camilla, would be expected to step in whenever the Queen needed him to represent her on future long-haul trips. In a stroke, she had given Charles, our longest-serving heir to the throne in British history the chance to show us his strengths on the world stage. Charles proved a success and since that moment has always accompanied his mother at CHOGM meetings.

To this day, the Queen remains remarkably physically and mentally fit for a woman of her age. When she has time she rides her horses, enjoys country walks and maintains a healthy diet. But it was time, she felt, to give the next generation their chance, and, for heir Charles, there was no better place to showcase his undoubted diplomatic skills than at the Commonwealth meeting.

In November 2015 Elizabeth and Philip returned to Malta for three days for the Commonwealth summit, a place where they had spent some of the happiest years of their married life. The Queen reportedly asked to see the Villa Guardamangia in Gwardamanġa, Pietà, her home for two years when Philip was based there with the Royal Navy, but the owners – the Ġużè Schembri family, who at the time were in a bitter legal wrangle with the Maltese government – refused to allow it. Elizabeth and Philip had previously visited the archipelago in the central Mediterranean in 2007 for their diamond wedding anniversary and last went inside the villa in 1992, during a previous state visit. The grand home, which was rented by Philip's uncle, Dickie Mountbatten, at the time the couple stayed there was purchased by the Maltese government in 2019 for £5.5 million and is now open to the public as an historical landmark.

The government stepped in amid fears that it could be sold to developers wanting to demolish it and build flats.

The Queen and Philip, joined by the Prince of Wales and the Duchess of Cornwall for the Commonwealth Heads of Government Meeting, were given a rousing welcome by the Maltese people in St George's Square in the centre of Valletta, where Elizabeth and Philip were officially welcomed by the Maltese President, Marie-Louise Coleiro Preca. She presented the couple with a watercolour of Villa Guardamangia by a local artist. 'Oh look, Guardamangia, that's very nice to have,' the Queen said, before adding that she felt the property, 'looks rather sad now.' They returned to the Maria Racecourse, home to the Malta Polo Club where Philip learned to play the sport, and also took a boat journey across Valletta Harbour, as they did in 1954 when they took the then five-year-old Charles with them.

The visit was not meant to be just a nostalgic trip down memory lane. In Malta, the Queen delivered an important address in which she thanked the Prince of Wales for his unstinting support and 'great distinction' with him standing alongside her. It was the clearest hint that Charles would take over the non-hereditary role as Head of the Commonwealth that she has held for more than 60 years. In Malta, the Queen made her position crystal clear. 'I feel enormously proud of what the Commonwealth has achieved, and all of it within my lifetime. For more than six decades of being head of the Commonwealth, a responsibility I have cherished, I have had the fortune of the constancy of the Duke of Edinburgh. To that, and to his many other Commonwealth associations, Prince Philip has brought boundless energy and commitment, for which I am indebted. Nor could I wish to have been better supported and represented in the Commonwealth than by the Prince of Wales, who continues to give so much to it with great distinction.'

Another key development was the Act of Remembrance in November 2017, when the Queen only watched as Prince Charles led the nation in honouring Britain's war dead. In an historic transfer of royal duties, the 91-year-old monarch stood beside

Prince Philip on a Foreign Office balcony as Charles, wearing the uniform of Marshal of the RAF, laid the first wreath on behalf of his mother. She and her consort, with whom she celebrated 70 years of marriage on 20 November, watched the service at the Cenotaph, central London, alongside the Duchess of Cornwall. On a neighbouring balcony the Duchess of Cambridge joined Sophie, Countess of Wessex, and the Queen's cousin Princess Alexandra to watch a ceremony that also marked the changing of the royal guard. In the corner of the balcony, Philip, at 96 one of the last survivors of the Second World War to be present at the service, looked frail and uncomfortable. Wearing the uniform of Admiral of the Fleet, he appeared to struggle to stand at times. A senior source said that Philip was determined to be there to witness his eldest son pay this historic tribute, despite being in extreme pain. 'His hip was causing him serious pain and he was suffering real discomfort that day, he was leaning against the wall to try to prop himself up. But he was to pay his respects to the fallen. Duty really matters to him.' Photographer, Arthur Edwards, who was there that day, took a shot of the duke puffing out his cheeks as he left the balcony. 'Yes, he was in real pain,' he said. 'You could see it etched across Philip's face.'

The Queen and the Commonwealth leaders confirmed Prince Charles's future appointment as head of the association at the following biennial summit held at Buckingham Palace and Windsor Castle in 2018. At the same summit the Queen said publicly that it was her 'sincere wish' to be succeeded by her son. At the start of the gathering of Commonwealth leaders, Charles too committed himself to his future role, delivering a speech in which he said the Commonwealth had been, 'A fundamental feature of my life for as long as I can remember, beginning with my first visit to Malta when I was just five years old.'

Securing Charles as her successor as the head of the Commonwealth was all part of a discreet but well-orchestrated campaign. It now seems very likely that not only Charles, but also Prince William and eventually Prince George will retain the role when they all become king though technically the decision rests with the individual leaders of all Commonwealth countries.

Throughout his nineties, although he maintained a regular regime of walking to keep active, Prince Philip inevitably suffered bouts of illness which accelerated his decision to retire from public life and spend his private time away from the spotlight at Wood Farm on the Sandringham Estate. But it was not without incident and just before Christmas on 20 December 2019, Philip was taken to King Edward VII's Hospital in central London for treatment relating to what the palace would only describe as a 'pre-existing condition'.

During a visit to flood-hit communities in South Yorkshire his son, Charles, was asked about his father's health. 'He's being looked after very well in hospital,' the prince replied. 'At the moment that's all we know.' During the visit, a woman in Fishlake asked him again, Charles responded, 'All right. When you get to that age things don't work so well.'

After four nights in hospital just before 9 a.m., and in time for Christmas, in a smart blazer, white shirt and tie he walked unaided to a waiting royal car, parked discreetly behind the hospital. Philip had once again defied the scaremongers.

27: BUMPY ROAD

'The path, of course, is not always smooth, and may at times this year have felt quite bumpy, but small steps can make a world of difference.'

The Queen, Christmas Broadcast 2019

The Queen famously referred to 1992 as an 'annus horribilis'. With typical understatement 27 years later the Queen described 2019 as being 'quite bumpy' during her annual televised Christmas broadcast. Within a few weeks of recording that message the journey got a lot rougher for the Royal Family, with potholes appearing everywhere. It had all the makings of 'Annus Horribilis II'.

At the heart of the difficult year for the Queen and Philip were serious allegations made against the Duke of York, who faced a fierce backlash after he performed badly in a disastrous interview on the BBC's *Newsnight* with the accomplished, journalist Emily Maitlis. His intention had been to subdue the growing public distrust towards him regarding his close connection to the dead convicted sex offender, the US financier Jeffrey Epstein. Despite telling the Queen that in his opinion it had 'gone well', the deluded duke was slammed for his shifty performance in the interview. Maitlis went on to win Network Presenter of the Year at the Royal Television Awards. Andrew, however, was left rueing the day that he agreed to do it as he had now lost what was left of his reputation. When she saw it, his friend Ghislaine Maxwell, daughter of newspaper baron Robert Maxwell, who was later accused of being Epstein's pimp and had urged Andrew not to do it, believed it was 'the beginning of the end.'"

Deeply concerned, Andrew had been accused by Virginia Roberts Guiffre that, when aged 17, she was forced to have sex with him, which she publicly described as 'disgusting'. The writing was on the wall for a compromised Andrew, who, despite saying he didn't remember ever meeting Ms Roberts Guiffre, stood down from carrying out royal duties amid a furious backlash. In a statement on the issue, Andrew said he 'unequivocally' regretted his 'ill-judged association with Jeffrey Epstein.' He went on to stress that he deeply sympathised with everyone who had been affected and wanted some form of closure on the matter. 'I can only hope that, in time, they will be able to rebuild their lives. Of course, I am willing to help any appropriate law enforcement agency with their investigations, if required,' he added. It was a case of too little, much too late.

In reality Andrew had effectively been fired by his mother and older brother. As one senior Royal Household figure explained: 'This was not about personalities, this was about protecting the institution of the monarchy itself.' The Duke of York's association with Epstein left the Queen and the Prince of Wales with little choice but to act decisively, which they did. Despite Charles being on the other side of the world at the time on a tour of New Zealand and the Solomon Islands, both had been monitoring developments with increasing concern. They both agreed there could be only one conclusion – that Andrew withdraw from the fray and from public life.

Prince Philip, now in retirement, left the decision making to his wife and his eldest son, the future king. Furthermore, he had grown more and more concerned about the impact on the monarchy of his second son's alleged louche behaviour which was

---

★ Maxwell was arrested in New Hampshire on 2 July 2020 on multiple charges related to the sexual abuse of young women and girls by Epstein and was denied bail. Her trial is expected to take place in the summer of 2021.

bringing the institution he was supposed to serve into disrepute. He could not understand Andrew's inability to lead a simple and relatively inexpensive lifestyle. Privately, he even blamed Sarah, the Duchess of York, after he was told she had introduced Andrew to Miss Maxwell in the first instance. Philip, throughout his long life, had always put duty to the crown first and had willingly made sacrifices for what he saw as the greater good. He couldn't understand why his second son had failed to grasp that simple premise.

A week before Prince Andrew faced his brother, Charles, he was summoned up to Sandringham to meet with his father. It was a strained meeting, but the duke made it clear that he didn't understand how Andrew had been so foolish as to fall into friendship with a man like Epstein. He had always been concerned by the way Andrew 'like a fly to the light' had kept the company of questionable people, but he felt his son should have seen through Epstein and given him a wide berth. Philip told Andrew that whatever the rights and wrongs of the case, he had 'no choice' but to bow to his older brother's decision and accept whatever outcome Prince Charles saw fit. The meeting was understandably tense but calm, close sources said, but Philip left his son in no doubt that the axe would fall and that he would have to step down from royal duties for the sake of the Queen, the monarchy and the institution they all served. Up until that point Charles had always been very supportive of his brother. Several years earlier, when the allegations first surfaced, the two had had a heart to heart and Charles told Andrew he totally believed he had not acted improperly. Of course, Andrew protested his innocence and Philip certainly didn't like the hysterical 'trial by the media', but he knew Andrew's actions, including the car-crash television interview, had now endangered the reputation of the institution of the monarchy itself.

When all three men eventually met, Prince Charles ensured it was all very civilised given the sensitivities of the situation. Afterwards, however, Andrew was left in no doubt from that moment he was out in the cold and that there was no way back for him in the near future. With Philip present, Charles reinforced the Queen's wish that Andrew step back from royal duties 'for the foreseeable future'. Of course, Andrew believed he was being treated harshly, as nothing has yet been proven against him, but as he agreed with his father, he accepted the decision. In reality he had no choice, he was out.

Meanwhile, just before Christmas 2019, the Prince of Wales had confided in the Queen and Philip about another developing situation brewing regarding Prince Harry and his wife Meghan and the pair wanting to live abroad and thus become only part-time royals. The Queen, at first, deferred to Charles on the matter and hoped he could resolve it without her having to become embroiled in the developing controversy.

In truth, Philip had not got off to the best start with Meghan Markle. It had been reported, when it became clear the couple's whirlwind romance was serious, that Philip had advised his grandson Harry against marrying Meghan and allegedly told him, 'One steps out with actresses, one doesn't marry them.' Philip's alleged comments were reported in *The Sunday Times* in a magazine article by journalist Sophia Money-Coutts about the so-called 'rift' between Harry and Meghan and Kate and William. Ms Money-Coutts, a former writer at society magazine *Tatler*, and daughter of retired private banker, Crispin Money-Coutts, 9th Baron Latymer, stuck by her story and Buckingham Palace decided not to comment on the matter further.

Despite him occasionally flouting royal protocol, the Queen had a soft spot for her grandson Harry. She helped him promote his Invictus Games, the sporting event he produced in 2014 to encourage injured veterans to compete. He invited his grandmother to take part in a promo video featuring the then US President, Barack Obama, and First Lady, Michelle Obama, in 2016, where the Queen feigned surprise that the president was keen to win. Harry told writer Angela Levin, 'You could almost see her thinking, "Why the hell does nobody ask me to do these things more often?" She is so incredibly skilled she only needed one take. Meanwhile, I was like a gibbering wreck. I was more nervous than anyone else,' said Harry.

Ms Levin commented afterwards, 'It also showed the Queen would do almost anything for her grandson. The feeling is mutual.' Harry said he absolutely adored his grandmother. What he did next shocked the entire Royal Family.

The Duke and Duchess of Sussex announced on 8 January 2020 that they would step back as 'senior' royals and work to become financially independent, planning to split their time between the UK and North America.

Philip has struggled greatly with what he saw as a lack of respect shown to the Queen by Harry, whose behaviour, he felt, had been unbecoming of a prince. 'Both Her Majesty and the duke have a soft spot for Prince Harry. But on this matter they both felt he and his new wife had behaved recklessly and without proper consideration to the consequences to the institution they had both signed up to serve, the crown. Yes, they thought their behaviour was unpredictable and showed a total lack of respect,' said a senior member of the Royal Household.

The Queen and Prince Charles then had to deal with so-called 'Megxit'. In October, Meghan launched legal action against the *Mail on Sunday* newspaper for 'unlawfully' publishing a private letter, and Harry publicly condemned the tabloids for behaviour that he said 'destroys lives'. Referring to his late mother, Princess Diana, Harry said, 'I lost my mother, and now I watch my wife falling victim to the same powerful forces.' In an emotional interview that aired soon afterwards, Meghan spoke about the toll of being a new mother under the glare of the tabloid newspapers. 'It's a very real thing to be going through behind the scenes,' she admitted. When asked whether the experience had 'really been a struggle', she replied with a subdued: 'Yes.'

The dramatic sequence of events led to the sixth in line to the British throne effectively resigning from his front-line role, 'After many months of reflection and internal discussions'. Harry and

Meghan genuinely believe they are helping to deliver a slimmed-down monarchy and have the ability to reach out to a younger and more diverse audience than other members of the Royal Family.

Harry originally contacted his father about the possibility of him and his wife spending more time in Canada and America just before Christmas, but was told he needed to come up with a thought-out plan. Harry sent a draft proposal about his future role to his father early in the New Year but was again informed that more time was needed to think through the complex implications, particularly over funding. Harry asked for a private meeting with the Queen at Sandringham as soon as he, Meghan and their son Archie, arrived back from their long Christmas break in Canada. He was told bluntly that while the Queen was happy to meet him, she would not under any circumstances be drawn into discussions on his wish list until he had first talked them over in detail with his father. Indeed, any talk of a meeting was subsequently blocked by courtiers. That said the Queen gave explicit instructions to Harry that neither he nor his wife should go public about their future plans at this time and until it had been agreed and signed off by her and the Prince of Wales.

Within days the situation had deteriorated further, when Prince Charles and Prince William, the next two direct heirs in line of succession, were only sent a copy of Prince Harry and Meghan's statement ten minutes before it was released and without any further consultation. It was a complete mess and Harry and Meghan were acting like loose cannons. Philip was spotted leaving Sandringham in the morning, after he was reportedly made furious by Meghan and Harry's intention to step back as senior royals. The Duke of Edinburgh, who was seen sitting on the passenger seat of his Land Rover wearing a seat belt, is understood to have said, 'What on earth are they playing at?' after the Sussexes issued their statement. One senior member of the Royal Household told me that the duke's fit of pique was due to seeing his wife unsettled and upset by the couple's behaviour.

'To say that the duke feels they let the side down would be a considerable understatement. He was furious and felt that the Queen and indeed his son the Prince of Wales had always given Prince Harry plenty of scope to live the life that he wanted. Yes, he was extremely disappointed by their behaviour and the way they tried to back both the Prince of Wales and Her Majesty into a corner by releasing that statement.' It was that Instagram post and the statement released on the couple's newly launched and unsanctioned website SussexRoyal.com that did the most damage and created an awkward atmosphere. 'It was a question of trust. There was a feeling that Harry and Meghan had knowingly breached that trust. It showed a total lack of respect.'

The pair said they wanted to become financially independent but equally they knew they would have to rely, at least at the outset, on funds from Harry's father's private income. Indeed, the combination of their demands and COVID-19 led to considerable cut backs in Charles's expenditure. The Sussexes' decision was to quit Britain and at first live in a rented mansion near Vancouver before renting Tyler Perry's hilltop home and then finally buying a £14 million 14,463-foot French-inspired estate in exclusive Montecito, LA.

The couple issued a statement which said, 'After many months of reflection and internal discussions, we have chosen to make a transition this year in starting to carve out a progressive new role within this institution. We intend to step back as senior members of the Royal Family and work to become financially independent, while continuing to fully support Her Majesty, The Queen.' Within months, on 2 September, *Forbes* reported that the couple had signed a multi-year agreement to produce content exclusively at Netflix. Although Netflix didn't disclose how much it is paying the couple, the streamer has a history of paying a high price to work exclusively with influential people. It reportedly paid *Black-ish* creator Kenya Barris $100 million, *Grey's Anatomy* creator Shonda Rhimes $150 million, *American Horror Story* creator Ryan Murphy up to $300 million, and *Game of Thrones* creators David Benioff and Dan Weiss $200 million for multi-year contracts. Whatever the figure Harry and Meghan received, reported to be £150 million, it was sizeable enough for them to pay off the £2.3 million of taxpayers' money spent renovating their home Frogmore Cottage in Windsor.

28: FINAL FAREWELL

*'In the event that I am reincarnated, I would like to return as a deadly virus,
to contribute something to solving overpopulation.'*

Prince Philip, 1988

Prince Philip never shied away from his feelings on the worrying
subject of global overpopulation. In 1988, he brought up the subject
when giving an interview to the German news agency, Deutsche
Presse-Agentur, when his questioner strayed onto the topic of
reincarnation. Philip was quoted as saying, 'In the event that I am
reincarnated, I would like to return as a deadly virus, to contribute
something to solving overpopulation.'

Different versions of his remark resurfaced and were circulated
on social media platforms during the devastating Coronavirus
outbreak. Another report quoted the duke as saying, 'If I were
reincarnated, I would wish to be returned to earth as a killer virus
to lower human population levels.' Given what happened in 2020
– when the COVID-19 global pandemic killed more than one
and a half million people, with nearly 70 million cases, creating
widespread unemployment and a devastating economic meltdown
– his comments about a deadly virus being a solution to world
overpopulation were something he probably wished he could have
taken back.

The Prime Minister, Boris Johnson, who would himself become
seriously ill with the virus, made a televised address to the nation on
23 March 2020, when he ordered a strict lockdown, to be enforced
by the police, in a bid to relieve the overwhelmed National Health

Service. From Downing Street, he warned that people would only be allowed outside to buy food or medication, exercise alone once a day, or to travel to work if absolutely necessary. All non-essential shops were told to close with immediate effect, along with playgrounds and libraries.

It was decided, with his full blessing, that Philip should be moved to a safe 'bubble' along with the Queen at Windsor Castle, where they would be cared for by a small number of staff to limit the chance of them contracting the virus. From Windsor on 6 April, the Queen delivered a powerful televised address, watched by more than 24 million in the UK, in which she spoke of how history would judge the nation, and said that, 'Those that come after us will say the Britons of this generation were as strong as any'. She went on, 'The pride in who we are is not part of our past. It defines our present and our future'. There were no gun salutes to mark her 94th birthday as she felt it would not be appropriate, the first time in her reign that there was no such salute, which usually takes place at Hyde Park and the Tower of London. The Trooping the Colour parade in June to mark the Queen's official birthday had already been cancelled.

Being forced to shield together in Windsor Castle for most of 2020 and 2021, and for a time at Balmoral, Scotland in August, in isolation from the rest of the Royal Family, Philip and the Queen spent much more quality time together. It gave the Queen what aides described as a 'new lease of life' in lockdown. The duke managed to help pull the Royal Family together and help his wife through some of the toughest times of her reign after the fallout of the Duke and Duchess of Sussex first fleeing to Canada and then settling in the USA, which was seen as a body blow for the monarchy that could do immense and lasting damage. When the Queen finally issued a statement on 19 February 2021, stripping the Sussexes of their royal patronages, including Harry's honorary military appointments, Philip was resting in hospital after a bout of ill-health. He was fully aware what was coming. The door that had been left ajar for the Sussexes in case they wanted to return to the royal fold was slammed firmly shut just days after the Queen had expressed her 'delight' that her grandson and Meghan were expecting their second child.* Perhaps the final straw was the announcement by the couple that they were to give a wide-ranging televised interview with their friend Oprah Winfrey to be broadcast on US network CBS for a Primetime special on 7 March. Nothing was off limits. Initially it featured Meghan discussing 'stepping into life as a royal, marriage, motherhood' and how 'she is handling life under intense public pressure.' Then she was joined by Prince Harry, and the couple talked about their move to the US and future plans.

Privately, in these troubled times, Philip gave the Queen the strength to carry on. It also sparked their desire to never again be apart for long periods, as they had been doing. They were rarely seen during lockdown, although they were pictured together during the surprise wedding of their granddaughter Princess Beatrice on 17 July 2020 to property entrepreneur Edoardo Mapelli Mozzi, at a private ceremony at The Royal Chapel of All Saints at Royal Lodge, Windsor.

Philip, albeit briefly, stepped back into his life of royal duty to carry out a military ceremony on 22 July 2020. It involved handing over the keys of Colonel-in-Chief of The Rifles, a merger of four infantry regiments that was formed in 2007 and is now the largest infantry regiment in the British army, to his daughter-in-law Camilla, Duchess of Cornwall, amid the sounds of bugles. Inevitably, the three-minute ceremony was reimagined to allow for social distancing, with Philip officially handing over the position at Windsor Castle, some 85 miles from where Camilla later took up the duty in a ceremony at Highgrove House.

Immaculately dressed, in a blazer, regimental tie and highly polished brogues, he appeared the picture of health as he walked out of the Equerries Entrance to stand tall in front of the cameras. As he stepped into the Windsor Castle quadrangle with a smile

---

* When born the child will be the Queen and Philip's tenth great-grandchild

and a cheerful wave, he seemed thrilled to be back on duty, joking about fitness with one bugler who described him admiringly as, 'All banter'.

'He asked me if that was all I did, the bugling, and I told him that we were assault pioneers as well,' said Lance Corporal Colin Streetin, 33, afterwards. 'He said, "Obviously keeping up your fitness then?" and then kind of looked me up and down and I was thinking, "Are you trying to say I am fat?!" That's what we were laughing about. He's a very fit man himself for 99. Just incredible.'

He was then saluted and thanked for his 67 years of service to The Rifles and their forming regiments by Major General Tom Copinger-Symes, the assistant colonel commandant, who gave the salute, telling him: 'All Riflemen, whether serving or retired would like to thank you for 67 years of continuous service, support and leadership to the Rifles and to our forming and antecedent regiments. And on this occasion, as you hand over your duties, as Colonel-in-Chief to her Royal Highness, the Duchess of Cornwall, we would like to wish you fair wind and following seas.' He later explained that the 'fair wind and following seas' was intended in honour of the duke's own distinguished naval service. With four members of the Band and Bugles of The Rifles sounding the Rifles 'Assembly' call and the 'No More Parades' call, the official elements of the ceremony came to a close. Speaking after the ceremony, Major General Copinger-Symes said: 'Clearly this is a mark of our respect for him and his fondness for soldiers and servicemen and women of all kinds. He is a military man through and through.' It summed Philip up perfectly.

Throughout his life, Philip always refused to allow his age to affect the way he lived. As he approached his 90th birthday, Prince Philip admitted it had finally caught up with him.

His reputation for being awkward with the press was justified. In an interview with the BBC's presenter Fiona Bruce in 2011 to mark the same milestone birthday, Philip was particularly uncooperative. At least he gave the unfortunate Ms Bruce a line when he admitted he was ready to slow down. 'I reckon I've done my bit,' he said gruffly. 'So I want to enjoy myself a bit now, with less responsibility, less frantic rushing about, less preparation, less trying to think of something to say. On top of that my memory's going. I can't remember names and things. It's better to get out before you reach your sell-by date.'

It was a modest summing up of a truly remarkable life. His decision to effectively walk away from public life and step down from public engagements didn't come for almost another six years after he first hinted at his desire. On the morning of 4 May 2017, the palace revealed that Philip, weeks away from his 96th birthday and with the Queen's full support, was to step down from his public role. Hours after the announcement, Philip was at his 26th public engagement of 2017, a service and lunch for members of the Order of Merit at St James's Palace. At the reception, the duke quipped to the late British-Lebanese mathematician Sir Michael Atiyah (d. 11 January 2019 aged 89) that he 'can't stand up much'.

With the odd exception, his final official engagement was due to be on 2 August 2017. The stage was set for the duke to bow out of public life to the sound of resounding cheers and a rousing rendition of *For He's a Jolly Good Fellow* played by the band of the Royal Marines for their Captain General on the forecourt of Buckingham Palace. He was there to take the royal salute and inspect an honour guard to mark the finale of the 1664 Global Challenge, a series of endurance feats to raise awareness of and funds for the Royal Marines Charity.

Among those he met were Corporal Will Gingell, 33, and Corporal Jamie Thompson, 31, who had run 1,664 miles over 100 days, and Sergeant Matt Burley, a physical training instructor, who swam 1,664 lengths underwater over 10 days. 'You all should be locked up,' Philip joked characteristically. It was the 22,219th solo engagement carried out by the duke since his wife became Queen in 1952. As far as Buckingham Palace could ascertain, his very first had been on 2 March 1948, a few months after his marriage to Princess Elizabeth, when he attended the London Federation of Boys' Clubs Boxing finals at the Royal Albert Hall. The Court

Circular recorded that the prince, then aged 26, presented the prizes.

It rained heavily on his final parade, necessitating a raincoat and bowler hat, which he duly raised and tipped above his head in response to the three cheers. I was commentating for the BBC who had decided to air the moment live, recognising its historic significance. The public duties might have ended but Philip's public life did not. He remained president, patron, and member of 780 organisations and continued to celebrate the milestones that came his way.

Almost immediately after the parade, Philip headed for rural Norfolk where he settled into the Grade II listed Wood Farm on the Queen's Sandringham Estate, making it his retirement home with the Queen's blessing. With its simple furnishings and open fires, it was a lot less formal than life at the palace or Windsor or Balmoral. It was still spacious and had been the Queen and Philip's bolt-hole away from Palace formality for years.

Prince John, the youngest son of George V and Queen Mary who suffered from severe epilepsy and possibly autism, resided at Wood Farm from 1917 until his death there in 1919. Before Philip moved in, the younger royals too had several times held private parties at Wood Farm. Divorced spouses of royals such as Sarah, Duchess of York were often put up there during holiday periods so they could be close to royal children without officially being at the Queen's festive holiday celebrations at Sandringham House.

Philip had always been content when he was at Sandringham. On her accession to the throne, the Queen asked him to take on the responsibility for the management of the 20,400-acre estate with its 62-mile perimeter. 'When the Queen succeeded we sort of chatted about who should do what,' he said, 'I suppose and I thought that if I could relieve her of the management of the estates it would save her a lot of time.'* He grew to love it and would to stay there during shooting weekends and hosted shooting parties

---

*   To Sir Trevor MacDonald in the ITV documentary, *The Duke: A Portrait of Prince Philip*.

on the estate, before making it his final home. He still had help: a page, housekeeper, chef, and a footman to watch over him. They all wore everyday clothes and insisted they were not liveried servants like those serving at the palace or Windsor Castle. His team of Scotland Yard Personal Protection officers was on hand too but for these elite armed officers the hurly-burly of Royal life in the mainstream began to feel like a distant memory.

An accomplished public speaker – he made 4,632 speeches at official meetings, conferences and receptions during his royal career, an average of around eight a month for 50 years – Philip enjoyed the less structured existence. He may have joked about his long life, but Philip was aware of his physical limitations. His life at Wood Farm gave him a kind of anonymity this very public figure had privately long craved. His pet projects kept him focused. He had his entire living quarters modernised too, organising for a new kitchen to be fitted at Wood Farm, the first for 30 years as well as a few other minor changes.

His sharp mind was always active. He spent his days reading works of literature he had always wanted to get round to, but had never had the time. He had a personal library of more than 11,000 books and during his life wrote on a wide range of subjects including the environment, technology, equestrian and animal subjects.

Philip loved to paint too, like his son Charles, the Prince of Wales. He had become an accomplished painter of watercolours and dabbled in oils and found it a perfect release. He had also enjoyed entertaining friends at Wood Farm, but never on a grand scale. If he did have time for television, he liked documentaries and cookery shows; the presenter, Mary Berry, was a particular favourite.

He kept himself busy overseeing the estate, and was thrilled in 2018 when he became the first person in Britain to successfully grow a crop of black truffles. He was said to be 'over the moon' that his 12-year quest to cultivate the delicacies on the Sandringham estate was finally realised. He had planted more than 300 £15 saplings impregnated with truffle spores on the royal estate in Norfolk back in 2006.

In retirement Philip had tried to keep as fit and active as possible. His secret was simple: regular exercise, a moderate diet and a good dose of sheer will power. Central to this was a regime of short but intensive exercise adopted by both the Duke of Edinburgh and Prince Charles, called the 5BX Plan. The plan, designed to improve the fitness of recruits for the Royal Canadian Air Force, can be carried out in a restricted space, with no warm-up or equipment required, using five basic exercises to strengthen every muscle in the body. In his final years he had to scale it down, but those close to him said he 'always took the stairs' whenever he could as it helped him maintain fitness. 'Lifts were never an option as far as he was concerned,' one staffer said.

He enjoyed the freedom this allowed him, without his equerry arriving each morning with his daily schedule, or with a camera and sound man capturing his every move. The Queen fully supported her husband's decision to quit public life. It was her way of showing her love and gratitude.

The monarch, five years his junior, felt her husband had earned a proper retirement. Living at Wood Farm meant he was not too far away, but far enough to be able to avoid the press whom he always had a fractious relationship with. As his wife, Elizabeth obviously missed him, especially at the breakfast table, which they always shared. They still spoke to one another daily on the telephone and spent extended holidays together when the Queen's schedule allowed. After all, Philip's free spirit had always been at the forefront of the Queen's mind. She never knowingly tried to restrict him. He had always been his own man.

One incident, however, seriously dented his confidence and reputation and could very easily have ended in tragedy. He was involved in a serious car accident with him at the wheel, which left him cut and bruised and deeply shaken. He had to be helped from the wreckage of his car following a crash in which his Land Rover overturned on its side. The accident resulted in two other people, the driver and passenger of the other vehicle, being treated in hospital with minor injuries. A baby strapped in the back seat of the other car was miraculously not injured.

Again, there were calls for him to stop driving and slow down. The press reaction infuriated him, but what bothered him the most was that he was at fault. It may only have been a momentary lapse of concentration, but it could have been fatal. The Buckingham Palace statement didn't tell the full story. It read: 'The Duke of Edinburgh was involved in a road traffic accident with another vehicle this afternoon. The duke was not injured. The accident took place close to the Sandringham Estate.' It did not reveal how lucky Philip and the others were to escape without major injury.

Barrister Roy Warne, 75, who was the first on the scene of the car crash and helped pull Philip from his overturned Land Rover Freelander said he had the duke's blood on his hands. 'I looked down and had the prince's blood on my hands. All I could think is, thank goodness there wasn't more,' he said. Later the palace confirmed Philip did not need hospital treatment.

The accident led to Philip voluntarily giving up his driving licence. Two days later Norfolk Police gave him 'suitable words of advice' after he was pictured driving without a seat belt. In a statement, the palace said, 'After careful consideration the Duke of Edinburgh has taken the decision to voluntarily surrender his driving licence.' He was not prosecuted for his part in the accident, but it was a low point in his retirement, and focused his family's and the nation's minds on his mortality.

His last major intervention in public life came during the Coronavirus pandemic in early 2020 when he was self-isolating with the Queen at Windsor Castle in accordance with Government advice. Prime Minister Boris Johnson had instructed all people in the UK, particularly the over 70s, to avoid all non-essential contact and travel as part of unprecedented peacetime measures aimed at trying to control the spread of COVID-19.

Queen Elizabeth, who had been at Buckingham Palace, then 93, and in the greater risk category, de-camped a half an hour drive down the M4 motorway to the castle. The duke, then 98, who had already been spending most of his time in the sanctuary of Wood Farm on the Sandringham estate, was flown by helicopter to

Windsor to join her – something which had been long scheduled so he could join his wife for the Easter break.

Science and technology had always been one of Philip's major interests. His patronages included the Industrial Society that he took on in 1952 and he enthusiastically visited many research stations, laboratories, and workplaces throughout Britain. In 1976 he initiated the Fellowship of Engineering, now the Royal Academy of Engineering, which promotes engineering excellence and education. Driven by his lifelong passion in science and huge interest in the pandemic, the duke delivered what was to be his last public statement as a heartfelt thank you to key workers who were helping to make sure, 'the infrastructure of our life continues' during the crisis.

In his tribute in April 2020, Philip said, 'As we approach World Immunisation Week, I wanted to recognise the vital and urgent work being done by so many to tackle the pandemic; by those in the medical and scientific professions, at universities and research institutions, all united in working to protect us from COVID-19. On behalf of those of us who remain safe and at home, I also wanted to thank all key workers who ensure the infrastructure of our life continues; the staff and volunteers working in food production and distribution, those keeping postal and delivery services going, and those ensuring the rubbish continues to be collected.'

His rare intervention, the first since his retirement, made front page news. But it was not only about reaching out to the nation – he had always left that to the Queen who had earlier made a televised public address of solidarity – it was about showing his lifelong passion in science and humanities to try and find a vaccine.

The pandemic also meant the plans he had signed off for his funeral, 'Operation Forth Bridge', had to be significantly altered in the event of him dying during lockdown.

In his life the duke, only the fifth consort to a reigning queen in British history, has put in quite a shift. During his many years of public duty and service, he undertook 223 solo visits to 67 Commonwealth countries and completed 385 visits to 74 other countries; an average of 12 countries per year. He fulfilled over 18,567 official engagements, excluding those when he was accompanying the Queen, an average of 371 each year. In 2001 he undertook 363 solo engagements in the UK and abroad. He made two round-the-world voyages aboard HMY *Britannia* visiting some of the remotest parts of the Commonwealth as the Queen's representative, travelling some 72,430 miles. The four-month voyage of 1956–1957 included visits to the remote South Atlantic locations of the Falkland Islands, South Georgia, Tristan da Cunha, Ascension Island and St Helena. He has chaired over 1,454 meetings and always took a hands-on approach to the organisations which he represented.

Some 75 prizes and medals are associated with him. He was made a Knight of the Order of the Garter and a Knight of the Order of the Thistle and also Grand Master and First or Principal Knight of the Order of the British Empire, founded in the twentieth century to reward the work and service of members of the general public.

Philip said before his death that he didn't want an extravagant public celebration should he reach his landmark 100th birthday on 10 June 2021. It was, after all, not his style. In an interview with the *Daily Telegraph* in 2000 when discussing the Queen Mother's 100th birthday, Philip made it clear he had no desire whatsoever to reach the same age. With a typically flippant remark, he said, 'I can't imagine anything worse, bits of me are falling off already.' Sadly, for the rest of us, he did not reach that milestone birthday and he got his wish.